GAME DAY!

Today in Cleveland Sports History

Published by Cleveland Landmarks Press, Inc.
14189 Washington Boulevard, Cleveland, Ohio 44118
www.clevelandlandmarkspress.com
(216) 658-4144

ISBN: 978-0-936760-07-0
Library of Congress Control Number: 2023935760
Book Design by John Yasenosky, III
Printed by Versa Press, East Peoria, Illinois

Table of Contents

Acknowledgments

An examination of the long list of the various effects of the Covid-19 pandemic would certainly include this book. If not for the multiple lockdowns, it probably never would have been written.

The two of us are both retired sports journalists, and – like much of the rest of the world in the spring of 2020 – we were looking for something to do. The usual source of entertainment in our lives had been sporting events, but few such contests were taking place at that point. Those that were did not have any or at least many spectators, and the idea of hanging out with a group of people during a pandemic didn't carry much appeal to either one of us.

Among the two of us, however, Budd had an idea. He had written a book called *Today in Buffalo Sports History* that was published in 2013 while he was working for *The Buffalo News*. Budd discovered that it was great fun to research a city's sports heritage, as he dug up some long forgotten or relatively unknown facts about Western New York athletics. When the book came out, it provided some readers with memories of events from the past, while for others it furnished a quick education on Buffalo's sports history.

A thought struck Budd: Was the concept portable? Could it be applied to other cities? The closest big city to Buffalo was Cleveland, brothers of sorts on the eastern end of Lake Erie. It's been said that the Midwest "starts" in both of those cities, and that they have similar histories. It didn't take Budd long to think of Larry, his classmate at Syracuse University. Larry had grown up in Akron, Ohio, and returned there after graduation to begin a long professional career in journalism there.

The two of us realized how equally frustrated we were in being sidelined by the pandemic, so the idea of researching the sports history of Northeast Ohio was undeniably appealing to both of us.

As we began our research, we relied on a variety of newspapers, magazines and websites in the process of collecting information. Anyone who writes a sports book must tip a cap to the people who work on such sites as baseball-reference.com, pro-football-reference.com, basketball-reference.com, etc. They are amazing resources. In addition, *Sports Illustrated*'s Vault is a wonderful way to look back at the big moments of the past. Many, many others have written about Cleveland's highlights and lowlights, and we owe them all a debt of gratitude.

We also reached out to a few individuals along the way, and appreciated their help and encouragement in the process. Thanks to George Bozeka, Vic Carucci, Kevin Chase, Mark Derringer, Rob McBurnett, Chuck Stevens and Tim Wendel. Of course, the nice words for the back cover written by Indians (and former Buffalo) announcer Jim Rosenhaus, retired Cleveland (and former Buffalo) sportscaster John Telich, and veteran Ohio sportswriter Terry Pluto, Larry's former co-worker at the *Akron Beacon Journal*, are greatly appreciated.

Sports images nowadays are much harder to secure – even historical ones. Many thanks go to Cleveland State University's Elizabeth Piwkowski, who helped provide images from the Michael Schwartz Library special collections. Brian Meggitt and Sarah Dobransky from the Cleveland Public Library and Sue Jaworski of the Buffalo State / SUNY library were extremely helpful in finding images in their databases, too. Finally, veteran photographer David Richard spent hours combing through his collection to find some incredible images, including our cover art. We appreciate his efforts and of course his expert skills.

Naturally, the biggest professional thanks go to Greg Deegan and Cleveland Landmarks Press. This isn't a typical sports book, featuring the life story of an athletic superstar. The authors appreciate the fact that Greg took a chance on it, and us.

To learn more about the book, visit our Facebook page, "Today in Cleveland Sports History." You'll read more about Cleveland sports history through the inclusion of items that had to be taken out of the book for space reasons. There, we also will tell you about book signing events, Zoom interviews, etc., and take your questions and comments about the book.

Larry Pantages and Budd Bailey

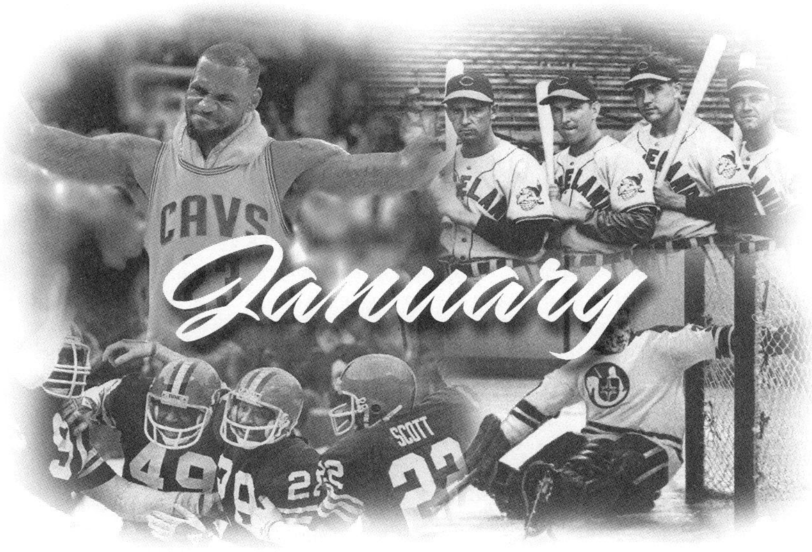

January 1, 1995 — Belichick defeats Parcells

Bill Belichick vs. Bill Parcells – could we ask for a better football matchup to start the New Year?

The renowned NFL coaches won two Super Bowls during their time together from 1983-91 with the New York Giants. Now Belichick of the Browns was in the fourth year of his first head coaching job, and Parcells had moved on to New England, leaving the Giants after the 1990 season and joining the Patriots in '93. On this day, they faced off in a first-round playoff game in Cleveland Stadium.

This was a competitive game that went back and forth for a while. The Browns took the lead for good in the third quarter as Leroy Hoard ran 10 yards for a touchdown. Matt Stover added a 21-yard field goal to give Cleveland a 10-point lead. New England got within seven on a Matt Bahr field goal, but couldn't move closer and lost, 20-13.

The Browns' defense put up a solid effort. The Patriots only ran for 57 yards. Drew Bledsoe was 21-for-50 for 235 yards and had three interceptions. Meanwhile, Vinny Testaverde was 20-for-30 for 268 yards and a touchdown. It was Belichick's only postseason win during his time from 1991-95 as head coach in Cleveland; he finished with a 36-44 record, including 1-1 in the playoffs.

January 1, 1958 — Running back Don Clark, whose career began at Central High School in Akron, rushes 14 times for 82 yards as Ohio State beats Oregon, 10-7, in the Rose Bowl to win the Buckeyes' second national championship. For the season, Clark led the Buckeyes in rushing with 737 yards.

January 1, 1968 — The Indiana football team, coached by Canton native Johnny Pont, reaches the Rose Bowl for the only time in school history. The Hoosiers lost to Southern California, 14-3.

2

January 2, 1984 — Kosar and Miami hang on, beat Nebraska

The 1984 Orange Bowl turns out to be one of the great college football games in history and also serves as Bernie Kosar's introduction to a national audience.

Nebraska arrived undefeated and ranked No. 1. The Cornhuskers had clobbered almost everyone they played, averaging 52 points per game. Meanwhile, Miami had lost its opener but won 10 straight after that. Kosar, who grew up in Boardman (near Youngstown), had been brilliant as a redshirt freshman at quarterback for Coach Howard Schnellenberger, who had spent two years on his way up in coaching as an assistant to Blanton Collier at Kentucky. Browns fans know Collier's place in history well.

The Hurricanes got off to a great start; Kosar threw two touchdown passes as they led, 17-0, after a quarter. Nebraska responded with 17 points to tie, but Miami completed two long scoring drives to go back in front, 31-17, in the fourth quarter. Then the fun began. The Cornhuskers got one score back quickly, and drove down the field for another touchdown to make it 31-30, with an extra point pending.

Now it was decision time for Nebraska Coach Tom Osborne. If he ordered his team to kick the extra point, a successful attempt would have tied the score at 31-31, and probably given Nebraska the national championship as the nation's only unbeaten team. Instead, he opted to go for two points. Quarterback Turner Gill's pass was broken up by Kenny Calhoun, and Kosar and the Hurricanes were national champions.

January 2, 1966 — The Packers beat the visiting Browns, 23-12. It's the last NFL Championship Game before the Super Bowl is born, and the first NFL game broadcast in color. It was also Jim Brown's last game for Cleveland.

3

January 3, 1987 — Browns refuse to be counted out

The next time the Browns fall behind in a playoff game, they can always use what became regarded as an NFL classic as an inspiration that postseason comebacks are always possible.

Cleveland trailed, 20-10, in the fourth quarter after New York's Freeman McNeil scored a touchdown. The Jets' radio announcer proclaimed that New York was headed to the AFC title game in a week. But Kevin Mack got a touchdown back for Cleveland. Then a roughing-the-passer call that has been long remembered by Jets' fans happened on a play by New York defensive lineman Mark Gastineau. And that led to straight-ahead kicker Mark Moseley, who was age 38 and brought in at midseason because of a knee injury to Matt Bahr, kicking a field goal in the final seconds of regulation for a 20-20 tie.

The Browns seemed poised to win in overtime, but Moseley missed a 23-yard field goal to waste an opportunity. The game went on and on, all the way into a second overtime. Finally, Moseley, who would retire after the season and a 16-year career, kicked a 27-yard field goal to give Cleveland the 23-20 win. Bernie Kosar finished 33-for-64 for 489 yards, as the Jets' defense was on the field for almost 100 plays.

January 3, 1973 — George Steinbrenner, a native of the west side Cleveland suburb of Rocky River, heads an investor group that buys the New York Yankees from television network CBS for $10 million. He had previously been rejected in an attempt to buy the Indians from owner Vernon Stouffer, who instead sold the club to a group controlled by Cavaliers owner Nick J. Mileti.

January 3, 2003 — Jim Tressel, who played quarterback in college at Baldwin Wallace College (now University) in Berea for his head coach father Lee Tressel, coaches Ohio State to a national championship in football with a thrilling 31-24 double-overtime win over the University of Miami (Florida). The win completes a 14-0 season and gives OSU its first national title in 34 years. Before coming to Columbus, Tressel led Youngstown State to four national titles.

January 3, 2011 — A 10-22 record over two years isn't good enough for Eric Mangini to retain his head coaching position with the Browns. Team President Mike Holmgren then hires Pat Shurmur, who takes the job with no experience as a head coach at any level. Shurmur would compile a 9-23 record in two seasons.

4

January 4, 1981 — Red Right 88 goes wrong

It seemed like the perfect set-up. The Browns won their first division title in nine years with an 11-5 record and nine of the victories are by seven or fewer points. Three came by three points and two came by one point. In three of the victories, the winning scores came with 16 seconds to play, 1:25 to go, and 5:35 remaining.

No wonder the team is nicknamed the "Kardiac Kids." Now it's on to the postseason after a drought of eight seasons, where a first-round NFL playoff game with the Oakland Raiders is being played in Cleveland Stadium – on a day of 4-degree weather conditions.

Ron Bolton opened the scoring for Cleveland by returning an interception 42 yards for a touchdown. Oakland responded with a 1-yard scoring run by Mark van Eeghen to take a 7-6 lead at the half. The Browns' Don Cockroft kicked two field goals to put Cleveland back in front but van Eeghen again answered in the fourth quarter and the Raiders led by 14-12 when the Browns got the ball at their 15-yard line with 2:22 remaining.

Brian Sipe, the league's Most Valuable Player for 1980, went to work. The march included a 29-yard pass play to Ozzie Newsome, a 23-yard pass to Greg Pruitt and a 14-yard run by Mike Pruitt. Now the Browns were facing second down at the Oakland 13 with 49 seconds left. No doubt, Cleveland was in field goal range. But the conditions for kicking were awful, and Cockroft had earlier missed two field goal attempts and an extra point.

Coach Sam Rutigliano told Sipe to call "Red Slot Right, Halfback Stay, 88," and throw the ball into Lake Erie if no one was open. If the pass attempt failed, the Browns would run on third down and then, if necessary, try a field goal on fourth down. But Mike Davis of the Raiders cut in front of Ozzie Newsome on Sipe's pass to the end zone for a game-clinching interception. Oakland went on to win the Super Bowl later in that postseason, adding to the heartbreak of the game as the Raiders became the first playoff wild card team to win a Super Bowl.

January 4, 1970 — The Browns fall one game short of advancing to the Super Bowl, losing 27-7 in Minnesota to the Vikings in the NFL title game.

January 4, 1986 – The Browns lose a lead and then the game, 24-21, to the Dolphins in Miami in the opening round of the NFL playoffs. Cleveland, which qualified in Marty Schottenheimer's first full year as head coach with an 8-8 regular-season record, had a 21-3 lead early in the third quarter, as Earnest Byner had two touchdown runs. But the Dolphins rallied, and Ron Davenport ran for a 1-yard touchdown with less than two minutes left to decide the outcome.

5

January 5, 2003 — Holcomb's heroic effort falls short

It's fair to say that Kelly Holcomb's career isn't widely memorable in Browns' history. He had an 8-16 record in his 24 starts, and mostly was a handy backup quarterback. Yet for one game, Holcomb was magnificent – and his timing was good, too.

Holcomb had replaced an injured Tim Couch as the starter for Cleveland, and the Browns figured out a way on the last day of the regular season to reach the playoffs for the first time since their 1999 expansion year. The Steelers were waiting in Pittsburgh for them. Maybe the home team wasn't great offensively, but the Steelers' defense under Bill Cowher usually made life difficult for opponents.

Holcomb had other ideas. He came out firing at the start, and didn't stop. Cleveland had a 14-0 lead in the first period, and still led, 33-21, with less than four minutes to play. But Hines Ward caught a Pittsburgh touchdown pass to narrow the lead to 33-28, and Chris Fuamatu-Ma'afala scored from three yards out in the last minute to give the Steelers the 36-33 win.

Holcomb went 26-for-43 for 429 yards and three touchdowns. He spent two more seasons in Cleveland, bounced to Buffalo and Philadelphia, and retired. The game turned out to be the Browns' only playoff appearance in the first 21 years of their revived history.

January 5, 1972 — The Cleveland Arena is sold out for the first time for a Cavaliers' game (it was the franchise's second season), and the packed house sees the Lakers win, 113-103, for their 32nd victory in a row. The attendance was 11,178. The Lakers went on to make it 33 in a row, the longest streak in NBA history.

January 5, 2011 — Two baseball stars who spent parts of their careers in Cleveland - second baseman Roberto Alomar and pitcher Bert Blyleven - are elected to the Baseball Hall of Fame.

January 5, 2011 — Former Cleveland area high school standout Jason Garrett (University School in Hunting Valley) is named head coach of the Dallas Cowboys.

6

January 6, 1990 — Matthews makes the last big play

The crowd at Cleveland Stadium not only saw a classic playoff game in sub-freezing temperatures when the Browns hosted the Buffalo Bills. They also saw the birth of an idea.

Fans might have thought they were watching a video game when it came to great moments. Bernie Kosar threw touchdown passes of 52 and 44 yards to Webster Slaughter for Cleveland. Jim Kelly of the Bills had four passes for scores as well. Buffalo running back Thurman Thomas caught 13 passes for 150 yards.

The Browns had the lead for the entire second half, but it was close. Buffalo worked without a huddle for the rest of the game, and piled up the yardage in an attempt to pull off a comeback. The offense was so effective that several NFL teams have made it an important part of their offensive strategy.

The Bills had one last chance to pull the game out in the fourth quarter in the last minute. Kelly found Ronnie Harmon in the end zone, but the running back dropped the ball. Then Kelly tried to hit Thomas over the middle, but linebacker Clay Matthews made an interception on the 1-yard line with three seconds left for the Browns that saved the 34-30 win.

January 6, 1979 — The Cleveland Force plays and wins its first home indoor soccer game, beating the Pittsburgh Spirit, 7-6 in overtime, at the Coliseum in Richfield.

January 7, 1963 — Modell fires Brown from Browns

Paul Brown ***was*** the Cleveland Browns. He had been the team's general manager and head coach since the team was formed in 1946. The team was named after him, and his move to leading a professional sports organization only added credibility to his long list of coaching successes.

Then in 1961, television and advertising business executive Art Modell, 35, bought control of the team. Brown discovered he had differences with the new boss from New York. The Browns' records in Modell's first two years were 8-5-1 and 7-6-1. The team had not played a postseason game in two years. Reportedly, Brown did not inform Modell of the trade in December 1961 that sent veteran running back Bobby Mitchell to the Washington Redskins for the rights to Heisman Trophy-winning back Ernie Davis of Syracuse.

When Modell announced the coaching change, which occurred while there was a 129-day labor strike going on at the daily Cleveland newspapers, he said, "This is not a firing. This is a reorganization. Paul will continue as a vice president."

Brown wasn't given any new duties. He once described himself as "a vice president in charge of I-don't-know-what." Brown's son Mike recalled his father saying, "They took my team away from me." Brown played a lot of golf until he became involved with the successful effort to bring an expansion team in the American Football League to Cincinnati in 1968.

January 7, 1961 — The Browns lose, 17-16, to the Lions in the first-ever "Playoff Bowl" game played in Miami. The postseason event was created to match up the two second-place finishers in the NFL's divisions during the 1960s. Cleveland played in three such games and lost them all.

January 7, 1971 — Nick Skorich is named the third head coach in Browns' history. He had been the team's offensive coordinator under Blanton Collier.

January 7, 2001 — Chris Palmer is dismissed as head coach of the Browns. The team went 5-27 in his two seasons after returning to the NFL in 1999 as an expansion franchise.

January 7, 2021 — The Indians trade the "face of their franchise," shortstop Francisco Lindor, and pitcher Carlos Carrasco to the New York Mets for shortstops Amed Rosario and Andres Gimenez, pitcher Josh Wolf and outfielder Isaiah Greene. Indians executives believed they could not afford to re-sign Lindor, a four-time All-Star.

8

January 8, 1983 — Browns bounced from jumbo-sized playoffs

The 1982 season was unique in National Football League history. It came with an odd ending, too, at least for the Browns.

A 57-day labor strike wiped out almost two months of the schedule. When the two sides finally settled, the teams agreed to play a nine-game regular season and increase the size of the playoffs to 16 teams from the usual eight. It meant that the Browns' 4-5 record was good enough to qualify for the postseason.

They were matched against the Raiders, the team that had bounced them from the playoffs two years before. Los Angeles (where the team had moved from Oakland in 1982) came in with an 8-1 record, so little was expected from the Browns. Still, they put up a fight. Late in the first half, Cleveland and Los Angeles were tied, 10-10, as Paul McDonald threw a 43-yard touchdown pass to Ricky Feacher.

But it was all Raiders from there. Marcus Allen and Frank Hawkins both rushed for touchdowns. Los Angeles finished with a 27-10 victory.

January 8, 2009 — Under the ownership of Randy Lerner, the Browns move on from Coach Romeo Crennel and hire former Jets' head coach Eric Mangini, who had been in that job for three seasons. Mangini had been fired on December 29, 2008, after the Jets lost four of their last five games and missed the playoffs.

9

January 9, 1988 — Wright's interception boosts Browns

It's a battle of division champions in the NFL playoffs as the AFC East titlists from Indianapolis (9-6) visit Cleveland (10-5). The game was tied, 14-14, in the third quarter and the Colts were driving for an apparent go-ahead score.

The ball was on the Cleveland 16 when quarterback Jack Trudeau dropped back to pass. As he released the ball, he was hit by linebacker Eddie Johnson. The ball had little zip on it, and Browns defensive back Felix Wright had no trouble picking off the pass. Cleveland marched down the field and scored, as Earnest Byner ran over the goal line on a 2-yard play. The Browns never looked back, winning by a score of 38-21.

"It (the interception) turned the game around, because they went down and scored," Colts running back Eric Dickerson told the *Washington Post*. "They scored right away. And I think, if we would have held them and gotten the ball back, we'd have scored. We should have scored on that drive. We should have gotten something, a field goal or a touchdown."

Bernie Kosar was an efficient 20-for-31 for 229 yards and three touchdowns, while Byner ran 23 times for 122 yards. Dickerson was held to 50 yards rushing on 15 carries.

January 9, 2019 — Freddie Kitchens is promoted from offensive coordinator to head coach of the Browns. Kitchens, who played quarterback in college at Alabama, came to the job after never having been a head coach at any level but had worked as an NFL assistant.

January 9, 2022 — Doug Dieken announces his final game as the Browns' radio commentator, ending a run that he had for 37 years. Counting his playing days, Dieken was associated with the team for 51 seasons.

10

January 10, 2021 — Browns earn playoff win in Pittsburgh

A generation of Cleveland football fans might have had its best-ever moment when the Browns defeated the Steelers, 48-37, in a first-round postseason game. Perhaps its second-best moment came earlier, when Cleveland took a stunning 28-0 lead before the first period had ended.

The history books needed some rewriting when this one was over. The Browns won their first playoff game since 1995, and their first road playoff game since 1969 (in Dallas). But here's why the result was particularly sweet: Cleveland had lost to the Steelers in its previous 17 trips to Heinz Field.

The Browns had the biggest first half by a road team in NFL history in rolling up a 35-10 lead through 30 minutes. Pittsburgh made the game interesting, cutting the margin to 35-23 at the end of the third quarter. But Cleveland responded with a pair of touchdowns to wrap up the historic win. And the Browns earned the victory without having head coach Kevin Stefanski on the sideline, as he was home after testing positive for Covid-19. Four interceptions of Steelers quarterback Ben Roethlisberger played a huge role in the outcome.

"I grew up (a Browns fan), so I know what this means," said special teams coach Mike Priefer, who was born in Cleveland.

January 10, 1965 — Colts' defensive end Gino Marchetti delivers a punishing hit on Browns' quarterback Frank Ryan, separating Ryan's shoulder, during the Pro Bowl. The incident sparks speculation that Marchetti was delivering a message about some sentiments that the Browns tried to run up the score on the Colts in the 1964 NFL championship game (a 27-0 win by Cleveland on December 27).

January 10, 2013 — Paul Dolan is approved by Major League Baseball owners as the primary control person of the Indians. He is the son of Larry Dolan, who purchased the club in 1999 from Dick Jacobs.

January 10, 2013 — The Browns hire Rob Chudzinski as their new head coach. He had been an assistant coach in Cleveland twice before, and had been serving as the offensive coordinator in Carolina.

11

January 11, 1987 — Elway drives Broncos past Browns

The Broncos trailed the Browns, 20-13, with 5:32 left in the fourth quarter of the AFC Championship game. Then Denver return specialist Ken Bell had trouble fielding a kickoff and the ball was downed on the Broncos' own 2-yard line, meaning a 98-yard drive would be necessary to tie the game. Broncos offensive guard Keith Bishop joked at that point, "We got 'em right where we want 'em," according to *Sports Illustrated*. The Browns seemed to have the best chance in franchise history to get to their first Super Bowl.

John Elway had other ideas. Four runs and three completed passes moved the ball to

Cleveland 40 with two minutes to go. After an 8-yard sack on a second-down play, Elway hit Mark Jackson for a 20-yard pass on third-and-18.

Another pass moved the ball to the Browns' 14, and Elway took off on a 9-yard scramble. On third-and-1, Elway completed a 5-yard pass to Jackson for a touchdown. Rich Karlis added the extra point, and the Broncos had tied the game, 20-20.

The Browns won the coin toss to receive the ball in overtime but failed on a third-and-two situation to get a first down and decided to punt. Then Elway hit Steve Watson on a 28-yard play to set up a field goal by Karlis with 5:48 gone in overtime. Elway thought Karlis had missed the kick, pulling it left. Karlis told the *Miami Herald*, "Oh, I had about a foot to spare."

January 11, 1967 — John McLendon wins the 500th game of his basketball coaching career, as Cleveland State edges Walsh, 24-22. He was the first black student of Dr. James Naismith, the inventor of basketball. McLendon, who also became the first black pro coach with the Cleveland Pipers of the American Basketball League in 1962, eventually became a member of the Basketball Hall of Fame.

January 11, 2008 — The name of the Indians' stadium changes to Progressive Field as the insurance company based in the suburb of Mayfield obtains the naming rights for 16 years, paying about $58 million.

12

January 12, 1946 — Rams allowed to move to Los Angeles

Talk about going out on top! The Cleveland Rams were the kings of the football world as the year 1946 began. They had won the NFL championship in 1945 by beating the Washington Redskins. Yet they had problems.

Owner Dan Reeves was suffering financial losses while running the Rams, which had entered the NFL in 1937. He was also facing competition from a new franchise called the Cleveland Browns in a new league called the All-America Football Conference, which had a lease to play games in Municipal Stadium. Reeves believed he was in no position to get into a bidding war for talent, and he had his eye on open territory.

The NFL owners met on this day, and Reeves had a bombshell for them. He applied for permission to move the Rams to Los Angeles. At that time, there were no teams in the league west of Chicago or Green Bay. The NFL turned down the request.

But Reeves persisted. He threw in financial guarantees that would help cover travel costs of teams that would play the Rams in Los Angeles. Eventually, they reached an agreement. Reeves reportedly said, "It's not that I love Cleveland less, but that I love Los Angeles more." It was the first time an NFL team moved after winning a title.

January 12, 1971 — John Johnson of the Cavs, playing in their 1970-71 expansion year, becomes the first team member to participate in an NBA All-Star Game. Johnson, the Cavs' initial first-round draft choice from Iowa who would average 12.9 points per game as a 6-foot-7 forward in a 12-year NBA career, appears for two minutes in the contest in San Diego.

January 12, 2020 — Kevin Stefanski is named the 10th Browns' head coach (not counting two interim appointments) since 1999. He had been the offensive coordinator with the Vikings, and was runner-up to Freddie Kitchens in a coaching search a year earlier.

13

January 13, 2016 — Browns hire Jackson as head coach

In the Browns' coaching carousel over the years, Hue Jackson's tenure in Cleveland might rank as the most disappointing. He arrived with a deep resume and good recommendations from the football world, and high expectations for his abilities in working with quarterbacks.

Jackson spent the 1990s coaching in college ball, serving as USC's offensive coordinator from 1997 to 2000. Then he moved to the pros, where he was the offensive coordinator for three teams before finally getting a shot as a head coach in Oakland in 2011. An 8-8 record wasn't good enough for the team's front office to keep Jackson past one year.

The veteran coach headed to Cincinnati, where he served in a variety of roles from 2012 to 2015. Jackson even won assistant coach of the year honors in the NFL in 2015.

But Jackson compiled records of 1-15 in 2016, and 0-16 in 2017. He stayed on through a 2-5-1 start in 2018, when the Browns decided a move was necessary. Jackson's 3-36-1 record gave him a winning percentage of .088 – the worst of any coach in NFL history who stayed with a team for at least 40 games. The Browns never won a road game under Jackson.

January 13, 1963 — Browns running back Jim Brown is chosen the most valuable offensive player for the second consecutive year in the NFL's Pro Bowl, played at the Los Angeles Coliseum.

January 13, 1982 — Former Indians player-manager Frank Robinson is elected to the Baseball Hall of Fame on the same ballot as then-all-time home run king Hank Aaron.

January 13, 2011 — Pat Shurmur gets his turn at coaching the Browns, becoming the sixth coach to be hired since the team resumed play in 1999. Shurmur, chosen by team president Mike Holmgren, had been serving as the offensive coordinator in St. Louis.

14

January 14, 1990 — Another year, another loss to Broncos

Old news: the Browns lose to the Broncos in the AFC Championship Game. New news: At least this version didn't have any last-minute drama to cause agony for months. Denver made it three wins in a row over Cleveland in the conference final, beating the Browns, 37-21, in Denver.

It wasn't easy for the Broncos, in spite of the score. Denver jumped out to a 10-0 halftime lead and had a 24-7 margin in the third quarter. The Browns fought back with a couple of touchdowns to make it 24-21 with a quarter to play.

But quarterback John Elway guided his team to 13 unanswered points. Elway finished 20-for-36 for 385 yards and three touchdowns. A banged-up Bernie Kosar was 19-for-44 and 210 yards with three interceptions.

"When we got close, we just didn't make it happen," a United Press International report quoted Kosar afterward. "We were taking numerous chances out there. It paid off in the third quarter. It didn't pay off in the fourth quarter."

January 14, 1951 — The NFL plays the first Pro Bowl – its version of an all-star game – in Los Angeles. Otto Graham of the Browns is the MVP in the American Conference's 28-27 win, and Cleveland's Bob Rice was one of the officials. Rice worked 19 years as an on-field official and was assigned to two Super Bowls.

January 14, 1961 — Barons' general manager Jim Hendry dies after a heart attack at age 55. Considered "the godfather of hockey statistics," he was elected to the Hockey Hall of Fame in 1968.

15

January 15, 2015 — Cavaliers roll away their troubles

The Cavaliers have star LeBron James back on their roster after a four-year absence, but appear in trouble with a 19-20 record. Cleveland has lost six games in a row and nine of its last 10.

According to the sports blog "Waiting for Next Year," Coach David Blatt had an idea. Instead of having a pregame shootaround for that night's game with the Lakers, the team's coach took the players to the Lucky Strike on Hollywood Boulevard in Los Angeles. Blatt had set up a group outing at a bowling alley, and the establishment had set off some lanes with curtains so that the team could have some privacy.

The Cavaliers spent about three hours at Lucky Strike. They bowled, ate and drank. It apparently was a good release from the pressures of the season. Suitably rejuvenated, the Cavs went back to work and beat the Lakers, 109-102. James had 36 points and Kyrie Irving added 22.

A night later, Cleveland downed the Clippers, 126-121. The Cavaliers won 12 straight games after the bowling adventure, and 14 of 15. Those 19-20 Cavs finished the season 53-29, so they closed with a 34-9 rush. Cleveland advanced to the NBA Finals later that year. Lucky Strike manager Ashley Aul, a Northeast Ohio native, took immediate credit for helping the Cavs turn around their season.

January 15, 1959 — Cleveland's Mark McCormack formally signs pro golfer Arnold Palmer to be his business representative, adding one of the biggest names in the sport to his list of clients. It's the start of McCormack's venture that eventually becomes known as International Management Group (IMG), which changed sports marketing throughout the world.

January 15, 2013 — The name of the Browns' home field is officially changed from Cleveland Browns Stadium to FirstEnergy Stadium. The *Akron Beacon Journal* reports the deal calls for the Akron utility to pay $102 million over 17 years.

16

January 16, 1972 — Battle of Ohio moves West

At first glance, something seems wrong about the description of the contest between the Cincinnati Royals and Cleveland Cavaliers on this date. The two teams had their usual lineups that night, but the location was anything but typical. The game was played in Las Cruces, New Mexico, of all places. That's the home of New Mexico State, and it's located on the southern edge of the state.

The NBA sometimes took its act on the road, setting up games at neutral sites to increase awareness and build fan bases. In this case, the Cavs were in the midst of an eight-game road trip. They had a few days off between dates in Houston and Milwaukee, so the schedule-maker sent them to Las Cruces.

This wasn't a great attraction; the Cavs were 15-31 and the Royals were 13-31. But it was an NBA game that counted. Nate Archibald, who played college basketball in nearby El Paso, must have felt at home in that part of the country. He had 41 points and 16 assists in the Royals' 128-108 win. John Warren and John Johnson had 24 each for Cleveland.

The Cavaliers lost all eight games on the trip, and 11 in a row overall. Cleveland made a few more trips to unusual locations in that time period – playing the Bucks in Madison, Wisconsin, and the 76ers in Hershey, Pennsylvania. By 1974, the league decided the extra travel wasn't worth it, and generally stopped scheduling such games.

January 16, 1966 - In what turns out to be his last NFL game, Jim Brown rushes 21 times for 65 yards and is named "back of the game" in the 1966 NFL Pro Bowl, the 16th all-star game. The game concluded the 1965 season as the East team, coached by Blanton Collier of the Browns, defeated the West, coached by Vince Lombardi, 36-7.

January 17, 1988 — 'The Fumble' leads to another loss

The Browns had suffered a painful loss to Denver in January 1987, in the AFC Championship game. They deserve credit for bouncing back a year later and reaching the same point in the playoffs. The Broncos were still the opponent, but this time the game was in Denver. What could be better than spoiling the Broncos' Super Bowl hopes in Mile High Stadium?

Denver did its best to take the suspense out of the game. The Broncos jumped out to a 21-3 lead at halftime. But Bernie Kosar threw three touchdowns in the second half, and the game was tied, 31-31, in the fourth quarter. Denver responded with a nice drive that led to a 20-yard scoring play from John Elway to Sammy Winder. The Broncos had to protect a seven-point lead with about six minutes left, almost what the Browns tried to do in the previous season.

Kosar marched the Browns down the field in response. He worked nicely with Earnest Byner on several pass plays as Cleveland reached the Denver 8. Then on a play called "13-Trap," Byner got outside and saw a little daylight ... when Jeremiah Castille stripped the ball away at the 3-yard line. Denver recovered, took an intentional safety, and won by a score of 38-33.

"I tried to split two guys and the ball just popped out," Byner said. "I knew I had the first down and the chance for the touchdown."

January 17, 1915 — With player-manager Nap Lajoie off to the Philadelphia Athletics, Cleveland's American League baseball team changes its name from the Naps to the Indians.

January 17, 2021 — A Browns' storybook season comes to an end with a 22-17 loss to the Chiefs in Kansas City in the divisional round of the playoffs. Cleveland rallied from a 19-3 halftime deficit, but couldn't catch the defending champions in spite of the Chiefs' loss of star quarterback Patrick Mahomes to a concussion in the third quarter.

18

January 18, 1950 — Indians' Feller gets his pay cut

By 1950, Bob Feller had been a baseball superstar for years, coming to the big leagues at age 17 in 1936. He had won 20 games five times, and never had a losing record. However, Feller only had a 15-14 record with a 3.75 earned-run average for the Indians in 1949. Those numbers didn't meet his high standards.

Feller went in to talk contract with General Manager Hank Greenberg. He asked to have his salary reduced by $20,000. If this wasn't the first time that someone had asked for a good-sized pay cut, it was at least a rarity.

Feller's new contract dropped his salary to $45,000. That was still the second-biggest deal for an Indian player. Player-manager Lou Boudreau supposedly received about $65,000. Greenberg also revealed to the media that Feller had been receiving attendance bonuses from Cleveland since 1938, but the new deal did not have that clause.

Feller went back to work at the reduced rate, and bounced back on the mound. He finished 16-11 with a 3.43 ERA. The right-handed pitcher even made his eighth and final trip to the All-Star Game in 1950.

January 18, 1963 — Browns' draft choice Tom Bloom is killed in a car accident in Western Ohio. He had recently signed a contract with the team, and had used his bonus money to purchase the car he was driving that day.

19

January 19, 1937 — Three Indians' alumni called to Hall

The Baseball Hall of Fame opened in 1936, and that set the stage for arguments over who should be inducted. Baseball had been played professionally at that point for more than 50 years, yet only five players were part of the Class of 1936: Ty Cobb, Walter Johnson, Christy Mathewson, Babe Ruth and Honus Wagner.

That meant the pool of potential inductees was deep in talent. A year later, eight more people – six players and two executives – were chosen. Happily for Indians' fans, three had strong ties to Cleveland.

Most fans knew the exploits of Cy Young, Tris Speaker and Nap Lajoie. Young won 511 games as a pitcher, a number that will never be topped. Speaker was an excellent hitter and a superb center fielder. Lajoie, a second baseman, has been called the first superstar in American League history.

They joined Morgan Bulkeley, Ban Johnson, Connie Mack, John McGraw and George Wright in the Class of 1937. The Indians' next player to go to Cooperstown was Bob Feller in 1962.

January 19, 1972 — Former Indians star pitcher Early Wynn is voted into the Baseball Hall of Fame along with Sandy Koufax and Yogi Berra.

20

January 20, 1965 — Welcome home, Rocky

Think of it as trying to make up for a mistake. In 1960, Indians general manager Frank Lane, who made a reputation for bold trades, sent popular right fielder Rocky Colavito to the Tigers for Harvey Kuenn. It sparked a strong negative reaction from fans. They feared the deal would cause the Indians to lose ground to the rest of the American League – and they did.

Now fast forward five years, and the Indians jumped at the chance to get Rocky back in their lineup. Cleveland dealt promising young outfielder Tommie Agee, veteran catcher John Romano and pitcher Tommy John, who jumped from Class D minor league ball to Class AAA in one year, to the White Sox. Chicago dealt outfielders Mike Hershberger (a Massillon native) and Jim Landis and pitcher Fred Talbot to Kansas City. The Royals shipped Colavito and catcher Camilo Carreon to Cleveland.

"I'm glad to be going home – and I do mean home," Colavito said. "Every year when I went into Cleveland with the Tigers or Athletics, I would say to myself, 'Wouldn't it be nice to be playing here again?' "

Colavito had two good seasons in his old / new home, but then his numbers fell off drastically. The Indians traded him in 1967 to the White Sox, and there were few protests this time. Looking back at the trade to bring him back, a high price was paid. Agee helped the New York Mets win the 1969 World Series and John won 288 games in a 26-year career.

January 20, 1999 — The Browns take their time in the hiring process, but finally select Chris Palmer as their first head coach of the newborn expansion team. Palmer, who turned 49 during the season, had been the offensive coordinator in Jacksonville with nine years' NFL coaching experience and 27 years overall.

January 20, 2003 — The Cavaliers fire John Lucas as coach after an 8-34 start to the season. Lucas, a former star NBA point guard and the No. 1 pick of the 1976 NBA Draft by the Houston Rockets, was in the second year of a three-year, $9 million contract. His overall record was 37-87.

January 21, 2003 — Johnson dies of cancer at 43

It's a very sad day in Browns Nation, as popular Browns linebacker Eddie Johnson, 43, dies after a two-year battle with colon cancer.

When his NFL playing career began in 1981, Johnson beat the odds just to be on the roster. He was a seventh-round draft choice from Louisville, but from 1984 to '87, he earned a starting spot alongside such teammates as Tom Cousineau and Chip Banks.

Coach Sam Rutigliano played a 3-4 defense, and Johnson earned his berth even though he was only 6-foot-1 and 220 pounds. Johnson picked up the nickname "The Assassin" for his tackling skills. After his 10-year career was over in 1991, he stayed in Cleveland and worked in the community. Browns' alumni leaders admired him for never declining a request, even when his illness surfaced.

"The biggest regret I have is not getting to the Super Bowl," Johnson said in an interview in 2000. Others certainly wished they had had the chance to spend more time with him.

January 21, 1978 — The Barons pile up nine goals – setting a team record for their time in Cleveland – in defeating Colorado, 9-4. Dennis Maruk has two goals for the Barons.

22

January 22, 2016 - Lue hired as Cavaliers' coach

Despite a winning record, the Cavaliers decide to make a coaching change in midseason – replacing David Blatt with Tyronn Lue.

The Cavs had a 30-11 record, good for first place in the Eastern Conference. Most coaches would get a contract extension in that situation. Blatt was the first coach in NBA history to be fired when leading the conference.

Lue had been serving as Blatt's assistant, arriving in 2014 with a four-year, $6.5 million contract, according to a report by Yahoo Sports. It was believed to be the highest salary for an NBA assistant coach in league history. Lue was considered by observers to be popular with core players on the team.

You might not remember this fact about Lue and the 2015-16 season: He finished the regular season with a 27-14 record. That was not as good as Blatt's ledger. Still, Lue and the Cavs did win a championship in 2016, so no one would disagree that everything worked out perfectly.

January 22, 1975 - Charlie Sifford, the first African American to play on the PGA Tour, signs a three-year contract to become the club pro at Sleepy Hollow Golf Club in Brecksville.

January 22, 1976 – Indians pitcher Bob Lemon is elected to the Baseball Hall of Fame. Lemon had a career record of 207-128.

January 23, 2014 – Browns hire Pettine away from the Bills

The Browns certainly did their due diligence when it came to hiring a new coach when they decided to make a change from Rob Chudzinski after his 4-12 season in 2013. The team went through about 15 candidates. There were reports that some, such as Todd Bowles and Josh McDaniels, simply didn't want the job. Meanwhile, Bill O'Brien, James Franklin and Ken Whisenhunt went elsewhere.

At the end of the process, they decided to hire Mike Pettine, the defensive coordinator for the Buffalo Bills in 2013.

Pettine had worked for Rex Ryan in Buffalo, and was credited with doing a good job. The Bills had one of the best defenses in the league. His 3-4 defensive philosophy figured to be a good match for the Browns' talent.

"We wanted to be thorough from the start, and we interviewed as many people as we could," team executive Joe Banner said. "From that group, we hired the best individual for this job. Our players and fans are going to really enjoy Mike Pettine and his leadership style. We're excited to have him out in front of our team, and we look forward to working closely with him." As for Pettine, he said, "I'll bet on myself."

January 23, 1962 – Bob Feller and Jackie Robinson are elected to the Baseball Hall of Fame. If you don't know who those two gentlemen are, you probably are reading the wrong book.

24

January 24, 1950 - Maxim wins boxing championship

If Cleveland native Joey Maxim (his real name was Giuseppe Antonio Berardinelli) wanted to win boxing's light heavyweight world championship, he'd have to travel to do it. The champion at the time was Freddie Mills, and he wanted the fight at London's Earl's Court Exhibition Centre. Maxim and his crew thus jumped on a boat to cross the ocean.

Mills became the world champion at the 175-pound weight limit back in 1948. He had fought once in 1949 in a non-title bout, so he had gone about 18 months without defending the belt. Maxim, meanwhile, probably would have gone to Antarctica for a title shot at this point. He entered the ring on this night with 87 pro fights to his credit, winning 67.

Mills was the big favorite, in part because he was fighting at home. But Maxim took care of business relatively easily. He scored a knockout in the 10th round to take the title. What's more, after the fight, he found three of Mills' teeth embedded in his boxing glove.

Maxim held the title for almost three years, eventually losing it to the legendary Archie Moore. Maxim finished with a record of 82-29-4, and lost eight of his last nine fights. He was selected for induction into the International Boxing Hall of Fame in 1994.

January 24, 1939 — George Sisler, a native of the Akron suburb now called New Franklin, is voted into the Baseball Hall of Fame. Sisler had a 15-year career and won two batting titles in 1920 and 1922 for the St. Louis Browns when he hit .407 and .420.

25

January 25, 1961 – Modell buys the Browns for $4 million

There was no reason for Cleveland sports fans to know who 35-year-old Art Modell was in 1961. He went into business as an executive in television broadcasting and advertising after serving in World War II. He had no apparent business connections to Cleveland, having worked in New York.

The Browns had been formed by Arthur "Mickey" McBride in 1945. McBride, who had interests in real estate, a horse racing news wire, and a taxi cab company, owned the team through 1953 before selling for a reported $600,000.

(As an aside, when the term "taxi squad" comes up regarding football rosters, it's a reference to players needed as replacements in case of injury. Those players might have been among a team's final roster cuts and some became McBride employees – perhaps even taxi drivers – as a way to keep them nearby.)

Various people and companies owned the Browns through 1960; the Nationwide Insurance Company was said to be the largest owner of stock with a holding of 30 percent or more, according to media reports.

Modell put together a group to buy the team for a reported $4 million. In his 2010 book *Crazy, With the Papers to Prove It*, Cleveland sportswriter Dan Coughlin reported Modell's share of ownership was 55 percent and he borrowed money to come up with that investment. On this day, it was announced Modell and company were becoming owners of the NFL team.

Coughlin's book reported that a former Browns player, running back Fred "Curly" Morrison, heard that the team's executives led by president Dave Jones, 74, were willing to sell. Morrison worked for CBS in advertising sales and his accounts included tire company clients, which brought him to Cleveland and Akron on business calls. His television industry connections led to finding Modell, Coughlin said.

Media reports said Paul Brown had eight years remaining on his contract to serve as vice president, general manager, and head coach. He had owned a part of the team before the transaction with Modell was completed, and retained it afterward.

January 25, 1977 — A Barons' sweater is worn in an NHL All-Star Game for the first time, as Al MacAdam is Cleveland's representative in the game played in Vancouver.

26

January 26, 1970 — Browns trade Warfield to Dolphins

Teams usually don't trade talented players like Paul Warfield. The high school star from Warren Harding who then played for Woody Hayes at Ohio State had come to the Browns as a rookie wide receiver in 1964, and made an immediate impact. Warfield caught 52 passes, nine for touchdowns. He remained a standout through the 1960s, averaging more than 20 yards per catch from 1966 through 1969.

However, heading into the 1970 season, the Browns decided they needed a young quarterback. Bill Nelsen was coming off a season in which the Browns went 10-3-1, and was selected for the Pro Bowl. But he was playing with several injuries from his past.

After studying the upcoming NFL Draft, Browns executives dealt Warfield to the Miami Dolphins, a team that had not posted a winning record in four years of play. The Dolphins did have their quarterback in Bob Griese, and what they needed was a target. Miami gave Cleveland its first-round draft pick, the No. 3 choice overall. In a separate deal, the Browns made a move to replace Warfield. They sent a previous No. 1 draft pick, running back Ron Johnson, along with Jim Kanicki and Wayne Meylan to the New York Giants for receiver Homer Jones.

The draft took place the next day. The Browns took Purdue quarterback Mike Phipps. It all worked out great for Miami, as Coach Don Shula followed Warfield to town and the Dolphins had a great run during the 1970s. Phipps sat on the bench his first two years, then posted a 10-3-1 record as a starter in 1972 before going 12-20-2 during the three seasons after that. Jones lasted only one season in Cleveland.

January 26, 1956 — Indians' General Manager Hank Greenberg is elected to the Baseball Hall of Fame for his playing career with the Detroit Tigers from 1930 to 1946 and the Pittsburgh Pirates in 1947. He joined the Indians' front office under owner Bill Veeck as an executive in 1948 and remained until 1957.

27

January 27, 1982 — Huston burns Warriors with 27 assists

The Cavaliers were awful in 1981-82. They only won 15 games, tying a team record for fewest wins in a season that originally was set by the first-year team of 1970-71.

But the Cavs had a reason to smile with the play of left-handed point guard Geoff Huston on this day. Huston was drafted by the Knicks in the third round in 1979, and bounced around the NBA in his career. He came to Cleveland in a 1981 deal with the Dallas Mavericks that cost the Cavs their first-round pick in 1985 and contributed to the creation of "The Stepien Rule," named for team owner Ted Stepien, that prohibits teams from having no first-round draft pick in consecutive years.

For the mid-winter game against the Warriors, Huston was more than worth that pick. He played 46 minutes and frequently drove to the hoop for baskets in scoring 24 points (10-of-17 from the field). Taking what the defense gave him, Huston completed pass after pass to pile up 27 assists. That set a Cavaliers team record and was only two off the NBA record of 29 (by Kevin Porter) at the time.

It led to a rare Cleveland victory, a 110-106 triumph over Golden State. It also sparked the Cavs to four wins in five games, their best stretch of the season. From there, the Cavaliers closed with a 4-33 record, including losses in their final 19 games.

January 27, 1969 — Cleveland native, Benedictine High School graduate and former Browns player Chuck Noll is named head coach of the Pittsburgh Steelers. At 37, Noll was the youngest head coach ever in the NFL at that time.

January 27, 1989 — The Browns hire Bud Carson as their new head coach, replacing the departed Marty Schottenheimer. The Rams' Fritz Shurmur was considered a strong candidate for the position.

January 28, 1957 — Akron's Fry tops Gibson in Australia

A player who wins one of the four "Grand Slam" tournaments in tennis is considered a special accomplishment. Win all four – Wimbledon, the French Open, the U.S. Open, and the Australian Open – and the player is an all-time great. Say hello, then, to Shirley Fry of Akron, who became one of the best players in tennis history. Speaking of statistics, she also won a doubles title at all four Slam events.

Fry was already good enough to be ranked among the top 10 American players in 1946, even though she wouldn't graduate from Rollins College in Winter Park, Florida, until 1949. Her first singles' slam win came in 1951 in France, as she defeated Doris Hart in three sets. Five years later at Wimbledon, Fry was too good for England's Angela Buxton, winning in straight sets.

That led her to Forest Hills, the home of the United States Open. Her opponent in the final was Althea Gibson, who earlier in the year had become the first African American to win one of the four majors. Fry beat Gibson, 6-3, 6-4. That left only one more mountain to climb, and she did it on this day. Fry again topped Gibson, 6-3, 6-4, in the Australian Open.

With that, Fry retired at age 29 – even though she had a chance to win all four Grand Slam events in a row. Instead she celebrated her run by getting married to Karl Irvin in Australia. Gibson went on to win at Wimbledon and Forest Hills later in 1957.

January 28, 1901 — The American League of professional baseball clubs is formed with the Cleveland Blues (or Bluebirds) as a member.

January 28, 1958 — The Browns use their seventh-round draft choice (No. 84 pick overall) on running back Bobby Mitchell of Illinois. Mitchell would go on to a Hall of Fame career. He spent four years in the backfield with the Browns before being traded to Washington for the rights to Heisman Trophy winner Ernie Davis. Mitchell was the first African American on the Washington roster, and stayed for seven seasons as a top wide receiver.

29

January 29, 1980 — Cavs outlast Lakers in marathon

Joe Tait was the play-by-play radio broadcast for more than 3,000 NBA games during his career with the Cavaliers. He called this game the most exciting of them all.

The Cavaliers were struggling in the first year of new head coach Stan Albeck with a 22-31 record. Albeck had been hired as the team's second head coach in its history, replacing Bill Fitch, who had resigned to accept the Boston Celtics' job. The Lakers had rejuvenated their franchise with the addition of Earvin "Magic" Johnson to go with players such as Kareem Abdul-Jabbar and Jamaal "Silk" Wilkes. The teams traded leads in the early going, and Cleveland put on the last spurt of regulation time. Mike Mitchell's jumper with 29 seconds left sent the game to overtime with a 114-114 score.

Michael Cooper scored for the Lakers with seven seconds left in the first overtime to force more basketball. The game went through a second overtime, and then a third. The Lakers led, 151-146, with less than two minutes left when reserve forward Bill "Poodle" Willoughby hit some big shots to put the Cavs ahead. But Willoughby was called for goaltending Norm Nixon's go-ahead shot with five seconds left.

Cleveland put the ball in the hands of Mitchell, who drove to the basket and was fouled by Jim Chones with two seconds left. Mitchell made both free throws, and then a Los Angeles heave missed the target, and the Cavs were a 154-153 winner. Mitchell finished with 34 points to lead Cleveland, while Abdul-Jabbar had 42 for the Lakers. "You don't unwind after something like this," Cavs guard Randy Smith said after the game.

January 29, 1963 — The Pro Football Hall of Fame, based in Canton, Ohio, where the league was founded in 1920, announces its inaugural class of 17 inductees. It includes 11 players (Harold "Red" Grange, Don Hutson, Earl "Dutch" Clark, Bronko Nagurski, Mel Hein, Pete Henry, Cal Hubbard, Sammy Baugh, John "Blood" McNally, Ernie Nevers, Jim Thorpe), along with five owner/executives (Earl "Curly" Lambeau, Bert Bell, Tim Mara, George Preston Marshall, Joe Carr) and an owner/coach (George Halas).

January 29, 1974 — Wide receiver Gerald Tinker goes to Atlanta in the second round (44th overall) in the NFL draft. As of 2023, it remains the highest a Kent State player has ever been picked.

January 29, 1982 — The Indians release pitcher Wayne Garland, who became one of baseball's first prominent free agents to change teams when he signed a $2.3 million, 10-year contract in 1976.

January 29, 2018 — The Indians announce they will drop the logo known as Chief Wahoo from their uniforms beginning in 2019.

30

January 30, 2004 — Reunion spotlights Kent State trio

Kent State University's "Varsity K" Hall of Fame induction banquet marks a special occasion that includes a reunion of three national figures from the college's athletic program back in 1958 – baseball's Gene Michael, football's Rick Forzano, and basketball's Bill Bertka.

Michael, who played basketball and baseball at Kent, was a graduate of Akron East High and is the only person to be a player, manager, general manager, coach and scout for the New York Yankees. Forzano, a graduate of Akron Garfield High, was head football coach at Navy and with the Detroit Lions. Bertka, a graduate of Akron Buchtel High, was general manager of the New Orleans Jazz and a longtime coach and scout with the Los Angeles Lakers.

One of Forzano's assistant coaches at Navy was Steve Belichick, father of Bill Belichick. When Forzano was the Lions' coach, he hired the 23-year-old Bill Belichick to his first full-time NFL job. Other assistants on Forzano's staff in Detroit were future head coaches Joe Bugel, Raymond Berry and Jerry Glanville.

Bertka helped the Lakers earn 10 NBA championship rings during his tenure with the franchise, including seven in a coaching capacity.

January 30, 1973 — Linebacker Tom Jackson of Louisville is a fourth-round draft pick of the Denver Broncos after participating in multiple sports at Cleveland John Adams High School. Jackson would go on to a 14-year NFL career and then spent 29 years as an NFL analyst for ESPN.

January 30, 1978 — Addie Joss is named to the Baseball Hall of Fame. His entire major league pitching career, including throwing the fourth perfect game in Major League Baseball history, was with Cleveland from 1902-1910.

January 30, 1995 — The Cavaliers retire No. 22 to honor star forward Larry Nance.

31

January 31, 1977 — Pair of Indians picked for Cooperstown

It's not often that a particular team has two players selected for the Baseball Hall of Fame. Yet that's what happened when the voting by the Veterans Committee was released, showing that Al Lopez and Joe Sewell were both chosen.

Lopez caught more than 1,900 games in his career, a record that lasted for more than 40 years. However, he was best known for his managing. From 1949 to 1964, only one manager that didn't wear a Yankees uniform led a team to the World Series. That manager was Lopez, who guided the 1954 Indians and the 1959 Chicago White Sox.

Sewell got his big-league chance under horrible circumstances, as he moved into the lineup when Ray Chapman died in 1920 when hit by a pitch. Sewell was known for making contact at the plate. In 1929, he went 115 games without a strikeout, and often had fewer than 10 strikeouts in a season.

The pair joined Ernie Banks, Martin Dihugo, Pop Lloyd and Amos Rusie as inductees that summer.

January 31, 1962 — The Cleveland Pipers of the American Basketball League announce that Ralph Wilson, the owner of the Buffalo Bills of the American Football League, will become the majority owner of the team. It was part of a plan to bring an NBA franchise to Cleveland, perhaps as part of a merger between the Pipers and the NBA's Syracuse Nationals. The announcement was premature, as an agreement had not been finalized.

1

February 1, 1956 — Jenkins leads the way at Olympics

It is a great day in the history of American figure skating. You can give some folks from Akron two-thirds of the credit.

Hayes Jenkins was the favorite for the gold medal entering the 1956 Winter Olympics in Cortina d'Ampezzo, Italy. He had won world championships in 1953, 1954, and 1955. Before his performance at the Olympics, coach Edi Scholdan gave him some advice: "Hayes, whatever you do, don't fall, because if you fall, you'll lose."

Jenkins followed orders, and won the gold medal. What's more, brother David won the bronze. Ronnie Robertson of Long Beach, California, finished between them for a 1-2-3 finish by the American team. They represented the first medals won by the United States in the '56 Games. Americans only won seven medals in the entire competition.

Later, Carol Heiss won the silver medal in women's ice skating singles. She did even better in 1960, winning the gold medal, as did David Jenkins. Romance was on the skaters' cards, too. Carol married Hayes Jenkins in 1960, and they settled in Northeast Ohio.

February 1, 1981 — Nate Archibald of the Boston Celtics wins MVP honors as the East beats the West, 123-120, in the NBA All-Star Game at the Coliseum in Richfield. Cavaliers' forward Mike Mitchell has 14 points in 15 minutes.

February 1, 1983 — Tony Rini, one of the best jockeys in the history of the Cleveland area, sees his career end after an accident at Oaklawn Park during a workout. Rini suffered a broken back and a paralyzed left arm. He won 2,438 races as a jockey, and went on to have success as a trainer after the incident.

2

February 2, 2011 — Three Indians honored together

The Caribbean Baseball Hall of Fame salutes players from that part of the world who achieved success in the sport. It's also a way of honoring those who have been standouts in the Caribbean World Series over the years, a regional championship that takes place in the winter months.

The Indians have had several players receive the honor. The Class of 2011 for the Hall, inducted on this day, was a particularly fruitful year. Roberto Alomar, Carlos Baerga, and Candy Maldonado all went in together. Baerga played in seven championship rounds, while Alomar was in four and Maldonado in three.

They have lots of company when it comes to Indians' alumni, including Rico Carty, Ruben Gomez, Minnie Minoso, Camilo Pascual, Orlando Pena, Juan Pizarro, Vic Power, Humberto Robinson, Vicente Romo, and Jose Santiago.

The Hall of Fame has been saluting these players since 1996, when Carty, whose nickname was "The Beeg Mon," was in the first class. He joined Pascual, Hector Espino, and Willard Brown at the front of the line.

February 2, 1969 — Former Indians pitcher Stan Coveleski and Yankee great Waite Hoyt are named to the Baseball Hall of Fame by the Veterans Committee. They joined Roy Campanella and Stan Musial as inductees that summer.

February 2, 1978 — Elmore Smith has a huge day for the Cavaliers, scoring 32 points with 24 rebounds, as they beat the Bullets, 110-93. Smith, a 7-foot center who was the third pick of the first round of the NBA Draft in 1971, had been acquired by Cavs coach Bill Fitch in an attempt to bolster the frontcourt after the retirement of Nate Thurmond. He averaged 12 points and eight rebounds a game in 1977-78, but then played only 24 games the next year and was out of the NBA in 1979 at age 30.

3

February 3, 1978 — O'Neill purchases the Indians

The Indians were in big trouble. They were out of money. There was talk about whether the team could remain in Cleveland. But then 78-year-old Francis "Steve" O'Neill appeared.

"The club was practically bankrupt," said Gabe Paul, part of O'Neill's group that bought the team. "They would have gone under had we not stepped in."

O'Neill picked up the nickname "Steve" after the catcher for the 1920 Cleveland Indians. He made his money in the trucking business, and was a part owner of the team from 1961 to 1973. O'Neill then sold that interest to join with Cleveland-area native George Steinbrenner in the purchase of the Yankees, but five years later he divested that share to take control of the Indians.

The new ownership group paid a reported $6 million for the team, and agreed to be responsible for $5 million in debts. The purchase represented a life preserver for a franchise that needed one. The transaction marked the return of Paul to Cleveland after he had helped Steinbrenner build a winner with the Yankees, in part with the acquisitions of Chris Chambliss, Graig Nettles and Dick Tidrow from the Indians. Paul said he would not be caught in putting a timetable on when the Indians' fortunes would turn around. "Timetables are alibis," he was quoted in the *Akron Beacon Journal*'s news report of the ownership change. "If you put a five-year timetable on it, you've got four years of comfortable sailing."

February 3, 2019 — Former Kent State quarterback Julian Edelman, who was switched to wide receiver in the NFL, is named Most Valuable Player of the Super Bowl as the New England Patriots defeat the Los Angeles Rams, 13-3.

February 4, 1973 — AHL Barons depart Cleveland

There was reason for some joy among Ohio hockey fans when Cleveland was awarded a franchise in the newly formed World Hockey Association in 1972. While the WHA wasn't the National Hockey League, it gave Northeast Ohio fans the chance to see some great players such as Bobby Hull and Gordie Howe.

But there was a snag. The Cleveland Barons of the American Hockey League were still around. Nick Mileti owned both teams, and soon came to the conclusion that the minor-league franchise wouldn't survive with the Crusaders in town. The Barons were stuck playing some home games on Saturday and Sunday afternoons, and attendance frequently dipped under 1,000 per game. On November 6, Mileti announced that an agreement had been reached to move the Barons to Lewiston, Maine.

The AHL's leaders essentially responded with a speedy "not so fast." The AHL, perhaps with a quiet push from NHL owners who weren't willing to do any favors for a WHA team owner, voted down the franchise shift. Mileti regrouped and eventually worked out a deal to move the team to Jacksonville, Florida.

Even so, it took a little time to complete the arrangements. The Barons limped to the finish line of the Cleveland part of their history. On this date, they played their final game in Cleveland. Richmond took a 5-1 decision before an announced attendance of only 435. The coach of the Barons was John Muckler, who would go on to win a Stanley Cup as coach of the Edmonton Oilers in 1990.

February 4, 1989 — Bill White, who had been a star National League first baseman from Warren and had played in college at Hiram, is named president of the National League. He held the position until 1994. Earlier in his life, White also was the first Black play-by-play broadcaster of a major league team as he worked for the New York Yankees.

February 4, 2004 — Michael Rowland, one of the top jockeys at Northeast Ohio's thoroughbred horse racing track, Thistledown, for almost a quarter of a century, is killed in an accident during a race at Kentucky's Turfway Park. Rowland won 3,997 races in his career.

February 5, 1991 — Browns hire Belichick as new head coach

After the Super Bowl early in 1991, there was one man who was considered the hottest NFL head coaching candidate. Bill Belichick had been the defensive coordinator of the New York Giants, where he was known as "Doom" or the "Voice of Doom," and helped them defeat the Buffalo Bills in Super Bowl XXV earlier in the year.

Now he was ready for a step up. Belichick received a five-year contract to become the new coach of the Browns, replacing Bud Carson. At 38, he became the youngest head coach in the league by six years. He was the youngest Browns head coach since Paul Brown, who was 37 when he took the job.

"There'll be some questions about my age and experience relative to this job and this type of responsibility," Belichick said. "When I came into professional football, I was 23 years old with the Baltimore Colts. I heard those same questions. I feel like all those questions have been met. I'll stand by my record."

Belichick coached five seasons in Cleveland, and only had a winning record once. When the Browns moved to Baltimore for the 1996 season, Belichick was told he'd be coaching the relocated franchise – only to be informed a week after the move that owner Art Modell would start in his new city without him. Belichick eventually landed in New England, where he became universally acknowledged as one of the greatest head coaches in NFL history.

February 5, 1984 — The Indians trade infielder Toby Harrah to the Yankees for pitcher George Frazier and outfielder Otis Nixon.

February 6, 1970 — Cleveland awarded an NBA team

Times were tough in the National Basketball Association around 1970. The league was in the midst of a war over players with the American Basketball Association, and the price of talent kept rising. Even though the NBA was in bigger markets and had better players overall, its teams were not doing well financially.

One way to bring in revenue was to add expansion teams, whose owners would pay for the chance to join the NBA, with those funds distributed among the membership.

The league had announced on November 5, 1969, that it would add two teams. It received several applications, and decided that two teams weren't enough. So franchises were granted to four cities – Buffalo, Cleveland, Houston, and Portland – on this day. The price tag started at $3 million but eventually rose to $3.7 million.

The first casualty of the decision was Houston. The owners couldn't meet the financial guidelines, and they dropped out. (Footnote: the Rockets franchise then moved from San Diego to Houston in 1971.) However, the other three cities immediately started work on preparing for their first season – choosing players in the college draft and finding benchwarmers from existing teams to fill out their veteran roster. After all, training camp was only seven months away.

February 6, 1973 — The Celtics only lost 14 games in the 1972-73 season, but one was in Cleveland as the Cavaliers took a 110-105 decision. Lenny Wilkens had 31 points to lead the Cavs.

February 6, 1995 — Former Thunderbirds owner John Kuczek is an apparent suicide victim in Salem, Ohio, one day before he is scheduled to start a jail term for his involvement in a federal securities fraud case. He had sold his interest in the Arena Football League team before the 1993 season, placing it in a trust for his grandchildren.

February 6, 2001 — Robert Smith, who starred at Euclid High School and Ohio State University, retires from his running back role at age 28 with the Minnesota Vikings. Smith played eight years in the NFL.

7

February 7, 2011 — Cavaliers' losing streak hits 25

It was a moment that became symbolic of the Cavaliers' 2010-11 season. Cleveland's 7-foot center Ryan Hollins lined up for a jump ball against 6-2 Dallas guard Jason Terry. And Terry got the tap.

The Cavs lost a 99-96 decision to the Mavericks, their 25th consecutive defeat. No matter how it was counted – over one or two seasons – it was the longest such skid in NBA history.

"We're in the record books, we all know that, something we don't want to be a part of, but you can't go back and turn back the hands of time," forward Antawn Jamison said to the Associated Press. "We've got to worry about moving forward. The most important thing is getting a win."

Cleveland fought back throughout the game, and had a chance to tie at the buzzer. But Anthony Parker's shot danced around the rim before falling away, and the Cavs had found a new place in the record books. The loss made them 1-35 in their previous 36 games. It was their first season since LeBron James left as a free agent to play in Miami.

February 7, 1981 — The Cavaliers send their 1980 No. 1 draft pick Chad Kinch and a No. 1 pick in 1985 to the expansion Dallas Mavericks for guard Geoff Huston. The deal by Cavs owner Ted Stepien and Coach Bill Musselman means Cleveland has none of its own first-round draft picks for the period from 1982 to 1986 and eventually leads to an NBA by-law change that becomes known as "The Stepien Rule," prohibiting teams from having no first-round draft picks in consecutive seasons.

February 7, 2005 — The Browns hire Romeo Crennel as head coach. The former Cleveland defensive coordinator (2000) had that same job with the Patriots when they won Super Bowls in both 2004 and 2005.

8

February 8, 2020 — Cavaliers add Drummond from Pistons

The Cavaliers were in need of talent during the 2019-20 season. They had a 13-39 record and were on a five-game losing streak. Then General Manager Koby Altman completed a major trade in an effort to change the situation.

The Cavs added center Andre Drummond of the Pistons. In return, Detroit acquired guard Brandon Knight and big man John Henson. In addition, the Pistons were given the right to flip second-round draft picks in 2023 if it helped them at the time.

Drummond had been to the All-Star Game twice in his playing career. He led the league in rebounds, offensive rebounds, defensive rebounds, and double-doubles. Drummond was a ninth overall draft pick of the Pistons, and had averaged 14.4 points and 13.8 rebounds a game in his career. Detroit thought Drummond might opt out of his contract, and they'd lose him without getting anything in return.

Weeks later, Drummond gave this reaction to the trade to the website SBNation: "For me, it was just a part of the game, a part of the business, and I just happened to be falling into it, so it was definitely a different experience for me. Do I have any hard feelings for Detroit? No. Do I have anything negative to say about it? No. Because at the end of the day, that was home for me."

February 8, 2009 — The Cavaliers lose to the Lakers, 101-91, for their first defeat at home for the season. Cleveland had won 23 in a row.

February 8, 2018 — The Cavaliers trade Isaiah Thomas, Channing Frye and a first-round draft pick to the Los Angeles Lakers for Larry Nance Jr. and Jordan Clarkson. The trade means a return to Northeast Ohio for the 6-foot-7 Nance, whose father was a frontcourt mainstay in the 1980s and '90s for the Cavs. Nance Jr. played at Revere High School in Summit County.

9

February 9, 1945 — Paul Brown joins new Cleveland team

Historical sources differ on exactly when Paul Brown agreed to become general manager and head coach of Cleveland's incoming new team in the All-America Football Conference. References are scattered through the first couple of weeks of February. The differences could center on: (1) the finalization of the agreement; (2) the signing of the contract, or (3) a public announcement. Since February 9 appears to be the most popular date that can be researched, that is the choice here for the day that Cleveland football changed forever.

Brown grew up in Massillon and became the head coach of his old high school football team there at age 24 in 1932. In nine years there, his teams went 80-8-2. Brown invented the concept of a football playbook during that time. That record earned him a job with Ohio State University in 1941. The Buckeyes won a national championship under Brown in 1942.

Brown went into the Navy during World War II in 1944 and coached football for one of the teams that played games against colleges and other service teams to build morale among the troops. That's when Cleveland business executive Arthur "Mickey" McBride came calling. He was the new owner of the AAFC team and was looking for someone to put together his franchise. Brown became an obvious choice. The deal was for a reported $17,500 per season.

Ohio State wasn't happy about this development, but Brown didn't look back. He continued to coach a team at the Great Lakes Naval Training Station near Chicago in 1945. In Brown's last game there, his team beat Notre Dame, 39-7. Then it was off to Cleveland to make football history.

February 9, 1971 — Satchel Paige becomes the first Negro League standout to be selected for the Baseball Hall of Fame. Paige joined the Indians in 1948 at age 41, and his 6-1 record helped Cleveland win the American League pennant.

February 9, 1996 — A legal settlement involving the NFL, the city of Cleveland and the Baltimore Ravens is reached. At an owners meeting in Chicago, a vote of 25-2 gives Art Modell approval to leave. Cleveland is promised a new franchise by 1999, and that team will be considered a continuation of the previous Browns team – with its name, history and colors.

February 9, 1999 — The Browns select 37 players in the expansion draft to stock their new franchise. Cleveland's first pick is center Jim Pyne of the Lions. Pyne would play guard for the Browns and is credited with helping his family become the first with three generations of pro football players. Pyne's father played for the Boston Patriots and his grandfather played for the Providence Steam Roller.

10

February 10, 1920 — Baseball sets a trading deadline

The Indians hoped that baseball's winter meetings in 1920 would give them the chance to acquire a left-handed starting pitcher. They failed in that quest, but the gathering was noteworthy for something that changed baseball.

The American League had gone through a messy incident in 1919. Boston pitcher Carl Mays was having a tough season, with no run support and a couple of off-field incidents. On July 13, he stormed off the field during a game in Chicago, and headed back to Boston. There he announced his strong wish to be traded.

That led to an argument among major league owners. In the end, Mays was traded to the Yankees and performed superbly down the stretch. During the offseason, though, the AL owners decided on this day to set July 1 as a deadline for transactions – the first such action of its kind in major league history. The date might have changed over the next century, but deadline deals have become part of the fabric of baseball ever since.

Meanwhile, the owners also banned the use of the spitball starting in 1920, although pitchers who had used the pitch in the past were allowed to continue throwing it until retirement. That was just fine with Indians pitcher Stan Coveleski, who was considered one of the best practitioners. It ended up helping Cleveland win the 1920 World Series.

February 10, 1994 — Future Hall of Famer Jack Morris signs a contract with the Indians as a free agent. The 39-year-old only stays with the team until August, when he was released.

February 10, 1989 — Lenny Wilkens, whose NBA playing career included a stop in Cleveland, is inducted for the first of three times into the Basketball Hall of Fame. The other honors came for his coaching achievements and for serving on the 1992 Olympic Games coaching staff.

11

February 11, 2013 — Bourn signs as free agent with Indians

The season to sign baseball free agents usually has ended by February. That is particularly true for the Indians, who aren't in the class of the big market teams when it comes to throwing around millions of dollars in the offseason.That's why it was a surprise when Cleveland announced the signing of center fielder Michael Bourn. The veteran agreed to a four-year, $48 million deal, with an option for an extra year. Bourn's signing came a month after the Indians gave New York Yankees free agent outfielder Nick Swisher a four-year, $56 million deal.

What was behind the sudden spending spree? In December, the Indians turned their in-house television broadcast company into a cash asset on their books by selling it to Fox Sports. *The Plain Dealer* reported the deal was for $230 million and accompanied by another $400 million for 10 years of broadcast rights.

Another major off-season change was replacing manager Manny Acta with two-time World Series winner Terry Francona. All of it was aimed at fixing what went wrong in 2012 when the record was 68-94.

"You notice the things that are happening with teams," Bourn said to MLB.com soon after the signing. "And I think in baseball you're either trying to win or you're trying to rebuild. It's one or the other. And I know what they're trying to do. They're trying to win. Of course I'm going to try to be a part of that."

February 11, 1973 — Cavaliers coach Bill Fitch makes national news during Cleveland's 115-107 loss to the Atlanta Hawks when he throws a chair at referee Bob Rakel.

February 11, 2009 — Maurice Williams scores a career-high 44 points in the Cavaliers' 109-92 win over Phoenix. Williams had been named to the NBA All-Star Game the day before.

February 11, 2011 — The Cavaliers end a record 26-game losing streak with a 116-109 overtime win over the Clippers.

February 12, 1984 — Details revealed on Browns substance abuse program

The rules for participation in a Browns players life skills program called the "Inner Circle" include attending three meetings a week and a commitment to total abstinence from alcohol and drug products.

Details about the program are revealed in an *Akron Beacon Journal* news report by pro football writer Ed Meyer. Leaders of the program are Coach Sam Rutigliano, Dr. Greg Collins of the Cleveland Clinic, ex-players Calvin Hill and Paul Warfield, and Tom Petersburg, a Cleveland leader of the spiritually-based group Athletes In Action.

Running back Charles White is the only publicly identified player in the group. The program was first revealed in July 1983, in *Newsweek* magazine.

Rutigliano said he would have preferred that the existence of the program had never been disclosed but after that occurred, he said he felt "maybe other teams will follow our lead."

February 12, 1989 — The Cavaliers have three representatives – Larry Nance, Mark Price and Brad Daugherty – in the NBA All-Star Game.

February 13, 1937 — Cleveland enters the NFL

There have been four American Football Leagues in the past century. One started and ended in 1926. The second began in 1936 and ended in 1937. A third played two seasons in 1940-41. The fourth lasted from 1960 through 1969 before it merged with the National Football League. This story of Cleveland's association with pro football has to do with the second version.

Cleveland joined AFL II in 1936. Player-coach Buzz Wetzel was a fan of Fordham University, and suggested Rams as a nickname for the team (the same as Fordham). It supposedly pleased sportswriters, because the name was an easy fit in headlines. Cleveland had success on the field, going 5-2-2. However, finances were a different story. Team executive Homer Marshman and his group lost money in that first year, and didn't see much of a future for the AFL. They decided to try to jump to the NFL when the more established league announced expansion plans in 1937.

Cleveland outbid Houston and Los Angeles for a team, as the league wanted to concentrate its franchises in the Northeast and Midwest. The entry fee was $10,000. Cleveland took over a spot in the league that had been held by the Cincinnati Reds, which folded in 1934. When the Rams were inserted into the Western Division, that gave the National Pro league, as it was called in newspapers, an even number of 10 teams.

Life in the NFL was tougher than the AFL. The Rams went 1-10, including 0-10 in their division, under coach Hugo Bezdek. The bright spot was that Johnny Drake was named the NFL's Rookie of the Year.

The Rams endured until 1946 when then-owner Dan Reeves moved the franchise to Los Angeles.

February 13, 1991 — Nick Saban resigns as head coach at Toledo to become the defensive coordinator for the Browns, joining Bill Belichick's staff.

February 14, 1996 — Browns fire Belichick before move

In hindsight, it looks extremely difficult to understand. Fire Bill Belichick, one of the greatest coaches in the history of the National Football League?

Only one team ever did it – the Cleveland Browns. To be fair, they weren't going to be the Cleveland Browns much longer. The franchise would soon be off to Baltimore to become the Ravens. But the final details weren't worked out when owner Art Modell decided to let Belichick go.

Bill was hired in 1991 as the youngest coach of the NFL. His best season was in 1994, when the team went 11-5 and reached the playoffs. But the Browns went backwards in 1995, as they finished 5-11. When Modell announced in November 1995, that the team would go to Baltimore, he said Belichick would remain as the head coach. But something went wrong in the relationship, and Modell decided to make the move. He told Belichick about the action on the 14th, and announced it the next day.

Belichick had a 37-45 record as head coach of the Browns. He landed as the head coach of the New England Patriots in 2000, and had six Super Bowl rings by the time the 2020 season ended.

February 14, 1942 — Yankees vice president George Weiss announces that it will no longer place one of its minor league teams in Akron. It ends a relationship that started in 1935 when New York placed an Akron team in the Class C Middle Atlantic League.

February 15, 1980 — Cavaliers' trade proves costly

The Cavaliers completed quite a few trades that didn't work out in the early 1980s. The worst one, though, might have been on this date.

The Cavs were going nowhere in Coach Stan Albeck's first year with a 24-37 record, and making the playoffs appeared to be a longshot. Meanwhile, the Los Angeles Lakers with a rookie guard named Magic Johnson already were pretty good and headed for the NBA championship. Tinkering with the roster, Albeck and Cavs general manager Ron Hrovat gave up guard Butch Lee, a former college star at Marquette, plus Cleveland's first-round pick in 1982 to Los Angeles for forward Don Ford and a first-round pick in the upcoming 1980 draft.

Cleveland's own first-round choice had been dealt to San Diego for guard Randy Smith so obtaining the Lakers' choice meant the Cavs would hopefully add another worthy asset heading into 1980-81.

As it turned out, it was the 1982 asset that was in fact named "Worthy" – as in James Worthy, the star forward from North Carolina. He ended up becoming the first pick of that draft and the Lakers got him thanks to the 1980 trade. Worthy is in the Basketball Hall of Fame.

February 15, 1983 — New York City real estate executive Donald Trump offers to buy the Cleveland Indians for $13 million. The proposal came in a letter to Indians' president Gabe Paul. The offer was rejected, in part because Trump was said to be ready to move the team to Tampa as soon as the transaction was completed.

February 15, 1989 — Dennis Maruk plays his last NHL game, a 4-2 loss by the Minnesota North Stars to the Detroit Red Wings. It's the last time that a player who had been with the old Cleveland Barons took part in an NHL game.

February 16, 2014 — Cavs are stars of All-Star show

If you like offense and showmanship in your basketball, the NBA All-Star Game is usually the place to be. In this particular edition, two representatives of the Cavaliers set the tone. LeBron James made a terrific backwards dunk on an alley-oop play that put the fans in the mood for fun. The Cleveland superstar had 22 points and led everyone on the East team with seven rebounds.

However, teammate Kyrie Irving was even more helpful. Irving had a fabulous shooting night, going 14-for-17 from the field, including 3-of-6 in three-pointers. He had 15 points in the fourth quarter, and helped carry the East to a 163-155 win in New Orleans. That made him the game's MVP.

At the time, the 318 points by both teams was an all-star game record. The two Cavs had some help. Carmelo Anthony set a record with eight three-pointers. The East outscored the West, 10-0, in the final two minutes to wrap up its first win after losing the previous three games.

"We wanted this win," James said to the Associated Press. "They beat us the last three years and they had a lot of bragging rights, so to be able to come through being down 18 was huge."

February 16, 1982 — The Cavaliers send forward Reggie Johnson to Kansas City for 21-year-old forward Cliff Robinson. Then, separately, they package center Bill Laimbeer and forward Kenny Carr in a deal with Detroit for center Paul Mokeski, forward Phil Hubbard and draft choices. Hubbard's arrival marks a return to the area where his career began as a star at Canton McKinley High School.

February 17, 1992 — Cavs finally beat the Bulls

Every Cavs' fan remembers Michael Jordan's buzzer-beater to eliminate Cleveland from the playoffs in 1989. What they might have forgotten, or at least tried to forget, was that it was the first of 13 straight wins by Jordan's Chicago Bulls over the Cavs. Cleveland seemed to lose in every way possible.

The Cavs were in the midst of a very good season in 1991-92, but they still hadn't beaten Chicago when the teams played on this date. This was another thriller, as the teams exchanged leads throughout the game. Jordan was terrific as usual, scoring 46 points on his birthday. But the Bulls had trouble with Cleveland's front line.

Craig Ehlo's two free throws put the Cavs up three, 113-110, with about 44 seconds left. Jordan answered with 34 seconds left with a jumper. Cleveland iced the clock but committed a turnover with six seconds to play. Everyone thought they knew what would happen next, but Mark Price denied Jordan the ball. That left the game in the hands of Scottie Pippen, who missed an off-balance shot. The Cavaliers earned that 113-112 win.

"Others have made a bigger deal of this losing streak than we have," Price said. "We knew it was a matter of time before we would beat them."

February 17, 2010 — The Cavaliers acquire Antawn Jamison from Washington and Sebastian Telfair from the Los Angeles Clippers in a three-team deal that sends Zydrunas Ilgauskas, Emir Preldzic and a first-round draft choice to the Wizards.

February 17, 2010 — The Browns release running back Jamal Lewis after two 1,000-yard seasons in three years with Cleveland.

February 18, 2020 — Beilein steps away from Cavs' job

It was a surprise when John Beilein came to Cleveland as an NBA rookie head coach after 12 successful years at the University of Michigan. It might have been a bigger surprise to see him leave less than a year into his first season.

Beilein seemingly had found a home in Michigan. He coached the Wolverines to nine NCAA tournaments, and was 67 years old. Analysts believed Beilein had a job in Ann Arbor for as long as he wanted. Instead, he took on the massive challenge of helping to rebuild a Cavaliers team that was trying to compensate for the 2018 loss of LeBron James. At some point, Beilein realized it was time to exit.

"This was my decision to step down and I truly appreciate the understanding and support of the front office during this time," he said. "I find losing very challenging and this year has taken a much bigger toll on me than I expected. I grew concerned for the consequences this toll could potentially take on my own health and my family's well-being down the road."

J.B. Bickerstaff, son of longtime NBA coach and executive Bernie Bickerstaff, was promoted to head coach. He had held the same position for the Memphis Grizzlies from 2017 to 2019. Bickerstaff signed a multi-year contract in March 2020.

February 18, 1909 — The Red Sox trade Cy Young to the Cleveland Naps for pitchers Charlie Chech and Jack Ryan plus $12,500.

February 18, 1986 — San Antonio guard Alvin Robertson records the NBA's second-ever quadruple double in a game with 20 points, 11 rebounds, 10 assists and 10 steals. The Spurs won, 120-114, over the Phoenix Suns. Robertson, of Barberton High School in Summit County, played in college at Arkansas, had an 11-year NBA career and was a member of the gold medal-winning U.S. Olympic team in 1984.

February 18, 1991 — The Indians lose an arbitration decision to pitcher Greg Swindell and are ordered to pay a salary of $2.02 million to him. That contract situation led General Manager John Hart to decide on avoiding that possibility in the years to come by signing young players to long-term contracts – a policy that stayed in place for more than two decades.

19

February 19, 1971 — Wesley lights up the Royals for 50

To Cavaliers fans of a certain age, Walt Wesley is fondly remembered as the first center of Cleveland's expansion team in 1970-71. His name also comes up when fans talk about shocking scoring explosions.

The former Kansas All-American was one of the best college players in the nation in his time. He and the Jayhawks almost knocked off Texas Western in the Miners' memorable run to the 1966 NCAA championship, losing in double overtime. Wesley was the sixth overall pick in the 1966 draft by the Royals, but then had difficulty finding playing time in Cincinnati.

Wesley had become a regular for the first time in the NBA because of expansion, and he averaged 17.7 points and 8.7 rebounds per game in 1970-71 for the Cavs. Boosting his scoring average was a game on this date against the Royals. He had an amazing 50 points in a 125-109 win for Cleveland. Wesley had 20 field goals and was 10-for-14 from the line. The 6-foot-11 center has the lowest career scoring average (8.5 points per game) of any NBA player who scored 50 points in a game.

Wesley's numbers fell a bit in 1971-72, and then he became a backup center for the next few years before retiring. Still, he'll always have that night against Cincinnati.

February 19, 2006 — Cleveland's LeBron James earns MVP honors in the NBA All-Star Game as the East beats the West, 122-120.

February 20, 1972 — Cavs break the Knicks' hex

The Cavaliers had been in the NBA for almost two years by this point, and still had yet to record a victory over New York. This was the night that changed.

In the early going, there was no way of knowing that this latest matchup would produce a different result. Even without the injured Bill Bradley, the Knicks had a 21-point lead before the first period was over. New York led, 32-13, after a period, and the crowd of 8,877 in the Cleveland Arena probably assumed it was going to be a long night.

But the Cavs fought back. They reduced the lead to 12 points, 56-44, at halftime, and came within one in the later stages of the third period. Jerry Lucas hit three straight shots for New York from there, and the Knicks led by a more comfortable six points after three quarters. In the final minutes, Cleveland had a 10-1 run to take control of the game, and held on for the 111-109 win. Austin Carr led the Cavs with 25 points.

"We took off like gangbusters," Lucas said. "It was too easy and we probably relaxed, and the momentum changed."

February 20, 1989 — The Cleveland Crunch indoor soccer franchise is approved to join the Major Indoor Soccer League. The Crunch succeeds the former indoor team called the Cleveland Force, which operated from 1978 to 1988. The Crunch eventually became a part of the National Professional Soccer League and won titles in 1993-94, 1995-96 and 1998-99. The teams played at the Coliseum in Richfield and the Wolstein Center at Cleveland State University.

21

February 21, 2008 — Cavs add experience with massive deal

The Cavaliers had high hopes entering the 2007-08 season. They were coming off a trip to the NBA Finals, but their expectations had been dashed after 54 games. Cleveland was 30-24 and seemed unlikely to have another long playoff run.

General Manager Danny Ferry thought more experience would help bolster the ability of LeBron James to lead the team. So he talked with a couple of other GMs and worked out an amazing trade. Get out a legal pad and you can keep track of who went where.

The Cavs sent Donyell Marshall and Ira Newble to the Sonics. The Bulls traded Joe Smith, Ben Wallace and a draft choice to the Cavs. Chicago dealt Adrian Griffin to Seattle. Cleveland shipped Shannon Brown, Drew Gooden, Larry Hughes and Cedric Simmons to the Bulls. The Sonics dealt Wally Szczerbiak and Delonte West to the Cavs.

Got it? The Cavs ended up dumping about a third of their roster. If nothing else, the Cavs woke up a bit. They reached the Eastern Conference finals again before losing to the Celtics in seven games.

February 21, 1962 — By a vote of 5-to-1, the Cleveland Pipers of the American Basketball League are reinstated to full member status in midseason. Team president George Steinbrenner defended charges of violating league rules in explaining that the folding of the Los Angeles Jets team caused the Pipers to be unable to travel to San Francisco for a game.

February 21, 1981 — Cavaliers owner Ted Stepien informs the NBA Board of Governors that he will consider moving his franchise to Minneapolis, Louisville, Cincinnati or Pittsburgh if attendance in Cleveland does not improve for the 1981-82 season.

February 22, 1977 — Barons avoid folding at the last minute

The Cleveland Barons – we're talking about the NHL team, not the AHL – never had much of a chance at success. They were moved to Cleveland from the California Bay Area only a few weeks before the start of the 1976-77 season, and had financial problems right from the start. Crowds were poor, and financial reserves dried up quickly.

By January 1977, owner Mel Swig was running out of money. He asked for a loan from the NHL Board of Governors, and asked his players to defer part of their paychecks for a few months. While negotiations went on, the Barons couldn't meet their payroll on January 31, 1977. It appeared possible the team would fold in midseason.

Sanford Greenberg, the manager of the Coliseum in Richfield, offered to buy the team around that time. But the transaction fell through by mid-February. The situation looked bleak.

However, a deal was concluded on this date that saved the season for the Barons. It was brokered by the president of the NHL Players Association, Alan Eagleson. The NHLPA came up with a $600,000 loan, while Swig supplied $300,000 and each NHL team came up with $20,000. That added up to $1.3 million, and salvaged the team and its season.

February 22, 1912 — Johnny Kilbane of Cleveland wins the world featherweight boxing title with a 20-round victory over Abe Attell in Vernon, California. About 100,000 came out to greet him when Kilbane returned to Cleveland. The win started an 11-year reign as champion.

23

February 23, 2004 — Cavaliers complete astounding rally

For a while, it looked oh-so-easy for the New Orleans Hornets. They shot 78 percent in the first quarter alone and took a 37-16 lead over the Cavaliers in Cleveland. Then it got worse – the Cavs fell behind by 25 points with 6:19 left in the half.

But the Cavaliers didn't give up. They cut the lead to 14 at the half, and then put together a 20-8 burst in the third quarter that got them within two. It was now anyone's ballgame. Then Jason Kapono went to work, hitting a pair of three-pointers in the fourth quarter to tie the game.

It was close the rest of the way, but Carlos Boozer wrapped the game up for the Cavs in the final moments. He scored on a dunk and two free throws, and Cleveland had a thrilling 104-100 comeback. It was the largest rally in team history.

Kapono finished with a career-high 19 points, including 13 in the final period. He went five-for-five from three-point land. It was Kapono's rookie year with his claim to fame being that he was the "other" Cleveland draft choice after the Cavs had taken LeBron James with the No. 1 pick overall. Boozer had 24 points, while James added 21.

February 23, 1985 — Indiana basketball coach Bob Knight, a native of Orrville in Wayne County, is ejected during a game against Purdue after receiving three technical fouls and throwing a chair onto the court. Knight's path to coaching in the Big Ten included a playing career for Fred Taylor at Ohio State, followed by one year of junior varsity high school coaching in the Akron suburb of Cuyahoga Falls before moving to Army (1965-71), IU ('71-2000) and Texas Tech (2001-08).

February 23, 1994 — Indians owner Richard Jacobs agrees to pay $10 million for the naming rights to the newly constructed baseball stadium in downtown Cleveland that will open in April.

24

February 24, 2011 — Cavs score a slam dunk in trade

It seems as if many of the transactions on these pages completed by the Cavaliers have not worked out well. Here's one that turned out to be a smash hit.

The Los Angeles Clippers had some major money tied up in the contract of Baron Davis, a good scorer for several teams who was just about at the end of his productive period in basketball. They convinced the Cavaliers to take Davis, as long as they threw in a first-round draft choice in 2011. The Clippers were not a horrible team that year, so the price tag sounded relatively fair.

In return, the Clippers picked up Mo Williams, a pretty good scorer by most measures, and Jamario Moon, someone who hadn't been in a starting lineup for some time. Throw in the cap room supplied by Davis' departure, and it's easy to understand the logic on Los Angeles' side.

Then the unexpected happened. The Cavaliers won the draft lottery. They had the first pick and used it on Kyrie Irving, the Duke guard. It's fair to say that without Irving, the Cavs don't win a championship in 2016. In addition, the Cavs used an amnesty clause in the collective bargaining agreement to release Davis. Cleveland still had to pay him guaranteed money, but they received salary cap and tax relief in the process.

February 24, 1917 — The Indians purchase Smoky Joe Wood from the Red Sox for $15,000. Wood had been one of the best pitchers in the game in Boston, but his shoulder had given out and his mound days were over. Wood mostly played outfield in Cleveland, and did well in spot duty, including contributions during the Indians' 1920 World Series championship season.

February 24, 1985 — The West picks up an 11-7 win in the Major Indoor Soccer League's All-Star Game at the Coliseum in Richfield. Stan Stamenkovic of the Baltimore Blast is named the game's MVP for the second consecutive year.

25

February 25, 1991 — Richardson wins world boxing title

Some of the best boxing alumni of the Youngstown-Warren area in Northeast Ohio were Kelly Pavlik and Ray "Boom Boom" Mancini, but don't leave out Greg "The Flea" Richardson.

Richardson grew up on the east side of town and came from an athletic family. He won national amateur titles in 1974. He took his time to turn pro, making that move in 1982. Slowly but surely Richardson piled up the wins, taking 17 straight bouts and capturing some minor titles in the super-bantamweight division (around 120 pounds).

He lost a title bout to Jeff Fenech in Australia in 1987, but kept at it. He was rewarded with another title shot against Raul Perez at the Fabulous Forum in California. Richardson used his athletic gifts there to come away with a decision that made him WBC champion.

He defended the belt once, but then lost to Joichiro Tatsuyoshi. Richardson finished his career with a 2-4-1 stretch, and retired after a good run.

February 25, 1978 — The Barons set a team record for most goals allowed in a game, as the Sabres earn a win by a 13-3 score in Richfield. Buffalo finished with a 50-26 advantage in shots, including a 26-7 edge in the third period. The Barons led, 2-1, before giving up 10 consecutive goals.

February 25, 1988 — The Cavaliers make a major midseason roster move with the trade of Kevin Johnson, Tyrone Corbin, Mark West, and two draft choices to Phoenix for Larry Nance, Mike Sanders and a draft choice.

26

February 26, 1916 — Indians purchase Gandil from Senators

This seemed like an innocent transaction. Cleveland paid a reported $7,500 in 1916 for the contract of Chick Gandil, a first baseman for the Senators. Yet the newcomer went on to play a role in one of the most notorious moments in baseball history, so his story deserves to be known.

Gandil came from St. Paul, Minnesota, and worked his way very slowly up the ladder. He landed with the White Sox in 1910 but didn't do well there and was sold to a minor-league team. Two years later, he turned up in Washington with the Senators, and this time he was ready. Gandil could get on base and quickly became one of the best fielders at his position in baseball. He was a starter for the next four years.

However, Gandil was said to be a chain-smoker, and that supposedly annoyed Washington manager Clark Griffith. It was off to Cleveland, where he only hit .259. The Indians sold him back to the White Sox after only a year in Cleveland, and Gandil helped his new team win the 1917 World Series.

Now comes the heart of the story. Gandil was alleged to have been one of the leaders of the attempt to fix the 1919 World Series. The first baseman's contract demand of $10,000 for 1920 was turned down by Chicago owner Charles Comiskey. Gandil and his wife went back to California – supposedly carrying $35,000 in proceeds from the "Black Sox" scandal. He never played in the majors again.

February 26, 1968 — A shakeup of the Indians' broadcast voices on radio and television continues as WJW-TV (Channel 8) in Cleveland announces the hiring of nationally known baseball announcer Mel Allen, who had been dismissed by the New York Yankees after the 1964 season. Allen, who worked in Cleveland only for one year, replaced former Tribe pitcher Herb Score, who moved to radio full-time and took over for Jimmy Dudley, who had done Cleveland play-by-play broadcasts for 20 years.

February 26, 1991 — Bill Veeck, who owned the Indians in 1948 when they won the World Series, is named to the Baseball Hall of Fame.

February 27, 1997 — Rockers add Woodard to roster

It's always nice to have a familiar name on the roster of a new professional sports team. That sort of recognition attracts immediate attention from fans. Maybe that's why the Cleveland Rockers signed Lynette Woodard on this day, shortly before their debut season of 1997 as a charter member of the Women's National Basketball Association. Woodard ranked as one of the legends in her sport. Besides, she could still play.

The 6-footer played in college at Kansas as a four-time All-American. In 1984, Woodard helped the United States win the gold medal at the Olympic Games in Los Angeles. She became the first woman to ever play for the Harlem Globetrotters in 1985, and also played overseas.

When the Rockers and the WNBA were formed, Woodard couldn't resist coming out of retirement at age 37. She was a starter for 27 of 28 games and averaged 7.8 points. The Rockers lost her rights to Detroit in the 1998 expansion draft, and Woodard played one more season there. Then it was back into retirement, followed by a trip to the Basketball Hall of Fame in 2004.

February 27, 1997 — The Bulls take a 49-6 record into a game with the Cavaliers, but Cleveland beats them, 73-70, as Michael Jordan's three-pointer at the buzzer rolls off the rim.

February 27, 2009 — The Browns trade former first-round draft pick Kellen Winslow Jr. to Tampa Bay for a second-round pick in 2009 and a fifth-rounder in 2010. Winslow was the No. 6 pick of the first round of the 2004 NFL Draft by Browns coach Butch Davis, who had recruited him to the University of Miami (Florida).

28

February 28, 1978 — Indians pick up Horton and Clyde

The Indians and Rangers came together for a trade at the start of training camp in 1978. While the deal didn't have a great impact on either team, the names involved certainly had some stories behind them.

Cleveland gave up pitcher Tom Buskey and utility player John Lowenstein. Buskey spent a month in the Rangers' organization, and was released just before the start of the season. Lowenstein was a platoon player known more for his sense of humor than his bat. Lowenstein once noted that no one had started a fan club for him in Cleveland, so he named himself president of the John Lowenstein Apathy Club. Hundreds wrote the Indians' offices to take the trouble to join. He also became known for one of ESPN broadcaster Chris Berman's memorable nicknames – John "Tonight, Let It Be" Lowenstein, a play on words for the beer named Lowenbrau.

Outfielder Willie Horton and left-handed starting pitcher David Clyde came to the Indians. Horton, the youngest of 14 children, first made the major leagues with the Tigers in 1963, and was a good-sized part of the Detroit offense for more than a decade. He was a star in 1968, hitting 36 homers as Detroit won the World Series that year. The Indians had hopes that Horton still had a little life in his bat. They saw no sign of that, and released him in July.

In 1973, Clyde became a legend in high school pitching circles, going 18-0 as a senior. The Rangers picked him first in the amateur draft, ahead of Robin Yount, Dave Winfield, and Fred Lynn. Then Texas rushed him right up to the major leagues. Clyde allowed only one hit in five innings in his initial start, but it was downhill from there. He pitched his last game for Texas in 1975. The Indians hoped they could unlock some of his potential, and he went 8-11 for Cleveland in 1978. But that was his best season, and the Indians traded him back to Texas in 1980.

February 28, 1989 — Rick Mahorn of the Pistons gives Mark Price of the Cavaliers a hard elbow to the head during their game in Cleveland. Mahorn is fined $5,000 but not suspended, while Price receives a severe concussion. He only missed two games, but the Cavs' record was 15-13 the rest of the season after a 42-12 start.

February 28, 1996 — The Raiders file a lawsuit against the National Football League for pushing them to move out of the Los Angeles area and into Oakland. Browns owner Art Modell is cited as one of the owners who had an interest in moving his team to Los Angeles.

29

February 29, 2008 — Browns acquire Williams from Packers

The Browns surprised just about everyone when they completed a trade for a defensive lineman from the Packers. Then the Browns themselves were surprised – and disappointed – about how things worked out.

Corey Williams was a sixth-round draft choice by the Packers in 2004. It took him a while to find a spot in the lineup, but he did well once he was established. The veteran had seven sacks in each of his last two years in Green Bay. Williams signed a franchise tag for $6.3 million for the 2008 season, but the Packers wasted no time getting out from under that. They traded him to Cleveland for a second-round draft choice on this day.

The Browns needed to sign Williams to a multi-year contract to make everything work, and they did so. The defensive player got a six-year deal worth $38.6 million. Williams, however, didn't turn out to be a good investment from the Browns' standpoint, as he didn't contribute much in the next two seasons. He was not a good fit in Cleveland's 3-4 defense either, particularly after moving to defensive end.

In 2010, the Browns decided to cut their losses, and save some money on the salary cap. They sent him and a seventh-round draft choice to the Detroit Lions for a fifth-round draft choice. Williams completed his NFL career by playing two seasons there.

February 29, 1956 — The Indians are sold to a group headed by William R. Daley, 63, president of an investment firm called Otis & Co. Daley's group included Hank Greenberg, who had been general manager since 1950, and Ignatius O'Shaughnessy, president of Globe Oil Co. The price tag is $3,961,800 – believed to be a record for the purchase of a major league team.

1

March 1, 1919 — Indians add Gardner and Jamieson

When the Indians completed a deal with the Athletics, it took a year to have its biggest benefit.

At the end of the 1918 season, it looked as if Charlie Jamieson's career was going nowhere. He had been waived by the Senators and had suffered through a poor 1918 season for the Athletics in which he only hit .202 in 110 games. Larry Gardner was a more proven commodity as an infielder in Philadelphia, but was 32 years old. The two were about to be linked in Cleveland history.

Jamieson and Athletics owner Connie Mack didn't agree on Jamieson's salary for 1919, and Mack sent Jamieson, Gardner and pitcher Elmer Myers to Cleveland for outfielder Braggo Roth and cash. Jamieson saw little playing time in 1919.

But everything changed in 1920. Jamieson was given a starting job by player-manager Tris Speaker. Meanwhile, the baseball itself was changed to produce more offense – goodbye, "Dead Ball Era." Jamieson became a star in the new circumstances, hitting .319 in a leadoff role. Gardner continued to play well, and the two helped Cleveland win the 1920 World Series. Mack called it one of his worst deals; the Indians considered it one of their best.

March 1, 1947 — The Indians start training camp in their new spring home of Tucson, Arizona, having left Clearwater, Florida. Team owner Bill Veeck was displeased with racial conditions in Florida. The Indians, who signed the American League's first Black player (Larry Doby) during the '47 season, would stay in Tucson from 1947-92.

March 1, 1997 — The Cavaliers retire uniform No. 43 to honor center Brad Daugherty.

2

March 2, 1989 — Cavs keep winning at home

On the previous December 13, the Cavaliers lost a 111-102 decision to the Lakers at home. That was no disgrace at the time. Los Angeles featured three players you might know in Kareem Abdul-Jabbar, Earvin "Magic" Johnson and James Worthy.

Still, the Cavs played as if they were annoyed by the outcome. They had three more home games in a row in that part of the schedule, and they swept through Detroit, Atlanta and Utah by at least 16 points in each game. Cleveland went on to win all of its home games for the rest of December, and for all of January and February.

March started out promising for the Cavs as well. They blasted San Antonio, 112-84, for their 22nd straight win at home on this date. Cleveland led by 15 at the half, and then put on another burst in the third period. Brad Daugherty and "Hot Rod" Williams had 22 points to lead Cleveland, which improved to 43-12.

The next home game was on March 5 against the Bucks, and Milwaukee won that game. It was the next-to-last home loss of the season for the Cavs, who were beaten by Detroit on April 18. The Cavs' home record for the season was 37-4.

March 2, 2001 — The Browns sign free agent quarterback Kelly Holcomb after his release from the Colts.

March 3, 1984 — Akron's Jakubick is nation's best

How many athletes can say they led the nation in something? Akron basketball player Joe Jakubick can.

He finished his college career with 42 points in a 99-88 loss to Illinois-Chicago. That raised his season's scoring total to 814 – an average of 30.1 per game. No one was better in 1983-84. Therefore, Jakubick, a 6-foot-5 guard, joined some great names on the list of the nation's best scorers: Stephen Curry, Glenn Robinson, Pete Maravich, Rick Barry, and Oscar Robertson.

Jakubick accomplished practically everything possible during his time in Akron. He set 25 school records and was the university's athlete of the year three straight times. Jakubick became Akron's all-time leading scorer, was the Ohio Valley Conference's Player of the Year twice, and was an all-conference pick three times.

Jakubick went in the seventh round to the Cavs in the 1984 NBA Draft, but didn't play any games for them in the regular season. Jakubick eventually went into high school coaching.

March 3, 1900 — Pro baseball in Cleveland will take a year off as part of an agreement with the National League and the new American League.

March 4, 1940 — Pace shows he's a champion in draw

George Pace belongs to an exclusive boxing club. He won a "world championship" not in the ring, but by a ruling from a governing agency of the sport. That takes some explaining.

The Cleveland boxer only had a 7-7 record after his first 14 fights, but he got new management in 1937 and started doing much better. Pace had a long run of wins in the next few years, as he found a comfort zone by fighting in Toronto. Pace was ranked as a top contender at that point. The problem was that bantamweight champion Sixto Escobar never seemed ready or anxious to fight him. The National Boxing Association got tired of that and simply stripped Escobar of the title, giving it to Pace.

The next move came down to money. The boxing governing body matched Pace against the New York State world champion (the New York group kept its own titles and rankings), Lou Salica, in Maple Leaf Gardens in Toronto on this day. The bout was ruled a draw.

Pace won his next couple of bouts, and then took on Salica again – this time in New York City. The Cleveland boxer lost a unanimous decision. Pace stayed busy through the end of 1941, but only fought once after the start of World War II.

March 4, 1964 — The Browns acquire defensive tackle Dick Modzelewski from the Giants for tight end Bobby Crespino.

March 4, 1972 — Rick Roberson hauls down 25 rebounds for the Cavs against Houston, setting a single-game team record that had not been broken as of 2023.

March 5, 2008 — James puts up 50 on scoreboard

Basketball was invented in Massachusetts but it didn't take long for Madison Square Garden to create its own niche as a special place for the sport. The history in that New York City hoop shrine is not lost on LeBron James, who made his own imprint there on this day.

Playing almost 44 minutes, he was 16-for-30 from the field, including 7-of-13 on three-pointers, and went 11-for-16 from the line. That added up to his first 50-point game in the NBA. James had eight rebounds and 10 assists as well, and he led the Cavs to a 119-105 win over the Knicks.

"I've dreamed about playing well in this building," James said to the Associated Press. "To get a standing ovation in the greatest basketball arena in the world – it was a dream come true for me. It's one of the best things that ever happened to me."

March 5, 1978 — Lee Kemp of Chardon High School and the University of Wisconsin is named the Big Ten Conference's outstanding wrestler after winning his third consecutive league title. He won three NCAA titles at 158 pounds and had a record of 143-6-1.

March 6, 1978 — Indians let a pitcher get away

The Indians' front office had its troubles in the late 1970s. Losing records resulted from mistakes in judging talent, but sometimes deeper problems surfaced. There was no better example than the case of Jim Bibby.

The 6-foot-5 Bibby was a big man – "holds eight baseballs in one hand" was one phrase that described him. He had bounced around the majors in the early years of his career, starting with the Mets and passing through the Cardinals and Rangers before coming to Cleveland in the Gaylord Perry trade of 1975. Bibby was 13-7 in 1976 as a starting pitcher, and 12-13 in 1977.

The problem was money. Reports were that Bibby had to ask the Indians several times after the 1976 season in order to get a bonus that was due him. After the 1977 season, it was the same story – Bibby hadn't received a $10,000 bonus. Finally, he ran out of patience and filed for arbitration – and, on this date, won his case. Bibby was a free agent, and the Indians had nothing to show for it.

Bibby signed with Pittsburgh later that March, and he was a swingman on the Pirates' pitching staff. A year later, Bibby went 12-4 and helped his team win a World Series.

March 6, 1981 — The Cavaliers, one of the most porous defensive teams in the NBA, give up 140 points to the San Diego Clippers in a 140-125 loss. Exactly one week later, the Cavs lose by that exact same score to the New Jersey Nets.

March 7, 2002 — Offensive lineman Tucker joins Browns

When Ryan Tucker was on the field for the Browns, he usually was one of their best offensive linemen. If he had been on the field a little more often, his legacy would be less mixed.

Tucker came out of Texas Christian to join the Rams in 1997, and worked his way into the starting lineup. He was a Super Bowl champion there, as part of the "Greatest Show on Turf." Tucker became an unrestricted free agent in the spring of 2002, and signed with the Browns.

Cleveland made him an immediate starter, and he stayed there for more than two years. He didn't miss a snap in the 2003 season. Then a knee injury cost Tucker half of the 2004 season, but he came back fully in 2005. Tucker missed part of 2006 with an undisclosed problem. He had to sit out some games in 2007 because he tested positive for a banned substance. Tucker missed more games because of injury in 2009.

The lineman decided to retire in March of 2010, but there was one last surprise coming. The NFL announced a day later – eight years to the day after Tucker signed with the Browns – that he had flunked another test and was facing an eight-game suspension if he returned.

March 7, 2007 — The Ravens' all-time leading rusher, Jamal Lewis, signs a one-year contract with the Browns.

March 8, 1982 — Daly was Stepien's bright spot

Ted Stepien made many management decisions while operating the Cavaliers from 1980-83 that were unsuccessful, controversial, even laughable to many veteran NBA observers. His moves were expensive, too, as fans stayed away and financial losses totaled $16 million to $20 million during his tenure.

But there was one move during those three years that was like a tiny salmon swimming upstream amid a negative tide – the hiring of Chuck Daly as coach.

On this day, it became public that Stepien had seen enough after three months of Daly's services. Although Daly had arrived in early December with a three-year guaranteed contract, a record of 9-32 in 41 games spelled the end.

Daly was not sad to leave a situation with a last-place team that had no first-round draft picks coming until 1987. Looking at the big picture with a smile during even difficult times, he would tell reporters, "This is America; you've got to love it." But at age 51, he worried that his misstep in choosing Cleveland for his first NBA head coaching position could be an unrecoverable mistake after he had built a resume with successful tenures at Duke, Boston College and Penn and in the pros as Billy Cunningham's assistant with the Philadelphia 76ers.

When Daly got another chance with the Detroit Pistons in 1983, he thrived in a stable situation and stayed nine years. He won two championships there, and also led the U.S. Olympic squad known as "The Dream Team" to the 1992 gold medal in Barcelona. The Basketball Hall of Fame recognized his talents with induction in 2006. Meanwhile, the Cavaliers didn't have a coach with a career record above .500 until Lenny Wilkens arrived in 1986.

March 8, 1900 — The National League, the premier circuit of organized baseball, announces in New York that it will shrink from 12 franchises to eight with the elimination of clubs in Cleveland, Louisville, Baltimore and Washington. The Cleveland Spiders had compiled a last-place 20-134 record for that season and ranked last in attendance for three consecutive years. Spiders players with unusual names on the '99 roster included pitchers "Crazy" Schmit, "Highball" Wilson and "Sport" McAllister. A news report said the Cleveland club would receive $15,000 to disband. The move means the circuit will go forward with teams in New York, Brooklyn, Boston, Philadelphia, Pittsburgh, Cincinnati, St. Louis and Chicago.

March 8, 1980 — Indians rookie Joe Charboneau is attacked outside of a Mexico City hotel and is forced to miss the first part of the regular season. Cleveland was in Mexico for exhibition games.

March 8, 1996 — Cleveland City Council approves the deal negotiated by Mayor Michael White with the NFL to create an expansion franchise to replace the team that moved to Baltimore.

9

March 9, 2017 — Browns add quarterback for nothing

The Browns complete a trade for a starting quarterback that costs them essentially nothing.

Brock Osweiler saw some action with the 2015 Denver Broncos at quarterback, in part because of an injury to Peyton Manning. Everyone thought Osweiler would become the full-time starter when Manning announced his retirement after the Broncos won the Super Bowl. Osweiler had other plans. He signed a four-year, $72 million contract with the Houston Texans. That didn't work out well for either party. Osweiler set a team record for most interceptions in a season with 16. The Texans couldn't wait to get rid of him and his contract.

The following spring, the Browns had plenty of room under the salary cap. They agreed to take Osweiler off Houston's hands, as long as they threw in a second-round and sixth-round pick. Then in the fall, Cleveland paid Osweiler $16 million and said, "See you later." He was a backup quarterback for other teams for two seasons.

Meanwhile, on this day, the Browns also sign guard Kevin Zeitler (five years, $60 million) and center J.C. Tretter (three years, $16.75 million).

March 9, 1897 — The Cleveland Spiders sign Louis Sockalexis, a Penobscot Indian. He proves to be a popular figure on the team, and the team begins to refer to itself as the "Indians." The club officially changed its name to "Indians" in 1915.

March 9, 2004 — With Coach Butch Davis in charge, the Browns move on from the quarterback debate involving Tim Couch and Kelly Holcomb by signing former San Francisco starter Jeff Garcia to a 4-year, $25 million deal. Garcia, 34, posts a 3-7 record as a starter in 11 games and is released after the season.

March 9, 2017 — Kyle Juszczyk, who played football at Cloverleaf High School in Medina County, gets a four-year, $21 million contract with $7 million guaranteed and a $5 million signing bonus with the San Francisco 49ers. It is the largest contract for a fullback in NFL history. On March 14, 2021, he gets a new five-year, $27 million deal, not fully guaranteed.

March 9, 2021 — Cleveland State's men's basketball team beats Oakland, 80-69, in Indianapolis to win the Horizon League tournament and earn a berth in the NCAA tournament for the third time in history. Torrey Patton had 23 points to lead the Vikings.

10

March 10, 2020 — Cavs end shortened season with loss

The Cavaliers dropped a 108-103 decision to the Bulls on a Tuesday night in March. It was the 46th loss in 63 games for the Cavs, so in that sense the game was nothing out of the ordinary.

A day later, the NBA announced that it was suspending its season indefinitely after discovering that Utah center Rudy Gobert had tested positive for the Covid-19 virus. Basketball had come to a screeching halt, with no obvious plan for a resumption.

The other active sports, such as the National Hockey League and Major League Baseball, quickly came to the same conclusion. It turned out that the Indians played their last exhibition game on March 9, an 11-7 win over the Giants.

The Cavaliers had hopes of finishing up some portion of the schedule later in 2020, but they were left out of the league's return in the summer. That meant they'd have to wait for several more months before they were allowed to play again.

March 10, 1977 — Wayne Garland, the Indians' big free-agent signing (10-year contract for $2.3 million) in the offseason, goes three innings and allows two runs against the Giants in his exhibition debut for Cleveland. He later revealed that this outing was his first sign that he had arm and shoulder issues. Garland tried to pitch through that season, but his time as an effective pitcher was essentially over.

11

March 11, 2016 — Browns release quarterback Manziel

It didn't take long for fans to go from feelings of excitement and exhilaration during the 2014 NFL Draft to the understanding that the relationship between Johnny Manziel and the Browns would not end well. They were right – his tenure was less than two years.

Manziel was a first-round choice picked in 2014 by the regime of General Manager Ray Farmer and Coach Mike Pettine. There was little doubt that he had shown talent in college, but he was under 6-feet and had some controversial moments at Texas A&M. His career got off to a bad start in training camp, when Manziel was fined $12,000 by the league for making an obscene gesture in a preseason game. Manziel got into the lineup to finish up a game with the Bills, and he started in Week 15 against the Bengals – as his team lost, 30-0. Manziel was injured in his second start, and was done for the year.

The second-year player eventually earned the starting spot in 2015 – until video surfaced of Manziel enjoying himself at a party in Texas during the bye week. That resulted in demotion to third-string status. Early in 2016, Manziel was investigated for a domestic violence incident with a former girlfriend. That was more than enough for the Browns, who released him on this date.

The Heisman Trophy-winning Manziel then spent some time in the Canadian Football League and the Alliance of American Football, playing little in each spot.

March 11, 1967 — The University of Akron runs into a basketball scoring machine named Earl Monroe (49 points with 12 rebounds) as the Zips fall 88-80 to Monroe's Winston-Salem (N.C.) State team in a NCAA College Division regional tournament final at Akron's Memorial Hall. The Rams went on to win the national title. The loss broke a streak of three consecutive seasons of Akron reaching the national tournament.

March 11, 1997 — NFL Commissioner Paul Tagliabue announces in a report to the league that the Browns franchise will start its own fresh record books and history. Tagliabue says the city of Cleveland will keep the colors, name, records and history of the Browns and that a new organization created as an expansion team will start play with new ownership for the 1999 season.

12

March 12, 1928 — Risko beats future champion Sharkey

Mesto Bohunico and his family emigrated from Austria to Cleveland, where they set up a bakery on the West Side. The young Mesto thought about a future of making dough in the boxing ring instead of in a store, so he became a prize fighter. It led to a long career that saw him fight some of the toughest names in the business.

Bohunico soon changed his name to Johnny Risko. He wasn't a flashy fighter, but always put in an honest day's work. Risko was ranked in the top 10 in the heavyweight division from 1925 to 1932.

Risko happened to fight two future heavyweight champions in 1925, losing to both Jack Sharkey and Gene Tunney. The latter called him one of the toughest men he ever faced in the ring. The pride of Cleveland had 17 bouts in 1926 and 24 in 1927. Then on this date, he got a rematch with Sharkey – in New York's Madison Square Garden, no less – and won a split decision.

That earned him a fight with another future champion, Max Schmeling, in 1929. Risko came out on the short end of a TKO. That probably ended his chances at a title shot, even though he did beat another future champion, Max Baer, on points in 1931 in San Francisco. Risko took two years off in 1936 and 1937, then came back to fight for three more years. His last fight was in 1940. "The Cleveland Rubber Man" – a tribute to his durability – finished his career at 68-46-6.

March 12, 1982 — The Kent State women's basketball team makes its first trip to the NCAA Tournament. The Golden Flashes are eliminated by Southern California, 99-55.

March 12, 1999 — The Kent State men's basketball team takes part in the NCAA Tournament for the first time. The Golden Flashes drop a 61-54 decision to Temple.

13

March 13, 2019 — Browns trade for Giants' Beckham

It comes as a surprise when Browns General Manager John Dorsey trades with the New York Giants to get wide receiver Odell Beckham Jr. The deal was part of Dorsey's move to strengthen the roster with a playmaker at a key position. Cleveland gave up a first-round draft pick (No. 17), a third-rounder, and safety Jabrill Peppers.

Beckham Jr. came into the league and made an impact right away, catching 91 passes for 1,305 yards in 2014. The receiver made a one-handed catch, while falling backwards along the sidelines, that's been called one of the greatest receptions in history. His receiving yardage total has exceeded 1,000 yards four other times in a six-year career; Beckham Jr. was hurt for most of the 2017 season.

He came to Cleveland with a big price tag, having signed a five-year, $95 million contract with the Giants in 2018. He was released in November, 2021.

March 13, 1960 — The Browns lose Frank Clarke, Ed Modzelewski and Leroy Bolden to Dallas in the expansion draft that helps stock the roster of Tom Landry's Cowboys.

March 13, 1981 — Cavaliers owner Ted Stepien decides to make a coaching change, and reassigns Bill Musselman to a front-office job. On the bench, General Manager Don Delaney, whose coaching experience consists of jobs at Dyke College and Lakeland Community College, takes over.

14

March 14, 1986 — Cleveland State shocks the hoops world

College basketball fans learned on this date that Cleveland State University not only exists, but belongs with the best the NCAA Tournament has to offer.

The Vikings started playing Division I basketball in 1972, and were a member of the Mid-Continent Conference starting in 1982. Still, Cleveland State had never been a part of the "Big Dance" until 1986, when it advanced to the NCAA Tournament under Coach Kevin Mackey with a 27-3 record. That earned the team a first-round date with Indiana, coached by Bob Knight.

The Hoosiers would go on to win the national championship in 1987. But they couldn't stop the Vikings in 1986. Clinton Ransey had 27 points and Eric Mudd added 16 for Cleveland State, which earned a stunning 83-79 win in a game played in Syracuse.

After that, the Vikings beat Saint Joseph's to advance to the Sweet 16. The run ended there with a one-point loss to David Robinson and Navy, but no one was complaining. Ken "Mouse" McFadden of CSU set a school record for career points and had his uniform number retired.

March 14, 1967 — The NFL and AFL stage their first common college player draft; the

Browns take Duke linebacker Bob Matheson with the 18th pick in the first round. Later in his career with the Miami Dolphins (including the team's undefeated season in 1972), Matheson becomes a focal point of the "53 defense" nicknamed for his uniform number.

March 14, 1983 — NBA Commissioner Larry O'Brien discloses that he has received written communication from Cavaliers owner Ted Stepien indicating a desire to move the franchise to Toronto. The next day, Stepien holds a news conference in Toronto and announces the team will move and be renamed the Towers.

March 14, 2018 — Joe Thomas announces his retirement. The offensive tackle had been the only lineman in NFL history to be named to the Pro Bowl in his first 10 seasons. Thomas was the third overall pick in the 2007 draft, and at one point he was on the field for 10,363 consecutive snaps.

15

March 15, 2001 — Kent State knocks off Indiana

It's often difficult to get Big Ten basketball programs to even schedule Mid-American Conference opponents, particularly if they have to travel to do so, since they have less to gain and more to lose.

The NCAA tournament, then, offers a great opportunity for MAC teams to play bigger rivals on a neutral court, and sometimes upsets happen. Take the case on this day, when No. 13 seed Kent State downed No. 4 Indiana, 77-73, in a first-round game played in San Diego.

The Hoosiers had a 12-point lead in the second half, but couldn't hold it. One of the problems was 18 IU turnovers. Trevor Huffman picked the right time for a big day, leading the Golden Flashes with 24 points – including 11 of the team's last 15 points down the stretch.

"We had a serious mindset coming into this," Huffman said. "I don't think too many guys on our team were surprised that we beat Indiana."

March 15, 1973 — Phil "Flip" Saunders is named district high school basketball player of the year in the Class A small school division as a senior at Cuyahoga Heights. He goes on to play in college at Minnesota and later coaches in the NBA with Minnesota, Detroit and Washington. Saunders dies in 2015 at age 60 from Hodgkin's lymphoma.

March 15, 1977 — The San Francisco 49ers confirm an agreement is reached for Edward J. DeBartolo Jr. of Youngstown to acquire the NFL franchise for a reported $16.5 million.

March 15, 1991 — The Browns sign kicker Matt Stover as a free agent. He becomes one of the best kickers in the league for the Cleveland / Baltimore franchise from 1991 to 2008.

16

March 16, 1954 — Willis ends a great football career

Bill Willis announces his retirement from the Browns. You'd have to say that his career was on the short side, but his accomplishments remain legendary nonetheless.

Willis was a 202-pound nose guard at Ohio State University during the early 1940s. He graduated in 1945, and thought he was headed for a coaching career at Kentucky State. But then Paul Brown called to see if he was interested in joining a new pro team called the Cleveland Browns. Willis welcomed the opportunity – especially since there were no African Americans in pro football at that time.

He showed up at the team's initial training camp with Marion Motley; they were the only Black players there. They integrated the sport during the 1946 season, almost a year before Jackie Robinson arrived in Brooklyn to play for the Dodgers in Major League Baseball.

Willis retired as a seven-time first-team All-Pro; he was a second-teamer in the other season. He was a cornerstone of Cleveland's defenses during that era with his speed and intelligence. That made him an easy choice in 1977 for the Pro Football Hall of Fame.

March 16, 1900 — Just days after the National League of baseball clubs moved to reduce itself from 12 to eight teams – dumping the Cleveland Spiders as part of its contraction – the up-and-coming American League executives meet in Chicago led by President Ban Johnson to discuss their future. Cleveland was represented by Jack Kilfoyl, owner of real estate and a men's "furnishings" enterprise, according to reports. The meeting led to the creation of an AL team called the Cleveland Lake Shores, which compiled a 63-73 record and finished sixth among eight clubs. Other AL teams were: Chicago, Washington, Milwaukee, Detroit, Boston, Philadelphia and Baltimore.

March 16, 1941 — The first Knights of Columbus indoor track meet, featuring local sprinter Stella Walsh, is held in the Cleveland Arena. It starts a tradition that lasts until 1971.

March 16, 1973 — Ground is broken on a new arena construction project in the township of Richfield in Summit County, 21 miles south of downtown Cleveland.

March 17, 1898 — Big-time boxing comes to Cleveland

Boxing got off to a slow start in Ohio. A state law banned it in 1830, and the rule wasn't changed until 1923. But that's not to say that boxing didn't happen in that span in Northeast Ohio. Reports said a bare-knuckle bout between Paddy Ryan and Charley McDonald in 1881 took place in the City Armory. Other clandestine fights happened out of the view of authorities, sometimes on Whiskey Island along the Cleveland waterfront.

Still, history has recorded a good-sized title fight between George "Kid" Levigne and Wilmington Jack Daly at the Central Armory. Civic leaders allowed the match to take place on a trial basis. Levigne, who was from Michigan, is considered the first lightweight champion in boxing history. He won the title in 1896, and this was his fifth formal title defense.

Daly is also quite a story. His real name was Cornelius J. Moriarty, and he is considered Delaware's first great fighter. Granted, that wasn't saying much, because boxing also was considered illegal in that state. It was banned completely in 1901.

Fans crammed into the Central Armory for the bout, paying as much as $10 per ticket. The bout was declared a draw. One report said Daly knocked Levigne around the ring for the duration but didn't get the verdict – perhaps because the referee had bet on Levigne.

March 17, 1907 — The Detroit Tigers, angry after Ty Cobb got into an argument with a groundskeeper, offer him in a trade to the Indians for outfielder Elmer Flick. Cleveland manager Nap Lajoie turns it down, and Cobb goes on to a Hall of Fame career that is mostly spent in Detroit.

March 17, 1940 — The Barons are knocked out of the American Hockey League playoffs on the last day of the regular season when they lose to New Haven, 4-3. George Patterson, who scored the title-winning goal for Cleveland the year before, tallies with 30 seconds left to eliminate his old team.

18

March 18, 2022 — Browns pay big price for Watson

In 2018, the Browns hoped they had a franchise quarterback for a decade when they drafted Baker Mayfield with the first overall pick in the NFL draft. Those hopes essentially ended on this day.

The Browns completed a massive trade with the Houston Texans to acquire another quarterback on this day. The price tag for Deshaun Watson was very high. Cleveland gave up three first-round draft choices, a third-rounder in 2023 and a fourth-rounder in 2024 for Watson and a fifth-round choice in 2024. Then they signed Watson to a massive five-year guaranteed contract worth $230 million.

Off-the-field issues surrounded the veteran quarterback. He had been cleared of allegations of harassment and sexual misconduct only a week before the trade, as a grand jury did not charge him with crimes. However, Watson still faced 22 civil lawsuits, and an NFL investigation into the situation was said to be still in progress.

In other words, this ranks as one of the biggest gambles ever taken in Cleveland's sports history.

March 18, 1970 — Cavaliers owner Nick Mileti chooses the University of Minnesota's Bill Fitch to be the first coach in the NBA expansion franchise's team history.

March 18, 1970 — Tony Horton ends his contract dispute with the Indians after management told him that if he didn't sign, they'd simply move Ken Harrelson to first base. The next day, Harrelson breaks his leg and is lost to the team until September.

March 18, 2020 — The Browns spend about $100 million in signing free agents Austin Hooper, Jack Conklin and Case Keenum to contracts.

19

March 19, 1974 — Jim Perry comes back to Cleveland

Jim Perry had a curious major league pitching career. When he was good, he was very good – and some of that took place in Cleveland.

Perry broke in with the Indians in 1959, and quickly claimed a spot in the starting rotation. He had a 12-10 record and finished second in the voting for American League Rookie of the Year. Perry tied for the league lead in wins with 18 the next season, and was also in double digits in wins for the next two seasons.

The Indians then decided they needed a lefty instead of a righty, so they traded Perry to the Twins for Jack Kralick. Perry filled a variety of roles for Minnesota in the coming years, and did them well. He didn't have a losing record until 1972. Along the way, Perry moved into the starting rotation in 1969 and won the Cy Young Award in 1970.

Perry spent 1973 with the Tigers, and then the Indians couldn't pass up the chance to pair him with his brother, Gaylord. Walt "No Neck" Williams and Rick Sawyer went to the Yankees in a three-team transaction on this day. Perry went 17-12 in 1974, his last good season. He retired after the 1975 season.

March 19, 1957 — The Red Sox offer $1 million for 23-year-old Indians pitcher Herb Score, but General Manager Hank Greenberg turns them down.

March 19, 1989 — The Indians deal outfielder Mel "The Gunfighter" Hall to the Yankees for catcher Joel Skinner and outfielder Turner Ward.

20

March 20, 1975 — Bonda takes over the Indians

Alva T. "Ted" Bonda might be thought of as just a footnote in Cleveland sports history. He deserves more recognition than that.

Bonda was part of a group that purchased the Indians in 1973, and on this day he was named the president of the team, taking over for Cavs owner Nick Mileti, who remained a general partner.

Bonda might be best remembered as the executive who pushed the team to hire Frank Robinson as its manager. He therefore gets an assist in Robinson's status as the first African American to manage a major league team. Bonda simply said it was "the right thing to do." The Indians could have moved before Bonda and his partners bought the team, and Bonda oversaw some difficult financial years. Bonda remained with the franchise after F.J. "Steve" O'Neill took control in 1978 and brought Gabe Paul from the Yankees to help.

"He was a fair man. He was a listener," Robinson said about Bonda. "He was always open and honest with me . . . He was a very low-key man, a very honest man and a very compassionate person."

March 20, 1956 — The Browns sign 26-year-old quarterback Vito "Babe" Parilli to a $12,500 contract. Parilli's NFL career would continue all the way to 1969, and he was a backup on Joe Namath's New York Jets team that won the Super Bowl.

21

March 21, 2002 — Flashes rank among elite

Major college basketball teams from the Cleveland area haven't had a great many significant moments on the national stage. Perhaps it's because so many of the area's best players have gone elsewhere to play – with Ohio State serving as the most obvious recipient of talent.

But there is the odd exception. A game that certainly qualified was the time that Kent State reached the Elite Eight. The Golden Flashes defeated Pittsburgh, 78-73 in overtime, at Rupp Arena in Lexington, Kentucky. It marked Kent State's first trip to the regional finals.

Trevor Huffman put Kent State ahead in overtime with a driving layup, and the Flashes were on their way to their 21st straight victory – the longest such streak in the country at that point. Huffman finished with 17 points. Antonio Gates, who would switch sports and become a top-flight tight end for the San Diego Chargers in the NFL, has 22 points for the Flashes.

Waiting was Indiana, which knocked off No. 1 seed and defending champion Duke in the other regional semifinals. The dream ended there, as Kent State lost an 81-69 decision and fell just short of the Final Four.

March 21, 1959 — Larry Doby, the second African American to play major league baseball in the 20th century when he joined Cleveland in 1947, sees his time as an Indian end as he is traded to Detroit for John "Tito" Francona.

March 21, 1961 — The ownership change of the Browns transitioning to New York City business executive Art Modell becomes official. Modell figured out a way to buy the Browns for almost $4 million. Reports said Modell spent $250,000 of his own money, borrowed about $2.7 million, and found partners for the rest, including beer company executive Rudolph Schaefer, whose holdings were reported to be larger than Modell's.

March 22, 1993 — Olin, Crews die in boat crash

It is a day off from work for the Indians in their first spring training in Winter Haven, Florida. The team moved their camp from Tucson, Arizona, where they had been since 1947. General Manager John Hart and Manager Mike Hargrove had developed a young nucleus that promised a better record was coming. They had added pitching to go with some potentially strong, young hitters.

On this "vacation" day, recently acquired pitcher Tim Crews invited players to a cookout at his ranch an hour's drive away.

As part of the evening's events, Crews, Steve Olin, and Bob Ojeda went for a boat ride and crashed into a dock at an estimated 40 miles per hour. Olin was said to have been killed instantly. Crews died the next morning. Ojeda survived because he had slumped in his seat a bit, but still suffered major injuries. An autopsy ruled that Crews was intoxicated.

These were the first deaths of an active major league player since Thurman Munson was killed in a plane crash in 1979.

March 22, 1972 — Cleveland sports entrepreneur Nick Mileti puts together an investment group that takes control of the Indians in a deal valued at $9.8 million. The majority owner had been Vernon Stouffer, a business executive with experience in the food, restaurant, and hospitality industries who took over in 1966 when the franchise was valued at $8.2 million, according to the *Akron Beacon Journal*'s report. George Steinbrenner had also been negotiating with Stouffer to buy the club. The deal means Mileti, at age 40, is in charge of the pro hockey Barons, the NBA's Cavaliers, as well as the Indians.

March 22, 1972 — Walt Wesley's shot with 14 seconds to go wraps up a stunning 124-120 win by the Cavaliers over the Lakers, who would go on to win the NBA Championship.

March 22, 1973 — Two teenage women's tennis players who would become legends in their sport meet for the first time as opponents in the Virginia Slims of Akron Tennis Open. Chris Evert, age 18, defeats Martina Navratilova, who was then 16, by 7-6, 6-3, in the $25,000 event played at University of Akron's Memorial Hall. It's the first of 80 matches between the two players (Navratilova won 43 of them).

23

March 23, 1995 — Browns open wallet for Rison

Andre Rison ranked as one of the National Football League's elite receivers after the 1994 season. He had caught at least 81 passes in each of the previous five seasons for the Atlanta Falcons, and had more than 1,000 yards four times. Rison was only 28 years old, and figured to have many more good seasons ahead of him.

Who could resist such a free agent? Not Coach Bill Belichick and the Browns. Cleveland was coming off a playoff season in 1994, and thought another offensive weapon would help them take the next step. They made him the highest-paid receiver in the history of the league when they signed him to a five-year, $17 million contract. "Finally I feel appreciated," Rison said after signing the deal.

That feeling didn't last long. Rison had a difficult 1995 season as he only caught 47 passes. He also got into a feud with Cleveland fans, who already were in a bad mood after the announcement in November that the team would be moving to Baltimore for the 1996 season. Rison threw some gasoline on the fire when he said, "We don't have any home-field advantage. I've never been booed at home. Baltimore's our home. Baltimore, here we come."

Rison bounced to four different teams over the next five seasons, but rarely displayed the ability that made him so coveted by the Browns.

March 23, 1971 — The Cavaliers finish with a 15-67 record in their first NBA season after a 114-112 loss to Portland.

March 23, 2002 — LeBron James and St. Vincent-St. Mary are tagged with their only Ohio high school state tournament basketball loss in his four-year career. The championship went to Cincinnati Roger Bacon, 71-63, at Value City Arena in Columbus. James had 32 points on 14-of-21 shooting with six assists, three rebounds and seven turnovers.

March 24, 1975 — Ali defeats a real-life Rocky

Muhammad Ali needed a bit of a rest. He had won the heavyweight boxing championship again on October 30, 1974, in an epic fight against George Foreman in Zaire, and it was time to defend the crown. The plan was to find someone who wouldn't provide too much opposition.

Enter Chuck Wepner. No one doubted Wepner's toughness; they didn't call him "The Bayonne Bleeder" for nothing. The nickname referred to Bayonne, New Jersey – Wepner's hometown. But Wepner certainly wasn't in Ali's class as a fighter, and he was 35. Still, the idea of picking up $100,000 to be an opponent for Ali was attractive.

The two met in Richfield at the Coliseum. In the ninth round, Wepner was given credit for knocking Ali down, which only seemed to annoy the champion. Ali picked up the pace in the final rounds, and scored a technical knockout in the 15th round.

The bout was quickly forgotten by almost everyone except actor / screenwriter Sylvester Stallone. He worked on a movie script that incorporated part of Wepner's story into it. The film eventually was called "Rocky," and was released late in 1976. In boxing terms, the movie was a knockout – winning a Best Picture Oscar. Wepner later filed a suit against

Stallone seeking compensation as the inspiration for the movie. News reports said the suit was settled.

March 24, 1962 — Dayton co-captain Garry Roggenburk, a 6-foot-6 forward from Cleveland St. Ignatius High School, helps the Flyers to the National Invitation Tournament title with a 73-67 victory over St. John's. He went on to become a major-league pitcher for Minnesota, Boston and Seattle.

March 24, 1974 — The Cavaliers beat the Knicks, 114-92, in their final home game in the Cleveland Arena. Lenny Wilkens scores 22 to lead the Cavs. The Arena was built for $1.5 million and opened in 1937 as the home of the American Hockey League's Cleveland Barons.

March 24, 1979 — Clark Kellogg of St. Joseph High School in Cleveland turns in one of the great performances in Ohio prep history in a 79-65 loss to Columbus East in the state championship game. Kellogg scored 51 points to set a title game record and had 24 rebounds. He went on to play at Ohio State and for the NBA's Indiana Pacers.

25

March 25, 1997 — Indians trade Lofton to Braves

Indians General Manager John Hart had a problem in the winter of 1997. He knew his team had a ton of talent, but it would be nearly impossible to keep the squad together for the long term. Albert Belle departed as a free agent after the 1996 season. Kenny Lofton was the next player who could walk away, as his contract would expire at the end of '97.

Lofton reportedly had turned down a five-year, $44 million deal in the offseason. Hart didn't want another star to walk away for nothing, so he quietly started to shop his center fielder. He found a possible trading partner in the Atlanta Braves, who were looking for ways to save a little money because they needed to sign pitchers Greg Maddux, Tom Glavine and John Smoltz.

The key figure in the deal became David Justice, a power hitter who missed much of 1996 with shoulder surgery. He could take Belle's spot in the lineup. Marquis Grissom also could come to Cleveland in the deal and play center field. The Braves wanted another player in the transaction, so pitcher Alan Embree was added. Done deal.

It all worked out rather well for the Indians. Lofton had a good season in Atlanta, and then returned to Cleveland as a free agent for four more seasons. Justice hit 20 homers in each of his four seasons in an Indians uniform. Grissom had a decent 1997 in Cleveland and then was traded to Milwaukee to make room for Lofton's return.

March 25, 1964 — The Akron Goodyear Wingfoots basketball team defeats the Phillips Oilers, 86-78, for the AAU national basketball championship in a game played in Denver. It is the Akron club's first Amateur Athletic Union championship which they would win again in 1967.

March 25, 1989 — The Indians acquire Felix Fermin from the Pirates for Jay Bell.

March 25, 1995 — The Browns trade up in the draft, giving Eric Metcalf and a first-round pick (No. 26) to the Falcons for a first-round pick (No. 10). Later when the draft occurs, the Browns end up with linebacker Craig Powell of Ohio State as their first-round choice.

26

March 26, 1953 — Browns and Colts complete massive trade

The Browns had done nothing but win in their football lifetime at this point – seven consecutive appearances in championship games. You wouldn't think a good-sized roster shake-up was needed at that point. However, Coach Paul Brown apparently disagreed.

That's why the two teams completed a 15-man swap that is the largest in NFL history. Ten went from Cleveland to Baltimore. You've heard of one of them – a defensive back named Don Shula. Here are the others: Harry Agganis, Bert Rechichar, Carl Taseff, Ed Sharkey, Art Spinney, Elmer Wilhoite, Gern Nagler, Stu Sheets, and Dick Batten.

Five players went to the Browns: center Tom Catlin, defensive tackle Don Colo, offensive tackle Mike McCormack, halfback John Petitbon, and guard Herschel Forester. McCormack turned out to be the biggest name for Cleveland, building a career that led to the Pro Football Hall of Fame.

The key player in the deal for the Colts was Agganis, one of the great athletes of his generation. Agganis had signed with baseball's Boston Red Sox after starring in college football at Boston University. The Colts hoped to lure him to Baltimore. Sadly, Agganis developed pneumonia and died of a pulmonary embolism on June 27, 1955. Baltimore did acquire some players in the deal who were on the Colts' 1958 championship team.

March 26, 1985 — Future Cavaliers draft choice John "Hot Rod" Williams and two Tulane University teammates and a student are arrested on charges of "fixing" college basketball games. A jury eventually returns a not-guilty verdict.

March 26, 2008 — LeBron James of the Cavaliers concludes a run of 49 straight games with at least 20 points as he gets 21 against the New Orleans Hornets.

March 27, 1939 — Boughner, OSU stop a game short of title

Richard "Dick" Boughner probably smiled when he watched the NCAA basketball tournament in the latter stages of his life. After all, he was there at the creation.

The tournament began in 1939. You wouldn't have recognized it, except for the ball and the baskets. It only had eight teams, and the championship game was played in Evanston, Illinois, after regionals in Philadelphia and San Francisco. The contest was not a sellout, but drew a crowd estimated somewhere around 5,000.

"To me, it was just another game," Boughner, an Akron native, told *The Sporting News* in 1988. "You go back to 1939, this was a brand-new tournament. In those days, your goal was to win the Big Ten, and to heck with everything else. Around comes this tournament — and who wanted to play another game?"

The finalists were Ohio State and Oregon. Boughner was one of the starters for the Buckeyes, along with All-American Jimmy Hull, Dick Baker, John Schick, and Bob Lynch. Harold Olson served as coach. Ohio State was 16-6 entering the game, 10-2 in conference play. Oregon was the opponent; the team known as the Webfoots was 27-5, 14-2 in the PCC. Oregon led almost all of the way, and won by a score of 46-33. Boughner, who was an All-City basketball honoree at West High School in Akron, also played football at Ohio State. He died in 2007 at age 90.

March 27, 1981 — A crowd of 20,175 fills the Coliseum in Richfield to say farewell to Cavaliers' radio announcer Joe Tait. Team owner Ted Stepien, who was feuding publicly with Tait, had announced that the broadcasts of the games would be changing stations heading into the 1981-82 season. Stepien later named Paul Porter to replace Tait. Two years later, after Stepien sold the team to Gordon Gund, Tait was rehired as the team's announcer.

28

March 28, 1990 — Jordan sets career-high against Cavs

The Cavaliers saw more than enough of Michael Jordan over the years. The Bulls' superstar always seemed to be in the way when Cleveland was close to an important win. What's more, he had the best game of his life on an individual basis against the Cavs on this night.

Jordan opened the game with 16 points in the first quarter, and added 15 in the second period. He had 51 by the time the third quarter was over, and added 10 more in the fourth. That adds up to 61 – but the Bulls and Cavs weren't done yet.

Jordan scored eight more points in the final five minutes. That totaled a career-high 69 points, as he shot 23-for-37 from the field. He also had 18 rebounds in 50 minutes in a 117-113 win for Chicago.

"I didn't think about being tired because I wanted to win the game," Jordan said. "I've been in that situation where I've scored a lot of points and we lost, and I didn't want that to happen. So I kept pushing myself, kept talking to myself, saying, 'Don't stop, don't stop. Keep going.' You feel better about the effort when you win."

March 28, 1990 — Native Clevelander Jesse Owens is posthumously awarded the Congressional Gold Medal by President George Bush.

March 28, 2015 — Kentucky improves to 38-0 with a thrilling 68-66 win over Notre Dame in the NCAA Tournament's Midwest Regional final at Quicken Loans Arena in Cleveland, thanks to two free throws by Andrew Harrison with two seconds to go.

29

March 29, 1971 — Cavs grab Carr with first overall pick

The Cavaliers' record of 15-67 in their first NBA season in 1970-71 was the worst in the league. Surely there had to be a reward for all of that suffering. And there was – they had the first draft choice in the NBA Draft.

The top pick came with a catch. Not only did the Cavs have to make the choice, but they also had to sign him. The rival American Basketball Association was competing for players in that era, and teams from the ABA were willing to spend big money as well.

Austin Carr certainly deserved consideration. He was an All-American for Notre Dame, a 6-foot-4 guard who averaged more than 34 points per game. The other possible choice was Sidney Wicks, the excellent forward from UCLA. Jacksonville's Artis Gilmore and Villanova's Howard Porter also were possibilities, but they both signed with the ABA. Carr became the Cavs' pick.

Carr had three very good years in Cleveland, but injuries changed the course of his career. He remained in Cleveland through 1980, and finished his playing days with Dallas and Washington. Carr eventually became a popular broadcaster in Cleveland, known as "Mr. Cavalier" and for sayings such as, "Get that weak stuff outta here."

March 29, 1962 — The Browns and Detroit Lions complete a major trade revolving around starting quarterbacks. Cleveland deals quarterback Milt Plum, halfback Tom Watkins, and linebacker Dave Lloyd to Detroit for quarterback Jim Ninowski, defensive end Bill Glass, and halfback Howard "Hopalong" Cassady.

March 29, 1979 — Luke Easter, one of the first African Americans to play major league baseball, is shot and killed during a robbery of $5,000 outside of a bank in suburban Euclid. At age 63, Easter was a union steward at the TRW company and had cashed payroll checks for workers.

March 29, 1984 — The Baltimore Colts move to Indianapolis, leaving the city without an NFL team after it began play in 1953. The city would get a replacement team in 1996 when Art Modell moves his Cleveland franchise to Maryland. On March 29, 1996, the franchise announces it will be named the Ravens.

March 29, 2006 — The Cavs reach the playoffs for the first time in eight years with a 107-94 win over Dallas. LeBron James has 46 points for Cleveland.

March 30, 1978 — Indians trade Eckersley to Red Sox

Dennis Eckersley wasn't initially happy when he was drafted by the Indians in 1972. He would have preferred the Giants or Dodgers. But soon he realized that the Indians offered a faster ticket to the majors. Eckersley joined the starting rotation, and he won 40 games in his first three years.

But in those years, the Indians' team executives often tried to leverage a star player for several newcomers who might help plug holes. So Cleveland traded him and catcher Fred Kendall to Boston for a package containing pitchers Rick Wise and Mike Paxton, catcher Bo Diaz and infielder Ted Cox. Cox had been a minor league Player of the Year.

Eckersley had five good-to-great years in Boston before faltering. He ended up in Oakland, reinventing himself as one of the greatest relief pitchers in baseball history. His plaque is in Cooperstown.

March 30, 1998 — The Indians trade promising first baseman Sean Casey to the Reds for established starting pitcher Dave Burba.

March 30, 2018 — LeBron James of the Cavaliers reaches double digits in points for the 867th consecutive time, breaking the NBA record set by Michael Jordan.

March 31, 1976 — Cavaliers sew up a playoff spot

Reaching the postseason playoffs is always a benchmark of success for pro sports teams born as expansion franchises. Sometimes the stars align and results come quickly. Other times, it's not so easy.

In the case of the Cavaliers, it took more than five years with plenty of heartaches. That's why this game isn't just another regular-season contest. The Cavs beat the New

Orleans Jazz, 110-101, in Louisiana, and were officially headed to the postseason.

The Cavs did enough to win this one, and in a balanced way. Cleveland outscored New Orleans in every quarter, but never by more than four points. Jim Cleamons had 18, Jim Chones and Austin Carr 17 each, and Campy Russell added 16.

The Cavs still had a division to clinch, and they had seven more regular season games to do it. But making the playoffs for the first time was a breakthrough all its own.

March 31, 1945 — The Cleveland franchise of the All-American Football Conference announces that Otto Graham is the first player to agree to terms with the team, which will debut in 1946.

March 31, 1993 — The Browns sign quarterback Vinny Testaverde as a free agent.

March 31, 1995 — Parma native Brian Holzinger captures the Hobey Baker Award as the best player in men's college hockey. He had been a standout for Bowling Green, and went on to a pro career that lasted nine seasons.

April 1, 1998 — Meno ranks with skating's best

Jenni Meno, a Westlake native, was by any standard one of the best figure skaters in the world. She started skating at about age 8 and moved from singles to doubles as a teen. Jenni had success with Scott Wendland, as the duo placed second and third at the U.S. Championships in 1991 and 1992.

Then Meno switched partners, skating with Todd Sand in 1992. They had a terrific run of success, highlighted with a second-place showing in the world championships on this day. That was a notch better than a pair of thirds earlier in the decade. Meno and Sand won three consecutive national championships together, and finished fifth (1994) and eighth (1998) at the Winter Olympics.

Jenni and Todd had one other memorable moment at the 1994 Olympics – they became engaged. Married in 1995, they were part of the "Stars On Ice" show for several years and now coach together.

April 1, 1964 — Indians manager Birdie Tebbetts suffers a heart attack. George Strickland becomes the interim manager of the team for the next three months.

April 2, 1993 — For once, the Price is wrong

It's almost unfair. Mark Price is one of the greatest free throw shooters in NBA history. The Cavaliers standout guard sank 2,135 free throws in his career. He finished with a 90.4 percent success rate.

Yet he's remembered in part for the one he missed on this day.

Price had made 77 straight free throws. That was one short of the NBA record held at the time by Calvin Murphy. Price stepped up to the line, shot ... and missed! It must have been quite a shock. The 6-foot guard did go 7-for-8 from the line in the loss to the Hornets, so he still had a pretty good day in that department. Cleveland lost the game, 114-113.

Price spent nine seasons with the Cavaliers, and averaged more than 16 points per game. He scored on more than 40 percent of his three-point attempts, and is considered one of the best long-range shooters in NBA history. As for the free throw record, Michael Williams of Minnesota later made 97 in a row split over two seasons (1992-93 and 1993-94).

April 2, 1994 — The Indians stage something of a dress rehearsal for the opening of Jacobs Field by hosting the Pirates in an exhibition game. Fans in attendance observe the policy of no smoking in the stadium and ushers are given business-size cards to hand to anyone violating the policy to explain the details.

April 3, 1966 — Indians miss out on Seaver

This was a great day for the New York Mets – but not so good for the Indians. Cleveland came ever-so-close to having Tom Seaver, a future Hall of Famer, on its roster.

Seaver was drafted by the Los Angeles Dodgers in the summer of 1965 after an excellent sophomore year at USC. The team turned down his $70,000 asking price, so Seaver went back to college. Then the right-hander was taken by Atlanta in the free-agent draft in January of 1966. In February, Seaver agreed to terms with Richmond, the Braves' minor-league affiliate.

The problem was that Southern California had already started its season with some exhibition games, and Seaver could not sign with a pro team once that happened. Commissioner William Eckert voided the contract with the Braves on March 2, and he was ruled ineligible to play for USC. That left him in limbo. Then Eckert opted to allow any team that was willing to match the Braves' offer to enter a special lottery for Seaver's rights.

Only three teams took part in that procedure: the Indians, Mets and Phillies. Eckert put the names in a hat, and pulled out a piece of paper with "Mets" on it. New York signed him to a $50,000 deal.

April 3, 1974 — The Indians trade 17-year-old prospect Pedro Guerrero to the Dodgers for left-handed pitcher Bruce Ellingsen, who did not make the Los Angeles club. Guerrero spent 15 years in the majors with a career batting average of .300. Ellingsen appeared in 42 innings in 16 games for one year.

April 4, 1994 — Indians open Jacobs Field in style

Cleveland hadn't been talking forever about a new stadium for the Indians; it only seemed that way. Municipal Stadium, which later became Cleveland Stadium when Art Modell took over its management, was the site of some good memories, of course. But it was more than 60 years old by this point, and had become considered far too large for baseball as an increasingly intimate fan experience. When 20,000 turned out, the building still seemed almost empty.

After Cuyahoga County voters approved a tax on tobacco and alcohol products, $84 million of the total cost of $175 million was raised for construction of a new ballpark. Jacobs Field (named after Indians owner Richard Jacobs) was located on the southern edge of downtown. President Bill Clinton flew in to throw out the first pitch and was accompanied by Ohio Governor George Voinovich and legendary pitcher Bob Feller. Then Game 1 was on.

Dennis Martinez had the honor of the first start in the Indians' new home. He allowed a run to the visiting Mariners without giving up a hit in the top of the first. In the top of the third, Seattle's Eric Anthony hit the first home run in the history of the stadium. Meanwhile, Randy Johnson didn't allow a hit in the first seven innings of the game. In the eighth, Cleveland finally broke through against Johnson to score two runs to tie the contest.

Both teams scored a run in the 10th, so the game moved to the 11th. That's when Wayne Kirby singled home Eddie Murray to send the sellout crowd home happy. Murray became the major leagues' all-time leader in games played at first base that day (2,369) and the Indians would go on to average 39,121 fans for each of their home games that first year.

April 4, 1970 — Cleveland's new NBA basketball team has a name: the Cavaliers. Jerry Tomko of Eastlake gets the credit for naming the team.

April 4, 1970 — Don Johnson rolls a 299 to just miss a bonus of $10,000 and a new car in the final match of pro bowling's Tournament of Champions at Riviera Lanes in Fairlawn, which was broadcast on ABC-TV. However, he does beat Dick Ritger to win the tournament and $25,000.

April 4, 2001 — The Indians' sellout streak of home games ends at 455 as the team has an unsold seat for the first time since June 7, 1995. The major league record lasts until 2008 when the Red Sox break it.

5

April 5, 2001 — Hart decides to leave Indians

It is not a happy day for Indians' fans as the best general manager in recent history announces he'd be leaving soon.

John Hart worked in the Orioles' organization before joining the Indians in 1989. He was the team's interim manager at the end of that season, but General Manager Hank Peters thought he'd be better in the front office than on the field. Hart became director of baseball operations in 1990, assisting Peters. The two started to put the pieces of a winning ballclub together.

That process continued once Hart took over as GM in the fall of 1991. Once he identified core players like Carlos Baerga, Charles Nagy, and Sandy Alomar Jr., he signed them to long-term contracts before they were eligible for salary arbitration. If the Indians guessed right, they'd have top talent at a bargain price. That's exactly what happened, as the Indians went on a great run starting in 1994 that saw them win six American League Central titles.

Hart said on this day that he planned to retire from the GM's spot after the 2002 season and take an advisory role. But that changed in the fall when the Rangers offered him the opportunity to take over that team. He took the job, but Texas didn't duplicate Cleveland's success under Hart. He also worked for the Braves at the end of his career.

April 5, 1976 — Wide receiver Paul Warfield returns to the Browns, signing as a free agent.

April 5, 1992 — Mark Price sinks a free throw during a game at home against the Knicks – the first of 100 in a row at home games.

April 5, 1993 — A crowd of 73,290 attends the Indians' final season home opener in Cleveland Stadium as the Yankees win, 9-1. In a pregame ceremony, Patti Olin and Laurie Crews were presented the jerseys of their husbands, Steve Olin and Tim Crews, who were killed March 22 in a boating accident during an off-day at spring training in Winter Haven, Florida.

April 5, 2021 — The Indians play before their home fans for the first time since 2019, as they lose to the Royals, 3-0, in their home opener. A crowd of 8,914 turned out for the game; fans were not permitted in Progressive Field in 2020 because of the coronavirus health situation.

6

April 6, 1975 — Cavs are close, but no playoffs

For a handful of hours, the Cavaliers were allowed to do a little dreaming. They had defeated the Knicks on April 3, 100-95, before 20,239 in the Coliseum to gain the upper hand on New York in the race for a wild-card playoff spot. The Cavs had never reached the postseason before, and now they had a chance.

When the Knicks lost on April 4 to Milwaukee, Cleveland had two roads to the playoffs. The Cavs could make it if New York lost to Buffalo on the final day of the season. Failing that, Cleveland could qualify with a win against the Kansas City-Omaha Kings.

The Knicks didn't go down without a fight. They improved to 40-42 with a 105-93 win over the Braves. That left the Cavs in a must-win situation in a game played in Omaha, Nebraska. The Kings were led by Nate Archibald, who scored 33 points in the game.

The contest came down to the final seconds. Cleveland trailed by one when Fred Foster took a shot that could have sent his team to the playoffs. However, the Kings' Ron Behagen blocked it, and the buzzer sounded. The Knicks were off to the playoffs, and the Cavs were done for the season in a dramatic but painful way. Foster never played for the Cavs again.

April 6, 1974 — The Indians become the first team to play the Yankees in Shea Stadium, losing 6-1 in the season opener. Yankee Stadium in the Bronx was renovated in 1974-75, forcing the team to move across town for two seasons of home games. Another "first" occurred during the game when umpire Marty Springstead called a ball without a pitch being thrown in the sixth inning against Gaylord Perry, invoking a new rule when a pitcher is suspected of doing something illegal.

April 6, 1992 — Paul Sorrento gets the first hit in the history of the new Oriole Park at Camden Yards – the first ever recorded in the $225 million facility. By comparison, the construction cost of Jacobs Field when it opened in Cleveland in 1994 was $175 million.

April 6, 1996 — Unhappy about having his photo taken by Tony Tomsic of *Sports Illustrated* magazine, Albert Belle hits Tomsic in the hand with a thrown baseball during pregame warmups. The incident was undisclosed by anyone for two weeks. Tomsic did not file a complaint with anyone. Tomsic said Belle shook his finger at him before the ball was thrown. Belle reportedly told Manager Mike Hargrove that the throw was an accident while he was playing long-toss with Manny Ramirez.

April 6, 2007 — Earl Boykins scores a career-high 36 points on 10-of-16 shooting from the field and 12-of-13 at the free throw line and adds nine assists but his Milwaukee Bucks lose, 115-102, to the Atlanta Hawks. He played pro basketball from 1998 to 2012 after starting his career at Cleveland Central Catholic High School and Eastern Michigan. At 5-foot-5, Boykins was generally considered the second-shortest NBA player of all-time, after Muggsy Bogues.

7

April 7, 1946 — Keiser wins Masters championship

The Masters golf tournament began in 1934 as something of an invitational event. A relatively small group of players gathered in Augusta, Georgia, to compete. The winners, therefore, were fairly well known in the first decade of play. That circle included Gene Sarazen, Byron Nelson and Jimmy Demaret.

Then came 1946, the first Masters since 1942 because of World War II. The top players were there, of course, and Ben Hogan was a favorite to take his first Masters. But the player who stole the show was a relative unknown – Herman Keiser.

Keiser had served as a club pro at Portage Country Club and Firestone Country Club in Akron before the war. Then he worked on the *USS Cincinnati* before being discharged in 1945. Keiser brought his clubs along during his service time, so his game only needed a little tune-up before he was ready to compete against other PGA players who traveled from city to city.

Keiser shot a 69 to tie for the lead after the first round, and a 68 put him five up after 36 holes. He maintained that margin through three rounds, but slumped to a 74 on the event's final day. Hogan had a chance to tie, but he three-putted the 18th hole to finish one shot behind. Keiser had won his only major championship. He played on the tour for the next several years, and then headed back to the Akron area for the rest of his life.

April 7, 1973 — The Indians use John Ellis as the first designated hitter in team history in the 1973 season opener, a 2-1 victory over the Detroit Tigers before 74,420. The crowd set a record for largest American League attendance on Opening Day; Cleveland had set the old record in 1948.

April 7, 1983 — Cavaliers owner Ted Stepien announces a deal to sell the franchise (along with his advertising company) to Coliseum owners Gordon and George Gund for a reported $21 million. The deal ended talk of the team moving to Toronto. Stepien's three seasons produced a 66-180 win-loss record, and the *Akron Beacon Journal* reported that his financial losses totaled $16.3 million in three years.

April 7, 1989 — The hapless Cleveland Indians are depicted in a Hollywood movie called "Major League," released on this day. The stars were Tom Berenger, Charlie Sheen, Corbin Bernsen, and Bob Uecker.

8

April 8, 1975 — Robinson helps his own cause

The Indians had acquired Frank Robinson from the Angels in a deal late in the 1974 season. The party line was that Robinson would add a handy bat in a playoff drive, but there were whispers that team executives had something else in mind – making him the manager in 1975.

The whispers were right. The Indians thought Robinson could draw attention to the team as major league baseball's first African-American manager. Cleveland offered him a reported $200,000 to be the player/manager in 1975, a $20,000 increase from his player's contract. Robinson took it.

This was his first day on the job – a 36-degree afternoon game at Cleveland Stadium that felt colder because of the wind. Jackie Robinson's widow, Rachel, threw out the first pitch. Frank Robinson wrote his own name in the lineup as the designated hitter in the No. 2 spot. After Oscar Gamble fouled out, Robinson came up and smashed a pitch from Doc Medich into the left-field stands for a home run. A crowd of 56,715 went wild.

The Indians went on to win 5-3. It couldn't have gone better for Robinson. "I feel better than I have after anything I've done in this game. Take all the pennants, the personal awards, the World Series, the All-Star Games together and this moment is the greatest... the greatest," he said.

April 8, 1939 — The Barons claim their first American Hockey League title by beating Philadelphia, three games to one, with a 1-0 victory. George "Popeye" Patterson scored the winning goal. Patterson and goalie Moe Roberts were still signing autographs at 1 a.m.

April 8, 1969 — Mike Hegan, who played high school baseball at St. Ignatius in Cleveland, hits the first home run in Seattle Pilots' history. They beat the California Angels, 4-3. Hegan was the son of Jim Hegan, who was the Indians' catcher from 1941 to 1957. Mike Hegan later would become a broadcaster of Indians games.

April 8, 1974 — Where was Major League Baseball Commissioner Bowie Kuhn on the night Hank Aaron hit his 715th home run in Atlanta to break Babe Ruth's record? Kuhn was in Cleveland, attending a dinner on what was to be opening night for the Indians. Kuhn had been in Cincinnati when Aaron hit No. 714.

April 8, 1993 — Carlos Baerga of the Indians becomes the first major leaguer to hit two home runs in the same inning from opposite sides of the plate. He powers Cleveland to a 15-5 win over the Yankees.

9

April 9, 1962 – Pipers win ABL championship

The American Basketball League has an odd place in pro basketball history. It was founded out of spite, as Harlem Globetrotters owner Abe Saperstein was upset that he was not allowed to buy an NBA team after the Trotters had helped support the established league for years by playing in doubleheaders. Some industrial and amateur teams got together to form the American Basketball League. The quality of play wasn't bad and the three-point shot was introduced.

The Cleveland Pipers joined the ABL for the 1961-62 season with George Steinbrenner as president and John McLendon as coach. McLendon, the first African American to coach a pro team, eventually brought one of his college players, Dick Barnett, to Cleveland. After a disagreement of some type, McLendon either resigned or was fired in January 1962, depending on the source. Former Boston NBA star Bill Sharman, another Hall of Famer who was one year removed from his Celtics career, was brought in.

The Pipers had a couple of other good players in Connie Dierking and Larry Siegfried, who would go on to long NBA careers. The team was too good for ABL competition. Cleveland won the championship, 3-2, in a best-of-five series with the Kansas City Steers. The deciding game was delayed a day over a problem with finding a place to play. The final score of the final game was 106-102.

The Pipers started to defend their title in the 1962-63 season, but dropped out of the league for financial reasons and the entire ABL folded on December 31, 1962. In 2015, longtime *Plain Dealer* sports columnist Bill Livingston chronicled the Pipers' story in a book titled, "George Steinbrenner's Pipe Dream: The ABL Champion Cleveland Pipers."

April 9, 1926 — The Cleveland Rosenblums win the first championship of the American Basketball League, as they finish a three-game sweep of the Brooklyn Arcadians with a 23-22 win.

April 9, 1985 — The Cavs can celebrate making the NBA playoffs after beating New Jersey, 114-100, as World B. Free scores 35 points. It is their first appearance in the postseason since 1978. Free, who changed his name from Lloyd Free in 1981, played four seasons and averaged 23 points for the Cavs.

April 9, 1987 — It had never happened since the 1800s – two 300-game winning pitchers appear in the same game for the same team. Phil Niekro got the start and the win and Steve Carlton earned a save with four innings of relief as Cleveland beat Toronto, 14-3.

10

April 10, 1976 — Cavaliers earn a banner with win

The Cavaliers make a key trade with the Chicago Bulls early in the NBA season to solidify their frontcourt with 6-foot-11 center Nate Thurmond. His veteran presence and the maturity of some young players combine to create the start of what would be called "The Miracle of Richfield."

The Cavs combined a winning record for the first time in franchise history with a playoff berth and then they went after a Central Division championship. To do that, Cleveland had to beat the New York Knicks in the last game of the home season at the Coliseum. More than 14,000 turned out, and a national television audience watched, too.

The Knicks put up a fight, and the game was up for grabs in the final minutes. But Austin Carr, Campy Russell and Bingo Smith made big plays down the stretch, and the Cavs were 99-94 winners.

Jim Chones led Cleveland with 25 points, and Russell added 23 points in 25 minutes. The Cavs lost their final regular season game to finish the season at 49-33, but it didn't matter. They had the tiebreaker, and the defending champion Washington Bullets made that academic by losing their finale to finish at 48-34.

April 10, 1965 — The first Firestone Tournament of Champions is held at the Bowlarama in Akron, and Billy Hardwick beats Dick Weber and Joe Joseph to capture the title. The T of C, or "Firestone" as it becomes known, was one of the signature events of the Professional Bowlers Association tour that was founded in 1959, led by Akron business executive Eddie Elias.

April 10, 1997 — The Akron Aeros, a Class AA Eastern League baseball affiliate of the Indians, play their first game in the new $31 million Canal Park built in downtown Akron. The Aeros were relocated from Canton, where they had played at Thurman Munson Stadium and were known as the Indians. In the first game, Akron wins, 13-2, as 21-year-old right-handed pitcher Jaret Wright gets the victory over the Harrisburg Senators.

April 10, 2003 — The Lake County Captains minor league baseball team plays its first home game in Classic Park in Eastlake. The game attracts 7,124.

11

April 11, 1948 — Barons start a winning streak

What a time Cleveland sports fans had in 1948. All those teams ever did was win. The Browns took the All-American Football Conference title again, and the Indians won the World Series for the second time in team history.

However, the Cleveland Barons of the American Hockey League started the parade in the spring. The fun part was how it happened.

The Barons looked like a good team in the early going of the 1947-48 season. They were 16-11-3 on January 1, the day that Cleveland engaged in a near-riot with the Pittsburgh Hornets. Virtually everyone in the building – players, fans, coaches and policemen – traded punches in that game. The Barons soon went on a 5-0-2 streak, but lost on January 24. Cleveland rebounded to finish the season without a loss with a 21-0-6 burst. The Barons finished the season 43-13-12, good for first place.

The Barons finally lost a game in the opening round of the playoffs, but that was only a speed bump in a five-game series win against Providence. Buffalo was even less of a problem in the finals, as Cleveland won in four straight. The Barons finished the season with a 29-1-7 run in capturing the Calder Cup.

April 11, 1980 — Rookie outfielder Joe Charboneau homers in his second major-league at-bat, but the Indians lose to the California Angels, 10-2.

April 11, 2014 — The movie "Draft Day" is released to the public. It stars Kevin Costner as the general manager of the Browns and is the story of how the team prepares for the NFL Draft.

12

April 12, 1916 — Speaker debuts for Indians

Tris Speaker was one of the greatest players in baseball in 1916. He had hit at least .300 for all seven of his years with the Red Sox. Speaker had a reputation as one of the best outfielders in the game. And he was not quite 28. Why would Boston even think of trading him?

Money was part of it. Team president Joe Lannin wanted to cut Speaker's $18,000 salary in half because his batting average had declined in the previous three years. Personalities played a role, too. Speaker was from Texas, and allegedly was a member of the Ku Klux Klan. The Catholics on the Red Sox didn't appreciate that.

Speaker was a holdout in training camp, so the Red Sox traded him to the Indians on April 9. The price was Sam Jones, Fred Thomas and money estimated at either $50,000 or $55,000. It was considered a bargain; the Yankees were said to be furious that Boston never gave them a chance to try to top that offer.

Speaker took his place in the Cleveland lineup in a game against St. Louis on this day. His performance was unmemorable – 0-for-1 with three walks in the Browns' 6-1 win. But Speaker warmed up to his new home, leading the league in batting average (.386), hits (211) and doubles (41) that year.

April 12, 1980 — Cleveland advertising executive Ted Stepien becomes the primary shareholder of the Cavaliers, acquiring 37 percent of the company's stock for $2.4 million.

April 12, 1990 — Tom Hamilton joins the Cleveland Indians' radio booth next to Herb Score for his first game, beginning a career that lasts for more than three decades.

April 12, 1992 — Matt Young of the Red Sox throws a no-hitter against the Indians, but doesn't get a win. Cleveland won the game, 2-1. In the second game, Roger Clemens holds the Indians to two hits. The Indians set a record for fewest hits in a twin-bill.

13

April 13, 2011 — Joe Tait's last game

Joe Tait bounced around at the start of his broadcasting career in the 1960s. He called games for the Rose-Hulman Institute of Technology football team in Terre Haute, Indiana; the Ohio Bobcats and University of Indiana football, and also hosted the Indiana Pacers' pregame show in 1969.

Then Joe found a home. He landed the radio announcing job with the Cavaliers during their expansion season of 1970-71. Tait stayed for all but two seasons of the next 41 years. Tait saw some great moments and some difficult moments, which comes with the territory. But he brought enthusiasm to the job every night. While Tait also broadcast Indians games, he became most well-known for his work with the Cavaliers.

It's interesting that he never worked with a color commentator. Joe controlled the entire broadcast, and had the ability to make it work. No doubt a generation of Northeast Ohio fans have been saying, "Sights it, shoots it, got it!" when someone sinks a free throw. Other memorable phrases were: "It's basketball time at the Coliseum!" and "Wham with the right hand!" and "Have a good night, everybody!"

Tait's final broadcast of more than 3,000 games came on this night, which was labeled "Joe Tait Appreciation Night." It included the raising of a banner that carried his name and an image of a microphone. The team even beat Washington to put a smile on everyone's face. As his last night on the job ended, the Cavs played "My Way" as part of a salute to him.

April 13, 1954 — The greatest regular season in Indians history (111 wins!) begins appropriately, as Cleveland blasts the White Sox, 8-2, in Chicago.

April 13, 1969 — Charles "Chuck" Taylor, perhaps best known for the Converse basketball shoe that was named for him and is still worn today by men and women alike, is inducted into the Basketball Hall of Fame in Springfield, Massachusetts. Taylor's playing career resume included a stint in Akron with the Firestone Tire & Rubber Company industrial team called the Non-Skids in 1921, the same year Taylor began working with Converse.

14

April 14, 1925 — Indians, Browns open with slugfest

There's never been an Opening Day quite like the one in St. Louis on this date. The Indians and Browns got together to start the season, and neither one could do much to stop the other team from scoring.

Cleveland set the tone in the top of the first by scoring four runs. The Indians stayed ahead by scores of 4-1, 5-1, 7-1, 7-4, 8-4, 8-7 and 9-7 before the Browns evened the game at 9-9 after five innings. St. Louis added four runs in the bottom of the sixth to lead, 13-9, and the margin looked safe for an inning.

Then came the top of the eighth, and the Indians got serious about winning. They scored 12 runs in all. Tris Speaker and Pat McNulty both had three-run homers in the uprising. Meanwhile, St. Louis committed five errors. Three were by center fielder Herschel Bennett. Only one of the 12 runs was earned.

The Browns got a run in the bottom of the ninth to leave the final score at 21-14. Care to guess the time of the game in Sportsman's Park? It was finished in a tidy 2 hours, 46 minutes. The Indians needed seven more games to score a total of 21 more runs after that.

April 14, 1911 — Indians pitcher Addie Joss, a future Hall of Famer, dies at 31 of tubercular meningitis.

April 14, 1937 — Baseball Commissioner Kenesaw Mountain Landis rules that the Indians had improperly "covered up" the contract of outfielder Tommy Henrich, and declared him a free agent. Henrich, nicknamed "Old Reliable" and a native of Massillon in Stark County, soon signed with the Yankees, and won five world championships there.

April 14, 1953 — Bob Lemon throws a one-hitter on Opening Day as the Indians beat the White Sox, 6-0, in Municipal Stadium. Minnie Minoso had the only hit for Chicago.

April 14, 1972 — Olympic 200-meter sprint champion Tommie Smith, one of two U.S. athletes who raised a clenched fist in a black glove on the medal stand at the 1968 Games during the playing of the national anthem, is hired as assistant athletic director and track coach at Oberlin College in Lorain County, west of Cleveland. His tenure at Oberlin would last six years.

15

April 15, 1976 — Bingo! Cavs win first playoff game!

The Washington Bullets topped the Cavs 100-95 in Cleveland's first-ever NBA playoff game, so that was the setting for Game 2 at the Capital Centre. Washington had a 10-point lead, 46-36, at the half, but the Cavs got all of those points back by the end of the third quarter via a 27-17 burst.

The game was close for the final 12 minutes. The Bullets were clinging to a 79-78 lead with less than a minute to go when Bobby "Bingo" Smith was called for traveling. If Washington could score (remember, no three-point shots at that time), they would appear to be in a commanding position not only to win the game, but the series.

But with six seconds to go, Bullets guard Dave Bing was called for palming the basketball. Jim Cleamons inbounded to Smith, who quickly launched a 27-footer. Bingo! Cleveland had an 80-79 lead with two seconds left. When Elvin Hayes missed a shot for the Bullets at the buzzer, the Cavs had evened the series.

April 15, 1972 — Buddy Bell makes his debut as a 20-year-old rookie with the Indians and becomes part of Cleveland's place in the history of three- and two-generation ballplayers in the major leagues. Bell is the son of Gus Bell, longtime National League outfielder, and the father of future major leaguers David Bell (who played with the Indians) and Mike Bell.

April 15, 2000 — The Browns have the first overall NFL Draft pick for the second consecutive year, and select defensive end Courtney Brown of Penn State. Thirteen of the first 19 picks that year eventually played in the Pro Bowl, but Brown was not one of them. He would go on to a six-year career (five with Cleveland and one season with Denver).

16

April 16, 1940 — Feller opens with a no-hitter

Bob Feller already was on a path to baseball greatness. In 1939, Feller had won 24 games to lead the league at age 20, and he topped the American League in strikeouts for the second straight year (246).

How much better could he become? He provided a clue after he was named Opening Day pitcher for the Indians when they played in Chicago against the White Sox. Feller's mother, father, and sister came from their hometown in Van Meter, Iowa, to watch.

It was a chilly day, and Feller had control problems early. He walked a batter in the first and two more in the second, but the White Sox couldn't capitalize. Cleveland put a run on the board in the top of the fourth on a triple by Rollie Hemsley. That would be all of the offense of the day for the Indians.

Feller worked through his early control issues and retired 20 batters in a row at one point, relying mostly on fastballs. With two outs in the ninth, Feller walked Luke Appling. Then Taft Wright hit a smash to second base, but Ray Mack came up with the ball and threw out Wright. After three one-hitters in his career, Feller had his first no-hitter. Eighty years later, it still was the only game in baseball history where a lineup had the same batting average at the start of its game as it did at the end.

Feller would throw two more no-hitters in his career – a 1-0 win over New York at Yankee Stadium on April 30, 1946, and a 2-1 victory over Detroit at Municipal Stadium on July 1, 1951. Feller's three no-hitters tied Larry Corcoran and Cy Young for the most in history, a record that would stand until Sandy Koufax broke it in 1965.

April 16, 1929 — The Indians become the first major league team to wear numbers on the backs of their uniforms on a regular basis as they defeat the Tigers, 5-4. The Yankees had the same idea, but their opener was rained out.

April 16, 2018 — James Harrison announces his retirement from the NFL after 15 seasons. The linebacker played in high school at Summit County's Coventry and Archbishop Hoban High and then in college at Kent State. He was a Pro Bowl selection five times and part of two Super Bowl champion teams.

17

April 17, 1960 — Indians trade Rocky Colavito

Mark Sommer of Buffalo wrote a book about Rocky Colavito that began with an anecdote. Ten-year-old Sheldon Green of Mayfield Heights was in the Loew's State Theater in downtown Cleveland when the theater manager took the stage with an announcement before the showing of a movie: "I regret to confirm that Rocky Colavito has been traded to the Detroit Tigers for Harvey Kuenn." Green, one of Rocky's biggest fans, was shattered. All of Cleveland felt the same.

Colavito was at the peak of his career. He was 26, and had hit at least 40 homers and driven in 100 runs in both of the last two years. What's more, Rocky was wildly popular with fans who hadn't enjoyed a World Series championship for 12 years.

The Indians' general manager was Frank Lane, who had a reputation for being willing to trade players for any reason at all. Some thought his reason was none other than to keep the team in the newspapers. He had succeeded Hank Greenberg after the 1957 season and had helped the Indians achieve an 89-65 season, good for second place, in 1959. Lane also watched players' salaries closely, as Colavito had to fight for a raise after a spectacular 1959 season. "It was ego – pure ego, that's why he traded me," Colavito told longtime Cleveland sportswriter and columnist Terry Pluto.

Lane explained that he received value for Colavito in acquiring Kuenn, the American League batting average leader, from Detroit. But looking back, some Indians observers said the franchise was never the same from that day in 1960 to 1995, when it finally reached the postseason after a 41-year drought.

April 17, 1989 — Akron native Tommy Hudson is inducted into the Professional Bowlers Association Hall of Fame. Hudson had a 14-year career, retiring in 1985, and won 10 PBA titles, including the 1977 PBA National Championship.

April 17, 1999 — The Browns take Kentucky quarterback Tim Couch with the first overall pick in the NFL Draft. That year is remembered for quarterbacks going in the first three picks, as Donovan McNabb (from Syracuse to the Eagles) and Akili Smith (from Oregon to the Bengals) follow Couch.

18

April 18, 1960 — Score dealt to White Sox

The reaction in Cleveland to a trade by the White Sox must have gone something like this: "You mean he's not done yet?" No, general manager Frank Lane wasn't done revamping the Indians roster. Only a day after Rocky Colavito was shipped to Detroit, Lane dealt veteran Herb Score to the White Sox for pitcher Barry Latman.

It was the latest heartache involving Score and Cleveland fans since May 7, 1957. Score arrived with the Indians in 1955 and was a sensation. As a rookie, he had a record of 16-10 and led the league in strikeouts. He was even better a year later, with a 20-9 record and a league-leading 263 strikeouts. It was the start of what promised to be a can't-miss Hall of Fame career. But everything changed on that May 1957 day. Score was hit in the face by a line drive by New York's Gil McDougald. He missed the rest of the season.

Score looked good in training camp in 1958, but suffered arm and elbow injuries that essentially washed out his season. A year later, Score struggled through a difficult 9-11 season. Score always said he had recovered from being hit in the head but there were theories that he changed his motion and then came the injuries. Now he was being traded to the White Sox, which was overshadowed as the Colavito deal lingered in fans' minds.

Score pitched through 1962, but couldn't reclaim his ability. He came back to Cleveland and began a memorable run as one of the team's broadcasters. His last game was at the end of the 1997 World Series, lost by the Indians to the Marlins. Score exited by saying, "And so that is the season for 1997. And there's very little else we can say except to tell you it's been a pleasure."

April 18, 1946 — When Jackie Robinson hits a home run for the Montreal Royals in his first minor league game in Jersey City, New Jersey, he is greeted at home plate with a congratulatory handshake from Youngstown native George "Shotgun" Shuba. A photograph of the moment becomes a memorable part of professional sports' embrace of the color line being broken. Shuba later joins Robinson as a teammate with the Brooklyn Dodgers.

April 18, 1982 — The Cavaliers lose the last game of the season, 116-113, to Detroit to finish the year with 19 consecutive losses and an overall record of 15-67, the same mark as their expansion year of 1970-71. The team went through four coaches (Don Delaney; Bob Kloppenburg – for one game; Chuck Daly and Bill Musselman).

April 18, 1989 — Minor-league pro baseball returns to the region as the Canton-Akron Indians play their first Eastern League Class AA home game in the newly built Thurman Munson Stadium in Canton. The stadium was built for $2.3 million with seating for 4,500 in the grandstand and another 1,300 in a bleacher area. The team, owned by Mike Agganis, was relocated from Burlington, Vermont.

19

April 19, 1969 — Harrelson comes to Cleveland

Can Ken Harrelson's baseball life be summed up in a few paragraphs? No chance. Let's say this, though: he became a center of the baseball universe the day the Indians acquired him.

Harrelson had been a decent player for the first few years of his career with Washington and Kansas City. In the summer of 1967, he was released by Athletics' owner Charles O. Finley after he called Finley "a menace to baseball." The Red Sox needed an outfielder then because of a season-ending injury to Tony Conigliaro. They signed "The Hawk," who helped them win a pennant. Harrelson then had a huge 1968 season with 35 homers and 109 runs batted in. He was on the cover of *Sports Illustrated* in a powder blue Nehru suit and Beatles hairstyle and became the most popular player on the Red Sox roster.

Conigliaro returned to the Boston lineup in 1969, and the Red Sox had a spare hitter. Boston traded Harrelson along with pitchers Dick Ellsworth and Juan Pizarro to Cleveland for pitchers Sonny Siebert and Vicente Romo and catcher Joe Azcue. It caused an uprising. Red Sox fans protested loudly, and Harrelson threatened not to report to

Cleveland. But eventually he got something extra in his paycheck and also wound up with a local TV show. He created another memory for fans with teammate Sam McDowell as they re-enacted the "Who's on first?" comedy routine made famous by Bud Abbott and Lou Costello.

Harrelson had a good season with 27 homers and 84 RBI for Cleveland in 1969, but broke his leg in an exhibition game the following spring. The Hawk was never the same. His career was over after the 1971 season. Harrelson soon moved into broadcasting, working with the Red Sox and White Sox – with a brief interruption to serve as Chicago's general manager for the 1986 season.

April 19, 1944 — Creighton Miller of Cleveland is the third overall pick in the NFL draft, as the All-American halfback from Notre Dame goes to the Brooklyn Tigers. However, high blood pressure ended his football career at that point. Miller would go on to help organize the NFL Players Association union in 1956 and served as counsel until 1968.

April 19, 1949 — Minnie Minoso makes his debut in the majors; the Indians' outfielder is the seventh player of color to reach baseball's top level. Minoso, who had a 17-year career and was scouted by Harlem Globetrotters' founder Abe Saperstein on behalf of Indians owner Bill Veeck, would later become known for appearing in a game in five decades – the '40s, '50s, '60s, '70s and '80s. His age was disputed but baseball-reference.com lists his ages at 50 and 54 when he appeared in games in 1976 and 1980 for the White Sox.

April 19, 1960 — Walt Bond, a 6-foot-7 outfielder who played in the Negro Leagues, makes his major-league debut with the Indians at age 22. Bond died of leukemia at age 29.

April 19, 1997 — Mike Vrabel of Stow in Summit County becomes a third-round NFL draft pick of the Pittsburgh Steelers after his career at Walsh Jesuit High School in Cuyahoga Falls and Ohio State University. Vrabel would play 14 years in the NFL and then become an NFL head coach.

20

April 20, 1945 — The Cleveland Browns' birthday

It's a day for cakes for the Cleveland Browns. The history of the organization essentially starts at this point.

The All-America Football Conference had been in the planning stages since 1944, but this was the day when the team was created. The majority owner was Arthur "Mickey" McBride, with the assist going to Cleveland businessman Robert Gries. McBride had been interested in buying the NFL Rams for quite a while, but couldn't get it done. Therefore, he was ready to enter the football business another way when the AAFC came along.

What's more, he already had a coach. Paul Brown had been a successful high school and college coach, and he was coaching an armed forces team in 1945. Brown was hired to put together the Browns even before the creation of the team was formally announced. The Rams had started investigating moving their team, and eventually went to Los Angeles, 12 years before the baseball Dodgers from Brooklyn would join them.

The AAFC had a problem putting together eight teams for a new league, but the final piece came together when New York Yankees owner Dan Topping agreed to field a team. The Browns and the league declared it was open for business on this day.

April 20, 1910 — Addie Joss of the Cleveland Naps throws the second of the two no-hitters of his career. The first was on October 2, 1908. Interestingly, both were 1-0 victories over the Chicago White Sox. One difference? The 1908 victory was also a perfect game.

April 20, 2016 — The Browns trade a first-round draft pick in 2016 (No. 2 overall) and a fifth-round choice in 2017 to the Eagles. In return, Cleveland acquires a first-round pick (No. 8) in 2016, third- and fourth-round picks in 2016, and first- and second-round picks in 2017. The Eagles later used the top choice to select quarterback Carson Wentz.

21

April 21, 1991 — Browns take Turner second overall

This must have been one of the best days in the life of football player Eric Turner. Turner was an All-American safety at UCLA. He was highly regarded by college scouts. Even so, it was something of a surprise when the Browns took him second overall in the NFL draft in 1991. Defensive backs usually didn't go that high. Jerry Stovall was a second overall pick by the Cardinals in 1963, the last secondary player to be chosen as high as second.

Turner signed for four years and $6 million, and went right into the Browns lineup. He might have had his best year in 1994 when he led the league in interceptions with nine. That was the year the Browns won a playoff game – something that didn't happen again for more than a quarter-century. The team moved to Baltimore in 1996, and Turner moved with it. He was cut after the '96 campaign for financial reasons. Then it was on to three more years in Oakland.

However, after that, Turner never played another down in the NFL. He apparently denied that he was seriously ill in an interview in early May of 2000. Only two weeks later, Turner died of stomach cancer at 31.

April 21, 1910 — The Indians play their first game in the reconstructed League Park, and lose to the Tigers, 5-0, before 18,832. Cy Young was the Cleveland starter, just as he was for the first big league game played on that site in 1890.

April 21, 1970 — Akron-based Goodyear Tire & Rubber Company announces it will discontinue its amateur basketball program that first began 52 years earlier in 1918. The team participated in the National Industrial Basketball League and national Amateur Athletic Union events, winning AAU titles in 1964 and 1967. It also won an event called the World Intercontinental Cup three years in a row from 1967-69 along with 16 various league titles. From 1953 to 1969 under Hank Vaughn as coach, Goodyear's record was 463-192. Goodyear would renew its association with organized basketball by becoming the sole Cavaliers' uniform jersey sponsor in a deal that news outlet *cleveland.com* reported was worth $10 million to the Cavs.

April 21, 2001 — Dwight Smith, a cornerback for the University of Akron from 1997-2000, is taken in the third round of the NFL Draft by the Tampa Bay Buccaneers. He would live up to the Bucs' judgment by returning two pass interceptions for touchdowns during their 48-21 Super Bowl win over the Oakland Raiders on January 26, 2003. In that same draft, Nate Clements of Shaker Heights and Ohio State University is taken with the 21st pick of the first round by the Buffalo Bills and goes on to a 12-year NFL career.

22

April 22, 1976 — More thrills for the Cavaliers

The adventure continued in the Cavaliers' first playoff series against the Washington Bullets. Now it's Game 5 in the Coliseum in Richfield before 21,312, a record for an NBA playoff game.

The first 47 minutes were close. Washington's late burst gave it a one-point lead, 91-90, with seven seconds left. All Elvin Hayes had to do was sink a couple of free throws, and the Bullets would take the series lead. He missed them both, giving the Cavaliers one last chance.

After a timeout, Cleveland quickly worked the ball to Bobby "Bingo" Smith, who threw up an airball from 14 feet. Somehow, guard Jim Cleamons caught the ball and put up a reverse layup that went in. Cavaliers 91, Bullets 90.

"I wish I could say I planned it that way. But I didn't," Smith said after the game.

April 22, 2001 — The Indians "retire" the number 455 to salute the fans who set a major league record with that total of consecutive home sellouts between 1995 and 2001.

April 22, 2006 — LeBron James plays in his first postseason contest, and has 32 points, 11 rebounds and 11 assists. That helps the Cavs beat Washington, 97-86.

April 23, 1902 — Welcome, Cleveland Bronchos

Cleveland was part of the brand-new American League in baseball in 1901, joining such cities as Chicago, Boston, Detroit and Philadelphia in the new rival to the National League. The problem was that the team struggled. The Blues – who apparently were sometimes called the Bluebirds – finished 58-82, good for seventh place in an eight-team league.

What should a team do in that situation? Change the name of the team, of course. Therefore, the Cleveland Bronchos took the field for the 1902 season. They made their debut on this date, and promptly lost to St. Louis, 5-2.

Why was the extra "H" inserted into Bronco? Apparently, broncho used to be considered a variant spelling of bronco. Perhaps the new name brought some luck with it, as Cleveland's team improved 69-67 in its first year. Then again, the acquisition of superstar Nap Lajoie might have had more to do with it.

"Bronchos" didn't prove to be too popular either, as it was dropped after the 1902 season. The team started to be called the Naps a season later, after Lajoie. And guess what? You can still see Bronchos now. That's the nickname of the sports teams of the University of Central Oklahoma.

April 23, 1952 — How about a game of dueling one-hit pitching performances: Bob Feller throws the 11th one-hit game of his Indians career but loses 1-0 to the St. Louis Browns, who received a one-hit effort from Bob Cain.

April 23, 1983 — A crowd of 19,106, the largest in the history of indoor soccer, turns out at the Coliseum for Cleveland's 7-5 win over Chicago.

April 23, 1989 — The Browns trade running back Earnest Byner to Washington for running back Mike Oliphant. Byner went on to win a Super Bowl with the Redskins and ran for almost 4,000 yards in five seasons there.

April 23, 2005 — Quarterback Charlie Frye becomes the highest-drafted player in Akron Zips history as he goes in the third round to the Browns (67th overall).

24

April 24, 1982 — Browns acquire Cousineau

Tom Cousineau certainly took a roundabout method to becoming a Cleveland Brown.

Cousineau grew up in Fairview Park and played at Lakewood St. Edward High School before moving on to college at Ohio State. He helped the Buckeyes win three Big Ten titles under Coach Woody Hayes. The linebacker was a tackling machine for the Buckeyes, and a two-time All-American. When the Buffalo Bills had the first draft pick in 1979, they zeroed in on Cousineau.

But Buffalo's front office was a little dysfunctional in that era, and somehow Cousineau slipped away to sign with the Montreal Alouettes of the Canadian Football League. Cousineau spent three years there, and then decided he wanted to come back to America. The Oilers made him a contract offer, which the Bills matched. Then Buffalo traded Cousineau to the Browns for draft choices.

He led Cleveland in tackles three times in four seasons. Cousineau, who never was chosen for a Pro Bowl, ended his career as a backup in San Francisco for two seasons. Meanwhile, the Bills used one of the Browns' picks to take a quarterback named Jim Kelly. You can learn more about his career at the Pro Football Hall of Fame in Canton.

April 24, 1889 — The Cleveland Spiders make their debut in the National League of baseball clubs, losing in Indianapolis, 10-3.

April 24, 1901 — The Cleveland Blues take part in the first game in American League history. They lose to the White Sox, 8-2, before 14,000 at the Chicago Cricket Club.

April 24, 1988 — Eight picks after the Browns choose linebacker Clifford Charlton of Florida as their first choice in the 1988 NFL Draft, the Detroit Lions select linebacker Chris Spielman, who starred at Massillon High School and then Ohio State. He goes on to have a 10-year NFL career, including attempting to play for the Browns' new expansion team in 1999 before injuries prevented it.

April 24, 1994 — The Cavaliers beat Boston, 117-91, in their last appearance in a regular season game at the Coliseum.

April 24, 2004 — The Cleveland Fusion, a women's football team, drops a 27-6 decision to the Columbus Comets in a game played in Cleveland Browns Stadium.

25

April 25, 1890 — Infants put one in the win column

There are stories of many professional athletic teams and leagues that have ties to Cleveland in the 19th century, but the tale of the Players' League is especially interesting.

Labor relations for baseball players in the 1880s were one-sided. The owners told the players what they would earn, and the players could accept it or not play. John Montgomery Ward, a pitcher and Columbia Law School graduate, started baseball's first labor union during that era. When progress for the players was glacial in nature, Ward put together a new league that offered star players a share of their new teams as an incentive to change leagues.

In terms of recruiting, the idea worked. Most of the sport's best performers jumped to the Players' League. The Cleveland Infants opened play in Buffalo on April 19, 1890, and lost by a score of 23-2. The Infants also lost their next three. However, they earned their first victory on this day with a 9-8 win over the Burghers in Pittsburgh. Cleveland had a Hall of Fame shortstop in Ed Delahanty and another standout in Pete Browning. The Infants had a record of 55-75 and finished seventh out of eight teams.

The Players' League may have had the stars, but it didn't have deep pockets. Three major leagues were one too many, and the National League and American Association were more equipped to win a war of financial attrition. The rival league collapsed after 1890.

April 25, 1964 — The Cleveland Barons win their ninth and last Calder Cup as champions of the American Hockey League. They finished a sweep of the Quebec Aces with a 5-2 win at the Cleveland Arena. The Barons were coached by Fred Glover, who had a six-year run with the team before moving to the NHL.

April 25, 1981 — How many baseball players can say they were drafted by big league clubs three times as a first-round pick? Scott Fletcher of Medina County's Wadsworth High School is one. He finally signs in 1979 and then plays in his first major league game as an infielder with the Chicago Cubs at age 22 on this day. Fletcher would enjoy a 15-year career with six teams.

April 25, 1993 — The Miami Dolphins use their first-round NFL Draft choice on Penn State star wide receiver O.J. McDuffie, who played high school football at Hawken School in the Cleveland suburb of Gates Mills. McDuffie goes on to play eight seasons with the Dolphins. In the eighth round, the San Francisco 49ers draft quarterback Elvis Grbac, a Cleveland Villa Angela-St. Joseph High graduate who played at Michigan. Grbac would have an eight-year NFL career.

26

April 26, 2018 – Browns take Mayfield first in draft

The 2018 NFL draft was expected to be dominated by quarterbacks. At least four were prime candidates to go among the first several picks: Josh Allen of Wyoming, Sam Darnold of Southern California, Baker Mayfield of Oklahoma, and Josh Rosen of UCLA. The Browns had the first pick.

Darnold was considered the favorite to go first, since many scouts thought he'd be ready to step into a pro-style offense quickly. The Browns kept quiet about their plans until word leaked out that Allen and Mayfield were believed to be the finalists. Still, there was some drama when Cleveland got ready to announce its selection.

With the direction of General Manager John Dorsey and Coach Hue Jackson, they went with Mayfield, a 23-year-old who was the first "walk-on" player ever to win the Heisman Trophy. He was considered undersized for an NFL quarterback at 6-foot-1, but there was no denying that he showed talent: his year-by-year numbers – 2015: 11-2 record; 3,700 passing yards; 36 touchdowns; 68 percent completions. 2016: 11-2 record; 3,965 yards; 40 touchdowns; 71 percent. 2017: 12-2 record; 4,627 yards; 43 touchdowns; 70.5 percent completions.

Mayfield had a good rookie NFL year, coming into the starting lineup early in the season and throwing 27 touchdowns. He took a step backwards in 2019, but rebounded in 2020 as the Browns reached the playoffs and won a game against the rival Pittsburgh Steelers.

April 26, 1974 — The Indians trade Chris Chambliss, Dick Tidrow and Cecil Upshaw to the Yankees for four pitchers – Fritz Peterson, Steve Kline, Fred Beene and Tom Buskey.

April 26, 1983 — With the No. 7 pick of the first round of the NFL Draft, the Kansas City Chiefs select quarterback Todd Blackledge of Penn State, who starred in high school at Stark County's North Canton Hoover. Blackledge is the son of Ron Blackledge, who held the Kent State head coaching post from 1978-80. With the 39th overall pick, the Buffalo Bills select linebacker Darryl Talley, who played at Cleveland Shaw High School and West Virginia University. Talley later plays for the Bills in their four Super Bowl losses as part of an 11-year career.

April 26, 1993 — Placekicker Daren Alcorn of the Akron Zips becomes what is called "Mr. Irrelevant" of the NFL Draft as the last player taken. He was picked by Tampa Bay but never played in the NFL.

27

April 27, 1994 — Crunch claims a championship

By 1994, it had been 30 years since any Cleveland team had claimed a championship of any kind. Hopefully, fans still have a soft spot in their hearts for the Cleveland Crunch.

The Cleveland Force had been a moderately successful indoor soccer team for a while in the 1980s and then folded in 1988. The city was given a second chance with an expansion team in the Major Indoor Soccer League. Kai Haaskivi brought back some of the top players from the days of the Force. The MISL collapsed in 1992, and three teams including the Crunch moved over to the National Professional Soccer League.

That team had two great scorers in Hector Marinaro and Zoren Karic, and a superb goalie in Otto Orf. The three players helped the Crunch reach the NPSL finals in 1993, only to lose to Kansas City. It was a case of "better luck next time" for Cleveland.

The Crunch made it back to the finals in 1994, and St. Louis was the opponent. Cleveland led the best-of-five series, two games to one, when Game 4 was played at Cleveland State. The Crunch trailed by 15-10 in the fourth quarter, but rallied to tie the game and send it to overtime. The Ambush had chance after chance in extra time, but Orf – playing with a torn hamstring – kept making saves. Finally in the second overtime, Marinaro scored from close range ... and Cleveland had a champion.

April 27, 1961 — The National Football League announces Canton, Ohio, will be the site of what will be called the Pro Football Hall of Fame. A meeting in the city in 1920 was a key to the start of what was first named the American Pro Football Association. Other cities considered for the hall's location were: Green Bay, Wisconsin; Latrobe, Pennsylvania; Los Angeles, and Detroit.

April 27, 1982 — Oliver Luck is the third quarterback selected (by the Houston Oilers) in the NFL draft, after Ohio State's Art Schlichter (Baltimore Colts) and Brigham Young's Jim McMahon (Chicago Bears). Luck played at Cleveland St. Ignatius High School and then at West Virginia University. Later he would become the top executive of the NFL's European pro football league. His son Andrew Luck would later become a top quarterback at Stanford and with the Indianapolis Colts.

April 27, 2017 — Defensive end Myles Garrett of Texas A&M is the Browns' first pick of the NFL Draft. They also choose Michigan safety Jabrill Peppers at No. 25 and then trade up to take tight end David Njoku from the University of Miami (Florida) in the No. 29 spot in the first round.

28

April 28, 2006 — James takes another step forward

LeBron James always has considered himself a student of basketball, so the idea of winning playoff games on the road required some experience. It didn't take long.

Not only did he get a win in his first road game, but he became the first NBA player ever to score 40 points in that situation. James had 41, including the game-winning shot, as the Cavaliers beat the Bullets, 97-96.

On the game-winning play, James went around Washington's Antonio Daniels, bumped into Michael Ruffin, and hit a four-footer while falling down with less than six seconds to play. When Gilbert Arenas missed an open three-pointer at the buzzer, Cleveland had taken a 2-1 lead in the series.

"I said I wouldn't have two bad games in a row," James told the media after the game. "I watched Game 2 over and over, and I saw the adjustment they made on me from Game 1 to Game 2. Me being the player I am, I had to counterattack, and I was able to do that."

April 28, 1901 — Cleveland pitcher Bock Baker sets a franchise record by allowing 23 hits in a game.

April 28, 2011 — The Browns receive five draft choices, including two first-round picks, from the Falcons for the sixth overall pick in the first round. Atlanta uses the selection on wide receiver Julio Jones.

April 29, 1976 — The Miracle of Richfield is born

Just when everyone thought the Cavaliers and Bullets couldn't provide any more entertainment in a playoff series, they did in Game 7.

Neither team led by more than seven. There were 16 lead changes and eight ties. Fittingly, the Bullets tied the game on a Phil Chenier jump shot with 24 seconds left. The stage was set for a frantic finish.

Point guard Jim Cleamons inbounded to shooting guard Dick Snyder, who dribbled to the left side of the court. He then threw a shot high off the glass that banked through the net. Cleveland had an 87-85 lead – but there were still four seconds left.

Washington tried to get the ball to Elvin Hayes, but the ball was knocked loose by Cleveland's Nate Thurmond. It was picked up in the corner by Chenier, and his long shot from a bad angle was off target. The Cavaliers had won their first playoff series, and many in the record crowd of 21,564 came down on the floor and tore down the baskets while celebrating with their heroes.

April 29, 1931 — Wes Ferrell of the Indians throws a no-hitter in a 9-0 win against the Browns, and helps his own cause with a home run.

April 29, 1952 — The Browns acquire linebacker Walt Michaels, who would later be the head coach of the New York Jets and the New Jersey Generals in the USFL, from the Packers for defensive tackle Forrest "Chubby" Grigg and rookie offensive linemen Elmer Costa and Dick Logan. Michaels eventually becomes one of the team's best-ever linebackers.

April 29, 1980 — The Browns take Heisman Trophy winner Charles White of Southern California with their first pick (27th overall) in the NFL Draft. Earlier in the first round, the Bills selected offensive lineman Jim Ritcher, a star at Highland High School in Medina County.

30

April 30, 1996 — Cleveland State hires Massimino

What was college basketball coach Rollie Massimino doing at Cleveland State, a university not known as a power?

It's an interesting question. Massimino had spent almost two decades coaching at Villanova, where he was part of the rise of the Big East Conference in the 1980s. The highlight, of course, was when the Wildcats pulled one of the great upsets in NCAA basketball history by beating Georgetown in the championship game in 1985. Massimino stayed at Villanova through 1992.

Then it was on to Nevada-Las Vegas, where he replaced Jerry Tarkanian. It lasted two seasons until it was revealed that his contract there violated school and state laws about financial disclosures. After two seasons off, Massimino landed the job with the Vikings. "I felt I wanted to coach. It didn't make any difference what it took. I wanted to be part of young people," he said.

"Coach Mass," who came to CSU on this day, stayed seven years, but couldn't consistently win. There were also off-court issues involving some of his players. Massimino's contract was bought out by the university. He spent his last 11 coaching years at Keiser University, an NAIA school in Florida. He died in 2017 at age 82.

April 30, 1952 — Quincy Trouppe had served as a manager of the Cleveland Buckeyes in the Negro Leagues from 1945-47. Now, at age 39, he makes his major-league playing debut with the Indians. His MLB career was brief – six games, 10 at-bats, one hit.

April 30, 1992 — The Cavaliers win their first playoff series since 1976, eliminating the Nets in four games. Cleveland takes the fourth game of the best-of-five, 98-89.

April 30, 2000 — Pavel Kokin of Russia sets a course record in the Cleveland Marathon by winning in a time of 2:10:29.

1

May 1, 1879 — Cleveland debuts in the National League

Cleveland missed out on a team when baseball's National League was formed in 1876. The city had to wait a few years, but when a franchise arrived, Kennard Street Park was the setting. The field was squeezed into a block that wasn't a perfect square, so that right field was close to home plate. How close? If you hit the ball over the fence in that direction, you'd only get a double.

This was the day when the Cleveland Blues played their first game in the National League. The NL had gone from six to eight teams for the 1879 season, and some of the old franchises were in new homes. The Blues opened the season with a home game against the Providence Grays, and it's safe to say there weren't any traffic problems for fans. The average attendance that year was 610.

No one knew it at the start of the game, but this looked like a mismatch on paper. The Grays were the best team in the league, and had Hall of Famers such as John Montgomery Ward, George Wright and Jim O'Rourke on the roster. Providence won the pennant by five games, and this was its first win of the season – a 15-4 decision over the Blues. Cleveland was managed by Jim McCormick – at 23, the youngest manager in major league history.

The game marked the debut of Blues shortstop Jack Glasscock. The Wheeling, West Virginia, native was one of the first players to signal the catcher as to who would cover second base in case of a stolen base attempt by an opposing runner. Jack's smarts didn't help the Blues get out of seventh place that season.

May 1, 1891 — The Cleveland Spiders defeat the Cincinnati Reds, 12-3, in the first game played in League Park. Cy Young is the winning pitcher. The facility will host Cleveland's major league baseball team through 1946.

May 1, 1955 — Indians pitcher Bob Feller throws the 12th one-hit game of his career as Cleveland defeats Boston 2-0. Sixty-seven years later, Feller remained tied with Nolan Ryan for the most one-hit games of any pitcher's career.

May 1, 1966 — Indians' left-hander Sam McDowell throws his second consecutive 1-hit shutout, beating the Chicago White Sox, 1-0. Six days earlier, McDowell beat Kansas City by 2-0, also throwing a one-hitter. McDowell's performances tied Whitey Ford's American League feat in 1955. In the National League, it had been done by Rube Marquard in 1911, Lon Warneke in 1934 and Mort Cooper in 1943.

2

May 2, 1930 — Sewell's streak snapped at 1,103

Baseball fans know that Cal Ripken Jr. set the major-league record for consecutive games played at 2,632. They also know that he broke Lou Gehrig's supposedly unbreakable record, which was 2,130. But those aren't the only long streaks of that kind in baseball history.

Joe Sewell of the Indians had played in 1,103 straight games, but he had to sit out the contest in Boston on this date because of the flu. His streak started in 1922, so it lasted more than seven seasons. Sewell had a 102-degree temperature, and decided it was wise to rest. The infielder essentially missed the next 12 games before returning to action.

Sewell reached the major leagues for all the wrong reasons. He was called up when Ray Chapman was hit by a pitch and killed in 1920. Sewell became a regular in 1921, and he stayed in Cleveland through 1930 before spending two seasons with the Yankees.

Sewell is known mostly for his bat control. He was one of the toughest players to strike out in major league history, fanning once every 62.5 at bats. Sewell whiffed only three times in the entire 1932 season. He was named to the Baseball Hall of Fame in 1977.

May 2, 1942 — The Indians win their 12th in a row, a 12-3 win over Washington with Jim Bagby Jr. getting the win. Cleveland lost to the Red Sox the next day.

3

May 3, 1994 — Jordan-less Bulls still beat Cavs

The Cavaliers didn't spend all of the 1990s losing playoff series to Michael Jordan and the Chicago Bulls. It only seemed that way. In fact, Michael could be off playing baseball, and Cleveland would have trouble with the Bulls.

That was the case in 1994, when Cleveland drew Chicago in the first round of the playoffs. The Bulls had won the first two games of the series by remarkably similar scores, 104-96 and 105-96. Chicago finished off the three-game sweep on this date with a 95-92 win in overtime.

Scottie Pippen was out of Jordan's shadow that year, and he turned in an excellent all-around performance in this game. Pippen scored 23 points with 11 rebounds in 47 minutes. Toni Kukoc came off the bench for 18 points in 21 minutes.

For Cleveland, Chris Mills had 25 points while Mark Price added 22. The Cavs' biggest problem was offense. They scored only 12 points in the fourth quarter and five in overtime. It wasn't enough.

May 3, 1952 — When Sam Jones comes on in relief for the Indians, he teams with catcher Quincy Trouppe to form the first all-African-American battery in major league history. The two had played for the Cleveland Buckeyes of the Negro American League.

May 3, 1979 — Bobby Bonds of the Indians hits the 300th homer of his career, and becomes the first major leaguer to have 300 homers and 300 stolen bases.

May 3, 1979 — Linebacker Tom Cousineau of Lakewood St. Edward High School and Ohio State University is the No. 1 pick in the NFL Draft by the Buffalo Bills.

May 3, 2010 — LeBron James goes back-to-back by winning his second consecutive NBA MVP trophy.

4

May 4, 1871 — Cleveland baseball leads the way

Professional baseball took a huge step forward in 1871 when the National Association of Base Ball Players was formed. The top players wanted to get paid to play, and they broke away from a league that also included amateur players to form this organized structure.

Cleveland had a team named the Forest Citys that was involved in the first game in NA history. The squad came together in 1869, and played an independent schedule just like its cross-state rivals, the Cincinnati Red Stockings. The Cleveland team opted to move into the National Association in 1871.

The Forest Citys opened the season on this day in Fort Wayne, Indiana. The first batter in National Association history was James "Deacon" White. He is a Hall of Famer who was the top catcher in baseball in the 1870s. White played for about 20 years, ending his career in Buffalo in 1890. He stood up for players' rights before it was popular. White also was a religious man in a rough-and-tough profession, and apparently thought the earth was flat.

White doubled that first time up, but didn't score. The Forest Citys were blanked, 2-0, by the Kekiongas. The rules were different then; you could get someone out if you caught a foul ball on the first bounce. But it was baseball, and you'd recognize it.

May 4, 1976 — Jim Chones suffers a broken foot in practice, diminishing the Cavaliers' hopes of beating the Boston Celtics in the Eastern Conference finals of the NBA playoffs. The Cavs had advanced by winning their first-ever playoff series over the Washington Bullets in what became known as "The Miracle of Richfield."

May 4, 1991 — The Indians pound out 20 hits in a 20-6 win in Oakland, as Chris James is 4-for-5 with nine RBIs (breaking the team record of eight). The next day, Cleveland is "held" to only 15 runs in a 15-6 win.

May 4, 2009 — LeBron James of the Cavaliers wins his first NBA MVP award for the 2008-09 season, his sixth year as a pro.

5

May 5, 2005 — Jones' shot is decisive for Cavs

Now this is the way to win a playoff series.

Damon Jones had not played in the first 47 minutes and 41 seconds of the game between his Cavaliers and the Washington Wizards. Jones was inserted into the lineup with Cleveland down, 113-112. Everyone thought LeBron James would wind up with the ball, since he made winning shots in Game 3 and Game 5.

The ball, however, went to Jones, who was open for a 17-footer with five seconds left. Bang! The Cavs had a 114-113 lead, and held on to win the first Game 6 in their history. Jones' performance might rank as one of the most unusual 14-second appearances in NBA history.

James had 32 points as he advanced in the playoffs for the first time in his life. "This is probably one of the best feelings I've had in a long time," he said. "I didn't want to come here and just be happy to be in the playoffs."

May 5, 1989 — Michael Jordan scores 50 but it isn't enough for the Chicago Bulls as the Cavaliers win, 108-105 in overtime, to even their NBA first-round playoff series at two games apiece.

May 6, 2016 — Frye's shooting stops Hawks

When it comes to deals at the trading deadline, the NBA doesn't take a back seat to Major League Baseball. You never know who might walk through the door and make a difference in a key situation.

On February 18, 2016, the Cavaliers added Channing Frye from Orlando. Two players and a conditional draft choice went elsewhere in the three-team swap. Frye was thought to be someone who could supply some offense coming off the bench. The 6-foot-11 forward did that in the regular season, chipping in 7.5 points per game.

He was not needed in the first round of the playoffs against Detroit. Then came Game 3 in the Eastern Conference semifinals with Atlanta. Frye scored nine points on three three-point baskets in eight minutes in the first half. Then when Kevin Love got into foul trouble later, Frye came back out and went wild. He had seven points in the third quarter, and added 11 points in the fourth quarter.

It added up to a career-high playoff output of 27 points on 10-of-13 shooting (seven of nine from long distance). The Cavs won going away, 121-103, to make it three consecutive wins in the best-of-seven series.

May 6, 1961 — Carry Back wins the Kentucky Derby in Louisville. The horse went on to take the Preakness as well, much to the delight of owners Jack and Katherine Price of Shaker Heights.

May 6, 1970 — Indians left-hander Sam McDowell strikes out 15 White Sox batters, but still drops a 2-1 decision in Chicago. It was part of a spectacular year in which "Sudden Sam" struck out 304 batters in 305 innings and won 20 games for the only time in his career.

May 7, 1989 — 'The Shot' beats Cavaliers at buzzer

The Cavs were considered the favorites over the Bulls in this first-round best-of-five playoff series, thanks to winning all six of their regular-season games. Chicago had a chance to put the Cavs away in four, but Michael Jordan missed some key free throws at the end of Game 4, and Cleveland evened the series.

It was on to Game 5 at the Coliseum. Both teams had their runs and it was 90-90 with three minutes left. With the Cavs down one, Craig Ehlo converted an out-of-bounds play with three seconds left to give Cleveland a one-point lead.

Everyone knew the ball was going to Jordan. Coach Lenny Wilkens chose to keep Ehlo on him defensively. Jordan took the out-of-bounds pass, drove to the foul line, jumped, hung in the air, and converted the shot. Then he turned and pumped his arm with glee. The Jordan legend had just added another building block at the expense of Cleveland.

May 7, 1957 — Indians pitcher Herb Score is struck by a line drive off the bat of the Yankees' Gil McDougald. Score suffered several facial injuries and missed the rest of the season.

May 7, 1995 — It takes 17 innings and a game-time of six hours and 36 minutes (both team records), but the Indians finally beat the Twins, 10-9.

May 8, 2014 — Browns gamble, take Manziel

The best player in the 2014 NFL Draft, at least at the time, might have been Jadeveon Clowney, Sammy Watkins or Khalil Mack. The most interesting player might have been Johnny Manziel.

The Browns owned two first-round draft choices. With one, they traded down and took Justin Gilbert, a cornerback from Oklahoma State. Later, Cleveland traded up with Philadelphia, and picked perhaps the most controversial player available.

Manziel was a sensation as a freshman quarterback for Texas A&M. He threw for more than 3,000 yards and ran for another 1,000 yards. No wonder he was the first freshman winner of the Heisman Trophy. Manziel was almost as good in 2013, and then he entered the NFL draft. He had considerable skills, but he was under 6-feet and his personality was somewhere between confident and arrogant, depending on your viewpoint. The Browns took a chance with the No. 22 pick.

In hindsight, Cleveland didn't get it right. Gilbert was a disappointment and was sent to the Steelers for a low draft choice. Manziel didn't have many good moments on the field, and was involved in some incidents off the field. It led to his release in March 2016.

May 8, 1937 — Ground is broken on construction of the Cleveland Arena. The cost of the building, said to have a design based on Maple Leaf Gardens in Toronto, is $1.5 million.

May 8, 1982 — Boxer Ray "Boom Boom" Mancini of Youngstown scores a sensational first-round technical knockout of Arturo Frias to win the World Boxing Association's lightweight championship in Las Vegas.

May 8, 1987 — The creation of an all-sports radio station program format in New York City is too much to resist for talk show host Pete Franklin, who announces he will leave WWWE for a two-year contract paying him a reported $600,000. Franklin had worked in the Cleveland market since 1967 and built a reputation as a host who was anything but boring.

9

May 9, 1983 — Stepien Era ends for Cavs

Cavaliers fans probably felt like doing a little singing on this particular day. "Oh Happy Day" would have been an appropriate choice.

Ted Stepien may not have been the worst owner in pro sports history, but he's in the conversation. The Cavs had records of 28-54, 15-67 and 23-59 during his ownership but new owners Gordon and George Gund were unwilling to purchase the club without the benevolence of a three-quarters majority of the NBA's other 22 owners.

It came in the form of allowing the Gunds to purchase first-round draft picks in 1983, '84, '85 and '86 that Stepien had traded away. It was decided the '83 pick would be No. 24, coming at the end of the first round; the '84 pick would be no higher than No. 12; the '85 pick would be no higher than No. 8, and the '86 pick would be one position lower than wherever the team's record would have placed them in the round. Approval of the plan came by an 18-5 vote from the NBA Board of Governors on this day in a meeting at the Chicago Hyatt O'Hare. If there had been just one more "no" vote, the unprecedented move to award extra draft picks to a team would have failed to pass. The purchase price was not disclosed but media reports said the Gunds might have paid the league as much as $2 million for the extra picks.

The Cavs needed some time to change course, but they made the playoffs in 1985 and put together some good teams over the next decade. In 1994, the team moved to a new home in downtown Cleveland. It was called Gund Arena at the start of its existence and could be thought of as a tribute to the brothers who rescued pro basketball in Cleveland.

May 9, 1995 — The Indians tie a major league record by scoring eight runs in the first inning without recording an out. They hit three homers, including a grand slam by Paul Sorrento, in the outburst. It's the first grand slam by an Indian in Jacobs Field history. Pitcher Orel Hershiser received the win, his first as a member of the Cleveland team.

10

May 10, 1969 — Browns agree to switch conferences

One detail was left to complete the merger between the American Football League and the National Football League. The expanded NFL was set to be split into two conferences, each with 13 teams. But the old NFL had 16 teams and the AFL had 10 teams. Which three teams would change sides?

No one wanted to leave the NFL for what was to be called the American Football Conference. The old league had bigger television markets and more prestige. The owners even threw an incentive on the table – $3 million to any team that switched. Commissioner Pete Rozelle gathered the owners on this day and said no one was going to be allowed to leave until it was settled. Baltimore went first, and agreed to move to capitalize on a new rivalry with the Jets caused by New York's upset win in Super Bowl III.

Then fate went to work. Browns owner Art Modell went to the hospital with a bleeding ulcer. There, he told Art and Dan Rooney of the Steelers that the Browns would move if the Steelers would go with them. Pittsburgh's owners needed convincing. Then Rozelle handed the Rooneys a slip of paper with the names of the teams in the AFC Central for 1970: Pittsburgh, Cleveland, Cincinnati and Houston.

That got Rooney's attention. The Steelers could continue their rivalry with the Browns, and develop a new one with Cincinnati and its coach Paul Brown. In addition, the $3 million would allow the Steelers to be more than a shoestring operation for the first time in forever. The deal was done.

May 10, 1992 — Larry Nance goes 13-for-16 from the field to lead the Cavaliers to a 114-112 win over the Celtics. It ties the best-of-seven playoff series at 2-2.

11

May 11, 1970 — Cavs assemble team in expansion draft

Cleveland was about to get a National Basketball Association franchise in the fall of 1970, as it was part of a three-team expansion of the league that included Buffalo and Portland.

After owner Nick J. Mileti was granted the team, his first step was to hire someone to run it. He turned to a college coach, Bill Fitch, from Minnesota. Fitch had previously coached at Bowling Green, which was Mileti's alma mater.

Now it was Fitch's job to get some players – first in the college draft and then by choosing real, live NBA players who were unprotected by their employers. That meant the Cavs would be taking reserves (such as the 8th, 9th, 10th and 11th best) from those rosters because the best players were allowed to be protected.

Fitch had a novel idea as part of his research. In the book *Vintage Cavs* by *Plain Dealer* and cleveland.com sports columnist Terry Pluto, Fitch said he gave his assistant Jim Lessig $20 to buy as many basketball trading cards as he could find. Pluto reported that the Topps card company only printed 99 NBA player cards in 1969-70, so there were some players available who were not pictured on a card.

Fitch and Lessig had about 48 hours to study the list of available players once the teams had submitted the names of players who were protected.

The Cavs picked Walt Wesley, a 6-foot-10 center, with their first choice. They also added Butch Beard, Bingo Smith, John Warren and McCoy McLemore. It didn't help the team in year one, as the Cavaliers' record was 15-67. But the team eventually improved enough to reach the playoffs for the first time in 1975-76.

May 11, 1971 — Steve Dunning of the Indians hits a grand slam off Diego Segui of the Athletics. It's the last grand slam hit by an American League pitcher until 2008, when Felix Hernandez of the Mariners did it against the Mets.

May 11, 1976 — Jim Cleamons has 18 points as the Cavaliers beat the Celtics, 83-78, in a hard-fought Eastern Conference finals playoff game at the Coliseum. Cleveland narrows Boston's lead in the series to 2-1.

May 11, 1991 - Indians outfielder Albert Belle throws a baseball at a fan who yells at him from 15 feet away, "Hey, Joey! Keg party at my house after the game." Belle, who had been known as "Joey" when he first came to the major leagues, is suspended for six games and forced to donate a week's salary to charity.

12

May 12, 1973 — Johnson exits basketball on top

It's difficult to imagine two pro sports stars could have ever been high school teammates, but Gus Johnson and Nate Thurmond played basketball together at Akron Central High School.

Both ended up in the Basketball Hall of Fame, but it was Johnson who might have been the better prospect in the early years of their careers. Thurmond was 6-foot-10 but really skinny in high school. Johnson was already on the way to blossoming at 6-foot-6 and 235 pounds.

Johnson went to college in Idaho, and was a second-round pick of the Baltimore Bullets. There, his enormous strength made an immediate impression. No backboard was safe when "Honeycomb" felt like dunking. He was part of some excellent Baltimore teams between 1963 and 1972.

Then the Bullets traded him to Phoenix, but he ended up with the Indiana Pacers of the rival American Basketball Association. There he was a backup forward, but was part of an excellent team. In the season's last game, Johnson helped quiet Kentucky center Artis Gilmore as the Pacers beat the Colonels, 88-81, on this day to win the ABA championship. It was Johnson's last game, and he exited on top.

May 12, 2008 – Indians second baseman Asdrubal Cabrera catches a line drive, steps on second to double up a runner, and tags a nearby baserunner for a third out. It's the 14th unassisted triple play in baseball history.

13

May 13, 2010 – James' time with Cavs starts to run out

When one clock read 0:00, another started counting down. That's one way of describing the situation with the Cavaliers and their star player, LeBron James, at the end of this particular night.

The Celtics had just defeated Cleveland, 94-85, in Game 6 of the NBA's Eastern Conference finals. That gave Boston the series. Kevin Garnett (22 points and 12 rebounds) and Rajon Rondo (21 points and 12 assists) led the way for Boston.

James and his Cavs' teammates had just finished another season where they had the best record in the league but couldn't reach the NBA Finals. And now James' contract was about to expire, and he'd be free to go anywhere. Thus the suspense began about his eventual destination, which figured to change the balance of power in the league.

"I want to win. That's my only thing, my only concern," James said to reporters after the game. "I've always prided myself – it's all about winning for me and I think the Cavs are committed to doing that. But at the same time, I've given myself options to this point."

May 13, 2015 – Corey Kluber strikes out 18 batters without a walk in a game with St. Louis. He's only the fourth pitcher to ever have 18 or more strikeouts without a walk.

May 13, 2019 – The Cavaliers surprise the basketball world by hiring John Beilein as their new head coach. Beilein, who was moving to the NBA at age 66, had been coaching college basketball at Michigan the previous 12 seasons.

14

May 14, 1968 – Browns add insurance at quarterback

The Browns appeared to be set at quarterback entering the 1968 season. Frank Ryan was coming off another good season, and he was only going to be 32 in the new campaign. That's why Cleveland's trade on this day didn't receive a great deal of attention.

The Steelers had a quarterback by the name of Bill Nelsen. Coming out of Southern Cal, he had been on the roster for five years, including 23 starts (a record of 6-15-2) in 32 games. He was considered a decent game manager with leadership qualities. But injuries had slowed his career and he had lost his job to Kent Nix.

The Browns had Gary Lane and Dick Shiner behind Ryan, but looking at Nelsen, they might have been looking for an upgrade. The Steelers needed a defensive lineman, and the Browns had one in Frank Parker. The 6-foot-5, 270-pounder had a promising start to his career but suffered a severe knee injury, and had been ineffective for two seasons.

The two sides completed the trade: Nelsen and safety Jim Bradshaw from Pittsburgh for Parker, Shiner and a draft choice. The low-key move ended up paying big dividends as Nelsen stepped in for Ryan and led the Browns to the NFL Championship game that season, and stayed in Cleveland for five seasons.

May 14, 1939 – A pitch thrown by Indians' Bob Feller is fouled into the stands and hits a woman around the eye. Bob Feller's mother required seven stitches; the incident took place on Mother's Day.

May 14, 1976 - The Cavaliers explode with a 33-17 fourth quarter in a 106-87 win over the Celtics to tie their NBA Eastern Conference finals playoff series, 2-2.

May 14, 2016 - Mixed Martial Arts fighter Stipe Miocic of Euclid claims the UFC heavyweight championship by beating Fabricio Werdum in Brazil. The bout aired three hours after ESPN televised a documentary on Cleveland's unsuccessful attempts to win sports championships.

May 15, 1981 – Barker is perfect in win over Jays

The Toronto Blue Jays looked quite lifeless on May 14, 1981. They dropped a 10-0 decision to the visiting Orioles for their second straight loss via shutout. Mike Flanagan pitched a relaxed five-hitter, and the Blue Jays went 0-for-6 with runners in scoring position.

A night later, it got worse. Much worse. Len Barker threw the 11th perfect game in baseball history, beating the Blue Jays, 3-0. Barker struck out 11 in a dominating performance. No Blue Jays batter reached a "ball three" count and he struck out seven of the last 11 batters. He improved his record to 3-1, and the Indians moved to 16-8 on the young season.

The night had some trivia attached to it. Barker was the first pitcher to throw a perfecto against a team with a designated hitter. Catcher Ron Hassey, who had been behind the plate when Dennis Martinez threw a perfect game in 1991, eventually became the first catcher ever to catch two of them in a career. This also was the last no-hitter by an Indians pitcher in Cleveland Municipal Stadium.

Barker's grandmother, Tokie Lockhart of Ona, West Virginia, was excited about the accomplishment, according to *Sporting News* reporter Bob Sudyk. This woman with high standards said, "Tell Len I'm proud. I hope he does better next time."

May 15, 1948 - An Indians' home game appears on television for the first time as WEWS-TV, Channel 5, broadcasts the contest with the White Sox. Van Patrick does the play-by-play announcing.

May 15, 2012 – Kyrie Irving of the Cavaliers is named the NBA's Rookie of the Year for the 2011-2012 season.

16

May 16, 1962 – Lucas pulls shocker by joining Pipers

Jerry Lucas was one of the first high school basketball stars to receive national attention. His teams at Middletown, Ohio, won two state championships and just missed out on a third. Lucas then became the subject of an intense college recruiting battle, eventually won by Ohio State. He was a three-time All-American and two-time player of the year. He helped the Buckeyes win an NCAA title in 1960.

But after the 1961-62 season, it was time to move on. Everyone couldn't wait to see how he'd do against the world's best players in the NBA. The Cincinnati Royals held his rights and offered a three-year deal worth a reported $100,000. But Lucas had options because the American Basketball League existed and a franchise in Cleveland led by George Steinbrenner wanted him, too.

So a contract with Lucas was signed, and the transaction was announced on this day. The deal was only worth $10,000 for basketball, but included stock options and a future job in the business world that added to its value.

Lucas never played a game with the Pipers, who folded later that year. He eventually joined the Royals, and also played for an NBA championship team, the 1973 New York Knicks.

May 16, 1939 — The Indians and Athletics play the first night game in American League history when they meet in Shibe Park in Philadelphia. Cleveland wins, 8-3, in 10 innings.

May 17, 1925 — Speaker celebrates No. 3,000

Washington Senators pitcher Tom Zachary had a habit of showing up at major moments in baseball history in the 1920s. This is the first of them.

Indians center fielder Tris Speaker was just back from Rochester, where he had received treatment for a dislocated knee. "The Gray Eagle" didn't show any signs of injury, as he went 3-for-4 as Cleveland dropped a 2-1 decision to Washington. One of those singles was the 3,000th hit of his great career.

Speaker was the fifth player to reach 3,000 hits. An estimated crowd of 20,000 was in attendance. Speaker wasn't done, as he piled up 3,515 hits in his career.

As for Zachary, he was still pitching for the Senators when they faced the New York Yankees late in the 1927 season. That's right – he gave up one of the most famous home runs of that time period. Babe Ruth smashed his 60th homer of the season to break his own record and set a mark that would last until 1961.

May 17, 1974 —The Cavaliers acquire Jim Chones from the Lakers for a draft choice.

May 17, 1992 — Larry Bird's great career comes to an end as his Celtics team loses to the Cavaliers, 122-104, in the seventh game of a playoff series.

May 18, 2008 — Pierce tops James in duel

The drama and suspense of a Game 7 is unmatched, no matter the sport. If fans want to be greedy, they might ask to see two great players performing on a high level on a big stage. On this day, Paul Pierce and LeBron James answered that call.

The Celtics and Cavaliers were tied, 3-3, heading into Boston in the second round of the playoffs. Boston kept taking leads, and Cleveland kept crawling back into striking distance. Pierce would make a shot and James would answer.

In the end, though, the future NBA champions of that season had just enough. Pierce finished with 41 points while James had 45. Pierce wrapped up the game with two free throws in the final eight seconds in Boston's 97-92 win. It was a series in which neither team could score 100 points in a game with only one exception (Game 3 for Cleveland).

"You play on the road, if you turn the ball over, which we did a little tonight, and give up second-chance points, it is going to be tough to win," Cavaliers coach Mike Brown said.

May 18, 1963 — Former Heisman Trophy winner Ernie Davis dies of leukemia at age 23. Davis had been acquired by the Browns in a trade with Washington shortly after the NFL Draft the previous fall.

May 18, 1976 — The Cavaliers' first-ever run through the NBA playoffs ends as Boston's 94-87 win gives them the Eastern Conference finals in six games. The Celtics go on to win the NBA title in a memorable series with the Phoenix Suns.

May 19, 2016 — Lue sets record for coaching wins

Coaching in the NBA playoffs is supposed to be difficult. Tyronn Lue was making it look easy in 2016.

Lue and the Cavaliers beat the Raptors, 108-89, in Game 2 of the Eastern Conference finals on this day. Cleveland had a 2-0 lead in the series. More importantly, it was the 10th consecutive win in the playoffs in Lue's coaching career. He broke Pat Riley's record for most consecutive postseason wins at the start of a coaching career.

"It's been great," Lue said after the game. The streak ended in the Cavs' next contest. "We've just got a great team and they're playing great basketball right now. We've just got to keep it going."

LeBron James made a little playoff history as well. The Cavs' superstar passed Shaquille O'Neal for fourth place on the all-time postseason scoring list. James also had his 15th career postseason triple-double. Kyrie Irving led Cleveland with 26 points.

May 19, 1954 — Al Rosen homers in his fifth consecutive game as the Indians beat the Red Sox, 5-3. No Cleveland batter will top Rosen's streak until 2002, when Jim Thome homers in seven consecutive games.

May 19, 1998 — The NFL announces it will be responsible for $15 million in cost overruns at the new Cleveland stadium for the Browns.

May 20, 1983 — Dokes keeps title with draw

When Michael Dokes met Mike Weaver in boxing for the first time, Dokes was awarded the win in a first-round referee's decision – even though Weaver didn't seem to be hurt after getting knocked down. The rematch in Las Vegas on this day was different.

The two went the 15-round distance. Dokes, an Akron native, started strong but then showed the effects of the Nevada heat and some extra weight. Weaver shook off some ring rust to be a worthy opponent.

It came down to a decision. Two judges ruled it a tie, while a third had Dokes ahead, 145-141. So it was declared a majority draw, since the winner of a decision must be ahead on two of the three judges' scorecards. It was the first heavyweight title bout to have such an outcome since Jack Johnson fought "Battling Jim" Johnson in 1913.

"This was the toughest fight I ever had," Dokes told *Sports Illustrated*. "He hurt me with that body shot in the ninth. ... I'll fight anybody, as long as it isn't Weaver. They'll have to strip my title first."

May 20, 1948 — The Indians defeat the Boston Red Sox, 13-4, helped by 18 walks from two Sox left-handers, Maurice "Mickey" Harris (who gave up seven) and Maurice McDermott (11). Attendance was 43,158 at Municipal Stadium as the Indians improve to 16-6 for the season.

May 21, 1979 — Fitch leaves Cavaliers' job

Bill Fitch was not a well-known college basketball coach when he was named in 1970 to run the new NBA expansion team in Cleveland. He had been the college coach of a mediocre team at Minnesota, and before that was in charge at Bowling Green, North Dakota (where one of his players was Phil Jackson) and Coe College.

The Cavs might have struggled with their win-loss record in the first few years, but Fitch had a spry sense of humor with the media and kept everyone amused while he worked at trying to build a winner. Finally, in the franchise's sixth year, the team reached the playoffs and won its first-round series that became known as "The Miracle of Richfield."

But the team couldn't win another playoff series after that. Now, after a 30-52 record in the ninth season, Fitch's resignation as coach was accepted by owner Nick Mileti.

Two days later, the Celtics hired him – and also arriving for the fall of 1979 was a rookie named Larry Bird. In 1981, the two became part of a championship team. Fitch's career continued as he totaled 944 career victories from 1970-1998, good for 11th place on the all-time wins list as of the summer of 2023.

May 21, 1931 — The Indians lose their 12th game in a row, this time by 7-6 at home to the Yankees. Cleveland couldn't top that record for more than 75 years.

May 21, 1992 - The Cavs hand Michael Jordan his worst playoff loss in what would become a total of 179 postseason games, taking a 107-81 win in the Eastern Conference finals.

May 22, 2003 — Cavs win an important lottery

One of the biggest moments in Cavaliers' history occurred in, of all places, Secaucus, New Jersey.

The Cavs were taking part in the NBA Draft Lottery, and everyone knew the stakes. LeBron James, nicknamed by *Sports Illustrated* as "The Chosen One" as a high school junior in Akron, was the prize for whichever team obtained the No. 1 pick.

James was at a hotel suite in Akron to watch the prime-time show from Secaucus. The drawing came down to three remaining teams for the first pick – Cleveland, Detroit and Denver. Finally, the last envelope was opened to disclose the team with the first pick, and it contained a Cavaliers logo.

The Cavs staged a party that night for the lottery, and former star Austin Carr was there – and he almost cried at the news. "It was a very emotional night, and it got to me," he said.

May 22, 2009 — With the Cavaliers facing a 2-0 deficit in the NBA Eastern Conference playoff finals on their home court, LeBron James hits a three-pointer at the buzzer to give his team a 96-95 win over Orlando. James finishes with 35 points. The Cavs would go on to lose the series, 4-2.

May 23, 1972 — Indians reach a peak, if only briefly

For a brief while, the Indians and their fans had come down with a case of pennant fever. It was unexpected for a team that had gone 60-102 the previous season.

It looked to be business as usual at the start of the season, as the team opened 4-6 under new manager Ken Aspromonte, whose Brooklyn, New York, accent would be remembered by fans later in the decade when the accent turned up again as Sam Rutigliano took over the Browns. But then Cleveland won four in a row and eight of nine to improve to 12-7. That put the Indians a half-game ahead in the American League East. And they kept playing well from there, going 6-3.

The last win came against the Yankees. Gaylord Perry improved to 8-2 on the young season, and he threw a four-hitter with five strikeouts. Ray Fosse had a big two-run single in support of Perry. At the end of this day, Cleveland found itself in first place by 2½ games.

But that proved to be the high water mark. The Indians lost their next four to fall out of first place ... for good. Cleveland was 19-19 on June 3, and 23-30 on June 20. The Indians eventually finished fifth with a 72-84 record, well out of the pennant race. In Aspromonte's three years as manager, Cleveland won 72, 71 and 77 games. So in hindsight, the little run in May was nice while it lasted.

May 23, 1901 — The Cleveland Blues, trailing 13-5 with two outs in the ninth, score nine straight runs to take a 14-13 victory over the Washington Senators.

May 23, 1981 — The Cavs sign Kansas City Kings guard Otis Birdsong to a five-year, $5 million agreement that was called an "offer sheet" under newly implemented NBA free agent rules. Kansas City later matches the Cleveland offer. But instead of keeping him, the Kings trade Birdsong to the New Jersey Nets.

24

May 24, 1993 — Wilkens walks away from Cavs

Lenny Wilkens was like a coach on the floor during his time as an NBA player. It was no surprise that he was an excellent coach, too.

Wilkens had coached for 13 seasons – and won one championship in 1979 with Seattle – when he took the Cavaliers' job in 1986. The Cavs were still rebuilding from the chaos of the early 1980s, and Wilkens, along with General Manager Wayne Embry, brought order and stability. He stayed seven years, and won at least 50 games in three seasons.

But the Chicago Bulls, led by Michael Jordan, were insurmountable in the playoffs. Other teams felt that same experience, too. So, with fond memories of his nucleus of players that included Brad Daugherty, Larry Nance, "Hot Rod" Williams, Mark Price and Craig Ehlo, Wilkens resigned on this day to try coaching elsewhere after seven mostly good years in Cleveland.

The Atlanta Hawks quickly signed him, and he spent seven more years there. Then it was on to Toronto and the New York Knicks. It added up to 2,487 games on the bench, with 1,332 wins. That was the record for coaching wins when he retired, although Don Nelson eventually broke it.

May 24, 1918 — Indians pitcher Stan Coveleski throws a complete game of 19 innings with six walks and four strikeouts as Cleveland defeats the New York Yankees, 3-2, thanks to a solo home run by outfielder Smoky Joe Wood.

May 24, 1958 — During an American Bowling Congress event in Syracuse, New York, about 100 top bowlers vote to form the Professional Bowlers Association. Sports business executive Eddie Elias of Akron is named legal counsel and treasurer for the group, which sought to model itself after the city-to-city tournament format created in pro golf.

May 24, 2010 — Mike Brown is fired as the Cavs' coach.

25

May 25, 1935 – Owens has an hour to remember

Jesse Owens might be best known for winning four gold medals in the 1936 Olympics in Berlin, and there's no doubt that it was a stunning achievement for the Cleveland native. Yet, that probably wasn't the most impressive accomplishment of his career.

Owens introduced himself to the world at the 1935 Big Ten Track and Field Championships in Ann Arbor, Michigan. Historians might call it the greatest 45 minutes in sports.

Owens had a bad back suffered in a bit of horseplay a few days earlier, and he didn't know if he could compete. He gave it a try. At 3:15 p.m., he tied the world record in the 100-yard dash at 9.4 seconds. At 3:25 p.m., Owens went 26 feet, 8.25 inches in the long jump to set a world record; it was his only jump. At 3:34 p.m., he ran the 200 in 20.3 seconds, breaking the world record by three-tenths of a second. At 4 p.m., Owens ran the 220 low hurdles in 22.6 seconds, the first man ever to break 23 seconds. He also was given credit for breaking world records for the 200-meter hurdle record and the 200 straightaway record.

In other words, he entered four events in less than an hour, and put his name in the books as the record holder in all of them.

May 25, 1981 — The Cavaliers land 7-foot free agent center James Edwards from the Indiana Pacers with a four-year, nearly $3 million offer.

May 25, 1992 — Mark Price overcomes some digestive difficulties and leads the Cavs to a gutsy 99-85 win over the Bulls to tie their playoff series.

May 26, 2015 — James returns to finals with Cavs

In the 2010s, LeBron James seemed to own the NBA Finals. He had spent four years with the Miami Heat, and his team reached the last round of the playoffs each time. LeBron switched teams and returned to Cleveland in 2014, and Northeast Ohio fans were hoping his streak would continue.

The Cavaliers went 8-2 in the first two rounds of the playoffs. Then they polished off the Atlanta Hawks in four straight games. Game 4 was played on this date, and Cleveland easily won the game, 118-88.

James had 23 points and averaged close to a triple-double in the series. He did his best to spoil the playoffs for the Hawks, who reached the conference finals for the first time since 1970. But LeBron was more concerned about Cleveland's second trip to the Finals.

"I understood what these people were going through, the people here," he said after the game. "Not only in Cleveland but Northeast Ohio and all over the world, who love and bleed wine and gold. To be at this point tonight, it's very emotional."

May 26, 1937 — Cleveland native Hugo Bezdek is named the first coach of the Cleveland Rams, who would play their first game in the National Football League that fall. His salary was a reported $7,500. Bezdek, who managed baseball's Pittsburgh Pirates in 1917-19, only lasted three games into the 1938 season.

May 26, 1993 — Carlos Martinez's deep fly ball caroms off the head of Texas Rangers outfielder Jose Canseco and lands over the fence for a home run. The play, which grew more famous over time as a fan favorite to watch on video, gave the Indians a 7-6 win.

May 27, 1972 — Penske gets his first Indy 500 win

The sports business career of Roger Penske turned a corner in 1972.

Penske was born in Shaker Heights and was frequently around cars growing up – buying them, fixing them, selling them at a profit. He became a top driver in various circuits in the early 1960s and retired in 1965.

The entrepreneurial spirit struck Penske in 1966, when he formed Penske Racing. It entered a car in the 24 Hours of Daytona race in 1966, and then in the 1969 Indianapolis 500. Along the way, he found a great driver in the making in Mark Donohue. The two teamed up on this day to win the Indy 500; Donohue's speed for the distance set a record that lasted for a dozen years.

Penske won 19 Indy 500 titles as a race team owner through 2023, and his reach extends into several other types of racing. He's also served on the boards of corporations, and his list of awards includes the Presidential Medal of Freedom.

May 27, 1986 — The Red Sox defeat the Indians in Cleveland, 2-0, in a game that was shortened to slightly more than five innings because of dense fog from Lake Erie. "That's what they get for building a park on the ocean," said pitcher Dennis "Oil Can" Boyd of the Red Sox after the game.

May 27, 2017 — The Indians unveil a statue of Frank Robinson, who in 1975 became baseball's first Black manager. His uniform No. 20 is retired.

May 27, 2018 — The Cavaliers go to Boston for Game 7 of a playoff series and leave with a 87-79 win that pushes them into their fourth straight NBA Finals.

May 28, 1966 — Indians continue surprising start

The view from the top was special for the Indians at this point in the 1966 season.

The Indians won their first 10 games to take the lead in the American League, and continued to play good baseball throughout the next few weeks. The team had good starting pitching in Sam McDowell, Sonny Siebert, Gary Bell, Steve Hargan and Luis Tiant, and had some power in Rocky Colavito and Leon Wagner.

On this day, the Indians knocked off the Twins, 2-1. Bell improved to 4-1 with a complete game win over the defending American League champions, and Pedro Gonzalez drove in two runs with a single. Cleveland moved 4½ games ahead of the field after that win.

However, it didn't last. McDowell, the ace of the staff, missed some time due to injuries and finished 9-8. The team did not have a .280 hitter in the regular lineup, let alone someone who reached .300. The Indians fell into second place for good on June 12, and they eventually finished fifth at 81-81.

May 28, 1973 — The Indians lose two games on the same day in an unusual way. First, they resume a game suspended two days earlier because of the 1 a.m. curfew rule. That game goes 21 innings and the Chicago White Sox win, 6-3. Wilbur Wood takes over in the 17th inning to get the win. Then the knuckleball-throwing Wood comes right back in a 4-0 shutout of Cleveland in the regularly scheduled game.

May 29, 1974 — Indians have big brawl in Texas

The Rangers and Indians played a couple of memorable games in 1974 within a week's time. They are remembered more for chaos than baseball.

In the eighth inning of the game with Texas on this day, Indians pitcher Milt Wilcox threw a pitch behind Lenny Randle of the Rangers. Randle then bunted the ball down the first-base line, and Wilcox fielded the ball and went to tag Randle. The Ranger infielder went out of his way to run over Wilcox in a violent way, and that caused the benches to empty. Indians catcher Dave Duncan had to be restrained from going into the stands after some fans.

Randle somehow wasn't thrown out of the game. The Rangers won, 3-0, as Jackie Brown pitched a three-hitter. Texas manager Billy Martin said he wasn't concerned about the two teams scheduled to play again, this time in Cleveland, less than a week after the Randle incident. Martin said the Indians didn't have enough fans to worry about.

That set up "Ten Cent Beer Night" – five days later – against the Rangers. The late NBC television journalist Tim Russert was in the stands as part of a crowd of 25,134 that night as the event turned rowdy. That game was forfeited to Texas in the bottom of the ninth when the umpires and Rangers outfielder Jeff Burroughs were assaulted.

May 29, 1946 — Eddie Klep becomes the first white player to play in the Negro Leagues, as he pitches seven innings for the Cleveland Buckeyes in an 8-6 win over the Chicago American Giants in Grand Rapids, Michigan.

May 29, 1955 — Larry Doby of the Indians becomes the first player to hit a home run past the outer wall in Kansas City's Municipal Stadium as Cleveland picks up a 4-2 win.

May 30, 1937 — Shute doubles his fun at PGA

It's not easy to win one major golf championship, let alone win the same one in consecutive years. That's why Denny Shute is in a small group in golf history.

Shute, who was born in Cleveland and later lived in Akron, had won the 1936 PGA Championship. He beat Jimmy Thomson, 3 and 2, in the match play event at Pinehurst in North Carolina. That brought him to the Pittsburgh Field Club a year later to try to defend his title.

Shute quickly moved through the field to the quarterfinals, where he beat Jimmy Hines, 4 and 3. Tony Manero fell in the semifinals, 3 and 2. That brought the tournament to the 36-hole final, where Shute faced Harold "Jug" McSpaden. It was too early in that era for television but what an exciting broadcast it would have been.

McFadden jumped ahead by winning three of the first five holes, but Shute fought back to be 3-up after 18. That margin only lasted until the 26th hole of the day. On the back nine the second time around, McFadden was up by two with only three holes left. Shute came back to force a tie and the match moved to sudden death. Shute parred the playoff hole, and became the champion when McFadden couldn't match it. No player was able to win two straight PGA titles again until Tiger Woods did it in 1999 and 2000.

May 30, 1953 — ABC-TV shows the Indians' 7-2 win over the White Sox in the first game of a doubleheader in Chicago. A total of 15 stations throughout the nation (there were many restricted markets) air the game, which kicked off the network's "Game of the Week" broadcasts. It starts a tradition that lasts for decades.

May 30, 1977 — Indians pitcher Dennis Eckersley wins a 2-0 no-hitter against the California Angels.

May 30, 1992 — Arena League football comes to the Cleveland area as the Thunderbolts debut in the Richfield Coliseum. The 'Bolts beat the San Antonio Force, 36-34, before 12,323 in the opener for the team that had moved from Columbus in the previous offseason.

31

May 31, 2007 — James scores final 25 points in win

Cavaliers star LeBron James was in his best clutch performance form on this night, Game 5 of a playoff series with the Detroit Pistons. James had 19 points early in the fourth quarter, but it seemed he was just getting warmed up. He had a couple of big baskets, including a drive with nine seconds left that tied the game.

Then it was on to overtime. James scored every point for the Cavs in the five-minute span, but they couldn't put the Pistons away. Chauncey Billups' two free throws sent the game to a second OT. James didn't slow down for a moment. He hit a crucial fadeaway three-point basket with 1:14 to go to tie the contest. Then he drove through the entire Detroit team for a layup with 2.2 seconds remaining to give Cleveland the lead. When the Pistons couldn't answer, the Cavs had the game.

James finished with 48 points, including Cleveland's final 25 points in a row. "We threw everything we had at him. We just couldn't stop him," Billups said.

May 31, 1986 — Bobby Rahal, a native of Medina, gets the checkered flag to win the Indianapolis 500 auto race. Rahal becomes the first driver to finish a full 500-mile race on that track in less than three hours.

May 31, 2018 — LeBron James sets a team playoff record with 51 points but the Cavaliers lose to the Warriors, 124-114 in overtime, in Game 1 of the NBA Finals.

June 1, 1984 — Mancini loses his boxing title

Ray "Boom Boom" Mancini of Warren attempted to keep his lightweight career going and recover from the shock of the death of one of his opponents, Duk Koo Kim. He had two successful title defenses after the incident in 1983 and 1984. After that, Mancini signed to fight Livingstone Bramble in Buffalo. It turned out to be quite an event.

In the run-up to the fight, Bramble tried to act in unusual ways in an attempt to unnerve Mancini. Bramble introduced an associate by the name of "Dr. Doo," who was said to be something of a witch doctor. In reality, it was Bramble's CYO basketball coach. The challenger dedicated the fight to Ethiopia and its war in the 19th century with Italy.

Bramble brought one other quality to the ring in Memorial Auditorium that night. He could fight. Bramble was known as a good defensive fighter, but he could punch as well. It was a good, close bout. After 13 rounds, Mancini was ahead on two of the scorecards. But Mancini got into trouble in round 14, and couldn't get out of it. The referee stopped the fight, and Mancini had lost the championship. Ray spent the night in a hospital and had 71 stitches placed around his eye.

Mancini lost a close rematch with Bramble, and a couple of other bouts as well. He finished his career with a 29-5 record. Bramble went on to hold the title for a little more than two years. Both became inductees into the International Boxing Hall of Fame.

June 1, 1999 — Mike Fratello is fired as coach of the Cavaliers after the team misses the playoffs earlier in the spring. Owner Gordon Gund also announces that Jim Paxson will succeed Wayne Embry as general manager.

2

June 2, 2007 — Gibson plays the starring role in win

The Detroit Pistons no doubt knew that LeBron James would be ready when his Cavaliers had a chance to reach the NBA Finals. The Pistons, though, probably never thought Daniel Gibson would be anything more than a supporting player.

Gibson turned in an amazing performance in leading the Cavs to a 98-82 win over Detroit to capture the Eastern Conference final in six games. He scored 31 points, with 19 coming in the fourth quarter. Gibson, nicknamed "Boobie," hit four huge three-pointers in that final period, and they gave Cleveland a large boost.

James had 20 points and 14 rebounds, helping his team rebound from losing the first two games of the series in Detroit. LeBron had scored 48 points for the Cavs as they won Game 5 in overtime. After that, the Pistons were determined to make sure James didn't beat them. So Gibson ended up becoming the savior.

"This is the best thing that ever happened to me, man," James said to the 20,562 in attendance. "But look here, look here. It doesn't stop." No, the San Antonio Spurs were waiting in the Finals that Cleveland had reached for the first time since the franchise was founded in 1970.

June 2, 1869 — The first professional baseball game in Cleveland history matches the Forest Citys (of Rockford, Illinois) and the Cincinnati Red Stockings at Case Commons. Cincinnati wins, 25-6.

June 2, 1994 — Kent State pitcher Dustin Hermanson is the No. 3 pick of the first round of the Major League Baseball draft by the San Diego Padres. Players chosen after Hermanson include Jaret Wright, Nomar Garciaparra, Paul Konerko and Jason Varitek.

June 2, 2003 — The Cavaliers pick longtime NBA player and coach Paul Silas to be their new head coach, which also makes him the first professional coach for incoming NBA rookie LeBron James.

June 3, 2018 — Curry guns down the Cavaliers

Arguments can go on forever about the best long-range shooters in NBA history but Steph Curry of Golden State showed on this date that he's in the conversation.

Curry scored 33 points in a 122-103 win over Cleveland in Game 2 of the NBA Finals. It gave Golden State a 2-0 lead in the series. Curry was ruthlessly efficient, converting on nine three-pointers to set a Finals record. Kevin Durant added 26 points while Klay Thompson scored 20, but Curry was the story.

"I mean, regardless of how the season went, that's a pretty cool deal to accomplish knowing who has held the record for – what is it, probably six, eight years? But at the end of the day, it's all about trying to get a win and doing whatever you can to make that happen," he told reporters after the game. The previous record was eight by Ray Allen of the Boston Celtics in a Finals game against the Los Angeles Lakers in 2010.

LeBron James had 29 points and 13 assists in almost 44 minutes and Kevin Love added 22 for Cleveland, which trailed most of the game.

June 3, 1988 — The Indians trade utility player Pat Tabler to the Royals for left-handed pitcher Bud Black.

4

June 4, 1944 — The NFL gets some competition

Arch Ward was sports editor of the *Chicago Tribune*, but he had a promotional, entrepreneurial spirit, too.

Ward gathered several businessmen, some of whom had been unsuccessful in their efforts to purchase a team in the National Football League, in St. Louis. History teaches that when the demand is greater than the supply of pro franchises in a particular sport, and expansion isn't used as a solution, a new league might appear. And that was the case on this day as the All-America Football Conference was created.

The next step came in November of 1944, when Jim Crowley – one of Notre Dame's legendary "Four Horsemen" – was selected as the AAFC's first commissioner. Now it became a matter of firming up a group of teams to play. With World War II going on, the league looked ahead and decided to start play in 1946.

Cleveland always was on the list where the new league wanted a team, even though the NFL Rams already played there. Arthur "Mickey" McBride was the owner, and he quickly picked Paul Brown (formerly of Ohio State University) to coach the team. Buffalo, Chicago, Los Angeles, New York and San Francisco were selected for the league early in the process as well, and they eventually were joined by Brooklyn and Miami. Those eight cities were ready in September, 1946, when the AAFC played its first games.

June 4, 1963 — Browns defensive back Don Fleming dies of electrocution while working a construction job in Winter Park, Florida, at age 25. His uniform number 46 is later retired.

June 4, 1967 — Some of the nation's most well-known African-American athletes – including Muhammad Ali, Jim Brown, Bill Russell and Lew Alcindor (later known as Kareem Abdul-Jabbar) – gather in Cleveland for a meeting to show support for Ali and to discuss racial issues. Ali had refused to be inducted into the U.S. military on April 28 and was convicted of evasion on June 20. Among the others who attended were football players Walter Beach, Bobby Mitchell, Sid Williams, Curtis McClinton, Willie Davis, Jim Shorter and John Wooten.

June 4, 1974 — The Indians try a promotion called "Ten-Cent Beer Night," but it becomes a historic embarrassment. An unruly crowd of 25,134 causes umpire Nestor Chylak to forfeit the tied game to the Texas Rangers in the bottom of the ninth inning after fans run onto the field and fights break out.

June 4, 1998 — The Indians issue an initial public ownership offering that allows people to buy stock in the franchise. When Larry Dolan, at age 68, buys the team for $320 million more than a year later, he also purchases all of the outstanding stock in order to have complete control of the team.

5

June 5, 2016 — Women's soccer draws a crowd

The United States Women's National Team was on top of the soccer world in 2015. The USWNT had captured its third World Cup title, more than any other nation. That level of success greatly increased the team's notoriety and profile.

Therefore, it was a good idea to show off the team, especially with the Olympics coming up soon. That led to Cleveland being chosen to host a friendly match between the United States and Japan at FirstEnergy Stadium, and fans responded nicely. A crowd of 23,535 turned out – the largest ever to see the U.S. national team in Ohio.

The event came only two days after a federal judge ruled that the team did not have the right to go on strike in its effort to receive improved wages and conditions from the U.S. Soccer Federation. Even so, the American squad did not appear distracted as it took a 2-0 victory in a game shortened by about 15 minutes because of a thunderstorm.

Julie Johnson opened the scoring in the 27th minute and Alex Morgan added some insurance in the 62nd minute. Team USA improved to 12-0-1 on the year. Alas, it lost in the quarterfinals of the Olympics to Sweden, 4-3, on penalty kicks.

June 5, 1984 — The Browns take running back Kevin Mack and linebacker Mike Johnson in the first round of the USFL Dispersal Draft.

June 6, 1983 — Gorman comes stormin' into town

Thinking they could use some power in their lineup, Indians executives work out a deal with the Brewers to pick up Gorman Thomas. It was surprising to those in Cleveland, but downright shocking to everyone in Milwaukee.

Thomas was the only first-round draft choice in the history of the Seattle Pilots, who played one year as an expansion team in the Pacific Northwest and then moved to Milwaukee (under new owner and future Commissioner Bud Selig) in 1970. Thomas became a regular in 1978 in center field, and found a home run stroke – 32 that year. He kept slugging for the next four years, and was part of a powerful Brewers lineup that had just reached the World Series the year before in 1982. What's more, he might have been the most popular player on that team – a blue-collar guy who loved interacting with fans.

Thomas got off to a horrible start to 1983, hitting under .200 two months into the season. That made the trade possible. Outfielder Rick Manning and starting pitcher Rick Waits came to Milwaukee in the deal, while the Indians received relief pitchers Ernie Camacho and Jamie Easterly to go with Thomas.

The deal didn't work out too well for the people involved. Thomas hit .221 with 17 homers for the Indians in a little more than half a season. He was traded to Seattle with second baseman Jack Perconte for second baseman Tony Bernazard before the 1984 season. Camacho and Easterly had some good moments on the mound for the Tribe. Manning stayed in Milwaukee through 1987. Waits wasn't too effective in bullpen duty in the next 2½ years.

June 6, 1935 — With stories circulating that the Indians were having trouble getting along with manager Walter Johnson, the team takes the unusual step of buying a large advertisement in three Cleveland newspapers. It says, in part, "We, the members of the

Cleveland Baseball Club, want the fans to know that we are not a team split wide open by dissension, arrayed against our manager," and it is signed by 21 players.

June 6, 1972 — Holding the second pick of the first round of baseball's amateur free agent draft, the Indians select shortstop Rick Manning of LaSalle High School in Niagara Falls, New York. Manning batted .614 in his senior year with 27 hits in 44 at-bats, three home runs, three triples and four doubles, 20 runs scored and 16 RBI. In the third round, Cleveland drafts pitcher Dennis Eckersley.

June 7, 1936 — No bullpens needed in marathon

The pitching matchup on this particular day in Yankee Stadium featured New York's Red Ruffing and Cleveland's Oral Hildebrand. Those who missed the first inning had plenty of chances to see them work after that, because they were part of an unusual baseball game in the Bronx.

The Yankees took a 2-0 lead in the bottom of the third on a home run by Ruffing, but the Indians rebounded to go up by 4-2 in the fifth. Then New York scored two runs in the bottom of the seventh to tie the contest. Before the estimated crowd of 35,000 knew it, they were in extra innings.

Ruffing and Hildebrand both pitched the first nine innings, and apparently were determined to try to finish what they started. The two hurlers worked the 10th, 11th, 12th, 13th, 14th and 15th without giving up a run. They were still throwing in the 16th, and Ruffing kept Cleveland off the scoreboard again. Hildebrand got Lou Gehrig and Joe DiMaggio out to start his half of the inning, but then gave up a homer to George "Twinkletoes" Selkirk. That gave New York a 5-4 win.

Ruffing allowed 10 hits in those 16 innings. It's interesting that he didn't have one strikeout in that game. It remains the longest start for a pitcher in the history of the Yankees, and that's not likely to change any time soon. Hildebrand gave up 12 hits and struck out five.

June 7, 1938 — Pitcher Johnny Allen of the Indians storms off the field in a game in Boston because of his sweatshirt. He had cut off the sleeves, but umpires thought the ragged edges of the shirt were causing a distraction.

June 7, 1998 — Dave Burba becomes one of the few Indians' pitchers to homer in the era of the designated hitter, when he goes deep against Scott Clingenbeck as Indians pitchers were required to bat in the game in Cincinnati.

June 8, 2018 — King James exits with loss to Warriors

The Chicago Bulls had what was called "The Last Dance in 1998," according to an ESPN documentary on Michael Jordan that debuted in 2020, when they won their sixth championship. The Cavaliers had their own, slightly altered version of that concept 20 years later.

Cleveland came up short in the NBA Finals, losing to Golden State on this date by a score of 108-85. It meant that the Warriors had finished a sweep of the Cavaliers to win their second straight title. It was the fourth consecutive time that the two teams had met in the Finals, and Cleveland finished 1-3.

Steph Curry had 37 points and Kevin Durant picked up the MVP trophy for the series. It was the first 4-0 result in the Finals since 2007; the Cavs lost that one to San Antonio.

LeBron James had 23 points in this contest and revealed after the game that he was essentially playing with a broken hand. It was the eighth consecutive season that he had competed in the NBA Finals, as he had led Miami there four times from 2011 to 2014. There would not be an encore for James, as he jumped to the Los Angeles Lakers as a free agent a few weeks after this game.

June 8, 1965 — The Indians select catcher Ray Fosse with their first pick in the major leagues' first Free Agent Amateur Draft, which was designed to cut down on wild spending by teams on young prospects.

June 8, 1975 — The Indians retire the uniform number of outfielder Earl Averill (No. 3), who had been voted into the Baseball Hall of Fame by the Veterans Committee earlier in the year. He played for Cleveland from 1929-39.

June 8, 2016 — Facing a 2-0 deficit to Golden State in the NBA Finals, the Cavaliers snap back with a 120-90 win in Game 3. LeBron James leads Cleveland with 32 points and 11 rebounds.

June 9, 2003 — Rupp has the goal of a lifetime for Devils

Pro hockey highlights are rare coming from players who are Northeast Ohio natives. Therefore, Mike Rupp's contribution to the history books needs to be celebrated.

Rupp, a native of the city of Brunswick in Medina County, southwest of Cleveland, played high school hockey at St. Edward in Lakewood, and he also played for Team Ohio Midget AAA. The center was the first-round draft choice of the Islanders in 1998, but didn't sign with New York. Two years later, the New Jersey Devils picked him in the third round.

Rupp spent 2½ years playing for the Albany River Rats of the American Hockey League. The Devils called him up during the 2002-03 season, which was a good year to join them. They reached the Stanley Cup finals, where they played the Anaheim Mighty Ducks. The home team won all seven games, and New Jersey won the title. Rupp had the honor of scoring the Cup-winning goal for the Devils. It was his first NHL playoff goal, making the forward the first player to have his first postseason score become a Cup winner.

Rupp saw a lot of NHL action over the years, as he played 610 games in his career. He finished with 54 goals in the regular season and two in the postseason. (The less important playoff goal came for Pittsburgh in an 8-2 loss to Tampa Bay in 2011.)

June 9, 1940 — Lawson Little's 70 defeats Gene Sarazen, who shot 73, in an 18-hole playoff to win the United States Open golf championship at Canterbury Golf Club in Beachwood.

June 9, 2002 — When the PGA Tour takes away one of its World Golf Championship events from Firestone Country Club in Akron for one year, it is replaced by the Senior PGA Championship. Crowd favorite Fuzzy Zoeller wins.

June 9, 2014 — Lonnie Chisenhall ties an Indians' team record by driving in nine runs in a 17-7 win over the Rangers.

10

June 10, 1959 — The Rock hits four big knocks

Rocky Colavito was at the top of his game in the summer of 1959, and the aura included becoming a celebrity in Cleveland. He was one of the best power hitters in baseball at that time, and some thought he had a chance to reach Babe Ruth's record of 60 homers in a season. Colavito took four steps toward that goal on this day during a game in Baltimore.

The outfielder walked in the top of the first and scored on a Minnie Minoso homer. In the third, his two-run homer made it a 6-3 lead for Cleveland. Colavito hit a solo shot off Arnie Portocarrero in the fifth. Then in the sixth, Tito Francona and Colavito went back-to-back to give the Indians a 10-3 lead.

Cleveland went quietly in the seventh and eighth, but Rocky still had an at-bat coming in the ninth. He certainly knew that he needed one home run to tie the major league record with four in a game. Ernie Johnson tried to get an inside fastball past Colavito, but it was crushed to left field. When the ball landed in the seats, Colavito had become the eighth player to hit four homers in a game, and the third to hit them consecutively. A crowd of 15,883 supplied a standing ovation.

"Somebody up there (in right field) threw beer on me," Colavito said to the *Baltimore Sun* after the game. "It hit me on the arm. I knew who it was, too. It made me a little mad. After I hit that fourth homer and went out to right field, though, he waved at me. Nice fella."

June 10, 1921 — Babe Ruth homers off Cleveland's Jim Bagby for his 120th career round-tripper. That makes him baseball's all-time leader – a distinction he'll hold until Henry Aaron breaks the record in 1974.

June 10, 1953 — Arthur "Mickey" McBride, who has owned the Cleveland Browns since their founding in 1946, sells the team to an investor group headed by Homer Marshman and David Jones for $600,000, the largest sale price for a franchise in NFL history. The previous high was $250,000 for the Philadelphia Eagles, according to the Associated Press. Marshman, the president of Cleveland-Sandusky Brewing Co., was the first president of the old NFL team in Cleveland, the Rams, in 1937.

11

June 11, 1995 — Kilbane joins boxing's best in Hall

Only the best of the best in the world of boxing are inducted into the International Boxing Hall of Fame in Canastota, New York. Cleveland's own Johnny Kilbane certainly deserved his plaque there, which was put into place on this date.

Kilbane had to grow up fast as a youngster, as his mother died when he was three and his father became blind when Johnny was six. Kilbane had to drop out of school in the sixth grade to help the family survive. Johnny had his first pro boxing match at 18, when he earned the sum of $8.

It took five years for Kilbane to reach his goal, but he eventually won the featherweight title in 1912 with a 20-round match with Abe Attell in California. When Kilbane got back to Cleveland, a crowd of 100,000 was waiting to honor him. It was one of the biggest receptions in the city's history at that time. Johnny remained the champion for 11 years. It's one of the longest runs in boxing history. His name became a verb in the language, as in "he chased after a heckler and 'Johnny Kilbaned' him on the spot."

Finally in 1923, Eugene Crique beat him for the title. Kilbane finished his career with a 51-4 record. From there, Kilbane kept busy in a number of areas. He did some refereeing, worked at a gym, taught physical education and worked in real estate. Johnny even was a member of the Ohio State Senate. He died of cancer in 1957.

June 11, 2016 — The Lake Erie Monsters finish a sweep of the final of the American Hockey League playoffs, beating the Hershey Bears in four straight games to win the Calder Cup. No player on the roster had more than 46 points.

June 12, 1880 — Sheffield's Richmond has perfect day

Lee Richmond might have been called the Pride of Sheffield at some point in his life. And why not? He accomplished a great deal during his baseball career, as well as his life. The little town in Lorain County must have been very proud.

Richmond was born in Sheffield and went to high school in Geneva and Oberlin. He enrolled at Brown in 1876, and played baseball and football there when he wasn't serving as class president. Richmond jumped between college ball and the pros in 1879, prompting a rewriting of the rules in such areas.

Richmond signed with the Worcester franchise of the National Baseball Association for $2,400. He stayed there for three years, winning about 80 percent of the team's games in that span. Richmond is considered the first effective left-handed pitcher in baseball history. He certainly was good on this date, as he pitched the first perfect game in the history of organized baseball in blanking the Cleveland Blues. That was pretty good for a guy who had been up all night participating in college graduation activities. The *Chicago Tribune* put it this way: "The Clevelands were utterly helpless before Richmond's puzzling curves, retiring in every inning in one, two, three order, without a base hit."

Alas, Richmond suffered an arm injury in 1883 and only played a brief bit of time in 1886 before retiring. He became a doctor during the 1880s, and then moved into teaching at Toledo High School. There he taught Greek, history, chemistry and mathematics among other subjects. Today we might call him a Renaissance man.

June 12, 1965 — Sal Bando hits a triple in the sixth inning and scores on a sacrifice fly for the winning run as Arizona State defeats Ohio State, 2-1, to capture the College World Series. Bando, a star in high school in the Cleveland suburb of Warrensville Heights, is named the tournament's Most Outstanding Player. He would go on to play 16 major league seasons.

June 12, 2007 — The Cavaliers fall short in their first home game in an NBA Final, losing to San Antonio, 75-72. Anderson Varejao misses a wild shot at the end of the game that could have tied it.

June 12, 2017 — The Cavaliers' bid to repeat as NBA champions falls short as the Warriors beat them 129-120 and eliminate Cleveland in the NBA Finals in five games.

13

June 13, 1984 — Indians help the Cubs reach postseason

Executing a midseason trade in baseball often comes down to a simple question – should a team give up part of its future in the form of prospects to acquire a player who can give that team a better chance of winning right away? One of the best examples of this sort of trade took place on this day.

The Chicago Cubs were the surprise leaders of the National League East as the 1984 season headed for its midpoint. However, the Cubs had a couple of pitchers – Dick Ruthven and Scott Sanderson – who were injured. Meanwhile, the Indians were stuck in the basement of the American League East. They had a pitcher, Rick Sutcliffe, who won 17 games for them in 1983. That made him an attractive target.

The Cubs decided to pay the price for Sutcliffe, pitcher George Frazier and catcher Ron Hassey. Cleveland received a pair of young outfielders in Joe Carter and Mel Hall along with minor leaguers Don Schulze and Darryl Banks. "We got two pitchers who are necessary additions to our staff, and the making of the trade rested on Hall being part of it," Cubs general manager Dallas Green said.

Carter turned into a star for Cleveland, and Hall had some good years as well. Meanwhile, Sutcliffe gave the Cubs a spectacular half-season. He was almost unbeatable, going 16-1 with a 2.69 earned-run average. The right-hander won the Cy Young Award for the National League, even though he was in the American League for 2½ months of the season. Sutcliffe led the Cubs to the National League Championship Series, where they were edged by the San Diego Padres.

June 13, 1914 — Mary K. Browne wins the third of three consecutive U.S. National Championships (now called the U.S. Open) in tennis by beating Marie Wagner in the final at Newport, Rhode Island. Browne went on to become the first women's tennis professional in history, and eventually moved to Cleveland, where she became a top amateur golfer.

June 13, 1940 — A group of 11 Indians players meet with owner Alva Bradley and ask that manager Ossie Vitt be relieved of his duties. When the story broke, the public sided with Vitt and the incident became known as "The Crybaby Mutiny."

June 13, 1999 — Cleveland heavyweight fighter Jimmy Bivins is inducted into the International Boxing Hall of Fame even though he never had a chance to win a title. Bivins had an 8-3 record against the world champions he did fight.

June 13, 2016 — The Cavaliers stay alive and narrow the NBA Finals to a 3-2 Golden State lead with a 112-97 win over the Warriors in Oakland.

14

June 14, 1978 — Barons pack for Minnesota

On June 14, 1977, Mike Crombeen became the first-round draft pick (fifth overall) of the Cleveland Barons of the National Hockey League. Exactly one year later, the Barons dropped out of the NHL.

The Barons' two-year stay in the Cleveland sports landscape had difficulties. The team moved from Oakland on relatively short notice, giving the franchise little time to market itself in the community. The Barons drew more than 10,000 fans only seven times in their first season. Also, it was an era when the World Hockey Association was in business, and that drove up player salaries throughout pro hockey. Owner Melvin Swig soon ran out of money, and team employees went unpaid for a few weeks. In the summer of 1977, the team was sold to brothers Gordon and George Gund, a family well-known in Cleveland.

Life was better in 1977-78, as the team received an infusion of money and picked up its play. A 15-game losing streak, though, took care of any playoff hopes. The Barons thought they had a poor lease at the Coliseum, and saw no way to change their financial situation in the Cleveland area.

Meanwhile, the Minnesota North Stars were going through similar problems of their own. There was talk of that team folding as well. Instead, the NHL decided to merge the Barons and North Stars and put the revised franchise in Minnesota under the ownership of the Gunds. Crombeen, who had spent the 1977-78 season in Cleveland, was claimed by the St. Louis Blues in a dispersal draft and had an eight-year NHL career. The North Stars eventually moved to Dallas.

June 14, 1962 — Future Basketball Hall of Famer John Havlicek signs to play with a Cleveland team – the football Browns, who gave him a long look at wide receiver. Havlicek was a seventh-round draft choice of Cleveland, even though he never played football at Ohio State. Havlicek was one of the Browns' last cuts, and he then signed with basketball's Boston Celtics.

June 14, 2007 — Cleveland's first appearance in the NBA Finals is a brief one, as the Cavs are eliminated by San Antonio in four straight games. Game 4 is an 83-82 win for the Spurs.

June 15, 1958 — Indians trade a future two-time MVP

Roger Maris was not a happy man in 1958, particularly when it came to a dispute with the management of his employer. The Indians' outfielder had to deal with a new general manager in Frank Lane, who at that stage in his career as an executive "was treating players like meat," in the words of baseball historian Bill James. Lane wanted Maris to go play winter baseball to learn how to become a center fielder, and Maris wanted to stay with his family. That caused a rift that reportedly never healed.

Then when the 1958 season began, Maris had a new manager in Bobby Bragan. They didn't get along, either. In those days, if you didn't get along with the GM and the manager, you had a chance to get lost easily in the shuffle. Maris hit .235 for the first 2½ months of the season, and his status as a top prospect on the Indians' roster was fading fast.

Lane never saw a player that he didn't think about trading, and he didn't change his reputation this time, either. The Indians sent Maris, Preston Ward and Dick Tomanek to the Athletics for Vic Power and Woodie Held. Maris' game picked up a bit during the rest of 1958, and he played even better in 1959. However, any time the Athletics ran out of money in that era, which seemed to occur frequently, they'd make a trade with the Yankees to pick up some cash. So it was off to New York in a seven-player deal.

You know what happened from there if you are a baseball fan. Maris won the Most Valuable Player award for the American League in 1960. Then in 1961, he cracked 61 homers to break Babe Ruth's one-season record – and won the MVP trophy again. Held and Power both had good years in Cleveland, but the loss of Maris was another line etched in fans' memories under the heading "what might have been."

June 15, 1962 — Harry Chiti, who had been traded to the Mets by the Indians for a player to be named later in April, is returned to Cleveland by New York. He therefore becomes the first player ever traded for himself.

June 15, 1980 — Indians outfielder Jorge Orta goes 6-for-6 in Cleveland's 14-5 victory over Minnesota on Jersey Day before a crowd of 25,182. It is the first time in 28 years an Indians player has had six hits in a game.

June 15, 1994 — Jim Thome of the Indians hits the first walk-off homer against Toronto. He eventually set an MLB record with 13 such round-trippers in his career.

16

June 16, 1986 — Sixers do the Cavs a big favor

The Cavaliers had a gift horse that arrived out of the blue one summer day in 1986. Luckily for them, they didn't look him in the mouth.

The Philadelphia 76ers owned the first pick in the college draft that year. They had a veteran center in Moses Malone in their starting lineup, but a young player to help him in the short term and maybe replace him in the long term seemed like a good idea. One such player available was Brad Daugherty of North Carolina, a 7-footer rated by scouts as having excellent NBA potential.

But the Sixers had other ideas, mostly because owner Harold Katz thought Malone was earning too much money. They completed a couple of trades on this day that revamped their lineup enormously. The first swap sent the first overall pick to the Cavaliers for center-forward Roy Hinson. Philadelphia thought Hinson was better than anyone coming out of college that year. Then General Manager Pat Williams traded Malone, Terry Catledge and a pair of first-round picks to Washington for Jeff Ruland and Cliff Robinson.

The Cavs definitely had the edge in their half of the deal with General Manager Wayne Embry doing the negotiating. Daugherty was a solid contributor in Cleveland for eight seasons before he was forced to retire because of injuries. Hinson's scoring average in Philly never topped the number he put up in Cleveland in 1985-86. Meanwhile, Ruland only started a handful of games for the Sixers because of knee trouble, while Malone stayed in the NBA for 10 more years.

June 16, 1962 — The Indians blow a 6-0 lead to the Yankees, but Jerry Kindall's dramatic two-run homer in the bottom of the ninth gives Cleveland a 10-9 win.

June 16, 2015 — Golden State wraps up the NBA championship, ousting the Cavaliers in the Finals in six games. The Warriors were 105-97 winners in the deciding game.

June 16, 2016 — The Cavaliers force a seventh game in the NBA Finals by beating Golden State, 115-101. LeBron James has 41 points and 11 assists for Cleveland.

17

June 17, 2002 — Mexico can't break through the 'Human Wall'

Brad Friedel of Lakewood might be the greatest men's soccer goalkeeper ever produced by the United States of America. The catch is that much of his best work was done overseas.

Friedel attended Bay Village's Bay High School, where he was an outstanding three-sport athlete. An all-state player in basketball, Friedel was invited to walk on to the UCLA basketball team. But Friedel stuck to soccer and led the Bruins to a national championship in 1990. He left UCLA early to pursue a pro career in Europe.

He found it across the sea, but he's best known here as a member of the United States National Team. Friedel was a backup in the 1994 World Cup, but took over the starter's job in 1998. Then in 2002, Friedel was back in goal for another World Cup, and he was sensational. The highlight came on this day when he earned a 2-0 shutout in the second round against Mexico. Friedel became the first goalie to stop two penalty kicks during regular play (as opposed to shoot-outs) in a tournament since 1974. That earned him the nickname of "The Human Wall."

Friedel retired from international play in 2005. However, he stayed in the Premier League in England until 2014. He played in 450 games in that league in his great career, which set a record for a player from North or South America.

June 17, 1960 — Boston Red Sox star Ted Williams hits the 500th home run of his storied career, a two-run blast off Indians pitcher Wynn Hawkins as Cleveland loses, 3-1, to the last-place Sox.

June 17, 1986 — The Cavs draft Brad Daugherty of North Carolina and Ron Harper of Miami (Ohio) in the first round of the NBA Draft, get Mark Price of Georgia Tech in a trade, and add Johnny Newman of Richmond in the second round. It's considered the greatest draft day package in team history. In that same draft, former Warrensville Heights and Ohio State star Brad Sellers is the ninth choice of the first round by the Chicago Bulls and goes on to a six-year NBA career.

June 17, 1993 — Mike Fratello gives up a broadcasting job with NBC to take over as the head coach of the Cavaliers, succeeding Lenny Wilkens.

June 18, 1950 — Indians score two early touchdowns

The Indians had done a good job of thrashing the lowly Athletics in the first game of a doubleheader at Municipal Stadium on a Sunday afternoon. They had won, 7-0, as Bob Feller threw a compact two-hitter with only two walks and two strikeouts. The second game was even more one-sided.

The Athletics went down 1-2-3 in the top of the first. Let's quickly recount what happened next, interjecting a score when needed. Dale Mitchell doubled. Bob Kennedy lined out. Luke Easter walked. Larry Doby walked. Al Rosen walked (1-0). Joe Gordon walked (2-0). Ray Boone walked (3-0). Jim Hegan singled (5-0). Mike Garcia singled (6-0). Mitchell walked.

Philadelphia pitcher Lou Brissie exited in favor of Carl Scheib. Kennedy walked (7-0). Easter singled (9-0). Doby singled (10-0). Rosen reached on an error (11-0). Gordon flied out to center. Boone homered (14-0). Hegan flied out. If you are scoring, that's 14 runs on six hits and one error.

The Indians added four more runs in the third, and scored three times in the eighth. It's interesting that Cleveland only made a couple of substitutions in the game, even though it was obviously well in hand after that first inning. The Indians went home with a 21-2 win; Mike Garcia might have had the easiest complete game win of his career.

June 18, 1985 — The Cavaliers choose Virginia Union star Charles Oakley with the No. 9 pick of the first round of the NBA draft but immediately trade his rights to the Chicago Bulls with Calvin Duncan for Keith Lee and Ennis Whatley. Oakley goes on to play 19 years in the NBA after a career that started at John Hay High School in Cleveland. Lee only stayed with Cleveland one more year and ended his NBA career after just three seasons.

June 18, 1991 — Cancerous growths in his left pitching arm require amputation for Dave Dravecky, a Youngstown Boardman High graduate who had an eight-year major-league career from 1982-89.

June 18, 2011 — Erica Rosa of Cleveland Heights wins the Manhattan Island Marathon Swim in New York, finishing in 7 hours, 29 minutes and 46 seconds.

19

June 19, 2016 — Cleveland has a world champion at last

Was it worth the wait? It sure felt like it. After 52 years, Cleveland had itself a major professional sports team champion. The Cavaliers won the NBA title by defeating Golden State, 93-89, in a game that left memories that will live forever in Northeast Ohio.

The Cavs did things the hard way. They were playing a team that had a regular-season record of 73-9. Golden State raced through the early rounds of the playoffs, and had a 3-1 lead over Cleveland. The Cavs fought back, taking Games 5 and 6 to even the series. Still, Game 7 was in Oakland, California, and winning there would be difficult.

The momentum went back and forth with neither team getting much of a lead, and players appeared exhausted as the clock wound down. Then came the shot of the game. Kyrie Irving had the ball a foot or two beyond the three-point line. He launched the ball over Steph Curry and scored with 53 seconds left. Cleveland had a 92-89 lead at that point, and the air came right out of the building. LeBron James added a free throw with 11 seconds left, and the Warriors had no more answers.

For James, who had a triple-double, it was a case of promise made, promise kept. "I'm coming home with what I said I was going to do," he said, adding, "I can't wait to get off that plane, hold that trophy up, and see all our fans at the terminal."

June 19, 1924 — George Burns of the Indians goes 6-for-6 with a triple, three doubles and two singles in the opener of a doubleheader against the Tigers.

June 19, 1942 — Mel Harder of the Indians strikes out Yankee superstar Joe DiMaggio three times in Cleveland's 5-4 home win. It was the only time in his career that DiMaggio struck out three times in a game.

June 19, 1977 — The Indians dismiss Frank Robinson as manager and name Jeff Torborg to the position.

June 19, 1994 — The Indians win their 18th home game in a row. The 6-5 triumph over Boston sets a team record.

June 20, 1998 — Lemon's No. 21 goes out of circulation

Bob Lemon must have had a lot of memories come back to him during this particular weekend in Cleveland. He was part of a big team celebration, and then individually honored on back-to-back days. It doesn't get much better than that.

On June 19, the Indians celebrated the 50th anniversary of their last World Series championship. Lemon, who won 20 games that season with a league-leading 10 shutouts, was part of that event. He was one of 15 players and staff members to return to Cleveland for the reunion. Others included Bob Feller, Larry Doby and Al Rosen. Lemon autographed a program from the game in which he threw a no-hitter that season.

A day later, Lemon had the honor of having his uniform number 21 retired by the Indians. He pitched 13 years for Cleveland, winning 207 games. Lemon made the All-Star team for seven straight years, and the Hall of Famer is the only man to manage a team to the World Series title after starting the season as the manager of another team (White Sox/Yankees). The Indians' manager in 1998, Mike Hargrove, switched his uniform number from No. 21 to No. 30 to salute Lemon.

The Indians picked a good date for the honor. It was the 50th anniversary of one of his most memorable outings. Not only did he throw a four-hit shutout as Cleveland blanked Philadelphia, 10-0, but Lemon also hit a home run in the game to raise his batting average to .372 for the season. He was one of the best hitting pitchers in baseball history with a .232 career batting average that included hitting five or more home runs in a season four times.

June 20, 1936 — Track star Jesse Owens of Cleveland sets a record with a 10.2-second performance in the 100-meter sprint at the NCAA championship meet in Chicago.

June 20, 1972 — Nick Mileti acquires a rescinded franchise in the World Hockey Association that had been designated for Calgary, making Cleveland the 12th team in the league.

June 20, 1995 — The sellout crowd is part of the story in the Indians' 9-2 win over the Red Sox. The franchise goes past the one-million mark in attendance for the season.

June 21, 1946 – Indians return to life through new owner

Baseball was about to turn fun again in Cleveland. Bill Veeck, 32, had just purchased the Indians for $2.2 million.

Veeck might have been the most popular owner in baseball history in the cities where he managed teams. On the other hand, he was not popular with fellow owners, who were often set in their ways. Veeck had owned a minor league team in Milwaukee during the early 1940s, and was an innovator in promotions and marketing in pro sports. (He eventually was named to the Baseball Hall of Fame.) With World War II now over and Veeck out of the military, he set his sights on the Indians.

Then the fun began. Veeck immediately put all of the team's games on radio, something previous ownership thought would hurt attendance. He brought in Max Patkin and Jackie Price, two baseball veterans who were also known for their comic talents. Veeck spoke to every group that would have him. By the end of the year, the Indians had broken the team's attendance record of 912,832, set in 1920, going over 1,000,000 for the first time, and the team was about to begin one of the great rides in its history, culminating in the 1948 World Series championship.

June 21, 1971 — A broken ankle suffered in spring training ruined Ken "The Hawk" Harrelson's 1970 season with the Indians and on this day, batting .199 more than a year later, the 29-year-old has had enough. He announces his retirement and says he wants to learn if his golf game is good enough to start a new professional career.

June 21, 1997 — The Cleveland Rockers play their first game as a member of the Women's National Basketball Association, losing to Houston by a score of 76-56.

June 22, 2016 — Northeast Ohio celebrates a championship

A championship in major team sports isn't just a matter of winning that last game. It also requires a giant celebration to allow everyone to enjoy that winning feeling for a few extra days. When it's 52 years in the making, as it was in Cleveland, then fans know it will be an event to remember. But when did anyone ever attempt to stage a party for 1.3 million people on three days' notice?

Mountains were moved to make it all work, since some vendors were tied up with work on the upcoming Republican National Convention. Even so, the city and the Cavaliers were ready, and it was as tasty a moment as possible.

The fans started showing up at 4 a.m. in order to get a good seat. The parade went from Quicken Loans Arena to a downtown mall area, and it featured 60 floats and the Ohio State University marching band. Jim Brown, who was part of the last Cleveland championship with the Browns in 1964, was there. He handed the Larry O'Brien Trophy, which goes to the NBA winner, to LeBron James during the rally.

And if the event didn't provide enough joy for Clevelanders, James had a bit of news for them as well. "I love it here in Cleveland. I have no intentions of leaving," James said to ESPN. "There are some technicalities to take care of that I'll leave up to my agent. That's right from the horse's mouth."

June 22, 1924 — Virgil Cheeves becomes the first Native American to play for the Indians since they began play in the American League in 1901. He starts the game but only lasts a few batters into the second inning.

June 22, 1976 — The Cleveland Crusaders of the World Hockey Association announce plans to move to Hollywood, Florida, where they will become the Florida Breakers. The plan soon falls through.

June 22, 2001 — The Indians acquire controversial pitcher John Rocker and Troy Cameron from the Braves for Steve Karsay and Steve Reed.

23

June 23, 2011 — Cavs take Kyrie Irving first overall

The Cavaliers had their fingers crossed when they completed a trade with the Los Angeles Clippers earlier in the season. They acquired the Clippers' first-round draft pick in a deal that sent Mo Williams and Jamario Moon to Los Angeles. The hope was for a good spot in the upcoming draft.

Luck was on the side of the Cavaliers when they won the NBA Draft Lottery. This was the day when Cleveland found out its reward. The Cavs took Kyrie Irving of Duke.

The guard from Elizabeth, New Jersey, was an interesting case. He was considered one of the best freshmen players in the nation in college, but a foot injury limited him to only 11 games for the Blue Devils. That proved to be enough to convince the Cavs that he was worth the top pick. "I didn't have any doubts about going No. 1. I was looking to the organization to pick who they felt was the right choice," Irving said.

It was an unusual draft, because of a strong list of players from Europe who were eligible. Some of the other players who went in the first round that year were Brandon Knight, Kemba Walker, Klay Thompson, Kawhi Leonard, and Jimmy Butler. But Irving made the pick historic in 2016 when he hit a basket that gave Cleveland the NBA Finals championship.

June 23, 1950 — Luke Easter of the Indians hits what is believed to be the longest home run in the history of Municipal Stadium – 477 feet. It's one of two homers for Easter in a 13-4 Cleveland win.

June 23, 1985 — Arnold Palmer wins his second straight Senior Tournament Players Championship, finishing 11 strokes ahead of the field at Canterbury Golf Club.

June 24, 2007 — Tracy closes the show with a third win

The Grand Prix of Cleveland, held from 1982 to 2007, achieved some fame on the motor sports circuit because the track was on the runways of a working airport, and the views of the lake and skyline were excellent.

If it had to go away, Paul Tracy was an appropriate person to win the final running. Tracy had won the event in 1993 and 2005, and then came through to take the 2007 event. He hadn't won between the 2005 and 2007 triumphs in Cleveland, going 23 races without a visit to Victory Lane.

Tracy had luck on his side. He avoided a couple of accidents along the way and worked his way up the field. On the final lap, Tracy held off Robert Doornbos to win by a half-second. "I'm kind of overwhelmed," Tracy said. "It doesn't seem like it came the right way, but I'll take what I get." It was his last win on the circuit.

The crowds were always good in Cleveland, but the event got tangled up in the battle between Championship Auto Racing Teams and the Indy Racing League at the time. When the two circuits merged in 2008, Cleveland's event was left out of the racing schedule.

June 24, 1922 — The American Professional Football Association changes its name to the National Football League. It is heading into its third fall season as an organized entity with six teams in Ohio – Akron, Canton, Toledo, Dayton, Columbus and the Oorang Indians of Marion.

June 24, 1930 — Ground is broken on a new sports stadium in Cleveland located on the waterfront of Lake Erie.

June 24, 1970 — After Yankees left-handed relief pitcher Steve Hamilton throws a blooper pitch – or "eephus" ball – that he calls the "Folly Floater," Indians first baseman Tony Horton fouls it off. Hamilton gives Horton another chance at the trick pitch, and Horton fouls out. He raises his arms in frustration as he walks back to the dugout and – just before reaching the first step – enters it on his hands and knees.

June 24, 1980 — A publicity stunt for Ted Stepien's Cleveland Competitors softball team goes completely awry. The idea was to throw softballs off the top of the Terminal Tower building downtown and have some of the Competitors catch them. However, the first toss dents a car on the ground, and the next two throws injure spectators.

25

June 25, 1952 — Maxim earns TKO of exhausted Robinson

Bring up the name of Sugar Ray Robinson, and a phrase quickly comes up: Robinson was one of the best pound-for-pound boxers in history. He was the total package, with enough style that the joke was he could have boxed in a tuxedo. Robinson already had claimed the welterweight title (147 pounds) and the middleweight title (160 pounds) during his career.

Still, there's always another mountain to climb in boxing, and Robinson decided to take on a big one in Joey Maxim. The Cleveland native was the light-heavyweight champion (175 pounds), and no former welterweight champion had ever moved up in weight so far to win another crown.

The fight was scheduled to take place in Yankee Stadium on June 23, but a severe rainstorm in New York City interfered with that date. It was backed up by two days. The storms had cleared out, but a heat wave then settled in. New York had one of its hottest days on record, but there was no rescheduling plan at this point.

For 10 rounds, Robinson put on a great show. He darted in and out, landing punches and then vanishing. But all of that required a lot of energy, and it wasn't a good day for that. Maxim realized that he needed a knockout in the late rounds to win, while Robinson refused to change his style. By the end of Round 13, Robinson's tank was empty. When the bell sounded, Sugar Ray was so disoriented that he didn't even know where his corner was. The fight was stopped – the only time Robinson lost by anything but a decision in his 200-fight career.

June 25, 1967 — Max Alvis of the Indians comes down with a serious illness on a plane ride from Minnesota to Boston. He is soon diagnosed with spinal meningitis, and the third baseman's career never reached the same heights again.

26

June 26, 2003 — Pick of James starts new era for Cavs

Trivia question: Who was the other guy taken by the Cavaliers in the 2003 NBA Draft? It was Jason Kapono of UCLA, best known for winning a pair of three-point shooting competitions.

Kapono wasn't the reason fans were excited about the draft, of course. The Cavaliers found themselves in the fortunate position of winning the NBA Draft Lottery in precisely the right year. It gave them the opportunity to take LeBron James. James was one of the most heralded players to turn pro directly out of high school basketball. During his junior year at Akron St. Vincent-St. Mary High School in February of 2002, he had been pictured on the cover of *Sports Illustrated* magazine with the headline "The Chosen One." A couple of his games were shown on national television.

Soon, James signed a three-year contract with Cleveland for a reported $10.8 million. That answered the question for those wondering if he'd do all right financially without a college degree. But his NBA deal was dwarfed by an endorsement contract with Nike worth a reported $90 million over seven years.

The 2003 player selection meeting was quite a draft, especially at the top. The choices at No. 3, 4 and 5 consisted of Carmelo Anthony, Chris Bosh and Dwyane Wade. Bosh and Wade are already Hall of Famers, and James and Anthony will be joining them eventually. The second choice turned out to be a story of a different type. Detroit passed up Anthony, Bosh and Wade to take Darko Milicic from Serbia. Milicic played in the NBA for 10 years, but never averaged 10 points per game. The 7-foot center probably came to the league too soon, as he needed more playing time to develop his skills.

June 26, 1916 — The Indians debut numerals on the sleeves of their players' uniforms in a major league first. Then, in 1929, the Indians become the first team to wear numerals on jersey backs. The Yankees planned to do it, too, but their opener on April 16 of that year was rained out.

June 26, 2009 — The Cavs acquire Shaquille O'Neal from Phoenix for Sasha Pavlovic, Ben Wallace, a draft choice, and cash.

June 26, 2014 — Andrew Wiggins of Kansas is the top pick (first overall) by the Cavs in the NBA Draft.

June 27, 2002 — Colon brings a haul of talent from Expos

In the summer of 2002, it looked as if the Indians' great run of winning teams was about to end. They had not finished a season with a losing record since 1993. But on the morning of June 27, they were 36-41 and appeared to be going nowhere.

General Manager Mark Shapiro thought it was time to rebuild, and he had an asset that could help the process. Bartolo Colon was a legitimate top starter, someone with a 99 mph fastball. He had won at least 14 games in each of the last four seasons, and was only 29. That meant he might be getting very expensive to keep in the near future. Meanwhile, the Montreal Expos were in a bit of a mess in terms of ownership, but they were above .500 and had a chance at a wild-card playoff spot.

The two sides worked out a deal. Colon and pitcher Tim Drew went to the Expos for three prospects – infielder Brandon Phillips, left-handed pitcher Cliff Lee and outfielder Grady Sizemore – and veteran first baseman-outfielder Lee Stevens, which was more a matter of finances than talent. The reaction in Cleveland was quick. How could the Indians trade one of the premier pitchers in baseball for three unknowns who had never played an inning in the majors?

The fans heard about them soon enough. While Colon went 10-4 in his half-season in Montreal and eventually won a Cy Young Award, the Expos still missed the playoffs. Meanwhile, Shapiro's return was excellent. Phillips was a good second baseman during a 17-year career, spent mostly with the Reds. Lee did his best pitching for the Indians, and had a nice 13-year career. Sizemore looked like a Hall of Famer for his first few years in Cleveland. Sadly, the outfielder suffered from a variety of injuries, including a couple of knee surgeries that occurred after a four-year run of stardom from age 22 to 25.

June 27, 1939 — Bob Feller throws a one-hitter to beat the Tigers, 5-0, in the first home night game in Indians history.

June 27, 1963 — Cleveland reserve outfielder Al Luplow makes what is considered one of the greatest catches in history during a game in Fenway Park. Red Sox batter Dick Williams launched what could have been a go-ahead three-run home run in the bottom of the eighth inning, but Luplow vaulted a five-foot fence, clipping the top with his knees and then went over it and snagged the ball out of view of fans but in sight of players in the bullpen.

June 27, 1986 — Cleveland Browns safety Don Rogers dies at age 23 of a heart attack caused by cocaine use. Rogers had been a No. 1 draft choice in 1984 and was heading into his third NFL season. His death occurred the day before his scheduled wedding.

June 27, 2013 — The Cavs, with the first pick in the NBA Draft for the second time in three years, use it on 20-year-old 6-foot-8 forward Anthony Bennett of UNLV. He averages 4 points a game in 13 minutes per game in 52 appearances as a rookie, then becomes part of a trade to Minnesota in a deal that brings Kevin Love to Cleveland. Bennett played four years in the NBA for four teams in his career.

28

June 28, 1922 — Graney completes his first act

You can think of the professional life of Jack Graney in two parts. Either way, he was closely associated with the Cleveland Indians throughout most of his entire adult life.

Graney broke into the Indians' lineup for good in 1910. He was a regular for the next several years, an outfielder who didn't have much power and never hit .300 in a season. Graney was the first opposing batter ever to face a young left-handed pitcher from Boston by the name of George Ruth. You know him as "Babe." Graney also was the first man up in the game when the Indians used numbers on their uniforms. Graney's last game was on this date.

He worked in a number of different areas for a decade, but saw his savings wiped out in the stock market crash of 1929. Then in 1932, the Indians needed a baseball announcer in a hurry, as they had just fired the former occupant of the job. A nervous Graney took over . . . and stayed for 21 years, retiring in 1953.

"I always tried to give the fans an honest account," Graney was quoted as saying in a Society for American Baseball Research article. "It was a tremendous responsibility and at all times I kept in mind the fact that I was the eyes of the radio audience. I was like an artist trying to paint a picture. I never tried to predict or second guess, even though I had played the game. I just tried to do my best, and I hope my best was good enough."

June 28, 1986 — The Indians' Phil Niekro and Angels' Don Sutton square off in a battle of starting pitchers who have won 300 games in their careers. It's the first such matchup in the 20th century.

June 28, 1988 — Michigan guard Gary Grant is the No. 15 pick of the NBA Draft's first round but is traded the same day with a 1989 first-round pick to the Los Angeles Clippers for big man Michael Cage. Grant would play 13 seasons in the league after starting his career at Canton McKinley High School.

29

June 29, 1934 — A baseball founding father dies

This date marks the death of Charles Somers, a former owner of the Indians who has been more or less forgotten after so many years away from his association with baseball. He lived quite a life in his 65 years.

His father started a coal company based in Cleveland and had mines in Ohio and Pennsylvania. Charles reportedly accumulated $1 million by age 31. Somers always liked baseball, so he bought the Grand Rapids, Michigan, franchise in the new American League and moved it to Cleveland. Somers also loaned money to several franchises, and established control of the new team in Boston until an investor could be found. In other words, he was a key figure in the birth of the league.

The Cleveland team had some hot starts through the middle of the 1910s, but not much success. Somers couldn't help but fire managers almost on a whim. The team finished last in 1914. An economic downturn in 1915 hurt his coal and shipping businesses, and debts piled up. Creditors took over the team and forced Somers to sell. That was essentially the end of his association with baseball.

But, Somers hadn't lost his touch when it came to business. He simply went back to work at accumulating another fortune, and when he died, his estate was worth an estimated $3 million.

June 29, 1977 — The Indians walk off the field in the nightcap of a twin-bill, thinking they had beaten the visiting Orioles, 4-3. But Baltimore manager Earl Weaver correctly points out that the umpires had misinterpreted a rule on fielding overthrows, and the "winning run" should not have counted. The Indians came back from the locker room, and went on to lose the game, 5-3, in 10 innings.

30

June 30, 1948 — Lemon turns out the lights on Detroit

This was a big day in the electronics industry, as the announcement came that the transistor had been invented. The device would replace vacuum tubes in radios, and eventually make it easy for fans to bring radios to baseball games and hear a description of a game they were watching.

On that same day, another famous scientific development – the light bulb – played a role in a bit of baseball history. Indians pitcher Bob Lemon pitched a no-hitter in Detroit, beating the Tigers, 2-0. Detroit was the last team in the league to put up lights, and they had only been in use for two weeks.

Lemon only walked three batters as he took over the league lead in wins with 11. It was the first season that he had been exclusively a pitcher; he had split his time with outfield duties previous to 1948. Lou Boudreau doubled home a run in the top of the first, and later scored on a sacrifice fly. That was it for the Cleveland offense, which was otherwise shut down by Hank Edwards.

George Kell of the Tigers was the game's final batter. He hit a comebacker to Lemon, who gloved it and made a gentle toss to Johnny Berardino at first for the last out. It was one of Lemon's 20 complete games that season. One other footnote: Berardino became an actor playing the character named Dr. Steve Hardy on the soap opera *General Hospital* after retiring from baseball, and has a star on the Hollywood Walk of Fame.

June 30, 1901 — Pete Downing throws the first no-hitter in the history of the American League, as the Cleveland Blues pitcher blanks the Milwaukee Brewers. Apparently an official scorer changed a hit to an error shortly after the end of the game, causing the game to be a no-hitter and starting some confusion that continues to this day.

June 30, 1971 — Mary Bacon becomes the first woman jockey to win 100 races; the milestone takes place at Thistledown in North Randall, near Cleveland.

June 30, 1995 — Indians designated hitter Eddie Murray becomes the 20th player and second switch-hitter (Pete Rose) to reach 3,000 hits. He singled in the sixth inning off Mike Trombley of the Twins.

June 30, 1999 — James Posey, who starred in high school basketball at Twinsburg in Summit County, is chosen 18th in the first round of the NBA Draft by the Denver Nuggets. Posey, a 6-foot-8 forward from Xavier, would play 12 years in the league with seven teams and later served as a Cavs assistant coach.

During the 1915 baseball season, the Cleveland Indians traded Joe Jackson, whose nickname was "Shoeless Joe," to the Chicago White Sox. Jackson had played five years and part of a sixth at the time of the trade. *(The Cleveland Press Collection, Michael Schwartz Library, Cleveland State University)*

Tris Speaker was one of baseball's greatest players during his time with the Boston Red Sox. When the Red Sox and Speaker couldn't agree on a salary for the outfielder, the Indians were more than happy to acquire him in 1916. Speaker continued his great career in Cleveland, and also managed the team for more than seven seasons. *(The Cleveland Press Collection, Michael Schwartz Library, Cleveland State University)*

Cleveland Indians shortstop Ray Chapman was a popular player and the team was in a battle for the American League championship on August 16, 1920, when he was struck in the head by a pitch from Carl Mays. It was the first pitch of the fifth inning for Mays, who threw using what was called a "submarine" delivery, meaning his throwing arm dragged low to the ground as he released the ball. Chapman died 12 hours after being hit. The death did not result in the immediate requirement that batters wear helmets, however. *(The Cleveland Press Collection, Michael Schwartz Library, Cleveland State University)*

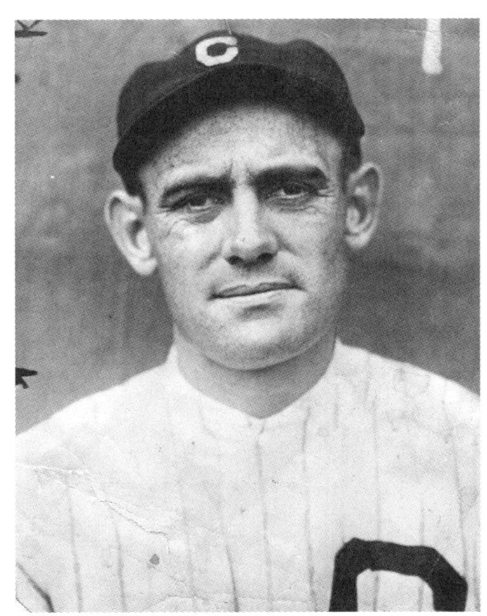

Larry Doby, shown here displaying his batting swing, became the first American League Black player when he was signed by the Cleveland Indians in 1947. In his first full year in the major leagues in 1948, he batted .301 with a slugging percentage of .490. He had 14 home runs, 66 RBIs, nine triples and 23 doubles as Cleveland won its first World Series since 1920. (*Cleveland Public Library/Photograph Collection)*

The pitching star of the Negro Leagues baseball organization was Leroy "Satchel" Paige, shown here in the Major League Baseball uniform of the Cleveland Indians, with whom he debuted on June 2, 1948. Paige was believed to be 42 that year. *(Cleveland Public Library/ Photograph Collection)*

The World Series champion 1948 Cleveland Indians featured a steady starting lineup throughout the year, with seven players totaling 500 or more appearances at bat. Shown here in an undated photo are, from left, Thurman Tucker; Larry Doby; Lou Boudreau; Joe Gordon; Allie Clark; Eddie Robinson; Ken Keltner; Jim Hegan, and pitcher Bob Feller. *(Cleveland Public Library/Photograph Collection)*

Soccer royalty turned up in Cleveland during the summer of 1968. Pele, considered one of the greatest players to set foot on the "pitch," led his club team, Santos of Brazil, to Ohio for a game against the Cleveland Stokers. The legendary scorer died on December 30, 2022 - less than two weeks after the epic World Cup final between Argentina and France. *(Photo by Paul Tepley, The Cleveland Press Collection, Michael Schwartz Library, Cleveland State University)*

When Cleveland sports entrepreneur Nick J. Mileti obtained a franchise in the fledgling World Hockey Association for the 1972-73 season, a priority was set on obtaining a top-quality goaltender. Gerry Cheevers had played five seasons for the Boston Bruins but at age 31, he did not have a contract for the upcoming year. The *Akron Beacon Journal* reported Cheevers' contract with the Bruins was for $45,000 but Mileti's offer was believed to be between three years and $500,000 up to six years for $1 million. Cheevers, shown here in a Cleveland Crusaders' WHA uniform, played 3 1/2 years before going back to the Bruins and the National Hockey League. (*Photo by Paul Tepley, The Cleveland Press Collection, Michael Schwartz Library, Cleveland State University)*

Cleveland Cavaliers coach and general manager Bill Fitch is shown during a team workout at the Coliseum in the Summit County community of Richfield. Fitch was hired by team owner Nick J. Mileti in 1970 and remained with the franchise for nine seasons,compiling a 304-434 record. He was named NBA Coach of the Year in 1976, when the Cavs made the NBA playoffs for the first time and won a series against the Washington Bullets before being defeated by the Boston Celtics in the Eastern Conference finals.
(Cleveland Public Library/Photograph Collection)

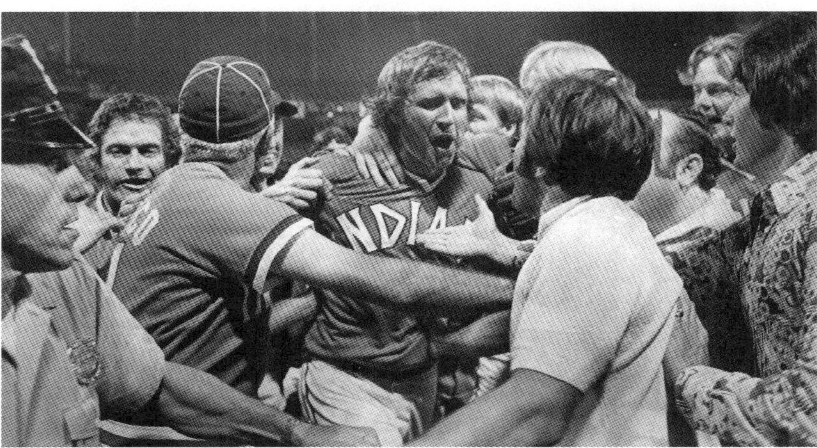

Cleveland pitcher Dick Bosman is mobbed by fans and teammates on July 19, 1974, after pitching a no-hitter against the defending World Series champion Oakland A's. The Indians won 4-0 at Municipal Stadium before a crowd of 24,302. It was the Indians' first no-hitter since Sonny Siebert had one in 1966.
(Cleveland Public Library/Photograph Collection)

Cleveland Indians second baseman Duane Kuiper chats with Cleveland Browns tackle Doug Dieken and Indians manager Dave Garcia (right). The seat from Municipal Stadium commemorates Kuiper's only major league home run, which was hit on August 29, 1977. *(Cleveland Public Library/Photograph Collection)*

Defensive players from the Cleveland Browns celebrate the team's only touchdown in the 14-12 playoff loss to the Oakland Raiders on January 4, 1981. From left, Henry Bradley (91) and Clinton Burrell (49) congratulate Ron Bolton (28), who had scored on a 42-yard interception. Also celebrating is Clarence Scott (right). (*Photo by Paul Tepley, The Cleveland Press Collection, Michael Schwartz Library, Cleveland State University)*

Cleveland Indians pitcher Len Barker is shown in the traditional postgame role of icing an elbow and throwing arm after a game. Barker made Major League Baseball history on May 15, 1981, in hurling a perfect game in a 3-0 victory in Cleveland against the Toronto Blue Jays.
(Photo by Paul Tepley, The Cleveland Press Collection, Michael Schwartz Library, Cleveland State University)

Major League Baseball at Cleveland Stadium in the 1970s, '80s and for four years in the early '90s featured many, many empty seats. The drought of American League pennant-winning seasons started in 1955 and continued through 1994.
(Courtesy of Larry Pantages)

A high leg kick was an integral part of the pitch delivery by Cleveland Indians starter Len Barker during his five seasons with the team in the late 1970s and early 1980s. Barker, who threw a perfect game in 1981, won 19 games in 1980 and 15 in 1982 for Cleveland. In 1983, he was traded to the Atlanta Braves for pitcher Rick Behenna and two position players – outfielder Brett Butler and third baseman Brook Jacoby – who would become steady performers for the Indians. *(Photo by Paul Tepley, The Cleveland Press Collection, Michael Schwartz Library, Cleveland State University)*

LeBron James gestures during a game while playing in high school in Akron for St. Vincent-St. Mary. During his four-year high school career from 1999 to 2003, James averaged 25.2 points, 7.9 rebounds and 5.0 assists while shooting 55.8% from the floor and 36% on 3-point attempts. He was named Ohio's Mr. Basketball three times. *(Courtesy of David Richard)*

Indians outfielder Kenny Lofton is carried off the field by backup catcher Eddie Taubensee after Cleveland came from 12 runs behind to win 15-14 over the Seattle Mariners on August 5, 2001. The Indians scored five runs in the bottom of the ninth inning to tie the game. *(Courtesy of David Richard)*

Travis Hafner, who played for the Indians from 2003 to 2012, follows the flight of the ball after a swing. In 2005, Hafner finished fifth in the American League voting for MVP as he had 33 home runs, 108 RBIs and 42 doubles. In 2006, he tied Don Mattingly for the single-season major-league record for grand slam home runs with six. (*Courtesy of David Richard)*

When the San Francisco Giants visited Progressive Field for a three-game series in 2008, former Indians fan favorite Omar Vizquel was saluted as Major League Baseball's all-time leader in games played at shortstop. Vizquel, who played for the Indians for 11 seasons from 1994 to 2004, finished his 24-year career in 2012 with 2,709 games at shortstop. *(Courtesy of David Richard)*

Two days before he turned age 41, Jim Thome was purchased from the Minnesota Twins and brought back to Cleveland and added three more home runs in the 2011 season to his franchise-leading total of 337. Shown here, fans and the scoreboard had signs saying, "Welcome Thome" with the "home" emphasized. Thome was a star at bat for Cleveland from 1991 to 2002. His career home run total of 612 ranked 8th on Major League Baseball's all-time list heading into the 2023 season.
(Courtesy of David Richard)

Cavaliers star LeBron James raises his arms in a mirror image of his pose depicted for years on the Sherwin-Williams building downtown. James and the Cavs celebrated winning the NBA's 2016 championship on June 21 along with a crowd estimated at 1.3 million people. The triumph marked the first major professional sports title for the city since the 1964 Cleveland Browns were NFL winners. (*Courtesy of David Richard*)

The Chicago Cubs celebrate winning the World Series of Major League Baseball on November, 2, 2016, with an 8-7 victory over the Cleveland Indians in Game 7. The Indians had a 3-1 series lead before the Cubs' spectacular comeback. *(Courtesy of David Richard)*

LeBron James is shown at center court in his 14th season as the Cavaliers used an image of the NBA championship trophy, named after former league Commissioner Larry O'Brien, on center court at Quicken Loans Arena in Cleveland during the 2016-17 season. *(Courtesy of David Richard)*

LeBron James is shown at Quicken Loans Arena as play continues with the ball near Cleveland's team bench. James' roster of teammates changed multiple times during his two tenures of service with the Cavs from 2003-2010 and again from 2014-2018. *(Courtesy of David Richard)*

During the 22-game winning streak in 2017 – the second longest in MLB history behind the 1916 New York Giants – the Indians outscored opponents by 105 runs, with starting pitchers posting 19 of the wins and a 1.77 earned-run average. The team batting average over the stretch was .306. The previous franchise record for win streaks had been 14, set a year earlier in 2016. (*Courtesy of David Richard)*

Cleveland Browns star running back Jim Brown reads the *New York Daily News* edition of Monday, Oct. 25, 1965, after his team defeated the New York Giants 38-14 the day before. The 1965 season was Brown's final year in pro football as he retired to begin a career as an actor. *(Courtesy of Buffalo State/SUNY Library)*

1

July 1, 2018 — Thanks for everything, LeBron

Hadn't we heard this before? LeBron James left the Cavaliers to sign with another team.

It was his second such move, of course, but this one came with somewhat less emotion after an NBA title was won in 2016, and one less television show for the announcement. James signed a four-year, $154 million contract with the Los Angeles Lakers.

The superstar was still at the top of his game in 2018, carrying the Cavs to the NBA Finals for the fourth consecutive season. So perhaps Cleveland's title in 2016 built up enough goodwill to allow Cavs' fans to be generous in wishing James well wherever he might go.

James thought he couldn't pass up the chance to rejuvenate one of the NBA's legendary franchises. "For me to be in this position now, the excitement that I have to be a Laker, I'm happy to be a part of it because I believe the Lakers (are) a historical franchise ... we all know that, but it's a championship franchise and that's what we're trying to get back to," he told Lakers.com.

July 1, 1951 — Indians pitcher Bob Feller beats the Detroit Tigers, 2-1, and throws his third career no–hitter.

July 1, 1962 — Picture this: Gene Green is in right field for the Indians against the White Sox in the fifth inning. With runners on first and third, the next batter flies to Green, who drops the ball, allowing a run. The scorer rules a sacrifice fly. After another single, the next batter flies to Green, who drops the ball to allow a run. The scorer rules a sacrifice fly. The next batter walks and the next batter flies to Green, who catches the ball. The crowd applauds and the scorer rules a sacrifice fly, the third of the inning - setting a major league baseball record.

July 1, 1963 — Arnold Palmer wins the inaugural Cleveland Open title in a playoff against Tony Lema and Tommy Aaron at Beechmont Country Club. The win is worth $22,000 for Palmer. The event would take place for 10 years. The list of the other winners is: Tony Lema, Dan Sikes, R.H. Sikes, Gardner Dickinson, Dave Stockton, Charles Coody, Bruce Devlin, Bobby Mitchell and David Graham.

2

July 2, 1952 — The NHL rejects Cleveland's bid

"The Original Six" is a nickname for the teams that were in the National Hockey League from 1942 to 1967: New York, Boston, Chicago, Detroit, Montreal and Toronto. The league came close to changing that title to "The Original Seven."

Cleveland was considered by some observers as one of the glamor franchises of the American Hockey League in that era, and was interested in moving up to better competition. The Barons owned their own players, and had ties to a couple of junior hockey league teams. Therefore, it would be easy to add them to the league as a new team without having an expansion draft.

NHL President Clarence Campbell said earlier in 1952 that the Barons almost certainly would be admitted into the league if they were able to come up with the necessary financing. A 72-game schedule for the seven teams was in the works. The fee was $50,000, although the team had to deposit $425,000 as an action of good faith and come up with more local ownership in its management group.

That proved to be a stumbling block. The league's Board of Governors opted to reject Cleveland's application for membership on June 17, but this was the day the decision was announced. The Cleveland market would have to wait until 1976 to watch NHL hockey in person.

July 2, 1904 — Edward Hennig, the first athlete from Cleveland to compete in the Olympic Games, finishes the gymnastics competition in St. Louis with two gold medals in Indian club swinging and the horizontal bars.

July 2, 1932 — The Western Open pro golf event, the third oldest tournament for professionals after the British Open (1860) and the U.S. Open (1895), is played at Canterbury Golf Club in the Cleveland suburb of Beachwood. Walter Hagen is the winner. The tournament also was played in Northeast Ohio at various locations in 1937, 1925, 1921, 1919 and 1902.

July 2, 1994 — Larry Doby's Indians uniform No. 14 is retired.

3

July 3, 1931 — Municipal Stadium opens for business

Imagine walking into Cleveland's newest sports palace on this particular night, located on what had once been a landfill right on the waterfront. You knew it would be big, but it was hard to comprehend just how big. Now you learned the answer – 78,000 seats was the largest stadium in terms of crowd capacity in the entire world.

The structure made financial history as well. Cleveland voters approved a bond issue of

$2.5 million for the new facility, making it the first publicly financed sports stadium. The final cost was about $3 million; it was a little over budget.

The building was ready for business two days after completion, and it had a big event as an opener. Max Schmeling of Germany was on hand to defend his heavyweight boxing championship against "Young" Stribling (so named because he started boxing at the age of 14). A crowd of about 37,000 attended – a huge gathering by most standards but one that didn't even fill half of the seats.

The boxers were evenly matched for several rounds. Then a right by Schmeling in the ninth left Stribling staggered. The challenger survived to move into the 10th round, but soon was knocked down by Schmeling. Stribling got off the canvas, but the referee stopped the fight.

July 3, 1947 — Indians team owner Bill Veeck signs Larry Doby, making him the second player after Jackie Robinson earlier in the season to break Major League Baseball's color barrier.

July 3, 1968 — Luis Tiant sets an Indians record with 19 strikeouts over 10 innings. Cleveland beats Minnesota, 1-0.

July 3, 1973 — Brothers Jim and Gaylord Perry face each other for the only time in their careers as the pitchers square off in Cleveland. Detroit wins the game, 5-4; Jim gets a no-decision while Gaylord takes the loss.

July 3, 1999 — Jim Thome hits the longest home run in the history of Progressive Field, a 511-foot blast against Kansas City.

July 4, 1982 — Rookie Rahal races to win

It was the first year for the Cleveland 500 race, part of the Championship Auto Racing Teams (CART) series of motor sports. Organizers couldn't have asked for a better finish. After all, everyone goes home happy when the hometown boy makes good.

The "boy" in question was Bobby Rahal, who claimed his first victory on the circuit. The win came in front of 55,000 at Burke Lakefront Airport, a unique layout. It was the only event held at an actual working airport; the facility was shut down in the week leading up to the race so that preparations could be made for the event.

Rahal was born in Medina and raced out of Columbus, so he had many of the fans on his side. He took his first lead 100 laps into the 125-lap event, as he patiently waited for the chance to move up front. Once he did, he stayed ahead of runner-up Mario Andretti. That's not to say he didn't worry about being passed on the final laps and falling short of the $38,000 prize for first.

"In the last 20 laps, I died every second,' Rahal told reporters. "I thought something was going to happen."

July 4, 1855 - The Ivanhoe Boat Club, formed earlier in the year, wins a special Independence Day race against the Ydrad Boat Club in one of the first sports competitions in Cleveland's history.

July 4, 2006 — The Indians have a star-spangled holiday as they blast the Yankees, 19-1, in Cleveland. Victor Martinez has five hits, and Travis Hafner hits two home runs and drives in four runs.

5

July 5, 1947 — Doby was second to none

As baseball events go, it wasn't much. A pinch-hitter struck out in his first trip to the plate in the major leagues. Yet, as soon as the batter's name was announced over the public address system, he was part of an historic cultural event.

The pinch-hitter was named Larry Doby. He was the first African American to play in the American League, and the second in major league baseball. Only Jackie Robinson – who joined Brooklyn at the start of the 1947 season – came before Doby.

Doby had been playing with the Newark Eagles of the Negro Leagues in 1947. Indians' owner Bill Veeck brought him to Cleveland right after the All-Star break. New Jersey reporter Bob Whiting broke the story a little ahead of what had been planned, so Veeck had to move up Doby's debut slightly. The Indians' players didn't say a word when Doby arrived at Comiskey Park in Chicago for the game, completely ignoring him. Doby struck out against Earl Harrist of the White Sox.

Doby played sparingly in 1947, but moved into the starting lineup the following year. He's remembered as the first Black player to hit a home run in a World Series (1948). Doby was an excellent player for the next decade with Cleveland and Chicago. In 1978, he became the manager of the Chicago White Sox – he was the second African American to manage as well. Doby went into the Baseball Hall of Fame in 1998.

July 5, 1954 — Bill Glynn drives in eight runs for the Indians on three homers, as Cleveland pounds Detroit, 13-6. It tied the franchise record for RBIs in a game. Glynn had five home runs in total that season.

July 5, 1994 — Mark Steinkerchner, who had been working Mid-American Conference football games since 1988 as a referee, is hired to work an NFL game. It's the start of a long career as a line judge from the Akron suburb of Copley. When he finally retired from officiating in 2021, he had been first among officials in seniority.

6

July 6, 2022 — Browns trade Mayfield

When Baker Mayfield was drafted No. 1 overall by the Browns in 2018, he was supposed to be the team's long-term answer to the quarterbacking problems that had plagued the team through its recent history. Instead, he turned out to be another of what seemed like an endless stream of bodies that went through a revolving door to somewhere else.

The divorce between the Browns and Mayfield became official when the team traded the four-year veteran to the Carolina Panthers. Cleveland received a conditional draft choice.

Hopes were high for Mayfield when he first arrived on the Browns' roster. He debuted for Cleveland in game three of 2018, leading the team to a win. Baker broke an NFL rookie record for touchdowns that season with 27. He later guided the team to the playoffs in 2020.

However, the Browns did not offer Mayfield a contract extension, and the quarterback was bothered by injuries during a disappointing 2021 season. When Cleveland acquired

Deshaun Watson in a trade with Houston, Mayfield's departure became close to a foregone conclusion.

July 6, 1931 — Billy Burke wins the United States Open golf tournament at the Inverness Club in Toledo, finally winning the title after a pair of 36-hole playoffs. Burke went on to become the club pro at The Country Club in Cleveland.

July 6, 1956 — Jim Busby of the Indians hits a grand slam in his second consecutive game to tie a major league record.

July 6, 1970 — Indians manager Alvin Dark moves Sam McDowell from pitcher to second base for two batters in a strategic move in the eighth inning of a game against the Senators. McDowell catches a force-out to end the inning, then returns to the mound in the ninth and finishes off the 6-4 win over Washington.

July 6, 1991 — The Indians fire John McNamara as their manager and replace him with Mike Hargrove.

July 7, 2008 – Sabathia heads to Milwaukee

The Indians had the reigning Cy Young Award winner in 2008 in CC Sabathia, as he led the team to the playoffs the previous season. The problem was that he was due to become a free agent at the end of 2008, and they didn't think they could re-sign him. Besides, Cleveland had fought through injury problems during the first part of 2008 and didn't think it could contend. Therefore, it was time to see what Sabathia might fetch on the trade market.

On the other side, Milwaukee appeared to have a chance to reach the playoffs, but needed pitching. So the Indians acquired outfielder Matt LaPorta, pitchers Rob Bryson and Zack Jackson, and a player to be named, who turned out to be Michael Brantley. Except for Brantley, Cleveland didn't do as well as it hoped on the transaction. LaPorta had shown power-hitting skills on his way to the majors but ended up splitting time in the minors each year he was with Cleveland from 2009-12.

Many wondered how Sabathia would do as he grew older. But if there were doubters about Sabathia's longevity, he proved them wrong after signing with the New York Yankees after the 2008 season, as his career lasted until 2019. He won 251 games, and when he retired, he was thought to have a good chance at induction into the Hall of Fame.

July 7, 1923 — The Indians become the first team to score a run in every inning as they beat Boston, 27-3, in Cleveland's Dunn Field. Twelve different Cleveland players scored.

July 7, 1942 — A special exhibition All-Star baseball game takes place in Cleveland. The American League stars, who had played the day before in New York in the "regular" All-Star contest, beat a team of Service All-Stars, 5-0, before 62,094 in Municipal Stadium. More than $130,000 was raised in aid for soldiers, sailors and their families.

July 7, 1948 — Satchel Paige signs a contract on his 42nd birthday to play with the Indians. The pitcher, who was purchased from the Kansas City Monarchs of the Negro

League, said, "I ain't as fast as I used to be," according to the Associated Press. "But I'm a better pitcher. I used to overpower them; now I 'out-cute' them."

July 7, 1956 — Shirley Fry of Akron defeats Angela Buxton, 6-3, 6-1, to win the women's Wimbledon tennis title.

July 8, 2010 — LeBron announces his Decision

When the NBA off-season arrived after the 2009-10 year, LeBron James was 25 and had been a pro for seven years. Now he was a free agent and had on his resume one trip to the NBA Finals, in 2007.

So it was time for James to plot the next step in his career after turning pro right out of high school at Akron St. Vincent-St. Mary in 2003. When he decided to leave Cleveland, in some ways it might be compared to a student learning about life away from home at college.

Once he chose Miami, where he would team with executive Pat Riley and assist in wooing new teammates Dwyane Wade and Chris Bosh, most would say the announcement was at best clumsy. Journalist Jim Gray came up with the idea of having a prime-time television news program to present James' next destination. The proceeds from the advertising on the show were to be directed to Boys' and Girls' Clubs, but that fact was buried under the hype.

Near the end of the show, an uncomfortable-looking James finally got to the point. "I'm going to take my talents to South Beach and join the Miami Heat," he said. The addition of Wade in the backcourt and Bosh as a big man would give Coach Erik Spoelstra a lineup that became an instant contender for the NBA title. James became the subject of angry words from Cavaliers fans – both in that moment and over the four years of his Heat career that included two NBA titles. But all would be eventually forgiven.

July 8, 1935 — Municipal Stadium hosts the third All-Star Game in baseball history. Jimmie Foxx homers in the American League's 4-1 win.

July 8, 1997 — Sandy Alomar Jr. thrills the home crowd in Jacobs Field by hitting a two-run homer in the All-Star Game, powering the American League to a 3-1 win. Alomar is named the game's MVP.

July 9, 2019 — Bieber is the star of stars

Playing in an All-Star Game in an athlete's home stadium or arena is a special event. The cheers are louder than for any of the other stars. For reference, ask Shane Bieber. He joined Carlos Santana and Brad Hand as the representatives of the Indians in the 80th All-Star Game, which was held at Progressive Field. It was the midseason classic's first visit to Northeast Ohio in 22 years.

It can be difficult to stand out in such games these days in baseball, particularly for pitchers. They usually get an inning at most to display their talents as managers want to make sure everyone participates. Bieber's big moment came in the top of the fifth inning.

It couldn't have gone better. Bieber, who was picked for the squad as an injury replacement, struck out Wilson Contreras, Ketel Marte and Ronald Acuna Jr. It took Bieber

19 pitches to retire the side, and he left with the home fans chanting his name. American League pitchers finished the game with a total of 16 strikeouts, so Bieber fit right in.

The AL had a 4-1 lead after seven innings, but the NL came within one when Mets' slugger Pete Alonso – the winner of the home run-hitting contest the night before – drove in two runs. That was as close as the Nationals got, and the Americans had their seventh straight victory. Bieber picked up the night's MVP trophy. "Really just tried to fill up the zone as much as I could and go out there and get three outs," he said.

As a footnote, the Alonso story had a Northeast Ohio moment all its own. His cousin, Derek Morgan, a high school assistant baseball coach at Summit County's Woodridge High, was his pitcher during the Mets' star's home-run derby barrage.

July 9, 1963 — Ken McBride, one of the greatest athletes in Cleveland West High School history, is the starting pitcher for the American League in the All-Star Game in Cleveland. The Los Angeles Angels hurler gave up three runs in three innings in the National League's 5-3 win.

July 9, 1970 — A small crowd of 11,152 comes to a routine Indians game but the attraction is a night for Lou Boudreau as a tribute to a career that was capped by the World Series victory of 1948. Boudreau's uniform No. 5 is retired.

July 9, 1986 — Cavaliers' general manager Wayne Embry hires Lenny Wilkens as the team's new coach. It's the first time in NBA history that African Americans have held both of those positions of leadership on an NBA team.

10

July 10, 1968 – Pele comes to Cleveland

Edson Arantes do Nascimento might be too long of a name to catch on with the sports-loving public. His nickname did much better: Pele. The name was synonymous with soccer for decades around the world.

He was part of one of the great soccer dynasties in history, leading Brazil to World Cup championships in 1958, 1962 and 1970; no other player has been a part of a title-winning team three times. Pele joined Brazil's national team at 16, and averaged about a goal per game in international or league play.

He turned up in Cleveland one summer day in 1968 as his Santos team was touring the United States, and it played the Cleveland Stokers in an exhibition game at Municipal Stadium. The Stokers of the North American Soccer League won the game, 2-1. A crowd of 16,000 turned out, setting a record for the Stokers. It was the last hurrah for the franchise, which folded after the 1968 season.

As for Pele, he came to the United States in 1975 and spent most of three years with the New York Cosmos. His name was enough to draw thousands of fans to stadiums around North America, and that was a key moment in the rise of the sport in the USA. Pele was named the player of the century by the International Federation of Football and also FIFA in 1999.

July 10, 1932 — Johnny Burnett of the Indians has a record nine hits in one game, but Cleveland still drops an 18-17 decision to Philadelphia in 18 innings at League Park.

July 10, 1947 — Don Black pitches a no-hitter for the Indians before 47,871 in Municipal Stadium; decades later, it was still the largest crowd ever to witness a no-hitter. On September 13, 1948, Black suffered an aneurysm during a game and never played again. He died at age 42 in 1959.

July 10, 1962 — By a vote of 7-2, the NBA's Board of Governors invites the Cleveland Pipers of the American Basketball League to join its league if it can meet certain conditions. The NBA had wanted to expand from nine to 10 teams for scheduling purposes, as well as to damage the rival ABL by adding the team that had signed Ohio State All-American Jerry Lucas. However, Pipers executive George Steinbrenner did not pay the entry fee in the coming weeks, and the expansion plan was abandoned.

11

July 11, 2014 — James decides to return to Cleveland

When LeBron James' four seasons in Miami had ended, no one could say it wasn't a successful partnership. The Heat won two NBA titles, and lost in the Finals in the other two years. But now James' contract was up, and the speculation was intense on what the future held.

The Cavs had some good young talent, while the Heat was getting old. James decided he could win in Cleveland. A deal was struck a few days into the free agency period. He only signed a two-year contract (reportedly worth $42.1 million according to Akron native and reporter Brian Windhorst of ESPN) that included an opt-out in 2015. The money was good, but the idea of coming home and trying to win a title proved irresistible.

"My goal is still to win as many titles as possible, no question. But what's most important for me is bringing one trophy back to Northeast Ohio," James wrote in an article for *Sports Illustrated*. "I looked at other teams, but I wasn't going to leave Miami for anywhere except Cleveland. The more time passed, the more it felt right. This is what makes me happy."

July 11, 1914 — The Red Sox beat the Indians, 4-3, and the win goes to a rookie pitcher who was appearing in his first major league game: Babe Ruth. The first batter Ruth faced was Jack Graney, who singled. Graney went on to a long broadcasting career in Cleveland.

July 11, 2002 — Charlie Manuel gets his answer to an ultimatum about his status as Indians' manager: he's fired and replaced by interim skipper Joel Skinner.

12

July 12, 1951 — Reynolds quiets the Indians

A crowd of 39,195 settled into their seats on a Thursday night in Municipal Stadium as the Yankees got ready to play the Indians. No one probably anticipated much offense. The pitching matchup had Allie Reynolds of New York going up against Bob Feller of Cleveland.

The tone was set in the first inning, when both sides went down in order. Reynolds had the first jam of the game when he walked two batters, but the Indians couldn't get a run across. Feller walked two in the top of the third, but escaped as well. The outs continued to pile up from there. Fans who looked at the scoreboard after five innings saw a 0-0-1 for the

Yankees at the end of the line score, while below it was a 0-0-0 for the Indians. A double no-hitter was in progress.

With one out in the sixth, rookie right fielder Mickey Mantle solved Feller with a double to center field. He didn't advance though. Then in the seventh, Akron native Gene Woodling homered to put New York ahead, 1-0.

Meanwhile, Reynolds kept getting outs. In the ninth, he set down pinch-hitter Bob Lemon, Dale Mitchell and Bobby Avila to complete the no-hitter. Reynolds struck out four and walked three, while Feller's four-hitter came up short of a victory.

July 12, 1936 — Dave Albritton of Cleveland and Corney Johnson finish in a tie for the high jump title at the U.S. Olympic Trials, jointly setting a world record at 6-foot-9.75.

July 12, 1954 — During the All-Star Game festivities held in Cleveland, Major League Baseball players announced the formation of an association. It was not called a labor union because no member dues were being charged. The first project of the association was creating a pension fund. In 1956, Bob Feller was the American League player representative to the owners and Ralph Kiner served for the National League.

13

July 13, 1963 — Wynn reaches the 300-win mark

There was something noble about Early Wynn's quest to reach one of the most magical milestones in pitching. Wynn broke into the majors at age 19 in 1939 with the Washington Senators, and he was still throwing more than two decades later. But in 1962, Wynn went 7-15 with a 4.46 ERA for the Chicago White Sox. He had won the 299th game of his career... but couldn't get No. 300 in the final four starts of the season.

Then the White Sox released him. He didn't have a team for the first two months of the season, and it looked like the milestone was gone for good. Then Indians manager George "Birdie" Tebbetts reached out to Wynn on June 1 and asked if he was interested in his second tour of duty in Cleveland. So Wynn was back on the mound on June 21 in a loss to Chicago. Wynn then had two no-decisions.

On this date, Wynn was the starter for the Indians in a game in Kansas City. Cleveland jumped out to a 5-1 lead, but Wynn gave up three runs in the bottom of the fifth to allow the Athletics to have a chance. Early exited the game knowing that he would be the winning pitcher if the Indians maintained the lead. They did, taking a 7-4 decision. "I was pooped," Wynn told the *Plain Dealer*. "Don't know why, but my legs felt it right from the start. I had good stuff, but I couldn't get it over the plate."

Wynn started only one more game that season, and finished with a 300-244 record for his spectacular career. He was elected to the Hall of Fame in 1972.

July 13, 1954 — Al Rosen of the Indians hits two homers – out of the six struck in the game – to lead the American League to an 11-9 win over the National League. The game is played in front of 68,752 in Municipal Stadium.

14

July 14, 1966 — Jim Brown announces his retirement

If Jim Brown wanted to do something dramatic, well, he was in the right place. Brown was in the United Kingdom in the summer of 1966, working as an actor for director Robert Aldrich's upcoming World War II movie, "The Dirty Dozen." Work had gone on for a longer than expected period of time.

That meant he probably would miss the start of training camp with the Browns, as his 10th NFL season was approaching. Owner Art Modell was concerned about that. He announced in June that Brown would be placed on the suspended list and fined for every day of camp that he missed.

The future Hall of Famer was not happy about that message. So Brown sent a letter to Modell in early July saying he would leave the Browns, and then made his retirement public at a news conference on this day.

The sports world was stunned. This was arguably the best player in the National Football League at that point in his career, and he wasn't even 30 years old yet. Few ever walked away from a situation like that – Barry Sanders' departure might be the closest comparison – but Brown was a man of his word and he called it a career. Brown did more acting in the years after football and was involved in a variety of other projects. As a little postscript to his football life, on December 12, 1983, he was pictured on *Sports Illustrated* magazine's cover wearing a Raiders uniform with a headline that speculated whether he could make an NFL comeback at age 47.

July 14, 1946 — In a game against Boston, Indians manager Lou Boudreau applies what became known as the "Williams Shift" against Red Sox slugger Ted Williams. Boudreau moved all four infielders to the right of second base. Williams hits a double against the new alignment.

July 14, 1970 — Pete Rose crashes into Indians' catcher Ray Fosse to score the winning run for the National League on the final play of the All-Star Game, causing a shoulder separation that hampered Fosse's batting prowess over the remainder of his career.

July 14, 1973 — Tom Weiskopf, who was born in Massillon and raised in Cleveland, captures his only major golf championship – the British Open at Troon. He finishes three shots ahead of Neil Coles and Johnny Miller.

July 14, 1976 — The California Golden Seals announce they are moving to Cleveland for the 1976-77 season, as the transaction is approved by the NHL.

15

July 15, 1994 — Belle's cork is popped

Remember Albert Belle and his corked bat? It is still a great story – not because Belle was caught cheating, but because of what happened once the whole episode gained momentum.

The Indians were playing a series in Chicago when Carlos Baerga drove in Kenny Lofton with the first run of the game in the top of the first. That brought Albert Belle to the plate for Cleveland. Chicago manager Gene Lamont told umpire Dave Phillips that the bat should be inspected because it might be illegal. Phillips confiscated the bat, and said it would be sent to the American League office.

Belle was not happy. He grounded into a fielder's choice. Then the story took on a legendary turn. Pitcher Jason Grimsley volunteered to retrieve Belle's bat and replace it.

To accomplish that, he had to climb into the duct work at Comiskey Park and invade the umpires' dressing room. There he switched Belle's bat for a Paul Sorrento model.

The umpires suspected something was up when they saw the Sorrento bat. When the investigation took place, the Indians handed over Belle's bat. It was found to be filled with cork, and the outfielder was suspended for 10 days. The punishment was later reduced to seven days. Five years later, Grimsley confessed to his part of the drama.

July 15, 1973 — Akron native and Buchtel High School and Kent State player Art Kusnyer is behind the plate as Nolan Ryan of the Angels throws his second career no-hitter. Kusnyer appeared in 139 games in his career for four teams in the 1970s.

July 15, 2020 — Myles Garrett signs a five-year contract extension with the Browns for $125 million. The deal makes him the highest-paid non-quarterback in the NFL.

16

July 16, 1987 – A prediction goes embarrassingly wrong

It might be one of the most famous magazine covers in Cleveland's sports history. The screaming headline read, "Believe it! Cleveland is the best team in the American League," as power hitters Cory Snyder and Joe Carter smiled in the portrait photo. It gave the Indians a booster shot of optimism as they got ready for the 1987 baseball season. Could this be the first year for a pennant or championship since 1954?

No, it wasn't. In fact, if anyone wanted to argue that *Sports Illustrated* does bring on a "cover jinx," this could be Exhibit A. The Indians started their season with two losses, beat the Blue Jays by a score of 14-3, and then lost the next seven games. Cleveland was already last in the American League East at that point, and wouldn't budge an inch upward for the rest of the season.

Naturally, when a season goes wrong, someone has to pay a price – and it's usually the manager. Sure enough, Pat Corrales lost his job on this day. Corrales had guided the Indians to an 84-78 record in 1986, but the team was 31-56 when he was dismissed. "Doc" Edwards took over for him, and did a little better the rest of the way (30-45).

Plenty went wrong that season, but the pitching staff had more than its share of problems. The team ERA was 5.71. Two of the starters – Steve Carlton and Phil Niekro – would end up in the Hall of Fame, but they were also well over 40 years of age during this season. Three pitchers finished with seven wins on the season to lead the team: Niekro, Tom Candiotti and Scott Bailes. Closer Doug Jones had eight saves for what was nicknamed "The Bullpen from Hell."

July 16, 2004 — Victor Martinez has his only three-homer game as an Indian, and Cleveland scores a total of 11 runs in the last four innings to take an 18-6 win over Seattle.

17

July 17, 1941 — DiMaggio's streak is snapped

New York Yankees star Joe DiMaggio recorded a hit in 56 straight games during the 1941 season, one of the great accomplishments in baseball history. The story of how the streak ended attracted plenty of attention.

DiMaggio had gone past the existing modern record of Summit County native George Sisler (41 games) earlier, so it might be said some pressure had been relieved. The streak was at 56 on this day when the Indians hosted the Yankees at Municipal Stadium, and a crowd of 67,468 turned out.

In the top of the first, DiMaggio hit a line drive down the third base line. Cleveland's Ken Keltner, playing deep, gloved it and threw out DiMaggio by a half-step. Three innings later, the Yankee outfielder took a walk from lefty Al Smith.

In the seventh, DiMaggio hit another smash down the third base line. Keltner was playing even deeper and closer to the line this time, and he came up with the ball smoothly. Keltner's quick throw to first beat DiMaggio for the out. That meant there might only be one more chance for DiMaggio to keep the streak going. But in his last at-bat, he bounced into a force play at second. When the Yankees couldn't send the game into extra innings, the streak was over.

July 17, 1979 — Sid Monge is the Indians' representative at the All-Star Game in the Kingdome in Seattle, won by the National League, 5-4. Monge, in the midst of the best season of his career, doesn't get to play as the American League only uses five pitchers.

18

July 18, 1919 — Babe's homer leads to a firing

Babe Ruth remains one of the most magical names in baseball history. He certainly made the Indians' chances of winning a game disappear on this day.

Ruth had been a standout pitcher for most of the first five seasons of his career. However, managers had figured out that his bat needed to be in the lineup every day. The 1919 season in Boston was a year of transition for Babe. He played plenty in the outfield but also pitched in 17 games. The Babe was in right field for the game this day at League Park in Cleveland.

The score was tied, 3-3, when the Indians came up with four runs in the bottom of the eighth. That probably should have been enough, but the Red Sox weren't done. They had scratched out a run when Ruth came to the plate. Manager Lee Fohl of the Indians brought in lefty Fritz Coumbe, who hadn't pitched in seven weeks, to face the Babe. Centerfielder Tris Speaker yelled during the switch that Fohl should have brought in a different pitcher. Ruth already had a two-run homer on the day, but he outdid himself this time with a grand-slam. It was the difference in a 9-8 Boston win.

As you might expect, Cleveland's fans did some serious second-guessing about that pitching change. The next day, Fohl resigned as manager, saying "I feel the fans are not for me." Apparently management agreed with Speaker's opinion of the move – he was named player-manager.

July 18, 1962 — Talk about slow starts! The Indians give up grand-slam home runs to Bob Allison and Harmon Killebrew in the first inning, and go on to a 14-3 loss to the Twins.

July 18, 1995 — Albert Belle sends everyone at Jacobs Field home happy with a rare ending to a game in the form of a walk-off grand slam. It gives the Indians a 7-5 win over the Angels.

19

July 19, 1910 — No. 500 for Cy Young

At long last, Cy Young looked as if he was starting to slow down. The legendary pitcher had enjoyed a fabulous run of 19 straight seasons with at least 13 wins, and 20 or more victories in 14 consecutive years.

But at 43, and now playing for Cleveland in the American League, Young had lost some of his effectiveness. He only needed three wins to reach 500 for his career, but entering the day's game with the Senators, Young had a record of 2-7 and was stuck at 499.

Off to the mound he went in Washington, and gave up a run in the bottom of the first. For quite a while, it looked as if that would be the only scoring of the game, as the Senators held the 1-0 lead in the ninth. But Cleveland scored twice in the top of the inning, and now Young needed three outs to get No. 500. He fell short, giving up a run, and the game went to extra innings.

The teams played a scoreless 10th, and in the 11th, the Indians took no chances. They scored three runs to make it a 5-2 game, and Young finished Washington off for the win. The immortal went on to win 11 more games in his career, bringing his career total to 511. He also had 315 losses – another major league record.

July 19, 1909 — Playing shortstop for an injured Terry Turner, Cleveland's Neal Ball catches Amby McConnell's line drive, steps on second base and then tags Jake Stahl, executing the first unassisted triple play in major league history.

July 19, 1974 — Dick Bosman's throwing error in the fourth inning is the only blemish as the Indians' pitcher no-hits the Athletics in a 4-0 win.

July 19, 1975 — Karl Wallenda, known as "The Great Wallenda," walks on a tightrope from foul pole to foul pole between games of a doubleheader involving the Indians and Angels in Municipal Stadium. The action provides more thrills than the Indians do, as they are swept by scores of 8-0 and 3-2.

July 20, 2004 — Hafner's bat sets off fireworks

It was "get-away day" for the Indians in Anaheim, California. Cleveland was finishing up a two-game series with the Angels before flying home to play the White Sox. Considering what happened in that series, it's a wonder that the Angels didn't give Travis Hafner a ride to the airport to make sure he had left town.

The Indians slugger started the game with a two-run homer in the top of the first off Aaron Sele. Then in the 10th, Hafner came through with a two-run blast off Troy Percival, the Angels' closer. It lifted Cleveland to an 8-5 win. The designated hitter went 3-for-4 with two homers and five RBI.

But he was just getting warmed up for the next day. Hafner hit a two-run homer in the top of the third, and connected for a third straight round-tripper in the fifth. He had one last going-away present for the Angels, hitting his third homer of the day in a 14-5 romp by the Indians. Hafner, whose nickname was "Pronk" (because some teammates said he was "part project, part donkey") finished 4-for-4 with six RBIs.

Do the math – the slugger had hit five homers in two games, tying an Indians record set by Earl Averill. But Hafner and the Indians lost their magic on the way home. Chicago beat Cleveland, 14-0, the next night in Jacobs Field.

July 20, 1987 — Phil Niekro picks up the 318th win of his great pitching career as the Indians defeat the Royals, 9-5. Niekro goes five innings and allows five runs. It turns out to be his last win as well, as the future Hall of Fame retired at the end of the 1987 season. Brother Joe had 221 victories, and their total of 539 is the most by any brothers in baseball history.

July 20, 1993 — Carlos Baerga hits the final grand slam in the history of Cleveland Municipal Stadium; Joe Boever of Oakland was the opposing pitcher.

21

July 21, 1985 — Dickinson enters golf's winner's circle

Judy Clark Dickinson must have felt like a bridesmaid on the LPGA tour for several years. Then, not only did she catch the bouquet by finally winning a tournament, but she got married in the same year.

The Akron native began playing on the women's tour in 1978. In 1980, she had her best tournament of her career with a fourth-place showing in the U.S. Open. Clark earned a second in at the Henredon Classic a year later, and duplicated it in 1984 at the Mayflower Classic. Still, there were no wins to her credit.

Finally, in 1985, she broke through at the Boston Five Classic. A second-round 66 was instrumental in giving her momentum, and Clark went on to a three-shot win over Donna Caponi and Jane Geddes. It became a true year to remember when she married PGA Tour player Gardner Dickinson.

Dickinson won two more titles in 1986 and a fourth in 1992. She's an advisor to the World Golf Hall of Fame, and has been active in community events for many years.

July 21, 1954 — While the Indians are playing to a rain-shortened 7-7 tie in Boston, the Yankees are losing to the White Sox, 15-3. That puts Cleveland into undisputed first place in the American League pennant race, and the Indians will stay there for the rest of the season.

July 21, 1996 — The Indians trade Eddie Murray to the Orioles for pitcher Kent Mercker.

22

July 22, 1996 — Ghaffari just misses a huge upset

It's not easy to beat someone considered the best ever in his sport. Matt Ghaffari knows that, but no one can say he didn't give it his best effort.

Ghaffari was born in Iran but moved to the United States as a child. He grew up in New Jersey and went to college at Cleveland State University, where he had a good but not exceptional record as a wrestler. But he found his niche in Greco-Roman wrestling, which is more restrictive than the freestyle version of the sport. Ghaffari qualified for the United States Olympic team in 1992, and then spent the next four years getting better. It was back to the Olympics in 1996 in Atlanta.

Waiting for him there in the super-heavyweight division was Aleksandr Karelin, considered the greatest wrestler of all time in that sport. Karelin hadn't lost an international match since 1987, and hadn't given up a point in 1988.

Ghaffari gave it his best, but came away with a narrow 1-0 loss in overtime. Still, it was good for a silver medal. Ghaffari is one of the greatest Greco-Roman wrestlers in American history. He still calls Cleveland home.

July 22, 1966 — Pro golfer Sam Snead finishes the second round of one of golf's "majors" – the PGA – with a 36-hole score of 139 at Firestone Country Club in Akron, giving him a one-shot lead. The surprise is that Snead is age 54 at the time. In the final two rounds, Snead shot 75 and 73 for a 287 total and ended the tournament in a five-way tie for fourth place, seven shots behind champion Al Geiberger. First-place prize was $25,000. Snead won $5,000.

July 22, 1988 — The Cleveland Force folds after 10 years in the Major Indoor Soccer League – only weeks after reaching the MISL finals.

July 23, 2021 — Welcome, Cleveland Guardians

Cleveland's American League baseball team had been called the Indians since 1915. The team had been the Cleveland Naps since 1903, after the team's superstar player/manager, Nap Lajoie. But when he was traded, the Indians were born.

The name lasted for more than a century. But the meaning and implications of words change over time, and the use of the word "Indians" angered many – particularly in Native American communities. Besides, a company has a problem when it is somewhat afraid to use its full business name.

The search began in 2020, with the announcement that the Indians tag would be dropped after the 2020 season. About 1,200 names supposedly were considered. One of the most popular ideas was the Spiders, which was used by a Cleveland baseball team from 1887 to 1899. But that name already was taken by the University of Richmond, and the team wanted something unique.

The Guardians certainly qualified. The name comes from the 43-foot "guardians of traffic" on the Hope Memorial Bridge, a short distance from the team's stadium. It's said to be a tribute to the loyalty of the people of Northeast Ohio – to each other, to the community, and to the team. The new name went into use as soon as the 2021 season was over. We'll see if it lasts a century.

July 23, 1979 — Dave Garcia is the pick to replace Jeff Torborg as the manager of the Indians.

July 23, 1996 — Future Ohio resident Dominique Moceanu is part of the United States' women's gymnastic team that wins a gold medal in Atlanta. Moceanu graduated from John Carroll University, married an Ohio State gymnast and became an author and businesswoman.

July 23, 1998 — Cleveland business executive Al Lerner announces he will bid to own the new expansion Browns franchise. Lerner is accompanied by former San Francisco 49ers executive Carmen Policy, ex-Browns quarterback Bernie Kosar and Cleveland Mayor Michael White.

24

July 24, 1911 – Top players gather to honor Joss

It has been called the first "All-Star" game in the history of major league baseball. That's because it wasn't a formal, planned contest, but rather a fund-raising game after a tragedy that hit close to home for the sport.

Addie Joss had been a mainstay for Cleveland's baseball team since arriving in 1902. During eight full seasons, he threw seven one-hitters and averaged about 20 wins per season – and never dipped below 10 wins in any of them. Joss' earned-run average over the years was 1.89, and he led the league in that category twice. Joss only pitched in 13 games in 1910 because of a sore elbow.

In an exhibition game in April 1911, Joss collapsed on the field. Eleven days later, he died of tubercular meningitis just after his 31st birthday. The Naps decided to organize a charity game to help Addie's wife, Lillian, and their two children. It was set for July 24.

A crowd of 15,272 jammed League Park for the game. Among the stars playing the Naps that day were Tris Speaker, Eddie Collins, Ty Cobb, "Home Run" Baker, Sam Crawford, "Smoky Joe" Wood and Walter Johnson. It might have been the greatest lineup ever assembled at that time. The All-Stars won the game, 5-3. The Baseball Hall of Fame later waived the 10-year service rule – the only time it has happened – to induct Joss.

July 24, 1952 — Harrison Dillard of Cleveland wins the 110-meter dash at the Olympics. Since he won the 100-meter dash in the London Olympics of 1948, Dillard becomes the first man to "double" in those two specialties. Dillard's performances in 1948 and '52 result in four gold medals won.

July 24, 1966 — Pro golfer Tony Lema, known as "Champagne Tony" because he would treat golf media members to champagne when he won, is killed in a crash that occurs on a small plane he boarded to leave Akron upon finishing his final round of the 1966 PGA tournament at Firestone Country Club. The casualties included Lema's wife and the pilot and co-pilot. Lema was traveling to Joliet, Illinois, to play on a Monday in a one-day, $12,000 event. An airline strike left Lema unable to fly commercially, which led to the decision to hire a charter.

July 24, 2020 — The Indians finally begin the baseball season, which had been delayed for more than three months because of the COVID-19 pandemic. Shane Bieber celebrates with 14 strikeouts in a 2-0 win over the Royals, setting a team record for whiffs on Opening Day.

25

July 25, 2018 — Love decides to stay in Cleveland

The Cavaliers and their fans needed a bit of good news in the summer of 2018. LeBron James had left the team after his second stay with the Cavs, signing with the Los Angeles Lakers as a free agent. It was clear that Cleveland had some rebuilding ahead.

Keeping Kevin Love in town became a top priority of Cavalier management. The team got the job done, with a contract extension of four years for $120 million. The deal would kick in during the summer of 2019, so Love was set to stay on the team through 2023.

"We got a little bit spoiled with four straight trips to the Finals," Love said to reporters. "But now we get to build this thing again." Then Love signed his contract in front of workers who were fixing up Quicken Loans Arena, and even posed for a selfie with all of them in thanks for their efforts.

July 25, 1930 — The Philadelphia Athletics record a pair of triple steals in their game with the Indians. More than 95 years later, it was still the only time in baseball history that such an event happened.

July 25, 1935 — Bob Feller signs his first contract with the Indians for a bonus of $1.

July 25, 1946 — Indians owner Bill Veeck announces the team will move its spring training site from Clearwater, Florida, to Tucson, Arizona, beginning in 1947.

July 26, 1972 — Crusaders sign Cheevers for first season

In the spring of 1972, Gerry Cheevers was on top of the hockey world. He had been the primary goalie for the Boston Bruins, who had just won the Stanley Cup in the National Hockey League by defeating the New York Rangers in the finals. It was Boston's second championship in three years. Certainly with players like Bobby Orr and Phil Esposito on the roster, there was a good chance that more titles were on the horizon.

However, the new Cleveland Crusaders of the new World Hockey Association were looking to lure top talent from the NHL to play for them in the fall. They found someone to listen to an offer in Cheevers, who perhaps realized that it would be difficult for the Bruins to pay everyone on their loaded roster. Cheevers accepted a contract offer on this date for seven years and $1.4 million, considered a ton of money. John McKenzie and Derek Sanderson also departed the Bruins for similar deals.

Cheevers was the obvious star for the Crusaders, playing their home games in the Cleveland Arena for two seasons. The franchise was owned by Nick Mileti, who had moved the Cleveland Barons of the AHL to Jacksonville to make room for the Crusaders. The WHA team had a mix of NHL players who weren't stars and some veteran minor leaguers who took this as a shot at the big time with more money. Cheevers was the best goalie in the WHA in 1972-73, and his team made it to the semifinals of the playoffs.

During the 1975-76 season, Cheevers returned to Boston when he was involved in a dispute over finances with the Crusaders' management. He stayed through 1980 before retiring, and later coached the Bruins.

July 26, 1998 — Larry Doby, who was the second Major League Baseball player to break the color barrier when he signed with the Indians in 1947, is inducted into the Baseball Hall of Fame.

July 26, 2020 — Pitcher Carlos "Cookie" Carrasco gets a 9-2 victory in the third game of the long-delayed Indians' 2020 season as he continues a comeback from a leukemia diagnosis in 2019. Carrasco struck out 10 Kansas City Royals in six innings while allowing five hits and two earned runs.

27

July 27, 2006 — Bentley's career ends abruptly

The second version of the Browns, who began play as an expansion team in 1999, didn't have many highlights in their first two decades of play. Not only were winning seasons quite rare (two times), but the franchise had several unlucky moments, too.

Such was the case on the first day of training camp in 2006. The Browns had targeted LeCharles Bentley, a center for the Saints, when free agency began in the spring. Bentley was considered by some as the best player available in the entire free agent class, a Pro Bowl-caliber player. He was a Cleveland native who went to St. Ignatius High School and then Ohio State. The offensive lineman signed for six years and $36 million. "I can die happy now. This has been my dream," he told reporters.

On the first day of training camp, there was a collision of bodies, and Bentley didn't get up. He had suffered a knee injury that team general manager Phil Savage called one of the worst in NFL history.

During rehab, Bentley developed a staph infection that did even more damage to his knee. He almost died, and thought about having an amputation. Bentley spent two and a half years trying to improve his knee, and did get cleared to play football by doctors. But he decided retirement was a better option. Bentley never played a game in a Browns' uniform.

July 27, 1974 — Browns' kicker and offensive tackle Lou Groza is inducted into the Pro Football Hall of Fame. Exactly 22 years later, Dan Dierdorf (Glenwood High School in Stark County) also receives football's greatest honor.

July 27, 1978 — Indians second baseman Duane Kuiper becomes one of three modern-day players to hit two bases-loaded triples in the same game. The others were: Elmer Valo of the Philadelphia A's in 1949 and Billy Bruton of the Milwaukee Braves in 1959. Cleveland beats the Yankees, 17-5.

July 28, 2000 — Sexson sent to Brewers for pitching

The Indians had a 51-48 record on the morning of July 28. That put them 10 games behind the leader in the American League Central. They had plenty of offense in such players as Manny Ramirez, Roberto Alomar and Jim Thome, but their pitching staff was thin.

The player the Indians chose to shop was Richie Sexson, a 25-year-old who had 16 homers at that point in the season. Sexson would be an attractive target for anyone looking for power. Cleveland was in the midst of a run where it always seemed to have extra hitting and not enough pitching.

So Sexson, Kane Davis, Paul Rigdon and Marco Scutaro packed to go to Milwaukee, while Cleveland acquired pitchers Bob Wickman, Jason Bere and Steve Woodward. It was one of the biggest trades in Brewers' history, and a good-sized one for the Indians as well.

The Indians did get better. They finished 90-72, but they just missed catching the teams in front of them for a wild-card spot. Wickman worked out quite well for the Indians, as he became their closer for the next few seasons. Wickman totaled 139 saves, which was the team record until it was surpassed by Cody Allen in 2018. Bere only stayed through the end of 2000, and Woodward was generally ineffective. Sexson hit 45 homers twice for the Brewers in three seasons, but saw his production decline in his 30s for other teams.

July 28, 1984 — Former Browns lineman Mike McCormack is inducted into the Pro Football Hall of Fame.

July 28, 1990 — The Indians retire uniform No. 18 to honor pitcher and coach Mel Harder.

July 28, 2006 — Jeremy Sowers throws his second straight shutout, the first Indian to do that since Dick Tidrow in 1972, as he beats the Mariners, 1-0.

29

July 29, 1996 — Baerga goes to Mets in trade

If there was a symbol for the rise of the Cleveland Indians during the 1990s, Carlos Baerga was it. He was acquired from the Padres in the Joe Carter trade, and eventually found a home at second base. Baerga was an All-Star in his third season with the Indians, and he became one of the most popular players on the roster.

But in 1996, the Indians weren't happy that Baerga showed up for training camp about 20 pounds overweight, which he blamed on injuries suffered over the winter. His offensive production dropped off in the first four months of the season, and so the Indians were ready to listen when the Mets brought up Baerga's name in trade talks.

Baerga and utility infielder Alvaro Espinosa went to New York and Cleveland acquired infielders Jeff Kent and Jose Vizcaino. Mets' general manager Joe McIlvaine said at the time, "I don't think a year ago we could've acquired Carlos Baerga."

Baerga spent two-plus years with the Mets, and never hit .300 there or had 10 homers in a season. He departed after 1998 and never was a regular again in the majors. Kent was traded to the Giants in November, and he turned into one of the best second basemen in the league over the next decade. The Indians gave up on Baerga at the right time in terms of baseball skills, but fans who had enjoyed his role in helping the Indians become a pennant winner in 1995 were still hurt to see him go elsewhere.

July 29, 1921 — To celebrate the 125th anniversary of the founding of the city of Cleveland, a baseball game is played featuring former well-known players. The teams were called the "Old-Timers" and the "Sand Lotters." Denton True "Cy" Young, at age 54, pitched two innings for the Old-Timers, who went on to win by 11-6. Young had retired from the major leagues 10 years earlier in 1911 at age 44.

July 29, 2009 — The Indians trade Cliff Lee and Ben Francisco to the Phillies for Carlos Carrasco, Jason Knapp, Jason Donald and Lou Marson. Lee went 7-4 for Philadelphia and helped the team reach the World Series that year.

July 29, 2013 — Jason Giambi strokes a walk-off homer in the Indians' 3-2 win over the White Sox at Progressive Field. At 42, he breaks Henry Aaron's record as the oldest player to ever hit a walk-off homer.

July 29, 2018 — Indians first baseman Jim Thome is inducted into the Baseball Hall of Fame. He is part of a class with Vladimir Guerrero, Chipper Jones, Jack Morris, Trevor Hoffman and Alan Trammell.

30

July 30, 1977 — Willis leads the way for Browns

This is the day on the calendar that has become closely associated with players with ties to Northeast Ohio reaching the Pro Football Hall of Fame in Canton. It wasn't quite an annual parade down the interstate for the induction ceremonies, but you get the idea.

Bill Willis had played for Paul Brown at Ohio State in college, and did well enough to be named to the College Football Hall of Fame. When it was time for him to graduate in 1945, African Americans hadn't played in the National Football League since 1933. But Paul Brown was involved in the formation of the Cleveland Browns of the rival pro league, the All-America Football Conference, and still knew about Willis. He was invited to camp, made the Browns roster and – along with teammate Marion Motley – integrated pro football in the first game of the 1946 season. Willis played eight seasons and was an All-Pro in all of them; this was the day he was inducted.

In 1983, Paul Warfield received his call to Canton. The native of Warren had been one of the premier receivers in the league during his career, with roughly half of it coming with the Browns. Warfield was traded to Miami in 1970, although he did finish his career in Cleveland. Leroy Kelly followed Warfield to the Hall in 1994. Kelly had big shoes to fill as he became a starting running back when Jim Brown retired. Kelly did fine, rushing for 1,000 yards and earning All-Pro honors for the next three seasons. At the time of his retirement in 1974, Kelly was fourth on the NFL's all-time rushing list.

Finally, Alan Page certainly didn't need to ask directions to attend his induction ceremony. He grew up in Canton and attended Canton Central Catholic High School. One summer he worked on the construction crew that built the Hall of Fame. Page played in nine Pro Bowls once he got to the Minnesota Vikings, and was the first defensive player in NFL history ever to be named the league's Most Valuable Player. From there, Page went into legal work, and became the first African American to serve on the Minnesota State Supreme Court.

July 30, 1962 — The plan to admit basketball's Cleveland Pipers to the NBA formally collapses, as the league formally votes to rescind its membership offer.

July 30, 1968 — The Indians start a rally in the bottom of the first inning of their game at Municipal Stadium against Washington when Dave Nelson singles and Russ Snyder walks. With a hit-and-run play signalled, Joe Azcue lines the ball to Ron Hansen at shortstop. Hansen steps on second and then tags Snyder after he passes second base for an unassisted triple play. It was the eighth such play in history and the first in 41 years. The Indians recover to win the game, 10-1. As for Hansen's night at the plate? Not so good – four strikeouts.

31

July 31, 1932 — Indians have new part-time home

It took a year, but the Indians finally got around to playing a home game in Municipal Stadium on this date. The facility had been open for a little more than a year, but Cleveland waited until this point to move some games to the era's "big house."

The Indians brought back names like Cy Young, Tris Speaker and Nap Lajoie. Tommy Connolly, the head of the umpiring office in the American League, even came back to duty for the game. Connolly was a walking historical marker, since he had been at the openings of Fenway Park, Comiskey Park, Yankee Stadium and Griffith Stadium.

Mel Harder of the Indians was the Cleveland starter that day, and he faced a lineup from Philadelphia with all-time greats such as Jimmie Foxx, Al Simmons and Mickey Cochrane. Lefty Grove of the Athletics was matched against Harder, so it was easy to anticipate a pitcher's duel. The 76,989 in the building certainly got one.

Neither side could score until the eighth inning. Cochrane singled home a run for Philadelphia, and that was all Grove needed. He pitched a four-hit shutout to earn a 1-0 victory. The Indians didn't play in Municipal Stadium very often for the next 15 years, using it only for games that figured to draw big crowds such as Sunday doubleheaders. That changed in 1947, when owner Bill Veeck moved all of the team's games there.

July 31, 1948 – Harrison Dillard of Cleveland claims the gold medal at the Olympic Games in London with a victory in the 100-meter dash.

July 31, 1963 - Four Indians batters in a row hit home runs off Los Angeles Angels pitcher Paul Foytack – Woodie Held, pitcher Pedro Ramos, Tito Francona and Larry Brown – in the sixth inning of a game with the Angels. Ramos hit another homer and earned the win in a 9-5 decision.

July 31, 1971 — Running back Jim Brown of the Browns is inducted into the Pro Football Hall of Fame.

July 31, 2010 — The Indians complete a three-team trade that sends Corey Kluber to Cleveland from San Diego. The Indians send Jake Westbrook to the Cardinals.

August 1, 1932 — Walsh stars in Olympics

The story of Stella Walsh should be an easy one to tell: Local athlete wins gold medal. It's more complicated than that for a number of reasons, and we can only scratch the surface here.

Walsh was born with the name Stefania Walasiewicz as the family lived in Poland at the time, but they soon moved to America and settled in Cleveland. With a new Americanized last name of Walsh, Stella went to South High School and soon became one of the top female sprinters in the country. She set a world record in the 100-yard dash.

Walsh was not an American citizen at that point, so she couldn't run for the USA in the 1928 Olympics. Walsh got a job in New York at the Polish consulate, adopted Polish citizenship, and ran for Poland in the 1932 Summer Olympics. She debuted as an Olympic athlete in the 100-meter dash on this day. On August 2, she won the gold medal, tying the world record in the process. After the 1936 Olympics in Berlin (silver medal), Walsh went back to America and competed there. She eventually became a citizen, and was inducted into the U.S. Track and Field Hall of Fame in 1975.

Walsh was killed as a bystander in an armed robbery attempt in Cleveland in 1980. An autopsy revealed that she had a disease called mosaicism, in which her sex organs were ambiguous in nature. A coroner ruled that Walsh was by most standards a female, and she lived her entire life that way. However, discussions continued over the years about her Olympic eligibility.

August 1, 1979 — The Browns reacquire defensive end Jack Gregory from the Giants for a seventh-round draft pick in 1980.

August 1, 1986 — The city of Cleveland comes down with a mild case of "pennant fever," as the contending Indians and the Yankees draw 65,934 for a twi-night doubleheader.

2

August 2, 1979 — Munson killed in plane crash

A plane crash at the Akron-Canton Airport shocked not only the people in Ohio, but everyone in New York and across Major League Baseball, as Yankees catcher Thurman Munson died.

Munson grew up in Canton and attended Lehman High School, where he was a standout in football, basketball and baseball. From there, it was on to Kent State University, and he became a first-round draft pick of the Yankees in 1968, thanks, in part, to scouting by former Yankee outfielder and Akron native Gene Woodling. Munson moved up through the minor leagues, and claimed a starting job in New York by the end of the 1969 season.

For much of the 1970s, Munson was a leader on and off the field for New York. He was selected as the team's first captain since Lou Gehrig. Munson helped the Yankees reach the World Series in 1976 and win it in 1977 and 1978. He became one of two catchers to win a Rookie of the Year award, a Most Valuable Player award, a Gold Glove and a World Series title. The other was Johnny Bench.

Munson had developed a love of flying, and often went home to see his family in Canton on off-days. He was practicing takeoffs and landings with a flight instructor and a friend on this day. The fourth and final landing went wrong, as the plane hit a tree stump and burst into flames. Munson was killed, while the two passengers survived.

August 2, 1936 — Dave Albritton, a teammate of Jesse Owens at Cleveland East Technical High School, wins a silver medal in the high jump at the 1936 Olympic Games in Berlin.

August 2, 1975 — Former Browns wide receiver Dante Lavelli of Hudson in Summit County is inducted into the Pro Football Hall of Fame.

August 2, 2014 — A statue of longtime Indians star first baseman Jim Thome is placed on the spot in Progressive Field where his 511-foot home run landed in 1999.

3

August 3, 1948 — Paige packs them in

A crowd of 72,434 almost filled Municipal Stadium on a Tuesday night for a game between the Indians and Senators. And why not? How many times do you get to see a legend pitch?

The mystery surrounding Leroy "Satchel" Paige started with the curiosity that no one was certain about his birthdate. He was said to be 42 when he signed with Cleveland. But no matter how old he was, the man could pitch – endlessly and accurately. Paige had played all over North America – Negro Leagues, Caribbean leagues, barnstorming teams, and more. Everyone agreed that he was one of the best pitchers ever, but he had never faced major league hitters regularly because there were no Black players in the majors until Jackie Robinson signed with the Dodgers in 1947. After some relief appearances, Paige started against Washington, and the crowd set a major league record for attendance at a night game. Paige did his job, earning the win as he allowed three runs in seven innings.

Paige had six more starts the rest of the season, and finished with a 6-1 record and a 2.48 earned-run average. He made a brief appearance in the 1948 World Series. Paige pitched for Cleveland again in 1949 and then with the St. Louis Browns in 1951, '52 and '53. He capped his career in 1965 when he appeared in one game for Charles O. Finley's Kansas City A's at age 58, throwing three innings of shutout ball against Boston. Carl Yastrzemski had the only hit off him.

August 3, 1936 — Sprinter Jesse Owens of Cleveland wins the 100-meter dash in 10.3 seconds at the Olympic Games in Berlin with the leader of Germany, Adolf Hitler, in attendance.

August 3, 1960 — The Indians and Tigers trade managers in a unique moment in baseball history. Cleveland gets Jimmy Dykes, while Joe Gordon goes to Detroit.

August 3, 1968 — Browns fullback-linebacker Marion Motley is inducted into the Pro Football Hall of Fame. Motley, a Canton native, played for Cleveland from 1946-53 and one season with Pittsburgh in 1955.

August 3, 1973 — The Cleveland Nets of the professional World Team Tennis league use the 11th overall draft pick in the sport's first draft to select Bjorn Borg of Sweden. Other picks included Nancy Gunter, Ray Moore, Clark and Carole Graebner, and Pancho Gonzalez. The league's first iteration lasted from 1974-78.

August 4, 1935 — Johnson exits as Indians manager

The managing career of Walter Johnson came to an abrupt end on this day, as the Indians let him go. Looking back, it was a match that just was not going to work out.

For many years, Johnson and the Washington Senators were inseparable. Johnson joined the Senators in 1907 at age 19. He won 20 games for the first time three years later, and quickly became the premier power pitcher of his age. Johnson won an astounding 417 games, with a record 110 shutouts.

After a year of managing in the minors, Johnson was named manager of the Senators in the middle of the 1929 season. He did well, winning at least 90 games between 1930 and 1932. But Johnson was out of work in 1933 when the Indians hired him in midseason.

He lasted for parts of three seasons. On June 6, 1935, with stories circulating that players were having difficulty getting along with Johnson, the team took the unusual step of buying a large advertisement in three Cleveland newspapers. It says, in part, "We, the members of the Cleveland Baseball Club, want the fans to know that we are not a team split wide open by dissension, arrayed against our manager," and it is signed by 21 players.

Johnson lost his job about two months later. Steve O'Neill took his place; Johnson never managed again.

August 4, 2007 — Browns' guard Gene Hickerson is inducted into the Pro Football Hall of Fame.

August 5, 1990 — Mucha earns first golf win

Not every pro golfer comes out of Florida, Arizona or California, although sometimes it seems that way. One such exception was a product of Parma Heights, Ohio.

Barb Mucha grew up more interested in bowling than golf, but then she entered a junior golf tournament as a 10-year-old . . . and won it. Barb was hooked. She went on to Valley Forge High and Michigan State University as she prepared for life on the LPGA Tour. Mucha turned pro in 1985.

She won six events on the rookie tour, and made the jump to the sport's highest level in 1987. Breaking through with a victory was her next challenge and she met that goal in 1990 at the Boston Five Classic. The final round was held on this day, and Mucha needed two extra holes to defeat Lenore Rittenhouse. She earned $52,500.

Four more tournament wins followed in the 1990s, the last coming in 1998. Mucha played in 321 tournaments on the tour, and finished in the top 10 a total of 115 times. That's why she earned more than $2.4 million.

August 5, 1967 — Coach and executive Paul Brown along with Cleveland / Los Angeles Rams owner Dan Reeves are inducted into the Pro Football Hall of Fame. Brown dies exactly 24 years later at 82.

August 5, 2001 — The Indians rally from a 14-2 deficit in the seventh inning to shock the Mariners, 15-14. Jolbert Cabrera's broken-bat single in the bottom of the 11th inning drives in the winning run.

August 5, 2017 — Former Akron Zips star defensive lineman Jason Taylor is inducted into the Pro Football Hall of Fame after a 15-year NFL career.

August 6, 1890 — Cy Young comes to Cleveland

The story of Denton True "Cy" Young's rise to baseball stardom has a touch of 19th century Americana in it. He was the son of a farmer in Gilmore, Ohio, located about 45 miles south of Canton. Young liked to throw rocks and took up baseball as a hobby when he became old enough to join teams. In 1888 and 1889, he was playing semipro ball in the Canton area.

Young signed with Canton of the Tri-States League in 1890, and he became known for his fastball. That's when people started calling him "Cyclone" . . . or Cy for short. He was a good pitcher on a bad team in Canton, and attracted attention from big league teams. The National League was going through a war with a rival circuit, the Players League, and needed reinforcements. Young was one such player. His contract was purchased by Cleveland for $300.

His first game for the franchise known during that era as the Spiders fell on this day against the Chicago Colts. Cap Anson, the Colts' player/manager, reportedly said that Young was "just another big farmer." Maybe he changed his mind at the end of the day. Young threw a three-hitter and won, 8-1.

Cy finished his rookie year at 9-7, and took a big step forward to a 27-22 record in his first full year in the majors. The story is well-known from there. Young won an astonishing

511 games in his career, with five 30-win seasons. He threw the first pitch in the history of the World Series (1903 for Boston). The top yearly award for pitchers was named for him in 1956, the year after he died.

August 6, 1937 — Joe DiMaggio's hit along the foul line in the 10th inning of a game with Cleveland is first ruled foul by one umpire, and then ruled fair by another. It prompts DiMaggio to score the winning run for the Yankees. The Indians later win a protest about the game.

August 6, 1965 — The Browns, coming off their 1964 NFL championship, defeat the College All-Stars 24-16 in an exhibition game at Soldier Field in Chicago.

August 7, 1992 — Thunderbolts exit playoffs

Consider yourself fortunate if you had the chance to see the Cleveland Thunderbolts in action. There weren't a great many chances to do so.

The Thunderbolts were part of the Arena Football League, and played their games at the Coliseum in Richfield. The franchise had played in Columbus in 1991, and suffered through a 0-10 record. John Kuczak bought the team after that and moved it to the Cleveland area. The Thunderbolts couldn't have asked for a better start, winning their first three games. But then the team lost six straight before closing the regular season with a 46-25 win over Albany.

The Thunderbolts qualified for the AFL playoffs, and were sent to Orlando for a first-round game. Cleveland hung around for a half on this day before the Predators scored 30 unanswered points in the second half. That led to a 50-12 win for Orlando. The team was led in both rushing and passing by former West Virginia quarterback Major Harris.

That playoff game was the high point in the team's history. The team went 2-10 in 1993 and 1994, and then gave up. The franchise moved back to Columbus.

August 7, 1993 — Bob Ojeda pitches his first game for the Indians after suffering head injuries on March 22 in a boat accident in Florida that killed pitchers Steve Olin and Tim Crews.

August 7, 1994 — WEWS-TV sportscaster Nev Chandler dies of colon cancer at age 47. The versatile and well-liked Chandler, who was known off the air for his humorous impersonations of Cleveland sports figures, was the Indians' play-by-play announcer from 1980 to '84 and the Browns from 1985 to '93.

August 7, 1999 — Tight end Ozzie Newsome is inducted into the Pro Football Hall of Fame.

August 8, 1948 — A packed Municipal Stadium

The Indians couldn't have had a better situation to attract crowds than during this summer weekend in 1948. They were in the midst of a pennant race, and the New York Yankees were coming to town. It was a good thing Municipal Stadium had the largest seating capacity of any ballpark in the major leagues.

The teams divided the first two games of the series, leaving the Indians tied with the Yankees in second place – a half-game behind Philadelphia. Then came a Sunday doubleheader, and 73,484 turned out.

In the opener, the Yankees jumped to a 6-1 lead as the game moved into the bottom of the seventh. But Johnny Berardino and Eddie Robinson both homered as part of a five-run rally, which included a two-run pinch-hit single by Lou Boudreau. Cleveland added two runs in the bottom of the eighth, and Satchel Paige picked up the win in an 8-6 victory. In the second game, Steve Gromek pitched a tidy seven innings of four-hit ball while Jim Hegan singled home the winning run.

The three-date series drew 188,081, setting an attendance record. By comparison, that was more than half of the attendance total for the St. Louis Browns for the entire 1948 season (335,564). The Indians' season attendance total of 2.6 million that year set a record that stood until the Los Angeles Dodgers opened Chavez Ravine in 1962.

August 8, 1993 — Indians slugger Albert Belle accomplishes the unusual feat of driving home two runners on the same sacrifice fly. The ball was caught beyond the fence, and both runners were allowed to score.

9

August 9, 1936 — Owens caps a great Olympics

When Jesse Owens of Cleveland arrived at the Olympics in Berlin, Germany, in 1936, he was already considered one of the great athletes of his day. This was the day when he became a sports legend.

The Nazi government in Germany wanted to host the sports showcase to demonstrate its prowess and supremacy over the rest of the world. The country had been hit hard by the Depression, bringing Adolf Hitler to power, and the Olympics were designed to show off a rebuilding nation.

But on an individual basis, there was no finer athlete than Owens, the youngest of 10 children, whose family had moved from Alabama to Cleveland when he was nine. On August 3, Owens won the 100-meter dash. The next day, Owens, whose given name was James Cleveland Owens, was the winner of the long jump. On August 5, he won the 200-meter sprint, defeating Mack Robinson – the older brother of Jackie – in the process.

There was only one goal left – a fourth gold medal in the 4x100-meter relay. Owens wasn't expected to run in the final, but he and Ralph Metcalfe were ordered to replace Jewish-Americans Marty Glickman and Sam Stoller in the lineup. The full story of the switch might remain shrouded in mystery, but it seems clear that someone from Team USA did not want to annoy the host country, with its anti-Jewish laws on the books. The new foursome easily won the gold medal, setting a world record in the process.

August 9, 1971 — Leroy "Satchel" Paige, the famous Black pitcher from the Negro Leagues whose major league career began in 1948 with the Indians, is inducted into the Baseball Hall of Fame.

August 9, 1976 — The Crusaders of the World Hockey Association move to Minnesota and become the second version of the Fighting Saints. The original team had folded the previous February.

August 9, 1981 — Baseball's All-Star Game had been delayed by a labor dispute, but finally takes place in Cleveland's Municipal Stadium. Mike Schmidt's homer in the eighth lifts the National League to a 5-4 win. Mike Easler of the Pittsburgh Pirates, whose 14-year MLB career had some of its formative days at Cleveland Benedictine High School, appeared in the game and had a hit. The game marked the start of the "second half" of the '81 season.

August 9, 1999 — The "new" Cleveland Browns make their first-ever appearance as they beat Dallas, 20-17 in overtime, in the Hall of Fame Game in Canton.

10

August 10, 1975 — Another major for Nicklaus

Jack Nicklaus had a memorable season with five pro golf event victories in 1975, and it included the PGA Championship at Firestone Country Club in Akron.

Nicklaus was the favorite entering the fourth major of the year, as usual. He had won the Masters in the spring, and just missed qualifying for the playoff to determine the winner of both the U.S. Open and the British Open. Nicklaus put up a 70 on the scoreboard in the first round, three shots back of leader Mark Hayes. The next day, Bruce Crampton stole the headlines with a 63, good for a three-shot lead over Hale Irwin and four shots over Nicklaus.

On Saturday, the Golden Bear took charge with a 67. Crampton shot a 75, and found himself four shots back of Nicklaus. It was never a good idea to spot Jack Nicklaus four shots in the final round of a major. Jack shot a comfortable 71, and Crampton's 69 left him two shots short.

It was the 14th major championship of Nicklaus' career; he would end with 18. Nicklaus also put up 19 runner-up finishes at the four majors (seven at the British and four each at the U.S. Open, Masters, and PGA). Crampton never did win a major title in a fine career. In fact, he finished second in such tournaments four different times – losing to Nicklaus in each of them.

August 10, 1963 — The all-Black New York Renaissance basketball team is named as an inductee in the 1963 Basketball Hall of Fame enshrinement class along with Bob Gruenig and William Reid. The Case Western Reserve University website case.edu notes that one "Ren" player in team history was 6-foot-5 William T. Smith, who was nicknamed "Wee Willie," and was a Rens player from 1932-36 while also playing in Cleveland for Slaughter Brothers Funeral Home.

August 10, 1984 — Alvin Robertson of Barberton High School in Summit County contributes six points, three assists, two rebounds and one steal as the United States Olympic basketball team defeats Spain 96-65 for the gold medal in the 1984 Games in Los Angeles. Robertson, whose college career had ended at Arkansas, was the Olympic team's seventh-leading scorer in eight games.

August 11, 1935 — Welcome to the Derby, Akron style

The words bring a smile and thoughts of America in a simpler time: Soap Box Derby.

The idea came out of the Depression. A reporter in Dayton, Ohio – Myron Scott – noticed some youngsters competing in homemade race cars without engines. He was so enchanted that he bought a copyright and convinced Chevrolet to become a national sponsor. The first competition was held in Dayton in 1934.

However, the Western Ohio city was a little flat for such purposes. The hills of Akron were better, and the location was more centrally located. The Derby found its first new home on Tallmadge Avenue in Akron. Maurice Bale, Jr. of Anderson, Indiana, won the initial race in that location in 1935 before a crowd believed to number more than 75,000. The event is best remembered for an accident, as announcer Graham McNamee was hit by one of the race cars.

The race continues to this day with only a couple of interruptions along the way. Girls were allowed to compete beginning in 1971, and celebrities from Ronald Reagan to Tony Stewart have watched the action over the years.

August 11, 1912 — Shoeless Joe Jackson steals second, third and home in the seventh inning to help the Indians beat New York, 8-3.

August 11, 1929 — Babe Ruth hits the 500th home run of his career in the game between the Indians and Yankees, played at League Park. Willis Hudlin gave up the round-tripper.

August 11, 1957 — The Indians retire No. 19 in honor of Bob Feller – the first player in team history to be saluted in that way. The first jersey retirement in baseball history honored New York Yankee player Lou Gehrig, who wore No. 4, on July 4, 1939.

August 11, 1962 — NFL Commissioner Pete Rozelle visits the site of the Pro Football Hall of Fame to turn the first shovel of dirt for construction in the $366,000 project. The meeting credited with causing the birth of organized pro football had taken place in Canton on September 17, 1920, and in 1961, the city was chosen as the location for the hall. Rozelle was accompanied at the ceremony by Mrs. Ralph Hay, widow of the Canton car dealer who helped organize the 1920 meeting.

12

August 12, 1979 — Browns add Alzado from Broncos

There aren't many sadder stories in the pro football history book than the one about Lyle Alzado, whose journey included becoming a fan favorite during a stop in Cleveland. On the day of his trade to the Browns, he told the *Akron Beacon Journal*: "I'm excited. I'm ready. Let's go to the Super Bowl."

Alzado grew up on Long Island, and finished his college football career at Yankton in South Dakota. A Denver Broncos scout happened to see some film of the defensive lineman, and convinced the team to draft him in the fourth round in 1971. Alzado worked his way into the starting lineup, and was a ringleader of the "Orange Crush" defense that helped Denver reach the Super Bowl in January 1978. He established a reputation for playing with a rage factor that even alarmed his teammates. Alzado considered a career in boxing at one point, and took on Muhammad Ali in an eight-round exhibition.

He played well during the 1978 season, but then got into a contract dispute and on this day was dealt to the Browns for three draft choices. Alzado said at the time, "There is nothing worse in this world than having people give up on you and not believe in you."

Lyle wasn't bad in his three years in Cleveland. He then was dealt to the Raiders and retired after the 1985 season.

Alzado's legacy was clouded by his use of steroids and human growth hormone in those years, which he later admitted in public. He died at 43 of brain cancer.

August 12, 1973 — Jack Nicklaus wins the PGA Championship at Canterbury Golf Club in Beachwood. He finishes four shots ahead of Bruce Crampton. It is his third of five PGA titles.

August 12, 1994 — The Indians appear on their way to reaching the newly arranged playoffs as well as challenging the first-place Chicago White Sox in the first year of play in the American League Central Division. Cleveland's 66-47 record is one game behind the White Sox when Commissioner Bud Selig and the team owners cancel the remainder of the 1994 season, including the playoffs and the World Series. The dispute goes on for 232 days.

13

August 13, 1932 — Barth goes for the gold

Boxing has had a tradition of competitors with their names changed or shortened. One example is Carmine DiBartholomeo, known in the ring as Carmen Barth. No matter what he was called, he was really good.

Barth worked his way up the usual ladder as an amateur. The Cleveland native (he grew up in the Collinwood neighborhood) won the city's Golden Gloves title, and also took a regional crown. That earned him a ticket to the Olympic Trials, where he took the middleweight title and qualified for the Games in Los Angeles in 1932.

Barth had a first-round bye at the Olympics, and beat Manuel Crux of Mexico in the quarterfinals and Ernest Peirce of South Africa in the semis. That put Carmen a win from the gold medal, and he got it by beating Amado Azar of Argentina. That made him the first Cleveland boxer to finish first in the worldwide competition.

The Olympic champion immediately turned pro, and had a lengthy career. In 1934, he had 16 bouts. He had one chance to win a title, but lost on a technical knockout to Freddie Steele in a bout held in Public Hall in Cleveland. Barth finished his career with a 48-15-4 record.

August 13, 1958 — Rocky Colavito comes in from right field and pitches three innings of relief in his only appearance as a pitcher as a member of the Indians. He allows an inherited run to score as Cleveland loses a 3-2 decision to the Tigers, who swept a doubleheader.

August 13, 2006 — The Indians' Travis Hafner hits his sixth grand-slam homer of the season, tying the major league record for a season set by Don Mattingly of the Yankees.

August 13, 2020 — LeBron James has only four assists in the Los Angeles Lakers' 136-122 loss to the Sacramento Kings in the final regular-season game of the 2020 season, but his average of 10.2 assists per game leads the NBA. It is the first time in James' 17-season career that he was first in assists. He won a scoring title once, in 2007-08, with a 30.0 average.

14

August 14, 1913 — It's not easy being Green

Consider yourself a Cleveland baseball expert if you know anything about a team called the Cleveland Green Sox. Yes, it was a professional team, but in a minor league – the Federal League.

About the only part of the team that isn't obscure is the name of the manager: Cy Young. Matthew Bramley owned the team. He made his money from the asphalt business but also owned Luna Park, an amusement park. That was where the Green Sox (reflecting the youth of the team) played in 1913.

Cleveland had a decent team. In mid-August, the Green Sox were challenging the Indianapolis Hoosiers for the league lead. But the Hoosiers finished a three-game sweep of Cleveland with an 8-7 win on this day, and that essentially ended the pennant hopes of the Green Sox. The team finished second at 64-54, 10 games back of Indy. Even a good squad, relatively speaking, couldn't excite the fans of Cleveland, as the team often drew less than 200 people to its games.

The Federal League decided to take on the big boys by becoming a third major league that fall, and wooed some players to join. However, the Cleveland franchise couldn't break even with minor league players, and was not ready to take another step up. The team dropped out of the league, was sold, and moved to Toronto to compete in a different league. The Federal League lasted two seasons before collapsing. The biggest reminder that fans have is Wrigley Field in Chicago, which was built to house its Federal League team.

August 14, 1958 — Vic Power steals home twice in the same game, helping the Indians to edge the Tigers, 10-9.

August 14, 2012 — The Indians play the 15,000th game in their history – second only to the Tigers – and beat Detroit, 12-1.

15

August 15, 1936 — Wilson medals in Berlin

Jesse Owens of Cleveland was the star of the 1936 Olympics in Berlin, and much was said about how he smashed Adolf Hitler's belief about a "master race." Yet there were 17 other African Americans on USA teams that year, and some came home with medals as well. One was Jackie Wilson, and he also represented Cleveland.

Wilson took part in the Olympic Trials in Chicago in boxing, and qualified as the bantamweight (118 pounds) representative. That sent him to the Games later in the summer. Wilson went on to win his first four matches on points. In the final, Wilson lost to Ulderico Sergo of Italy on points, so he had to settle for a silver medal.

Wilson went on to avenge the loss to Sergo by beating him in a special series of bouts between fighters from the U.S. and Europe. Then it was on to a pro career, and he got as high as No. 2 in the rankings. Wilson never got a title shot, and only fought a few times in Cleveland as apparently he had moved to Los Angeles by then.

Cleveland had another boxing medalist in those games. Lou Laurie graduated from East Technical, and went into amateur boxing. He made it to Berlin and finished third to pick up a bronze medal. Laurie was known for his style and he won an award in Berlin as the most clever boxer.

August 15, 1950 — Joe Louis records the final victory of his fabulous boxing career, taking a unanimous decision against Cleveland's Jimmy Bivins in Baltimore's Memorial Stadium. Bivins had a career record of 86-25-1, and went up against such fighters as Archie Moore, Ezzard Charles, Joey Maxim and Jersey Joe Walcott.

August 15, 1989 — Left-handed pitcher Dave Dravecky, a native of Youngstown, suffers a broken bone in his upper arm and appears in his final major league game. Dravecky had made a comeback after surgery to remove cancer in his arm. He had an eight-year career with the San Diego Padres and San Francisco Giants.

August 15, 1993 — Nolan Ryan wins the 324th and final game of his career, as his Rangers beat the Indians, 5-3, in Cleveland.

16

August 16, 1920 — Chapman killed by thrown ball

American League fans were enjoying a terrific pennant race in this particular August, as the Indians, Yankees and White Sox were all in the chase. Cleveland was starting a long road trip on this day, and the first stop was New York's Polo Grounds. It was something of an overcast day in New York, and there was rain for a few innings until it stopped for the rest of the day.

Carl Mays was the pitcher for the Yankees. He had an 18-8 record, using a submarine style that probably resembled the style used by 2000s pitcher Chad Bradford. Mays was known as a pitcher who was not afraid to throw inside to batters. The Indians scored three runs off him in the first four innings.

Ray Chapman led off the top of the fifth for Cleveland. On the first pitch of the at-bat, he was struck on the left side of the head. Chapman collapsed, and umpire Tommy Connolly called for a physician from the crowd. Chapman returned to his feet, and was walking to the clubhouse in center field when he collapsed again and had to be carried by his teammates.

Chapman was taken to a nearby hospital. The Indians went on to win the game, 4-3, but there was no celebrating. Chapman survived brain surgery, but passed away the next morning before his wife could get to New York from Cleveland. "I would give anything if I could undo what has happened. Chapman was a game, splendid fellow," Mays said.

August 16, 2002 — Vonda Ward of Macedonia captures the IBA women's world's heavyweight boxing championship with a 10-round decision over Monica McGowan in Canton. Before deciding to try that sport, Ward was a basketball star at Garfield Heights Trinity High School and then played for legendary college coach Pat Summitt at the University of Tennessee.

17

August 17, 1951 — Browns knock off All-Stars

The Browns enjoyed their offseason as champions of the National Football League in the first seven-plus months of 1951. Their first order of business as the defending champions was to play a special exhibition game to get the '51 campaign off to a proper start.

Arch Ward, sports editor of the *Chicago Tribune,* had come up with the idea of starting the season with a game between the champs of the NFL and the best college players who would be joining the pros as rookies after the game. Ward had previously conceived the idea for baseball's All-Star Game in 1933. The Bears and All-Stars played to a scoreless tie in the game's debut in 1934 before almost 80,000 at Soldier Field in Chicago.

The All-Stars' biggest name on the field in the 1951 game was Kyle Rote from SMU, who would go on to have a fine career with the Giants. His first look at the pros didn't start too well. He fumbled near the end zone, a play that led to a safety by Cleveland to open the scoring. Later in the first half, Dub Jones scored a touchdown as the Browns had a 12-0 lead at the half. It got worse from there. Otto Graham threw a couple of touchdowns, and Cleveland eventually won, 33-0, before 92,180.

The contest became less and less competitive over the years. The All-Stars' last win came in 1963 against Green Bay. Fans might imagine what Vince Lombardi's reaction to that was. The 1976 game was cut short by a savage thunderstorm. That was the final game of the series, as the NFL decided teams wanted their players to be in training camp on Day One.

August 17, 1914 — Nap Lajoie offers to resign as the manager of the Naps, who are suffering through a disappointing season. James McGuire replaces him five days later.

August 17, 1988 — Harry Lee "Butch" Reynolds Jr. of Akron sets a world record of 43.29 seconds in the 400-meter dash. The record lasts more than 11 years. Reynolds also wins a silver medal in the 400 and a gold as part of the 4x400 relay at the 1988 Olympic Games.

August 18, 1962 — Browns' Davis hears a roar

Browns' owner Art Modell comes up with an idea to try something new in pro football by staging a doubleheader of preseason games on this day. Detroit took on Dallas while the Browns went up against visiting Detroit. It's an experiment that lasted several years in Municipal Stadium, but this is the one that people remember – and not just because it was the first.

Heisman Trophy winner Ernie Davis of Syracuse had been unable to play in the College All-Star Game earlier in the month because of illness. He was hospitalized, and the winning Packers voted to give Davis the game ball. On August 9, the Browns held an off-the-record news conference to tell the media that Davis had been diagnosed with leukemia and was given six to 12 months to live. Even Davis hadn't been told at that point.

Davis was not restricted to the hospital and visited a few Browns' practices. Then came the big surprise during the introduction of the Browns' starting offensive lineup for the preseason game with the Lions. Davis was introduced as something of a ceremonial 12th starter. He took the field in street clothes as 77,683 gave him a five-minute standing ovation. Modell compared it to the reception Lou Gehrig received in Yankee Stadium when he was honored in 1939.

That was the only time Davis appeared on a football field with the Browns. Davis died on May 18, 1963, and the Browns retired uniform number 45 in his honor.

August 18, 1934 — Earl Averill reaches base nine straight times in a doubleheader in Philadelphia, with four straight walks in the first game and five consecutive hits in the second. The future Hall of Famer died exactly 49 years later on August 18, 1983.

August 18, 2018 — The Indians retire uniform No. 25 to honor Jim Thome.

August 18, 2022 — After months of negotiating, all sides agree to a suspension of Browns quarterback Deshaun Watson. He agreed to be suspended for 11 games and pay a $5 million fine in the light of several accusations of sexual misconduct during massage sessions. Watson also agrees to undergo mandatory evaluation by behavioral experts.

19

August 19, 2016 — It happens every century

On August 13, 1916, Braggo Roth scored on an inside-the-park, walk-off home run to give the Indians a win over the St. Louis Browns. Those who didn't see the play had to wait for 100 years and six days for Cleveland to do it again.

The Indians trailed the Blue Jays, 2-1, entering the bottom of the ninth. Toronto had its elite closer, Roberto Osuna, on the mound. Osuna got Carlos Santana to foul out for the first out of the inning. Then Jose Ramirez hit the ball over the right field fence, and the game was tied, 2-2.

Up came Tyler Naquin. He hit the ball deep to right field, and outfielder Michael Saunders couldn't catch up to it. The ball bounced away from Saunders in right-center, and center fielder Melvin Upton Jr. had to chase it down. Just as Upton started to throw the ball, he slipped. Naquin was waved home. He slid head-first into the plate to easily beat the throw, and the Indians were 3-2 winners.

"That was a pretty cool moment," Naquin said to MLB.com after the game. "I almost fell down there for a second. I wanted to just keep running."

August 19, 1966 — George "Birdie" Tebbetts resigns as the Indians' manager, and is replaced on an interim basis by George Strickland. Cleveland had won 14 of its first 15 games that season. Working in Cleveland from 1963-66 was the third and final stop of Tebbetts' managerial career after previous assignments in Cincinnati and Milwaukee.

August 20, 2004 — Munz caps her Olympic career

If you had told Diana Munz of Moreland Hills about five years before this day that she'd have won three Olympic medals at this point, she might have laughed or she might have cried. But she probably wouldn't have believed it.

Munz was a promising 17-year-old swimmer when her car was broadsided by a delivery truck that ran through a red light at an intersection. Four vertebrae in her back were compressed – she essentially had a broken back. Doctors were worried that she'd be paralyzed from the waist down. Perhaps only the strong back muscles she had developed from swimming saved her from that fate.

Munz's rehab was done in a pool, and it led to developing a competitive edge for the sport. In what doctors called a miracle, Munz improved to the point where she qualified for the 2000 Olympics in Sydney. There she was part of an Olympic gold-medal winning team in the 4x200-meter freestyle, and she won an individual silver medal in the 400-meter freestyle.

But that wasn't enough. Munz kept at it for four more years, and won a bronze medal in the 400-meter freestyle on this day at the 2004 Olympics in Athens. She retired in 2005.

August 20, 1938 — Indians catcher Henry Helf catches a baseball dropped from the top of the 708-foot Terminal Tower in Cleveland. It was estimated that the ball was traveling 138 miles per hour. The publicity stunt breaks a record set in 1908 when Gabby Street caught a ball dropped from the top of the Washington Monument (555 feet).

August 20, 1974 — The Nets of World Team Tennis are eliminated in the opening round of the playoffs by the Philadelphia Freedoms, 49-44. The Nets were coached by Cleveland's Clark Graebner, who also played for the team. Cleveland finished 21-23 in its first season.

August 20, 1995 — Jose Mesa of the Indians picks up his 37th consecutive save from the start of the season to set a major league record. His scoreless ninth inning gives Cleveland an 8-5 win over Milwaukee.

21

August 21, 1915 — Shoeless Joe shipped to Chicago

Say it ain't so! The Indians trade one of the great hitters in baseball history in Joe Jackson!

There is a story behind the trade, of course, and money takes center stage. The Naps, as they were known at the time, added Jackson in a trade with the Athletics before the 1910 season. He spent that season in the minors, and then came up to Cleveland for good in 1911. Jackson promptly hit .408 with 233 hits. The next two seasons were almost as good, and in 1914, he "slumped" to a .338 average.

By 1915, owner Charles Somers was on the verge of going bankrupt, and he decided to trade one of his two stars – Jackson or Ray Chapman. Somers was afraid that Jackson would jump to the rival Federal League for more money, so he was the logical choice. The Indians signed Jackson to a three-year contract, and then dealt him on this day to the White Sox for Bobby Roth, Larry Chappell, Ed Klepfer and $31,500. Financially, it was the biggest deal in baseball history at that point.

Jackson always hit with the White Sox, never less than .300 in a full season there. But other issues soon developed. Jackson was allegedly offered thousands to be part of an effort to fix the 1919 World Series. The story broke late in the 1920 season. Jackson and the other players were acquitted on all charges, but Commissioner Kenesaw Mountain Landis banned all of the accused players from baseball for life. Jackson left the majors with a career .356 average.

August 21, 1948 — The Indians break the record for consecutive scoreless innings against an opponent, topping the mark of 41 set by the Cleveland Blues in 1903.

August 21, 1986 — The Indians promote left-hander Greg Swindell from their Class AA minor league team after making him the No. 2 pick in the baseball draft earlier in the summer. The Boston Red Sox find Swindell's pitches to their liking and go on to a 24-5 victory. In 3 ⅔ innings, Swindell gives up six runs (four earned) on six hits with three walks.

August 21, 1999 — The new Cleveland Browns Stadium, built for a reported $283 million, stages its first event with a preseason game between the Browns and Vikings.

22

August 22, 2017 — Cavaliers send Irving to Boston

Kyrie Irving was part of a championship team when his Cavaliers won the NBA title in 2016. It didn't take long for those good feelings to come to an end.

Irving went to the Cavaliers management in June of 2017 to tell them that he wanted to be traded. The news came after the Cavaliers reportedly had talked about trading Irving in a three-way transaction with Phoenix and Indiana. There was also talk that Irving wanted to be the undisputed leader of the team, something that observers said he believed wouldn't happen in Cleveland with LeBron James in town.

It's tough to figure out exactly what the timeline was, but fans did see the result of his request. Irving was sent to the Celtics on this day for a large package of talent – Isaiah Thomas, Jae Crowder, the Brooklyn Nets' 2018 first-round NBA draft pick and Ante Zizic.

That was big news at the time, but the deal didn't have a huge impact on either franchise. Irving stayed in Boston for two seasons, and jumped to the Nets as a free agent. Thomas and Crowder were gone from Cleveland by the 2018 trading deadline. The draft choice became Collin Sexton, and he worked out pretty well as he has become one of the bright young stars in the NBA. Sexton was later dealt to Utah. Zizic was a reserve during his time with the Cavs and out of the league in 2021.

August 22, 1951 — Joey Maxim of Cleveland defends his light-heavyweight boxing title with an exciting 15-round decision over Irish Bob Murphy in New York.

August 22, 1962 — The Browns release their seventh-round draft choice, a receiver named John Havlicek. The move works out well for him, since he had been a first-round pick by the Boston Celtics of the NBA. Havlicek became a member of the Basketball Hall of Fame.

August 23, 1936 — Feller debuts as starter

Plenty of kids have summer jobs during their high school years. Bob Feller had a particularly interesting one when he was 17. He was a pitcher for the Cleveland Indians.

Feller is one of the great prodigies in baseball history. The right-hander was between his junior and senior years in high school when the Indians asked him to throw three innings of an exhibition game against the St. Louis Cardinals on July 6, 1936. He struck out eight batters. Even Dizzy Dean thought Feller couldn't miss.

Feller was supposed to spend some of that summer pitching semi-pro ball in Cleveland, and he also sold peanuts for the Indians at League Park. But Feller received a promotion by the Indians – directly to the major leagues. At first, he was given relief duty in July and August.

Then on August 23, it was decided to give Feller a starting assignment. Manager Steve O'Neill had Denny Galehouse warming in the bullpen in the first inning, if needed. Galehouse was something of a local player, coming from the Wayne County community of Doylestown, southwest of Akron. Feller started by striking out the side in the first inning. He didn't stop piling up strikeouts until he had pitched a complete game. Feller whiffed 15 St. Louis batters, one shy of the American League record, in a 4-1 win.

August 23, 1972 — The Cavaliers acquire guard Lenny Wilkens and forward Barry Clemens from Seattle in a deal for guard Butch Beard.

August 23, 2014 — The Cavs add forward Kevin Love to their roster in a trade with Minnesota. The Timberwolves get Anthony Bennett, Andrew Wiggins, and a trade exception.

August 23, 2014 — League Park, the former home of the Indians, is brought back to life with an artificial surface. High schools and youth leagues use it for baseball and softball games.

24

August 24, 1919 — Lightning strikes for Caldwell

League Park was the setting for one of the most unimaginable moments in the history of baseball. That's because despite its unique nature, it had no effect at all on the record book.

Dark clouds had moved in from Lake Erie late in the game between the Indians and the Philadelphia Athletics. Cleveland had a 2-1 lead, and pitcher Ray Caldwell was in great form. He had recorded the first two outs in the top of the ninth inning, and only needed to retire one more batter for a complete game win.

Then, kaboom! A bolt of lightning came out of the sky and struck the ground somewhere in the infield. The force was so great that Caldwell was knocked to the ground, and everyone was worried that he might have been killed by the strike. Those on the field said they could feel electricity passing through their bodies.

Caldwell picked himself up, checked to make sure his body parts were working properly, and went back to work. Joe Dugan hit into a ground out, and Caldwell had his victory – moments before the rain picked up considerably. No one could say he didn't earn that particular win.

August 24, 1957 — The Brooklyn Dodgers make the last player sale in their history as a New York franchise, selling Vito Valentinetti to the Indians.

August 24, 2008 — LeBron James, wearing uniform No. 6, scores 14 points and gets six rebounds as the United States' men's basketball team defeats Spain 118-107 for the gold medal at the 2008 Olympics Games in China.

25

August 25, 1967 — One run on no hits

The American League staged one of its greatest pennant races in 1967, and four teams went down to the final week before a winner was determined. The Indians weren't one of them, but they played a role in the race for one of the contenders in an unusual game.

Cleveland hosted Minnesota in a doubleheader on this day. The Twins needed 10 innings to take the opener, 6-5. Then Dean Chance took the mound for Minnesota in the nightcap. Chance was a former star at Northwestern High School in West Salem in Wayne County, southwest of Cleveland, and he always had friends and family in the stands when he pitched against the Indians.

Chance had a rough start. He walked the first two batters, and a third reached base on an error with one out. Chance struck out Max Alvis, but the ball got away from catcher Jerry Zimmerman, and Lee Maye scored for the Indians. From there, Chance and Sonny Siebert were in good form. The Twins tied the score at 1-1 in the top of the second on an outfield error, and took the lead when Siebert balked Cesar Tovar home.

It stayed that way until the bottom of the ninth, when everyone noticed Chance had a no-hitter going in spite of the run scored by Cleveland. The Indians' Vic Davalillo, Chuck Hinton and Tony Horton went down quietly on sliders, and Chance had his no-hitter.

August 25, 2011 — The Indians purchase Jim Thome from the Phillies.

26

August 26, 1955 — Wertz is stricken by feared illness

The word polio – short for poliomyelitis – created fear in people's hearts and minds during the first half of the 20th century. It had paralyzed hundreds of thousands of children and was every parent's nightmare.

Dr. Jonas Salk developed a vaccine in 1955, but that didn't always result in the end of the problem. Imagine the thoughts of Vic Wertz of the Indians when he started to come down with a high temperature and severe pain shortly after playing in a game on August 24 of that year. He was examined by a doctor, and two days later came the diagnosis – polio.

Wertz's condition did not cause paralysis but was still serious. "I honestly didn't think of baseball. My fear was that I'd be a cripple and all that meant to my future," he told *The New York Times*.

Wertz needed a few weeks before he could even walk again, and lost 20 pounds in the process. The first baseman/outfielder received 14,000 letters, many from children. But eventually he recovered, and showed up in spring training looking to play baseball again. He did that, and hit a career-high 32 home runs.

August 26, 1960 — Harvey Kuenn of the Indians fouls a ball off his foot and breaks it in batting practice, abbreviating his only season with the team after coming to Cleveland in the trade for popular star Rocky Colavito.

August 26, 1990 — Firestone Country Club's South Course always had a reputation as a tough layout on the PGA Tour. But Jose Maria Olazabal, 24, put together a fine weekend at the NEC World Series of Golf. He shoots 67-61-67-67 for a record 18-under 262 to take the $198,000 first prize.

August 27, 2004 — Mack vaults into history

In the 1896 Olympic Games in Athens, William Hoyt of the U.S. won the gold medal in the pole vault. Four years later in Paris, Irving Baxter of the U.S. won the event. That was followed by a win by Charles Dvorak of Team USA in St. Louis in 1904. Americans won every men's pole vault in the Games through 1968.

The streak ended in 1972, but America can still produce top vaulters. One of them is Tim Mack, who learned his craft at St. Ignatius High School in Cleveland.

Mack first attempted to reach the Olympics in 2000, finishing eighth in the trials. He kept competing and improving for the next four years, and had become one of the best in the world in 2004. Mack won at the Trials to earn a ticket to Athens, where Hoyt had gotten the streak started.

Mack improved on his performance of 5.90 meters in the Trials, clearing 5.95 meters to win the gold medal and set an Olympic record. Teammate Toby Stevenson finished second. The meet record has since been broken, but as of 2021 Mack was still the last American to be part of his country's great winning tradition in the pole vault.

August 27, 1850 — The first harness racing meet in the area's history starts at the Forest City course. It lasts five days and is organized by the Cleveland Jockey Club.

August 27, 2004 — LeBron James plays three minutes and hits one 3-point shot attempt for Coach Larry Brown as USA Basketball loses, 89-81, to Argentina in the semifinals of the 2004 Olympic Games in Athens, Greece. The defeat means the U.S. settles for the third-place bronze medal.

August 27, 2011 — Jim Thome hits his first home run since returning to the Indians. It's No. 602 in his career and No. 335 as an Indian.

August 28, 1983 — A great deal for the Indians

Late August was the time in the 1980s for pennant contenders to make one last attempt to bolster the lineup for the stretch drive of September. If a waiver deal was made and the incoming player was on the roster as of September 1, he would be eligible to participate in the postseason. It's also a time for teams to try to move players who will be free agents at the end of the season.

Those two factors were in play when the Indians and Braves talked about a trade. Cleveland had a pitcher named Len Barker, who was best known for throwing a perfect game two years earlier. Barker was 8-13 with a 5.11 ERA while fighting an elbow injury, and he already had told Cleveland's front office that he was not interested in returning to the team for 1984.

The Braves, meanwhile, were battling the Los Angeles Dodgers in the National League West. Barker could serve as a veteran arm to help Atlanta win the division. The deal was made – with the Indians getting outfielder Brett Butler, pitcher Rick Behenna, third baseman Brook Jacoby and $150,000.

It was later called the worst deal in the history of the Braves. Barker didn't return to perfect game form with the Braves. Butler became one of the best leadoff men of his era, piling up 2,375 hits in his career. Jacoby started at third base for the Indians for seven years, and made two All-Star Games.

August 28, 1926 — Dutch Levsen of the Indians wins both ends of a doubleheader, throwing complete-game four-hitters in two wins against the Boston Red Sox. Levsen did not strike out a batter that day.

August 28, 1987 — Browns linebacker Chip Banks heads to San Diego in a trade with the Chargers. The two teams flip first- and second-round draft choices.

29

August 29, 1977 — Kuiper goes deep, for once

Duane Kuiper stepped up to the plate 3,754 times in his 12-year career. He finished with 917 hits for a career batting average of .271. Kuiper was considered an above-average defensive second baseman for the Indians in the 1970s. It's funny, then, that he's remembered for a one-time-only achievement in his baseball life: one career home run.

Kuiper came up in this game with no home runs in his career, the longest active streak of at-bats of any player without a round-tripper (1,381). Former Kent State star Steve Stone was pitching for the White Sox, and Kuiper hit Stone's 1-0 pitch into the second row of the right field stands. The drought was over.

"When I got back to the dugout, I tried to think back," Kuiper said after the game. "Did I touch all the bases? I knew it would happen. Eventually it has to happen. It was a big thrill."

When he retired, no player had fewer home runs while recording at least 2,500 at-bats in his career.

August 29, 1903 — The Indians and St. Louis Browns are on the same train when it derails because of a missed signal. No one suffers severe injuries, but Addie Joss – who was knocked cold in the incident – becomes ill after making one more start and misses the rest of the season.

August 29, 1983 — Indians owner Francis "Steve" O'Neill dies at age 83. It takes O'Neill's estate about three years before a group headed by two brothers – Richard "Dick" Jacobs and David Jacobs, natives of Akron – complete a purchase of the team. O'Neill, whose nickname was Steve after the onetime Indians catcher, served as principal owner of the franchise since 1978.

30

August 30, 1946 — The Browns get going

The summer of 1946 is the start of a new era for pro football in America. Many of the country's best players had been in military service during World War II. Now the war was over, and an athletic field was a place where talented men could see what their abilities were capable of.

The National Football League was facing competition from a rival as the All-America Football Conference was about to be born. A franchise was placed in Cleveland and former Ohio State University coach Paul Brown was given the task of putting it together. His first signing was a quarterback named Otto Graham, and many other talented players followed.

Still, it was difficult to know what level of talent Brown had assembled until his team actually played a game. The Browns got over that hurdle on this date, when they took part in their first and only preseason game. The Brooklyn Dodgers supplied the opposition, and the game was held at the Rubber Bowl in Akron.

The Browns won, 35-20, before 35,964. For the record, the first touchdown scored in the franchise's history was by Fred Evans, who caught a short touchdown pass from Cliff Lewis. It was the start of a 35-0 run by the Browns. Yes, Cleveland looked ready to play that day, and they proved it during a superb inaugural season.

August 30, 1910 — Tom Hughes throws what could have been the first no-hitter in the history of the New York Highlanders as they take on Cleveland, but the score is tied, 0-0. The teams go to extra innings, and Hughes comes up on the wrong end of a 5-0 decision in 11 innings.

August 30, 1951 — The Browns trade Art Donovan and Sisto Averno to the New York Yanks for a couple of draft choices. Donovan eventually becomes a star with the Baltimore Colts and is inducted into the Pro Football Hall of Fame.

31

August 31, 2004 — A big shutout over the Yankees

The Indians were about out of the pennant race in the American League Central when they played the Yankees on this date. New York was in the midst of another very good season, one that would see them win the division title. So the game represented a chance for Cleveland to be a spoiler.

The Indians put up three runs in the first inning on a bases-clearing triple by Travis Hafner. They scored three runs in the second inning, and three more in the third. At that point, the Indians led by a score of 9-0. Omar Vizquel already had three hits in the game. Cleveland took the fourth inning off, but scored six more in the fifth. Vizquel had four hits at that point.

The Indians only scored a single run in the sixth, but Vizquel had another hit. So it was 16-0 after 5 ½ innings. Cleveland was quiet in the seventh and the eighth, but Vizquel moved to 6-for-6 on the day with a single. Jody Gerut and Victor Martinez hit homers as part of a six-run ninth inning. The only drawback was that the Yankees finally got Vizquel out in the ninth, preventing him from becoming the first American Leaguer in history to have seven hits in a nine-inning game.

The final score was 22-0, tying the major league record for largest shutout. The headline in the *New York Daily News* the next day was, "Stinkees!" It also was the worst loss in Yankee history. New York announcer John Sterling said with a laugh about the Yankees' day, "Well, at least no one got hurt."

August 31, 1994 — Even though the baseball season is under suspension because of a labor dispute, the Indians acquire Dave Winfield from the Twins for a player to be named later. When the season does not resume and the trade is left meaningless, the Indians' front office buys dinner for its Minnesota counterparts as compensation.

August 31, 1999 — Trailing by 12-4 entering the bottom of the eighth, the Indians score 10 runs and beat the Angels, 14-12. Eight of the runs in the rally came after two were out.

August 31, 2020 — The Indians and the San Diego Padres choose different paths to finalize their rosters for the remainder of the virus-shortened 2020 season. Cleveland gives up starting pitcher Mike Clevinger, outfielder Greg Allen and a player to be named for six players – Josh Naylor, Cal Quantrill, Gabriel Arias, Austin Hedges, Joey Cantillo and Owen Miller.

September 1, 2022 — Cavs take a bold step

The Cavaliers hadn't been particularly relevant in the NBA once LeBron James left in 2018. But after three dreary seasons, a 44-38 season in 2021-22 gave the team some hope for the future. It was enough to convince Cleveland's front office that the team was close to becoming a possible title contender.

The Cavs then acted to take that step in a huge way. Cleveland acquired guard Donovan Mitchell – three-time All-Star – from the Utah Jazz. Suddenly, the roster had a powerful look to it.

The price tag was heavy. The Cavs gave up Lauri Markkanen, Ochai Agbaji and Collin Sexton in the swap. Cleveland also gave up three first-round draft choices (2025, 2027 and 2029), and agreed to swap picks (2026 and 2028) in the transaction.

Mitchell had averaged 25.9 points per game in 2021-22. He was scheduled to move into a starting lineup that also included Darius Garland, Isaac Okoro, Evan Mobley and Jarrett Allen. Suddenly, the possibilities for the Cavs' immediate future had come into focus.

September 1, 1980 — The Browns trade a second-round draft choice in 1981 and a third-round pick in 1982 to the Buffalo Bills for guard Joe DeLamielleure, a future Hall of Famer.

September 1, 2008 — Cliff Lee wins his 20th game of the season for the Indians with a five-hit shutout of the White Sox. He went on to finish 22-3.

2

September 2, 1972 — Wottle comes from behind to win

If anyone were to create a list of the greatest runs in the history of track and field, Dave Wottle's performance in the 1972 Olympics certainly deserves to be on it.

The Canton native had qualified for the Games in Munich with a world-record performance in the 800 meters at the Olympic Trials earlier that year. Still, he wasn't considered the favorite in the race. It was a strong field, and Wottle had been having some knee problems that prevented him from full workouts that summer.

When the race started, Wottle – wearing a distinctive golf cap – was soon in last place, eight to 10 meters back. Then he was in sixth place with a half-lap to go, and in fourth place with 100 meters left. Wottle put on his characteristic kick and kept passing people. Finally, he caught leader Evgeny Arzhanov of the Soviet Union just before the finish line. Wottle didn't know he had won a gold medal until the result flashed on the scoreboard.

Wottle had attended Bowling Green State University before the Olympics called. He eventually became a college track coach and then an administrator. If you've never watched his greatest athletic moment, it's available on YouTube.

September 2, 1949 — A movie named "The Kid From Cleveland" about baseball and a teenage fan is released by Republic Pictures. There are 17 Indians players and officials included in the cast, including Bill Veeck, Lou Boudreau, Bob Feller, Satchel Paige and Tris Speaker.

September 2, 1990 — Blue Jays pitcher Dave Stieb throws a no-hitter against the Indians in a 3-0 win in Municipal Stadium. It's the last no-hitter in stadium history.

September 2, 2006 — Kevin Kouzmanoff of the Indians hits a grand slam in his first major league at-bat in a game against Texas.

September 3, 1920 — A tribute to Ray Chapman

The death of Indians shortstop Ray Chapman after he was hit by a pitch in the days of no batting helmets was a shock to the baseball world. The incident occurred in the first game of a 15-game road trip and the club took a train back to Cleveland for Chapman's funeral before resuming the road trip in Boston.

On this day, the Indians played their first home game without Chapman. The game was preceded by a memorial service with a crowd of 15,000. The flag was placed at half-staff, a choir sang "Lead, Kindly Light," and a bugler from Chapman's Navy Reserve unit walked to the shortstop position and played "Taps."

Perhaps the game was an afterthought as Cleveland dropped a 1-0 decision to Detroit. Ty Cobb drove in the only run.

A 175-pound bronze plaque was made to honor Chapman, and it hung in League Park and then Municipal Stadium. Then it got lost for years, before it was discovered in Jacobs Field – sitting in a storage room. The Indians had it cleaned, and it found a new home in Heritage Park beyond the bullpens in the stadium. The bottom reads, "He Lives In The Hearts Of All Who Knew Him."

September 3, 1996 — Hillsborough County voters in Florida, which includes the city of Tampa, approve a 30-year sales tax by 53 to 47 percent to pay for a $168.5 million new stadium for the NFL Buccaneers franchise. The vote quashes rumors that the Buccaneers might have relocated to Cleveland.

September 3, 2019 — Indians pitcher Carlos Carrasco returns to the mound in Progressive Field for the first time after being diagnosed with leukemia. His appearance is a human triumph over medical adversity, even though he gives up four runs in the eighth inning in a 6-5 loss to the White Sox.

4

September 4, 1991 — Thome breaks in to the majors

The odds are against a 13th-round baseball draft choice reaching the major leagues. And so Jim Thome's rise up the Indians' organizational ladder was a nice surprise. It led to him showing up for work at the Metrodome in Minneapolis on this day, and he was penciled into the starting lineup as a third baseman.

He had spent the season playing AA and AAA ball, and displayed a good average but not a lot of power – seven homers. It appeared Cleveland had little to lose in giving playing time to the youngster, since the team had a record of 43-88.

Thome struck out in his first at-bat in the majors against the Twins' David West. But in the fourth, he singled for his first big league hit against Tom Edens. Thome later came around to score. After a fly out in the fifth, he singled to get his first RBI for the Indians to complete a 2-for-4 day.

Thome wasn't quite done with the minors at that point. He spent parts of 1992 and 1993 there before coming up to the majors for good. He became one of the most feared sluggers in the game and finished with 612 homers – 337 in Cleveland. He was a first-ballot choice for the Baseball Hall of Fame in 2018.

September 4, 1953 — "Jack Graney Night" is celebrated at Municipal Stadium, as the Indians' announcer is saluted for 22 years on the team's radio broadcasts. Graney was the first ex-player to become a sports announcer, starting early in the 1932 season.

September 4, 1994 — Tom Tupa, a native of the Cleveland suburb of Brecksville, becomes the answer to a trivia question as the first NFL player to score a two-point conversion. The run comes in the first quarter of the Browns' 28-20 win over the Bengals in Cincinnati.

September 5, 1949 — Tragedy in the Ohio skies

The National Air Races were a fixture on the calendar for Northeast Ohio. They arrived in Cleveland in 1929, and attracted huge crowds as well as many national celebrities. The fans watched a variety of events over the years. One was the end of a race from Los Angeles to Cleveland. Another was a more compact competition featuring planes that flew around pylons as fast as possible.

But there were major risks involved. Accidents cost pilots their lives in 1934, '37, '38 and '39. More problems followed in the 1940s, accompanied by near-misses. Then in 1949,

Bill Odom took part in the Thompson Trophy race on a seven-pylon course in a P-51 Mustang. Odom was more of a long-distance flyer than one who navigated tight turns.

Odom rounded a turn at too steep of an angle. The plane flipped over, and headed directly into a housing development. Odom crashed into the house at 429 West Street in Berea. He died in the accident, along with a mother and her young child. The father and another child were outside of the house and spared.

Berea soon passed a law prohibiting air races from taking place over its territory. Other cities and municipalities followed. Perhaps the mix of faster airplanes and suburban expansion had the potential to lead to such a tragedy, but it took Odom's accident to spark protective action.

September 5, 1921 — Elmer Smith of the Indians finishes an unprecedented batting spree, collecting seven straight extra-base hits (four homers and three doubles) over two days.

September 5, 1954 — Tommy Bolt wins the Rubber City Open, the first pro golf tournament staged at Firestone Country Club in Akron. Fred Hawkins finishes second.

September 5, 1976 — Crowd favorite Jack Nicklaus wins the first World Series of Golf tournament played in a PGA Tour-like traditional four-day format. Nicklaus' first prize was $100,000. It was his last victory at Firestone Country Club in Akron.

September 5, 1977 — A crowd of 28,184 in Municipal Stadium enjoys the Indians' doubleheader sweep of the Yankees, by scores of 4-3 and 5-4. They also take home a souvenir promotional item created by radio talk show host Pete Franklin: it's an "I Hate the Yankees Hankee."

September 6, 1972 — Berger killed by terrorists in Munich

The horrific events in Munich, West Germany, during the 1972 Olympic Games were a stark reminder that life can be fragile even for the world's top athletes.

David Berger was born in Cleveland and graduated from Shaker Heights High School. He won an NCAA weightlifting title for Tulane as a junior. After graduation, he received a law degree and finished fourth in the 1968 U.S. Olympic Trials as a middleweight. Then Berger emigrated to Israel, where he qualified for that country's Olympic team in 1972.

Berger was eliminated from the competition in a preliminary round. A few days later, he was part of the kidnapping of several Israeli athletes and officials by the Black September group in the Olympic Village. It ended in a firefight at the airport. ABC-TV broadcaster Jim McKay remembered later that he realized that he was in essence talking directly to Berger's family when official word came about the fate of the hostages: "They're all gone."

The Ohio Parks' David Berger National Memorial is in the Cleveland suburb of Beachwood and was dedicated to the memory of Berger and the other 10 athletes who died.

September 6, 1946 — Bill Willis, a defensive lineman, and Marion Motley, a fullback/linebacker, take part in the Browns' first game in the newly formed pro football league called the All-America Football Conference. It's a 44-0 home win over Miami. The two players became the first Black Americans to play professional football in that era.

September 6, 1990 — The Cavaliers match a free-agent contract offer from the Miami Heat, and keep John "Hot Rod" Williams on the roster. The deal is for $26.5 million over seven years, and makes Williams the NBA's highest-paid player at the time.

7

September 7, 1963 — Canton's Hall opens its doors

The story of the National Football League essentially began in Canton in 1920, when several potential team owners met to form the circuit. It was that piece of history that led to the idea of locating the Pro Football Hall of Fame there.

The Canton newspaper, *The Repository*, published an editorial in December of 1959 saying that pro football deserved a Hall of Fame – and it should be in Canton. It took less than two months for the people of Canton to rally around the idea. In another three months, the NFL officially approved Canton as the site.

That was the easy part. The organizing committee needed land to build a suitable structure, and a design, too. The proposal eventually came together, and a groundbreaking ceremony took place on August 11, 1962. From there it took a little more than a year for the facility to open.

Let's salute the original class of inductees here: Sammy Baugh, Bert Bell, Joe Carr, Earl "Dutch" Clark, Harold "Red" Grange, George Halas, Mel Hein, Wilbur "Pete" Henry, Robert "Cal" Hubbard, Don Hutson, Earl "Curly" Lambeau, Tim Mara, George Preston Marshall, Johnny "Blood" McNally, Bronislau "Bronko" Nagurski, Ernie Nevers and Jim Thorpe.

September 7, 1935 — The Indians pull off a rare 5-6-4-3 triple play against the Red Sox. Joe Cronin's line drive bounces off third baseman Odell Hale's head to shortstop Bill Knickerbocker. He catches it and flips to Roy Hughes at second, and the ball then goes to Hal Trosky at first for the triple play.

September 7, 1981 — Brian Sipe throws a team record 57 passes, but the Browns still can't keep up with the Chargers in a 44-14 loss. Sipe had 31 completions for 375 yards with two touchdowns and two interceptions.

8

September 8, 1995 — Indians return to the playoffs

The Indians turned Cal Ripken into a supporting player during this game. That wasn't easy to do in 1995.

Two days earlier, Ripken had broken Lou Gehrig's streak for consecutive games by playing in No. 2,191. That was an emotional night, and it was followed by a big parade in Baltimore the next day. But Ripken was back at work a day later in Cleveland. The Indians' fans gave Ripken huge ovations when he took the field at the start of the game, and when game No 2,192 became official.

But Cleveland had bigger things on its mind. The Indians had the chance to wrap up the American League Central Division title, and thus qualify for the playoffs for the first time since 1954. Since Cleveland led by more than 20 games at the time, it was a matter of "when" instead of "if."

The Indians did it with a 3-2 win. Orel Hershiser pitched well and Eddie Murray drove in two runs with a single. As the championship banner was raised after the game, the song "The Dance" by Garth Brooks was played over the stadium's sound system. It was a tribute to relief pitcher Steve Olin, who had been killed two years before in a boating accident during the team's first spring training camp in Florida. For those who knew the connection, tears flowed freely.

September 8, 1939 — Bob Feller becomes the youngest pitcher to ever win 20 games, as the 20-year-old beats St. Louis.

September 8, 1998 — Al Lerner, chairman of credit card company MBNA, is approved as the new owner of the expansion Browns. The price tag is $530 million, a record for a sports franchise at that time. The vote was 29-0 of the other NFL owners – with one abstention belonging to Al Davis of the Oakland Raiders. One of the other groups bidding for the team was led by Charles Dolan of New York, assisted by entertainer Bill Cosby and retired Dolphins coach Don Shula.

September 8, 2002 — The Browns drop a 40-39 decision to the Chiefs in a game remembered for Dwayne Rudd's helmet toss after a penalty that made the game-winning field goal much easier.

9

September 9, 1962 — Nicklaus wins first World Series

Two guys named Walter Schwimmer and J. Edwin Carter got together and thought up the idea of a two-day golf tournament. They wanted to name it the World Series of Golf and bring together the winners of golf's "majors" – the Masters, the U.S. and British Opens, and the PGA – for 36 holes with a first prize totaling $50,000, an unheard-of amount in that era. Schwimmer was a television producer based in Chicago. Carter had worked for the PGA. And so let it be written, let it be done.

The biggest decision was where to hold the event – and it was decided that Firestone Country Club in Akron offered a splendid venue for color TV from the 13th to the 18th holes on the recently redesigned South Course. NBC signed up for the broadcast and big corporate names Zenith Radio (of Chicago) and Amana (an appliance company from nearby Iowa) became sponsors.

And who qualified for the first event? Why, none other than Arnold Palmer, Gary Player and Jack Nicklaus, who were on their way to earning the nickname "The Big Three" in the early 1960s. They won all of the major championships in golf in 1962; Palmer had taken two of the titles. During a practice round on Friday, news coverage in the *Akron Beacon Journal* noted that Palmer had jokingly referred to Nicklaus as "Baby Beef."

Palmer shot a course record 65 to take the first-round lead. However, he slumped to a 74 on day two. That opened the door for Nicklaus, who finished with a two-day total of 135. That was four shots ahead of both Palmer and Player.

The rest of the PGA Tour was playing in Denver that week. Bob Goalby was the winner of that tournament and his award was $4,300. Nicklaus won four titles during the time that the World Series was staged in this format until 1975. Then, in 1976, it became a four-day event and brought together players who had won something, somewhere over the previous year. Nicklaus won the first expanded World Series event, too, with first prize of $100,000. In 1984, international players who had won an event were added to the field.

September 9, 1931 — Municipal Stadium hosts its first-ever football game – an exhibition contest between the Cleveland Indians of the NFL and the semipro Pennzoils. A crowd of about 35,000 watches the Indians win, 10-0.

September 9, 1956 — Akron native Shirley Fry wins the U.S. Open tennis championship in New York, beating Althea Gibson, 6-3, 6-4.

September 9, 1979 — After blowing a 20-0 lead, the Browns beat the Chiefs, 27-24, on a late pass from Brian Sipe to Reggie Rucker. In 1980, the team would earn the nickname of "Kardiac Kids" for games such as this.

10

September 10, 1967 — Graebner falls just short of major

Northeast Ohio doesn't have a reputation as a tennis hotbed, perhaps because of its climate. Therefore, the success stories in the sport deserve to be celebrated – and Clark Graebner was one.

He became a three-time state champion in high school at Lakewood High School in 1959, '60 and '61. Clark played amateur tennis at the highest level starting in 1960, and quickly developed a reputation as having one of the hardest serves in the sport.

Graebner might have peaked in 1967, when he met John Newcombe in the finals of the U.S. Open on this day. Newcombe was a little better, winning in straight sets – 6-4, 6-4, and 8-6. It was Graebner's only appearance in a Grand Slam singles final.

But he and Dennis Ralston did win the doubles title at the French championships in 1966, and at one point he was ranked seventh in the world. Graebner was a big part of several U.S. teams that won the Davis Cup as well. He also was part of a memorable match with Arthur Ashe at the U.S. Open in 1968 that was the basis for John McPhee's praised book, *Levels of the Game.*

September 10, 1937 — The newest member of the NFL, the Cleveland Rams, are defeated 28-0 by the Detroit Lions in their first game. The Rams would win their second game and then lose all the remainder for a 1-10 season.

September 10, 1989 — The Browns hand the Steelers a 51-0 shellacking on the Opening Day of a new NFL season.

September 10, 1992 — Browns defensive back Frank Minnifield receives $50,000 as one of four players found by a jury in Minneapolis as a victim of an unfair NFL free agent system. The legal case was known as the Freeman McNeil lawsuit because the New York Jets' running back was a lead individual in the filing.

September 10, 1995 — The Browns and Indians play home games nearby each other for the first time in their respective stadium and ballpark. Both are winners, the Browns by 22-6 over Tampa Bay and the Indians by 5-3 over the Orioles.

11

September 11, 1952 — Indians keep chasing Yankees

History has forgotten how good the Indians of 1952 were. They took part in a thrilling pennant race with the Yankees that featured a closing rush by both teams.

Cleveland was in the middle of that battle on this date, when it hosted the Philadelphia Athletics. Only 7,903 turned out, but they saw a great pitcher's duel. Harry Byrd of the A's only allowed five hits over eight innings. But one of them was a home run to Bobby Avila, a solo shot in the fourth inning.

That was enough for Mike Garcia. He allowed only two hits in pitching a complete game shutout. Garcia walked two and struck out three in winning his 20th game of the season.

With the win, the Indians moved to within a half-game of the Yankees. They had gone 9-2 in September and looked poised to try to break New York's pennant-winning streak of 1949, '50 and '51. But despite going 11-3 during the rest of the season to finish 93-61, it wasn't good enough. New York closed with a 12-2 record – including a win over the Indians on Sept. 14 – to take the American League pennant by two games. New York had 95 wins, Cleveland had 93.

September 11, 1956 — Bob Lemon earns his 200th career pitching victory, a 3-1 triumph over Baltimore.

September 11, 2007 — The Browns trade quarterback Charlie Frye to Seattle for a draft choice. The move comes only after he had started in Cleveland's opening game, going 4 for 10 with an interception and five sacks before departing in the first half of a 34-7 loss to Pittsburgh.

September 12, 1954 — Indians crush Yankees' hopes

A script for a better day for Cleveland's baseball fans couldn't have been written by Hollywood. It was a situation that was filled with optimism. The Indians were to host the Yankees in a Sunday doubleheader at Municipal Stadium. Cleveland had a 6½-game lead over New York with about two weeks left in the season, so it was a chance to do major damage to the Yankees' small hopes of winning a sixth straight title.

The fans of Ohio noticed. The game drew a crowd of 86,563. That was a record for a major league game, one that would not be broken until the Dodgers played in the Los Angeles Coliseum later in the decade. What's more, it turned out perfectly for the home team.

Bob Lemon went the distance in the opener for Cleveland, allowing six hits and one run. Al Rosen drove in two runs with two hits, and the Indians were 4-1 winners. Then in the nightcap, New York scored twice in the top of the first, but Cleveland replied with three in the fourth. Early Wynn was magnificent, allowing three hits in nine innings and striking out 12 in the 3-2 win.

The Yankees fell 8½ games back with 10 games to go. Manager Casey Stengel knew his team's hopes were done. He quickly dressed after the game and left the park without talking to anyone, an unusual move for the loquacious skipper. The Indians' play had left him speechless.

September 12, 1948 — The Browns defeat the Bills in Buffalo, 42-13, in the first game telecast back to Cleveland through the DuMont Network. Bob Neal and Stan Gee were the announcers.

September 12, 1965 — Two Cleveland quarterbacks – Otto Graham of the Browns and Bob Waterfield of the Rams – are inducted into the Pro Football Hall of Fame in Canton. Another enshrinee is Guy Chamberlin, who played end and was a coach (58-16-7 in six seasons). Chamberlain played in Canton in 1922 and '23 and in Cleveland in 1924.

September 12, 1974 — The Indians purchase Frank Robinson from the Angels; Cleveland later sends Ken Suarez and Rusty Torres west to complete the waiver deal.

13

September 13, 2017 — A record win streak for Indians

On August 23, 2017, the Indians dropped a 6-1 decision to the Red Sox. That was four losses in seven games for Cleveland. The Indians still had a 4½-game lead in the American League Central, but there was no sign that anything special was about to take place.

A day later, Kansas City came to town for a three-game series. Not only did the Indians sweep those games, but they didn't allow a run in any. Cleveland was off and running.

The Indians kept winning, and winning, and winning. They had won a preposterous 20 games in a row entering this day's game with the Tigers. No. 21 would set the American League record. Cleveland was aggressive at the plate right from the start, as Jay Bruce hit a three-run homer in the bottom of the first. The Indians added a couple of single runs later on, and the pitching staff did the rest in a 5-3 win.

"I think they're enjoying themselves. They should. It's pretty special," manager Terry Francona said about his team, which won one more game before losing to Kansas City on September 15.

September 13, 1883 — Hugh Daily throws a no-hitter for the Cleveland Blues in a 1-0 win over Philadelphia. His nickname was "One Arm," as a hunting accident ripped off his left hand.

September 13, 1936 — At age 17, Bob Feller sets the American League strikeout record and ties Dizzy Dean for the major-league record with 17 in a 5-2 complete-game win for the Indians over the Philadelphia Athletics. Feller walked nine batters in the game.

September 13, 1946 — The only inside-the-park homer in Ted Williams' career gives the Red Sox a 1-0 win over the Indians in Cleveland, and – coupled with a loss by the Tigers later in the day – the American League pennant.

14

September 14, 1971 — A long night at the office

There were no requests for refunds when the Senators met the Indians in a twi-night doubleheader at Municipal Stadium – even though the fans only saw one game decided.

The first game was over in less than two hours. Vince Colbert threw a nifty four-hitter as Cleveland beat Washington, 3-1. After an appropriate break, the second game began. The

Indians had a 5-2 lead and seemed poised for a sweep. But the Senators came up with three in the top of the ninth, and the game went into extra innings.

Neither team could score in the 10th inning, or the 11th, or the 12th, or the 13th, and so on. Washington used eight pitchers in the game through 16 innings, while Cleveland had seven. Finally, the umpires decided enough was enough, and suspended the game.

The contest went so long that it had to be completed in a different stadium. The scene shifted to RFK Stadium in Washington, since the teams didn't have any more dates on the schedule in Cleveland. The Senators scored three runs in the top of the 20th, the Indians could only respond with one, and Washington came away with a time-consuming 8-6 win.

September 14, 1923 — First baseman George Burns completes an unassisted triple play for the Red Sox in their game with the Indians. Burns catches a line drive, tags the runner off first, and sprints to second before Riggs Stephenson can return to the bag.

September 14, 2003 — Baltimore Ravens running back Jamal Lewis rushes 30 times for an NFL record 295 yards and two touchdowns in a 33-13 victory over the Browns. The record lasts four years until Adrian Peterson of the Minnesota Vikings gets 296.

15

September 15, 2018 — Indians clinch another division crown

Playing a home game against the Tigers with a chance to clinch a division title, the Indians leave no doubt about the outcome.

Cleveland scored six runs in the bottom of the first, five in the bottom of the second, and two more in both the third and the fourth. The Indians at that point had scored 15 runs and made only 12 outs. It was much more than enough, and Cleveland cleared the bench in picking up a 15-0 victory.

They had eight extra-base hits, and five pitchers shared the shutout. Mike Clevinger earned the win, perhaps the easiest of his career, in improving to 12-8. It was the team's third straight American League Central title.

"I'm savoring every moment of this," Michael Brantley said to reporters after the game. "This never gets old to me. This is a lot of hard work that this group has put in to get to this point. It's all well-deserved, well-earned, and I'm glad to be a part of it."

September 15, 1991 — The Browns had never played a hotter game in Municipal Stadium than this one against the Bengals. The temperature was a steamy 88 degrees. Cleveland picked up a 14-13 win.

September 15, 2002 — The Indians decide not to exercise a contract option to keep pitcher Jaret Wright heading into the 2003 season. He came up to the big leagues at age 21 in 1997, and is best remembered as the starting pitcher of Game 7 in that year's World Series. Wright's career ended in 2007 after he spent time with San Diego, the Yankees, the Braves and the Orioles.

16

September 16, 1950 — Browns make a statement

The schedule-maker for the National Football League must have had a sense of humor.

The Cleveland Browns were entering the NFL after dominating the All-America Football Conference from 1946 to 1950. Someone wanted to waste no time in seeing just how good these Browns were.

Therefore, opening night for the NFL season was on a Saturday, and the Browns drew the task of playing the two-time defending champions – the Eagles – in Philadelphia. Some called it "The World Series of Football," and it might have been the most talked-about game of its time.

The Eagles were missing some key pieces, such as standout running back Steve Van Buren. Also, there was a discussion about whether they were overconfident. Coach Earle "Greasy" Neale supposedly didn't even scout the Cleveland team. If true, that proved to be a mistake, as the Browns spotted the Eagles a field goal and then scored four straight touchdowns.

The final score was 35-10, shocking the 71,237 in attendance and many more nationwide. Otto Graham finished 21-for-38 for 346 yards. If there was any doubt that the Browns and the AAFC were for real, it had been erased in emphatic fashion.

September 16, 1980 — The Cavaliers trade their first-round draft pick in 1984 to the Mavericks for guard Mike Bratz. The pick by Dallas would later become Sam Perkins of North Carolina. It's the first major roster move by the new Cleveland management team of owner Ted Stepien and Coach Bill Musselman.

September 16, 1987 — The Indians' Joe Carter joins the 30-30 club, as his 30th stolen base of the season matches his 30 homers. Carter becomes the 10th player to accomplish the double.

September 16, 2007 — Derek Anderson rises out of obscurity to throw five touchdown passes as the Browns win a 51-45 shootout over the Bengals.

September 17, 1920 — Football takes a big step forward

Professional football wasn't too professional after the end of World War I. The college version of the game was clearly the king, leaving financial crumbs to the so-called pros. Some leagues were barely getting by in the Midwest with teams in small cities, but there was little organization. In addition, bidding wars often took place for the best players, meaning that it was difficult to make a profit as an owner. If the game was going to grow, something needed to be done.

Ralph Hay decided to act. He was the owner of the Jordan and Hupmobile auto dealership in Canton, and – more to the point – he was the owner of the Canton Bulldogs, the champions of the Ohio League. Hay brought a few other owners together in a meeting in his showroom on August 20, and the outline of an association came together.

The word went out from there. Who was interested in forming a less regional league? Eleven teams were represented at a meeting on this day that was again held at the Canton showroom. People came from Illinois, Indiana, Ohio and New York. Among those attending were George Halas and Jim Thorpe.

The men formed a league called the American Professional Football Association, and chose Thorpe to be the president. Play would begin later that year. It only took a little more than a week for the APFA to have one of its teams play a game, as the host Rock Island Independents blanked the St. Paul Ideals, 48-0. Head-to-head matchups soon followed, and more teams joined the league during the season to increase the membership to 14. There would be many bumps in the road, especially in the early years, but pro football had started to move forward.

September 17, 1938 — The Rams make their home debut of their second NFL season before 7,446 in Shaw Stadium (a facility in East Cleveland still used by Shaw High School), but fall to the Chicago Cardinals, 7-6.

September 17, 1970 — Indians pitcher Sam McDowell wins his 20th game, a 6-2 victory over Detroit. He and the team celebrate with champagne – not the best idea for someone who had battled alcohol problems. McDowell never won 20 again.

18

September 18, 1954 — Win No. 107 puts Indians on top

In each of the five years after their 1948 World Series championship, the Indians won between 89 and 93 games. Those totals might have been enough to win a pennant here and there, but the Yankees were in the midst of one of the great runs in history – five straight championships from 1949 to 1953 with Akron's Gene Woodling as one of manager Casey Stengel's important platoon players.

But whether it was good fortune or just working harder, Cleveland found some magic in 1954 and this was the day that the Indians made their American League pennant official.

Fewer than 7,000 turned out in Briggs Stadium in Detroit to see the crowning of the new champions. The Tigers scored a run in the first inning and held on to the lead until the seventh. Then pinch-hitter Dale Mitchell – you might remember him as making the last out in Don Larsen's 1956 World Series perfect game – cracked a home run to give Cleveland the lead. That was followed by another home run by Jim Hegan.

The Tigers got one of the runs back in the bottom of the seventh, but Ray Narleski got the last seven outs in relief. It was Cleveland's ninth win in a row, a streak that eventually reached 11, and its 107th win of the season on the way to 111, the most in the American League until the 1998 Yankees recorded 114.

September 18, 1908 — Bob Rhoads throws the first no-hitter in Indians' history, beating the Red Sox.

September 18, 1975 — Frank Robinson, the Indians' player-manager, has his last at-bat in the majors – a pinch-hit single.

September 18, 2018 — A statue of Jim Brown is unveiled outside of FirstEnergy Stadium. He is the first Browns player to be so honored.

September 18, 2022 — The Browns give up 14 points in exactly 60 seconds during the last two minutes after taking a 30-17 lead, and somehow lose a 31-30 decision to the Jets at FirstEnergy Stadium.

19

September 19, 1945 — Feller is back in form

Bob Feller went almost four years between major-league starts for a cause infinitely more important than ballgames – service to his country in World War II. He had been a dominating performer before departing, as he won 76 games from 1939-1941.

When he returned to the Indians in 1945, fans wondered how Feller would find his rhythm and mastery of the art of pitching. He answered that question quickly. In his first start of the season on August 24, he pitched a complete game victory, 4-2, over the Tigers and ace Hal Newhouser. Feller had 12 strikeouts.

Feller's best start of the 1945 season came on this date. He allowed a bloop single to Jimmy Outlaw of the Tigers, and went on to throw a one-hitter as Cleveland won, 2-0. It was one of 12 one-hitters in the right-hander's great career.

Feller made nine starts that year, and went the distance in seven. He struck out 59 in 72 innings. Feller eventually piled up 266 pitching wins in his great career, no doubt missing a chance for 300 because of his military service.

September 19, 1983 - The Browns score 16 straight points in the fourth quarter to beat the Raiders in Los Angeles, 19-16.

September 20, 2018 — Mayfield guides Browns to win

The question was: Would the Browns ever win again? The team's last win had come on December 24, 2016, and the record was 0-18-1 in that stretch.

They played the Jets on this day, a team that would go on to a 4-12 record. So there was hope entering the game, but some of it disappeared when starting quarterback Tyrod Taylor suffered a concussion and had to leave the game.

Baker Mayfield trotted into the contest for the Browns. He was the No. 1 pick in the NFL Draft earlier in the year, and represented a new beginning for the franchise. When the former Oklahoma college star entered, Cleveland was losing 14-0 late in the second quarter.

Mayfield went 17-for-23 for 201 yards in his pro debut. More importantly, he led the Browns on a long drive in the fourth quarter that was climaxed by a 1-yard touchdown run by Carlos Hyde with a little more than two minutes left. The Jets couldn't answer, and the Browns were 21-17 winners. The winless streak was over, and the Mayfield Era had started. Later that season, he cemented the start of his NFL brand by saying, "I woke up this morning feeling dangerous."

September 20, 1945 — The Cleveland Buckeyes wrap up the Negro League World Series title by finishing a four-game sweep of the Homestead Grays with a 5-0 win. The game is played in Shibe Park in Philadelphia.

September 20, 2000 — Swimmer Diana Munz of Moreland Hills and Chagrin Falls High School claims a gold medal as part of the U.S.'s 4x200-meter relay team at the Olympics in Sydney. The team sets an Olympic record with a time of 7:57.80. Munz also won a silver medal in the 400-meter freestyle.

21

September 21, 1970 — It's Monday Night Madness

The idea of a Monday Night Football game had been tried out by the National Football League a few times in the late 1960s. It didn't do too well in the television ratings, and there wasn't much enthusiasm from NBC and CBS about adding football to its prime-time lineup.

ABC didn't have such worries, though. That network could afford to gamble and begin an association with the NFL. Browns owner Art Modell stepped forward to offer to host the first game televised nationally as the Browns met the New York Jets.

The game was supposed to be a showcase for Jets' quarterback Joe Namath, who had become nationally known in January 1969 when he led New York to a Super Bowl upset victory over the Baltimore Colts. However, the Browns were the better team on this night. Cleveland scored the first 14 points and never looked back. The play of the night was provided by Homer Jones, who returned a kickoff 94 yards for a touchdown to start the second half. Linebacker Billy Andrews capped the night with a 25-yard interception for a score. The Browns won, 31-21.

The score was eventually forgotten but the debut of pro football on Monday began a cultural phenomenon. Announcers Keith Jackson, Howard Cosell and Don Meredith became broadcasting superstars. The games expanded the audience for NFL football, and having pro football on ABC from 1970 to 2005 represented a milestone in the league's growth and popularity.

September 21, 1967 — The Akron Vulcans, a new member of a 16-team minor league pro football association called the Continental Football League, fold their operation. The team had sold 700 season tickets at $28 apiece for games at the Rubber Bowl. The team started 1-3, and the *Akron Beacon Journal* reported that the franchise had amassed $70,000 in debts. The team had hired well-known football names Tobin Rote as general manager and Doak Walker as head coach.

September 21, 1997 — Indians pitcher John Smiley breaks his arm throwing a curveball in the bullpen. Smiley, who had been on the disabled list with tendinitis, never pitched in the majors again.

September 22, 1959 — Indians fall short of pennant

You could call the American League standings between 1947 and 1958 at best predictable, and at worst boring. The Indians won the pennant in two of those seasons, and the Yankees won all the others. The National Football League's idea of "on any given Sunday" – meaning a lowly regarded team could win something – did not apply here.

When the end of the dominant run by those two teams finally occurred, it was only appropriate that one of them was on hand to watch it. The White Sox had a chance to wrap up the flag on this day, and a crowd of 54,293 came to Municipal Stadium in Cleveland to see if the Indians could stop it.

Alas for those fans, the White Sox were the better team. Former Indian Al Smith and Jim Rivera hit solo homers for Chicago, while pitcher Early Wynn, another ex-Indian, was effective in going almost six innings. Bob Shaw and Gerry Staley cleaned up on the mound, and the White Sox were winners. Jim Perry took the loss for Cleveland, which finished second that season.

The White Sox went on to lose to the Dodgers in the 1959 World Series. Then the American League returned to normal, as the Yankees won the next five pennants.

September 22, 1954 — Don Mossi, who later becomes known for his relief expertise, pitches a complete game to beat the White Sox for the Indians' 110th win of the American League season – tying the Yankees' AL mark.

September 23, 2007 — Browns somehow lose to Raiders

It seemed like the Browns figured out new ways to lose during much of the first two decades of the 21st century. They may have overdone it on this day.

The Browns had the better record when they played the Raiders, who were on an 11-game losing streak. This matchup was all Oakland during the first part of the game. The Raiders took a 16-0 lead with about two minutes left in the first half. However, Cleveland came back with 10 points before halftime to close the gap.

The game see-sawed the rest of the way. Oakland took a 26-17 lead with about eight minutes to play. Derek Anderson ran for a score with 3:33 left, and the Browns were within two. Cleveland got the ball back, and set up for a potential game-winning field goal. Phil Dawson lined up for the kick, struck the ball, and it went through the uprights. It looked like a Browns win.

But wait. Oakland coach Lane Kiffin had called timeout just before the snap on the field-goal attempt. Dawson had to kick the ball again, and on Take Two, Tommy Kelly blocked it. This play stood, and the Raiders had found a new way to beat the Browns, 26-24.

September 23, 1949 — Indians owner Bill Veeck stages a solemn "funeral" and buries the 1948 championship pennant behind the center field fence under a cardboard "tombstone" that says "1948 Champs" after the Indians are eliminated from the 1949 pennant race.

September 23, 1983 — Akron's Michael Dokes suffers a 10th-round knockout at the hands of Gerrie Coetzee to lose the World Boxing Association heavyweight title. The bout was held in the Coliseum in Richfield.

September 23, 1997 — Sandy Alomar Jr.'s walk-off single gives the Indians a 10-9 win over the Yankees and their third straight American League Central title. Cleveland had trailed, 9-2, at one point.

September 24, 1994 — The Coliseum in Richfield exits

Most major arenas in the United States are located near population centers – usually downtown. The Coliseum that opened in Richfield, Ohio, in 1974, was, well, different.

The owner of the pro basketball (Cavaliers) and pro hockey (Barons and Crusaders) franchises in Cleveland had an idea in the early 1970s when it was time to replace the Cleveland Arena downtown that dated to November 10, 1937. Nick Mileti found land in Richfield in northern Summit County that he decided was both a population and geographic center of the Northeast Ohio region. It worked well for major attractions and when the sports teams were hot. The building opened on October 26, 1974, with a Frank Sinatra concert.

But when the time came for a new baseball stadium in Cleveland, the sentiment of leaders in the city and Cuyahoga County had changed. Now they believed a basketball arena should be part of the pitch to voters to fund the project for two facilities. And they approved a tax on the sale of tobacco and alcohol products to provide the funding.

So it was time to close the Coliseum after 20 years of service. Roger Daltrey of The Who played the last concert there, and that is often associated with the building's ending. However, the Lumberjacks of the International Hockey League still had three preseason games to play in the Coliseum.

The final one came on this date. The Detroit Vipers were 5-4 winners; Jock Callander of the Lumberjacks had the last goal in the building's history. The Coliseum remained empty until 1999, when it was demolished. Now it's an empty field, part of the Cuyahoga Valley National Recreation Area.

September 24, 1916 — Marty Kavanaugh hits the first pinch-hit, grand-slam homer in American League history, and it powers the Indians to a 5-3 win over the Red Sox in Cleveland's League Park.

September 24, 1979 — The Browns score three quick touchdowns in the first quarter and go on to beat Dallas, 26-7, in a battle of unbeatens shown on *Monday Night Football.*

September 24, 1980 — After Cavaliers guard Clarence "Foots" Walker does not report to training camp in a contract dispute, he is traded by Coach Bill Musselman to the New Jersey Nets for guard Roger Phegley. Walker did not report because he said the previous Cavs' ownership had promised a contract renegotiation.

25

September 25, 2022 — Guardians capture division

Cleveland's baseball team had a new nickname in 2022, the Guardians. It was a squad that was the youngest in major league baseball entering the season, and therefore few expected much of a team.

Yet the Guardians hung around the top of the American League Central, as the favored Chicago White Sox never could get going. That gave the young team time to grow up a little. When the calendar turned to August, Cleveland was ready. The team took a share of the division lead on August 9, and never took a step backwards. An 18-3 run made a title inevitable.

The Guardians claimed the championship banner after a 10-4 win over the Texas Rangers. Such players as Emmanuel Clase, Andres Gimenez, Steven Kwan, Triston McKenzie and Josh Naylor rose to the occasion. It was all so unexpected, and therefore all so sweet. Cleveland had its first division title since taking three in a row from 2016-18.

"This team's good. We're not just young. We're pretty good," said starter Cal Quantrill, the team leader with 14 wins, after the game. "I don't think anybody's excited to face us right now. We're playing our best baseball. We're playing baseball the right way."

September 25, 1954 — The Indians set an American League record with their 111th win, an 11-1 victory in Detroit.

September 25, 1955 — Outfielder Ralph Kiner's major league career ends as he plays his last game with the Indians, finishing with a strikeout against Detroit. Kiner, who led the National League in home runs every season with Pittsburgh from 1946-1952, batted .243 with 18 homers and 54 RBI in 113 games for Cleveland. Kiner was voted into the Baseball Hall of Fame in 1975.

September 25, 1980 — The Cavaliers trade starting forward Campy Russell to the New York Knicks for reserve forward Bill Robinzine.

26

September 26, 1977 — Browns work overtime in win

The National Football League added an overtime period in 1974 to help turn some ties into outcomes with a decision. The Browns took their time in testing out the new rule, and they certainly picked a big stage to do it.

Cleveland was coming off an opening week win against the Bengals when they hosted the Patriots on *Monday Night Football* – their first prime-time appearance in four years. It was a noteworthy game. The Browns scored all of the seven points tallied in the first quarter, the Patriots had a 17-0 edge in the second quarter, and the Browns answered with 10 of their own in the fourth quarter.

The scores came at a faster rate in the fourth quarter. Russ Francis of the Patriots and Greg Pruitt of the Browns had touchdowns, and John Smith of New England and Don Cockroft of Cleveland had field goals. The score was 27-27 when time expired. Overtime!

The Browns won the coin toss, took the kickoff and marched right down the field behind quarterback Brian Sipe. Cockroft sent the fans home happy with a field goal for a 30-27 win.

September 26, 1941 — Bob Feller throws a one-hitter in a 3-2 win over the Browns in his last game of the 1941 season; he enlisted in the Armed Forces in December to participate in World War II and did not pitch again until 1945.

September 26, 1954 — Indians second baseman Bobby Avila goes 1-for-2 in the season's final game to clinch the American League batting title with a .341 average. Ted Williams hit .345 but did not have enough plate appearances to qualify for the title.

September 26, 1970 - Infielder Rich Rollins plays the last game of his 10-year major league baseball career, spent mostly with the Minnesota Twins followed by brief stops with Seattle, Milwaukee and Cleveland. Rollins played at Parma High School (while there, he worked as a popcorn vendor at Indians' games) and at Kent State before making the majors.

27

September 27, 1914 — Lajoie's landmark hit has an asterisk

Many standards of statistical excellence have changed in baseball over the years. For example, it's become much more difficult to win 300 games but easier to hit 500 home runs. The exception might be 3,000 hits in a career. Hitting that number is worth a celebration in any era.

The story of Nap Lajoie's 3,000th hit is unusual, probably unmatched in baseball history. That's because no one is completely sure when it actually happened.

Lajoie's approach of the 3,000-hit landmark certainly was news. When the superstar of the Naps doubled in a game off Marty McHale on this date against New York, it was believed that it was No. 3,000. He was only the third player to hit that number at the time, joining Cap Anson and Honus Wagner, and it caused a celebration.

But, according to a note in former *Plain Dealer* baseball writer Russell Schneider's book *The Cleveland Indians Encyclopedia*, a baseball historian did some counting. He claimed that nine of Lajoie's earlier hits apparently were "misplaced." No. 3,000 therefore came earlier, on September 17 in a game against Boston. Therefore, there's a small cloud over this date. However, the September 27 date is the one widely recognized.

September 27, 1940 — Tigers' pitcher Floyd Giebell tops Indians' ace Bob Feller, 2-0, to give Detroit the American League title and eliminate Cleveland. Giebell only won two other games in his major league career. Indians' fans "celebrate" the end of the home season by throwing fruit and vegetables from the stands to the field. Future Cleveland manager Birdie Tebbetts is hit in the head by a basket of green tomatoes in the incident.

September 27, 1947 — The New York Cubans finish off the Cleveland Buckeyes, four games to one, in the Negro World Series in a game played in Cleveland. The starting pitcher for that game is Luis Tiant Sr., whose son becomes a star with the Indians two decades later.

September 27, 1968 — Nick Mileti, a lawyer working for the city of Lakewood, enters the sports business in Cleveland by buying the Cleveland Arena and the Cleveland Barons of the American Hockey League for a total price estimated between $1.8-$1.9 million. Mileti's previous sports experience consisted of promoting a 1967 college basketball game at the Cleveland Arena between Niagara, with star guard Calvin Murphy, and Bowling Green, coached by Bill Fitch.

September 27, 2020 — Shane Bieber of the Indians wins baseball's Triple Crown for pitchers, as he finishes the season leading all major league pitchers in wins, earned-run average, and strikeouts.

28

September 28, 1964 — The Davis Cup comes to Cleveland

The Davis Cup is the oldest team competition in tennis. It dates to 1900, when the United States played Great Britain. A trophy for the winning team was donated by Dwight Davis, one of the participants who later served U.S. President Calvin Coolidge as Secretary of War and was the governor general of the Philippines under President Herbert Hoover. "The Davis Cup" stuck as a name.

The event grew over the years, and received a boost when the pros were allowed to play in 1973. The best comparison to the Davis Cup might be the Ryder Cup, although the golf event only takes a week of the schedule while the tennis competition takes place over the course of months.

Cleveland has hosted the finals four times over the years, and this marked the first one. The U.S. met Australia for the title at the Harold Clark Courts. Chuck McKinley and Dennis Ralston teamed up for America, while Fred Stolle and Roy Emerson comprised the Aussie side.

The winner must take three out of five matches (four singles, one doubles), and this final came down to the last match. Emerson lost the first set to McKinley, but then won three straight. Australia had won the Cup for the 12th time in 15 years.

September 28, 1948 — More than 60,000 fans turn out for "Joe Early Night" at Municipal Stadium. The night watchman had written to Indians owner Bill Veeck and asked why "average" fans were never given a day, so Veeck responded by saluting the World War II veteran.

September 28, 1952 — Broadcaster Ken Coleman does the play-by-play of the Cleveland Browns for the first time, describing a 37-7 win over the Rams. Coleman stayed through 1965, and described every game in the career of legendary superstar Jim Brown. He also worked on Indians' games for a decade.

September 28, 2002 — Jim Thome hits his 52nd and last home run of the 2002 season, setting a team record. Thome had broken the old mark the day before; Albert Belle had hit 50 homers in 1995.

September 29, 1954 — Mays robs Indians with "The Catch"

It might not have been the best catch in the history of baseball, but it might be the most famous. Sadly for Cleveland, it came against the Indians.

The play came in Game 1 of the 1954 World Series in the Polo Grounds in New York. The game was tied, 2-2, in the top of the eighth inning, but Cleveland was threatening with two runners on. Giants' pitcher Don Liddle came on in relief. His fourth pitch to the Indians' Vic Wertz was clobbered – a blast that would have been out of most ballparks.

However, the oddly shaped Polo Grounds was very shallow down the lines and very deep to dead center. Giants' center Willie Mays took off and somehow ran the ball down to catch it after it traveled an estimated 425 feet. Then Mays turned and fired the ball back to the infield. Cleveland's two runners didn't expect Mays to catch it, and they had to return to their bases.

Liddle was replaced at that point. Supposedly, he went to the dugout and said to coach Freddie Fitzsimmons, "Well, I got my man." The Indians didn't score again and the Giants went on to win in extra innings.

September 29, 1977 — Earnie Shavers, considered one of the hardest punchers in boxing history, falls short of an upset of champion Muhammad Ali as he drops a 15-round decision in Madison Square Garden. Shavers was from the Northeast Ohio city of Warren.

September 29, 2002 — The Steelers beat the Browns, 16-13 in overtime, in a bizarre finish in Pittsburgh. Cleveland blocked a field goal attempt that the Steelers recovered, but officials ruled that since the ball didn't cross the line of scrimmage, Pittsburgh could try again. The ensuing kick was good.

September 29, 2007 — Kelly Pavlik of Youngstown knocks out Jermain Taylor in the seventh round to win the WBC and WBO middleweight boxing world championships. The fight was held in Atlantic City, New Jersey.

30

September 30, 2020 — Indians' season ends painfully

The 2020 season was unique in the history of the Cleveland Indians and the rest of Major League Baseball, thanks to a worldwide health pandemic that delayed the start of play and shortened the baseball season to 60 games. As for the Indians, they would finish play in an unusual way.

They drew the New York Yankees in the opening round of the playoffs, participating in a best-of-three series. Cleveland had lost the first game, 12-3, leaving the team in a must-win situation. The Indians scored four runs in the first inning of Game 2 to take a big, early lead.

But New York scored six straight runs to take the lead. Back and forth the game went, and the Indians took a 9-8 lead on a single by Cesar Hernandez in the bottom of the eighth. Cleveland was three outs away from evening the series.

The Yankees, though, wouldn't go away. Gary Sanchez tied the game with a sacrifice fly off closer Brad Hand, and D.J. LeMahieu put New York ahead with a single to center. The Yankees captured a 10-9 victory that took four hours and 50 minutes to complete – the longest nine-inning game in major league history. And that didn't include two rain delays around the start of the night.

September 30, 1937 — Johnny Allen wins his 15th straight game of the year and his 17th over two years (the latter set an American League record) as the Indians beat the White Sox, 6-4.

September 30, 1951 — Grand River native Don Shula debuts as a player for the Cleveland Browns in a 24-10 win over San Francisco. Shula played seven years in the NFL, and then moved on to coaching – where he won more games than anyone in league history.

September 30, 1956 — In the Browns' opener against the Chicago Cardinals, Coach Paul Brown uses a radio to dictate plays to quarterback George Ratterman. The devices were banned from NFL games a few weeks later.

September 30, 1995 — Albert Belle smashes his 50th home run of the season as the Indians beat the Royals, 3-2. He became the first player ever to have 50 homers and 50 doubles in the same season, and he did it in a year shortened from 162 to 144 games because of a labor dispute.

October 1, 1978 — Indians delay Yankees celebration

The 1978 American League East playoff race was one of the most memorable in history, as the Red Sox and Yankees ended up in a tie and needed a one-game playoff to settle matters. However, the Indians played a supporting role in the story.

The Red Sox were almost unstoppable in the first few months of the season and built a double-digit lead in the standings over the Yankees, who were dealing with major injury problems. But the roles were reversed in the final weeks, as New York stormed back to take first place when Boston was hurting. Just when it looked like the Yankees were set to go to the playoffs, the Red Sox caught fire again and closed the gap.

That brings us to the last game of the regular season. The Indians were in New York to play the Yankees, who were one game ahead of the Red Sox. Boston needed to win while New York lost. Rick Waits was the starting pitcher for the Indians, and he picked a great time from a Boston standpoint to be sharp. Waits threw a complete game, allowing two runs on five hits. His teammates did the rest, knocking Jim "Catfish" Hunter out of the game in the second inning. It added up to a 9-2 victory.

When the game was over, the Red Sox were moments away from blanking the Blue Jays, 5-0. The scoreboard posted a message that announced the playoff game would be held in Fenway Park the next afternoon. Then the scoreboard put up a simple message: "Thank you Rick Waits." The results set up an epic game the next day, as the Yankees beat the Red Sox, 5-4. It wouldn't have happened without the efforts of Waits and the Indians.

October 1, 1946 — Bob Feller finishes his season with 348 strikeouts, a mark that stands for 19 years.

October 1, 1989 — Matt Bahr's 48-yard field goal attempt clears the goal post by "two coats of paint," in his words, as the Browns beat the Broncos, 16-13, on the last play of the game.

October 1, 1995 — The Indians set a major-league record by winning the American League Central Division by 30 games. The old mark was 27½ games by the 1902 Pirates.

2

October 2, 1908 — Naps' Joss achieves perfection

Fans of good pitching hopefully were in attendance at League Park in Cleveland on this day. They were treated to two of the greatest performances ever seen on that field.

Ed Walsh pitched for the White Sox, and he was sharp. Walsh pitched nine innings, allowed four hits and one run, and struck out 15. Even Cleveland fans cheered him. But it wasn't good enough to win.

Addie Joss also threw nine innings, but didn't allow a run or a hit, and he didn't give up a walk. Joss pitched a perfect game as the Naps beat Chicago, 1-0. Joss only needed 74 pitches to throw the fourth such game in history as of that time.

The Naps' righty won 24 games that season, and his 1.16 ERA led the league. His nine-year career resulted in a record of 160-89 with a 1.89 ERA, but it was cut short when he died of tubercular meningitis early in 1911. The Baseball Hall of Fame usually is restricted to players who participated in the majors for 10 seasons, but the rule was waived to induct Joss in 1978.

October 2, 1938 — Bob Feller strikes out 18 Tigers batters in setting a record for strikeouts in a game.

October 2, 1954 — The New York Giants defeat the Indians, 7-4, to complete a four-game sweep of the World Series, a stunning conclusion to a regular season that saw Cleveland win 111 games.

October 2, 1974 — Running back Willie Spencer of Massillon High School in Stark County scores five touchdowns for the Memphis Southmen in a 47-19 victory over the Jacksonville Sharks in a World Football League game. Spencer later played one year with the Minnesota Vikings and two with the New York Giants from 1975-78.

October 2, 2013 — The Indians qualify for the playoffs in manager Terry Francona's first year with the team, but fall to the Rays, 4-0, in the American League wild-card game.

3

October 3, 1993 — Closing time on the lakefront

Municipal Stadium, which opened July 1, 1931, after being built with $2.5 million raised in a 1928 bond issue approved by Cuyahoga County voters, wasn't always thought of as a charming baseball cathedral. Ken Harrelson called it the worst stadium in the majors at one point, and part of the problem was that its immense size with a seating capacity of 78,000-plus wasn't a good fit for baseball.

But it was home for 4,197 games by the Indians. The last one came on this date, and 72,390 turned out. It was the third consecutive crowd of 70,000-plus on the weekend.

The White Sox were the opponents that weekend, and they were busy tuning up for the playoffs. Chicago's Frank Thomas and Cleveland's Albert Belle were fighting for the RBI title. Belle took the individual honor but the White Sox won the game, 4-0. Drew Denson of the White Sox had the last hit in the stadium's history.

And that was it, at least in the baseball sense. Mel Harder, who threw the first pitch in the building in 1932, threw the "last pitch" after the game. Bob Hope, once a part-owner of the Indians, sang "Thanks for the Memories." The team would move south onto East 9th Street to the new facility called Jacobs Field the following spring. So the Browns remained as the occupant for the '93, '94 and '95 seasons before moving to Baltimore. Municipal Stadium was demolished in 1996.

October 3, 1936 — Cleveland native John Heisman dies of pneumonia at age 67 in New York City. Two months later, the Downtown Athletic Club of New York renames a trophy in his honor that is presented to the nation's best college football player. Heisman coached two years (1893 and '94) at Buchtel College, the forerunner of the University of Akron.

October 3, 1948 — The Indians lose the last game of the regular season, 7-1, to the Detroit Tigers before 74,181 at Municipal Stadium. That brings the club's home attendance total for the year to 2,620,627, setting a baseball record that stands for 14 years until 1962 when the Los Angeles Dodgers move from the Coliseum into the newly built Chavez Ravine and attract 2,755,184 fans.

October 3, 1995 — Tony Pena's homer off Zane Smith in the bottom of the 13th gives the Indians a thrilling 5-4 win over the Red Sox in the first game of the American League Divisional playoff series. The game takes five hours and one minute to play.

October 3, 2021 — Cleveland's major league baseball team plays its last game with the nickname of the Indians, and the name exits with a 6-0 win over Texas. "The Guardians" are scheduled to debut at home on March 31, 2022, against Kansas City.

October 4, 1948 — One game for a baseball title

A great playoff race between the Indians, Red Sox and Yankees came down to the last game of the season. The race was so close that an extra day was needed to settle matters, as Cleveland headed to Fenway Park to play in Boston in a one-game playoff.

The pitching matchup offered a pair of surprises. Indians skipper Lou Boudreau went with knuckleballer Gene Bearden, even though he had only one day's rest and was left-handed in a stadium that favored right-handed hitters. Counterpart Joe McCarthy chose Denny Galehouse (a native of Doylestown, just southwest of Akron), bypassing veterans such as Mel Parnell or Ellis Kinder for the team's fifth starter.

Indians owner Bill Veeck said he was never so sure that one of his teams would win as he was that day, because Boudreau had come through all year. That's why he ordered a victory party to be set up at a Boston hotel for after the game. Veeck's hunch was right. The Indians jumped to a 4-1 lead on Galehouse – McCarthy never was completely forgiven in Boston for that decision – and the Red Sox never got too close the rest of the game.

The final score was 8-3, as Bearden threw a five-hitter with six strikeouts. Boudreau was 4-for-4 with two home runs as he played like a league Most Valuable Player. That award was confirmed in the offseason. And the Indians were off to the World Series for the first time since 1920.

October 4, 1959 — Jim Brown carries 37 times to set a Browns record; he runs for 147 yards and two scores in a 34-7 win over the Chicago Cardinals.

5

October 5, 2007 — Indians provide science lesson

This was the day when the baseball fans of Cleveland and America learned what a midge was, and how it could affect a baseball game.

The Indians led the Yankees, one game to none, when the teams took the field at 5:07 p.m. for Game 2 of the playoff series. Andy Pettitte and Fausto Carmona (whose real name is later revealed to be Roberto Hernandez) were the pitching matchup, and it was a good one. Melky Cabrera's homer in the top of the third gave New York a 1-0 lead through 7½ innings.

Reliever Joba Chamberlain took over in the bottom of the eighth, and he was joined on the mound by a swarm of midges – flies that don't belong to the mosquito family. Bug spray didn't work, and Chamberlain seemed a bit unnerved. He promptly walked a batter and threw two wild pitches – the second of which scored Grady Sizemore from third. Tie ballgame.

It stayed that way until the bottom of the 11th. Travis Hafner was the hero for Cleveland, singling home Kenny Lofton for a 2-1 win. The Indians went on to win the series in four games.

October 5, 1964 — Drag racer Art Arfons, 38, of Springfield Township near Akron, averages 434.02 miles an hour on runs at the Bonneville Salt Flats in Utah to set a world land speed record. His racer is named the "Green Monster."

October 5, 1986 — After 16 consecutive years of losses, the Browns finally win in Pittsburgh's Three Rivers Stadium, 27-24.

October 5, 1997 — Sandy Alomar's homer off Mariano Rivera in the bottom of the eighth ties the ALDS game with the Yankees, and Cleveland wins it in the ninth, 3-2, to even the series at two games each.

October 5, 2014 — The Browns pull off the biggest comeback in the team's road history with a 29-28 win over the Titans in Nashville. Cleveland had trailed, 28-3, late in the first half. Brian Hoyer (Cleveland St. Ignatius High School) threw two touchdowns to Travis Benjamin in the final seven minutes to finish the comeback.

6

October 6, 1995 — Indians conclude an historic sweep

Winning a playoff series hadn't been particularly common in Cleveland during most of the 20th century. Therefore, the first one that ended a drought should be celebrated.

The Indians had been spectators since 1954 when they met the New York Giants in the World Series. Before that, there had been a one-game playoff series against the Red Sox in 1948 and then the World Series win over the Boston Braves that same year.

So in this first-round series against the Red Sox, it appeared as if the Indians wanted to make up for lost time. It took 13 innings for Cleveland to take Game 1, and that seemed to take a little starch out of Boston. The Indians captured Game 2, 4-0, before the best-of-five series moved to Cleveland.

Charles Nagy was in good form, allowing one run in seven innings. The game was decided in the top of the sixth, when the Indians plated five runs to make it 8-1. Cleveland's stars came through in that inning, as Paul Sorrento, Sandy Alomar Jr. and Carlos Baerga drove in runs.

The Indians' bullpen finished up, as the sweep was concluded with an 8-2 victory. Cleveland's pitching staff finished that series with a team ERA of 1.74.

October 6, 1997 — The Indians defeat the Yankees, 4-3, in the fifth and deciding game of their playoff series in the first round of the postseason.

October 6, 2007 — The Lake Erie Monsters make their debut in the American Hockey League in Quicken Loans Arena, playing the Grand Rapids Griffins. The Monsters lose, 3-2.

October 6, 2012 — The Indians hire Terry Francona as their new manager. Francona had been the skipper of the Boston Red Sox when they won championships in 2004 and 2007.

October 7, 1976 — NHL hockey comes to town

Cleveland-area hockey fans had been thirsting for a team in the National Hockey League for a couple of generations. Their dreams finally came true on this night.

Oakland, California, had been granted a team in the 1967 expansion, but it never thrived there. The team often had financial problems and never had a great record. Finally, the franchise was put out of its misery when it moved to Cleveland. Its new home was the Coliseum in Richfield.

The first sign of potential problems might have come when the attendance figure came out for the first game: 8,899. Still, those fans saw a competitive game with the Los Angeles Kings. Fred Ahern had the first goal in Barons' history, scoring in the third period. He ended up with four goals on the season. Dennis Maruk added a goal a few minutes later to give Cleveland a 2-1 lead. But Tommy Williams scored the tying goal with 6:21 left, and the Barons had to settle for a 2-2 tie.

At least Cleveland hockey fans had a chance to see two good goalies that night. Gilles Meloche had 26 saves; he and Maruk probably are considered the best players ever to suit up for the Barons. Rogie Vachon had 27 stops for the Kings.

October 7, 1948 — The Indians tie the World Series at a game each by beating the Braves in Boston, 4-1, as Bob Lemon bests Warren Spahn. The game makes television history, as it is broadcast into several cities in portions of the country and thus becomes the first contest shown on a "national network."

October 7, 1977 — The Cavaliers are awarded Knicks guard Walt "Clyde" Frazier as compensation for the loss of playmaking guard Jim Cleamons signing with New York as a free agent. Frazier was an integral part of the Knicks' championship teams in 1970 and 1973 but reports said he was not favored by first-year Coach Willis Reed.

October 7, 1979 — It's a crazy day for 5-foot-7, 165-pound kick and punt returner Dino Hall of the Browns as they lose 51-35 to the Steelers. Hall sets a team record with nine kick returns for 172 yards (including a dropped ball that turns into a Pittsburgh touchdown). He also had 58 yards on two punt returns. Hall's NFL career spanned 1979 to 1983, all with Cleveland.

8

October 8, 1895 — Spiders win a title, sort of

Of course, Indians fans all remember 1948 and 1920. But you can go back more than a century for some other happy memories.

The Cleveland Spiders were part of the National League in 1895. They finished with an 84-46 record, good for second place. The Spiders were led by center fielder Jesse Burkett, who hit .409, and pitcher Cy Young, who had a 35-10 record. Normally, that would be the end of the story, but Pirates owner William Temple had proposed a series between the top two teams in the league. The winner would receive the Temple Cup, an $800 piece of hardware.

The Baltimore Orioles had finished first in the National League in 1894 and 1895, and they already considered themselves league champions. They played for the Temple Cup as if it were an exhibition matchup in both years. Baltimore won a total of one game in the two best-of-seven playoffs. It came in Game 4 against Cleveland in 1895, as they won, 4-0, and their fans reportedly threw rocks and eggs at the Spiders.

But eventually the series was concluded, and Cleveland captured Game 5 by a score of 5-2 to win it. If you'd like to identify the likely Most Valuable Player of the series, Young would be a good choice since he won three games. The Temple Cup was handed out for two more seasons, and Baltimore won both. Then the idea was discontinued. Fans can view the Cup at the Baseball Hall of Fame in Cooperstown.

October 8, 1916 — Professional football debuts in Cleveland as the Indians defeat the Carlyle (or Altoona) Indians, 29-7, in an Ohio League game played at League Park.

October 8, 1923 — Jack Trice, considered a top football prospect during his days at East Technical in Cleveland, dies from injuries suffered during a game between his Iowa State team and Minnesota two days earlier. He was the second African American to play football for a major university, and Iowa State named its stadium for him in 1997.

October 8, 1953 — Indians star Al Rosen is part of a postseason exhibition baseball tour with Jackie Robinson. The team is told by Birmingham, Alabama, police commissioner Eugene "Bull" Connor that it will not be permitted to play in the city because of an ordinance prohibiting "mixed" athletic events.

October 8, 2007 — It's on to the American League Championship Series for the Indians, who eliminate the Yankees with a 6-4 win in Yankee Stadium. Cleveland moves into the ALCS for the first time since 1998. Meanwhile, it was the last game for Joe Torre as manager of the Yankees.

9

October 9, 1910 — A batting race to the finish and beyond

An entire book was written about the race for the batting championship of the American League in 1910. Let's try to boil it down to a few paragraphs.

Nap Lajoie of the Cleveland Naps trailed Ty Cobb of the Detroit Tigers by nine points entering the season's last day. The winner was to receive a new Chalmers automobile. Lajoie was to play a doubleheader, against the St. Louis Browns, while Cobb took a single game off. St. Louis manager Jack O'Conner supposedly hated Cobb, and told his third baseman to play back on the outfield grass.

Lajoie, not one to look a gift horse in the mouth, started bunting in order to pile up the base hits. He went 4-for-4 with three bunt singles and a triple. It was more of the same in the nightcap – four straight hits. When Lajoie reached on an error in his fifth at bat, coach Harry Howell of the Naps offered the official scorer a bribe to change the play to a hit.

When the official results came out, Cobb was declared the winner by .385 to .384. The Chalmers company decided to give each player a car. O'Connor and Howell were banned from baseball for life. Then in 1978, historian Pete Palmer discovered that Cobb had a 2-for-3 game double-counted, and Lajoie should have won the batting title. The revised statistics are used in most reference sources, but Cobb is still considered the batting champion by Major League Baseball. In other words, it's still a mess more than a century later.

October 9, 1920 — Cleveland hosts the first World Series game in its history and the joy of that day is only enhanced by a 5-1 win over Brooklyn.

October 9, 1948 — Larry Doby's home run is the difference as the Indians beat the Braves, 2-1, in Game 4 of the World Series. Doby becomes the first African American to go deep in the Fall Classic. A photo of winning pitcher Steve Gromek hugging Doby after the game became a symbol of integration in Major League Baseball.

October 9, 1949 — The Browns' 29-game unbeaten streak comes to an emphatic end, as the 49ers beat them, 56-28.

October 9, 1997 — Marquis Grissom, weakened by the flu, somehow hits a game-winning homer to give the Indians a 5-4 win over Baltimore in Game 2 of the ALCS.

10

October 10, 1920 — An eventful day at the ballpark

An 8-1 baseball game might be thought of as boring. The Indians' win over Brooklyn in Game 5 of the best-of-nine series probably qualified, but there were enough significant incidents in the game to fill a few lines of the history books.

After a quiet top of the first inning, the first three Indians in the batting order delivered hits. That left the bases loaded for Elmer Smith, who came through with a home run to make it a 4-0 Cleveland lead. It was the first grand slam in World Series history, and it thrilled the sellout crowd in League Park.

In the bottom of the fourth, Cleveland had a runner on third with one out, so the Robins opted to intentionally walk Steve O'Neill to set up a play. Pitcher Jim Bagby foiled that strategy by hitting a home run to make it a 7-0 game. It was the first time a pitcher had hit a home run in a World Series game.

Finally, the Robins showed some life, putting the first two runners on base. Pitcher Clarence Mitchell followed with a line drive up the middle. Second baseman Bill Wambsganss caught the ball on the fly, stepped on second for a second out, and tagged the other baserunner for a third out. The unassisted triple play never occurred again in the next century of World Series history.

October 10, 1920 — The Cleveland Tigers play their first game in the new American Professional Football Association, a direct ancestor of the NFL. The Tigers tie the Dayton Triangles, 0-0.

October 10, 1948 — A crowd of 86,288 jams into Municipal Stadium in the hopes of seeing the Indians win the World Series title. They go home disappointed as Warren Spahn tops Bob Feller as Boston beats Cleveland, 11-5.

October 10, 1999 — The Red Sox set a major league record for most runs and biggest victory margin in a postseason game as they beat the Indians, 23-7.

October 10, 2016 — Terry Francona's "new team," the Indians, beats his "old team," the Red Sox, 4-3, to finish a three-game sweep of Boston in the opening round of the playoffs.

October 11, 1948 — The Indians rule the baseball world

This might have been the best day for the Indians in their history. It certainly sparked one of the great parties in the city.

The Indians came into Game 6 with a 3-2 lead over the Boston Braves in the World Series, having missed a chance to clinch the title in front of the home crowd in Game 5. Bob Lemon took the mound for Cleveland against Bill Voiselle. If Boston could even the series, Braves' ace Johnny Sain was waiting to pitch in Game 7.

A Joe Gordon homer put the Indians ahead, 2-1, and Cleveland had a 4-1 lead in the eighth. But Boston fought back with two in the bottom of the inning to cut the lead to one. Relief pitcher Gene Bearden needed three more outs to earn the Indians their first title since 1920 and second overall.

Bearden walked Eddie Stanky, and pinch-hitter Sibby Sisti was asked to bunt pinch-runner Connie Ryan over to second. But Sisti bunted the ball up in the air, which led to a Cleveland double play. Tommy Holmes ended the game with a flyout to left, and the Indians were champs. Indians fans took to the streets in celebration, and hundreds of thousands were there for an impromptu parade staged when the team's train arrived in Cleveland.

October 11, 1946 — The Browns fly to New York for a Saturday night game with the New York Yankees. It was the first time a pro sports team had used air travel for a game, and the Browns flew to their games for the rest of the season.

October 11, 1997 — Cleveland's Marquis Grissom scores on a passed ball on a suicide squeeze play and the Indians take a 2-1 win over the Orioles in their playoff game. Baltimore catcher Lenny Webster insists that batter Omar Vizquel fouled off the pitch but his protests do not change the outcome of the 12-inning game.

October 11, 2015 — Josh McCown sets a Browns record by throwing for 457 yards in a game against the Baltimore Ravens.

October 11, 2017 — The Indians let a two-game lead slip away in the playoffs to the Yankees and lose to New York, 5-2, in the fifth and deciding game of the first round of the postseason.

October 11, 2020 — LeBron James is the first NBA player to be named Most Valuable Player of an NBA Finals series for three different teams as his Los Angeles Lakers beat the Miami Heat, 106-93, for the championship.

October 12, 1920 — Coveleski gives Indians first title

Indians' baseball fans had high expectations entering this World Series game against the Brooklyn Robins. Cleveland had dropped two early games in the best-of-nine series, but now had a 4-2 lead entering Game 7. And Stan Coveleski was on the mound, with two Series wins already to his credit. Fans filled League Park to see their favorites win a title.

The Robins' Rube Marquard was supposed to oppose him, but he was caught scalping tickets in a hotel lobby before Game 4. Reports said the veteran wanted $400 for eight tickets that cost a total of $52.80, but he made the mistake of trying to sell them to a policeman. Marquard didn't start another game in the Series, so Burleigh Grimes was called to open Game 7 for Brooklyn.

Both teams started slowly offensively. Cleveland took the first lead in the fourth when a throwing error plated Larry Gardner. An inning later, player-manager Tris Speaker tripled home Charlie Jamieson to make it a 2-0 game. Then in the seventh, Jamieson doubled home Coveleski to make it 3-0.

The pitcher did the rest. He only needed 70 pitches to go the distance, which is partly why it only took less than two hours to play the contest. The final out came on a fielder's choice, and the fans poured on the field to congratulate their heroes. For the first time, the Indians were on top of the entire baseball world.

October 12, 1982 — The Cavaliers and forward Cliff Robinson agree on a $2.4 million, five-year contract. At a news conference, Robinson says he would prefer to play elsewhere.

October 12, 2004 — Hector Marinaro announces his retirement from professional soccer. He scored 1,223 goals and added 702 assists for 1,925 points in just 685 games in 19 years, and won six league MVP awards along the way – most of them for Cleveland teams.

13

October 13, 2007 — Indians explode in Boston

Runs were not hard to come by when the Red Sox and Indians met in the American League Championship Series. The winning team in the seven-game series scored seven runs in six of the games, and it scored in double digits four times.

Game 2 in Boston, though, might have been the most bizarre. The Indians and Red Sox were tied, 6-6, through 10 innings. Neither side had been able to score since the sixth. Then the 11th inning began and Cleveland exploded.

Let's review what happened. Grady Sizemore singled, Asdrubal Cabrera walked, Trot Nixon singled, Javier Lopez threw a wild pitch, Victor Martinez was intentionally walked, Ryan Garko singled, Jhonny Peralta doubled, and Franklin Gutierrez homered. It added up to seven runs on five hits.

The Indians found themselves up, 13-6. Joe Borowski finished the Red Sox off in the bottom of the 11th with a double play, and Cleveland was a winner. The Indians had evened the series at a game each, and had the home field advantage as they headed back to Cleveland.

October 13, 1998 — The Indians lose the final three games of their best-of-seven series with the Yankees, exiting the playoffs with a 9-5 loss in Game 6 of the ALCS.

14

October 14, 1970 — Cavs begin with a loss

The NBA's schedule-maker certainly didn't do the Cavaliers any favors at the start of their first season in the league. The Cavs were slated to go on a six-game road trip to the West Coast, which would have tired out any team – let alone one in which the players barely knew each other's names.

First, though, was an Opening Night stop in Buffalo to play the Braves. The two teams joined the Portland Trail Blazers as the three new kids in the 17-team league, and they were matched against each other to start their NBA lives. A crowd of 7,129 turned out in Memorial Auditorium for the game.

Sadly for the Cavs, they were rarely close in this contest. Nate Bowman put Buffalo ahead, 12-10, in the first quarter, and the Braves never looked back. Buffalo went on to a 29-18 lead after the first quarter and a 56-42 advantage after 24 minutes. The Cavs eventually lost by a score of 107-92.

Bobby "Bingo" Smith gave a sign of things to come by leading Cleveland with 21 points. John Warren (14) and Johnny Egan (12) were the only other Cavs in double figures. They couldn't stop Donnie May, the former Dayton standout, who had 24 points for Buffalo. Dick Garrett, a starter for the Lakers the previous spring, had 20.

October 14, 1968 — Akron middleweight boxer Doyle Baird fights world champion Nino Benvenuti of Italy to a draw before 3,017 at the Rubber Bowl. Two judges scored the 10-round non-title fight even while a third judge had Baird ahead by one point. Promoter Don Elbaum estimated his financial loss in the bout at $17,000 after committing $20,000 to Benvenuti as prize money and another $5,000 for expenses.

October 14, 1984 — Ozzie Newsome catches a team-record 14 passes, but his Browns still lose to the Jets, 24-20.

15

October 15, 1899 — Spiders limp to the finish line

There must have been a sigh of relief at the end of this day from everyone connected with the Cleveland Spiders of the National League. After all, it had been a long, long season.

Their story represents a lesson about the dangers of owning more than one team in a league. Frank Robison owned both the St. Louis Browns and the Spiders at that time, and he thought a good team in St. Louis would do better financially than a good team in Cleveland. So he stripped the Spiders of much of their talent. Hall of Famers Cy Young, Jesse Burkett and Bobby Wallace all packed for St. Louis, and they were joined by a few other very good players.

The results were predictable. St. Louis jumped from 12th place to fifth, while Cleveland set records for ineptitude with a 20-134 record. Cleveland lost 30 of its first 38 games, and Robison responded by sending his best player, Lave Cross, to the Browns. The Spiders lost 24 in a row at one point, and had one two-game winning streak. Their top pitcher, Jim Hughey, finished with a 4-30 record.

The Spiders finally finished their season with a doubleheader against Cincinnati. After losing the opener, 16-1, manager Joe Quinn picked an amateur player who was a cigar store clerk to pitch the nightcap. Eddie Kolb gave up 19 runs on 18 hits in a 19-3 loss. It was his only major league appearance. The team finished with one win and 40 losses in its final 41 games.

October 15, 1968 — The Indians lose six players in the American League expansion draft. Seattle selects outfielders Tommy Harper and Lou Piniella and infielder Chico Salmon, while Kansas City takes Billy Harris, catcher Fran Healy and pitcher Mike Hedlund.

October 15, 1997 — Tony Fernandez's only home run in 150 postseason at-bats leads the Indians to a 1-0 win over the Orioles and a ticket to the World Series.

16

October 16, 1957 — Indians make a change at the top

It's not often when one of the owners of a business gets fired from a job. Yet that's the short version of what happened to Hank Greenberg.

When the Indians were sold in 1956, Greenberg became a good-sized shareholder (19%) in the team. He was also Cleveland's general manager, and in the midst of a good run, long before the concept of "big market" and "small market" cities was born. The Indians had been a pennant contender for most of the 1950s and reached the World Series in 1954. But attendance fell from 1.3 million that year to 722,256 in 1957. That season also ended with a 76-77 record – the first time the team had been under .500 since World War II.

The club's board of directors took a vote about Greenberg's status on this day and Greenberg was fired. Greenberg abstained from the voting. He stayed with the team for a while, and reportedly was part of an attempt to move the franchise to Minnesota. That plan was vetoed by the rest of ownership.

Greenberg then sold his shares of ownership and got back together with Bill Veeck, the former Indians owner who was running the White Sox at the time. They won a pennant together in Chicago in 1959, but both exited the franchise in 1961. That was essentially it for Greenberg and baseball, although he did purchase a small share of the White Sox in the mid-1970s. And how did the Indians fare after Greenberg's exit? Well, they never won as many as 90 games again until 1995.

October 16, 1964 — After a long discussion, the Indians' corporate board of directors decides not to move to another city and commits to stay in Cleveland for another 10 seasons.

October 16, 2012 — New Browns owner Jimmy Haslam says that team president Mike Holmgren will depart the organization at the end of the 2012 season. Holmgren, the former Super Bowl-winning coach in Green Bay, had been brought in by former owner Randy Lerner with a five-year, $40 million contract. He left with a $16 million payout remaining on his deal and a Browns' record of 12-31 in his tenure.

17

October 17, 1995 — A pennant for the Indians

The Indians enjoyed a great regular season in 1995, finishing 100-44 in a year shortened by labor issues. Still, they hadn't been to a World Series since 1954, and a spot was on the line if they could win one more game.

It certainly didn't figure to be easy. Cleveland had a 3-2 series lead on Seattle, which eliminated the Yankees in a thrilling first-round series. Randy Johnson was the starter for the Mariners, and he was coming off a remarkable 18-2 season.

But the Indians had Dennis Martinez ready for Game 6, and he was good, too. Martinez went 12-5 in 1995, the last time he reached double digits in wins. The veteran had been around long enough not to be worried about a loud crowd in Seattle's Kingdome that day.

The pitchers matched zeroes until Kenny Lofton drove in a run in the fifth for Cleveland. In the top of the eighth, two runs scored on a passed ball (Lofton came in all the way from second on a rarely seen play) and Carlos Baerga added a homer. That was enough, as Julian Tavarez and Jose Mesa closed out the shutout, the game and the series in a 4-0 triumph. Next stop, Atlanta.

October 17, 2004 — Jeff Garcia and Andre Davis combine on a 99-yard pass play for the Browns that ties an NFL record for longest completion. It was Davis' only catch of the day; Cleveland wins the game, 34-17.

18

October 18, 1987 — Replacement Browns earn a win

The game between the Browns and the Bengals came in the midst of one of the most bizarre periods in the history of professional football. It featured the biggest win of all time by the Browns over the Bengals, but some people might say it carried a giant asterisk.

The National Football League and its Players Association was having one of its biggest fights, and the players walked off their jobs in late September. That way, they'd have a couple of paychecks in the bank before taking the ultimate step: refusing to play. So the league opted to recruit "replacement players" to fill the rosters. Exit – Bernie Kosar, Kevin

Mack and Earnest Byner in the Browns' backfield. Enter – Jeff Christiansen, Larry Mason and Major Everett. Cleveland split its first two games with the new players.

By the third week of the walkout, some players were becoming anxious to return to the playing field and crossed picket lines to do so. One was veteran quarterback Gary Danielson, who joined the Browns.

The Bengals didn't have a great deal of talent, and Danielson knew how to take advantage of the situation. He threw four touchdowns to beat the Bengals, 34-0. Perry Kemp, who went on to play four seasons in Green Bay, had two of the scoring catches.

October 18, 1974 — Former Akron Central High School star Nate Thurmond records the first NBA quadruple double as the Chicago Bulls' center gets 22 points, 14 rebounds, 13 assists, and 12 blocked shots. The Bulls beat the Atlanta Hawks 120-115 in overtime.

October 18, 1974 — Portland needs four overtimes to beat the Cavs, 131-129, in a game marked by the debuts of Jim Chones, Dick Snyder, Campy Russell and Foots Walker for Cleveland.

19

October 19, 2016 — Indians advance to Series

It hadn't been an easy season for the Indians. They had lost such players as Michael Brantley, Carlos Carrasco and Danny Salazar to injuries. Still, they reached the American League Championship Series against a Toronto Blue Jays team that had expended a lot of energy with a long closing burst to reach the playoffs and then went through an emotional playoff series with Texas.

It turned out to be a close series in terms of runs, but not in terms of wins. Cleveland won the first three games by a total of five runs, as the pitching staff only allowed three runs. The Blue Jays bounced back to win Game 4, but they still had a big hill to climb.

The Indians started Ryan Merritt in Game 5; he was only making his second start in the major leagues. Merritt did exactly what Cleveland wanted, throwing 4⅓ innings of scoreless two-hit ball. Bryan Shaw, Andrew Miller and Cody Allen did the rest, completing the shutout.

Meanwhile, Mike Napoli doubled home a run in the top of the first, which was enough to win the game. But Carlos Santana and Coco Crisp added home runs, and that was it. The Indians finished with a 3-0 victory, and a date to play the Chicago Cubs in the World Series.

October 19, 1968 — Madeline Manning of Cleveland becomes the first woman in American history to win a gold medal in the 800-meter run. Her time in Mexico City is 2:00.9, an Olympic record.

October 19, 1980 — On third-down-and-20 with 25 seconds left, Brian Sipe hits Dave Logan with a 46-yard touchdown pass to give the Browns a 26-21 win over the Packers. Logan was a third-round draft choice in 1976 from Colorado and played eight years with the Browns. He was the rare athlete who was a pro draft pick in baseball, football and basketball.

20

October 20, 1968 — Browns hand Colts a rare loss

Trivia question: How many teams defeated the Baltimore Colts during the 1968 season (which included a playoff game in 1969)? The answer is two. This is the difficult one to remember.

The Browns came into the game in a bit of trouble. They had lost the previous week to the St. Louis Cardinals to fall to 2-3 on the season. That was a step down for a team that had gone 9-5 in 1968 and played for the NFL title. The Colts didn't figure to do Cleveland any favors. Baltimore was 5-0 entering the game.

Even so, the Browns were in top form. They took an early lead on a short pass from Bill Nelsen to Leroy Kelly and never trailed. Nelsen threw three touchdown passes by the third quarter, and Kelly finished with 130 yards rushing and another score. The final was 30-20, and it really wasn't that close.

However, the Colts got their revenge in the playoffs, and that put them in the Super Bowl against the New York Jets. You might have heard about how that turned out.

October 20, 1865 — The Oberlin Penfields beat Forest City, 67-28, in one of the first baseball games – or intercity sports events – ever played in Cleveland. The game is called after seven innings because of darkness.

21

October 21, 2007 — Indians let opportunity get away

A realistic chance for the Indians to reach the World Series for the third time in 13 years slips away – and it hurts.

The Indians had lost two straight games after taking a 3-1 lead in the best-of-seven series against Boston, and Game 7 was in Fenway Park. The Red Sox scored single runs in the first three innings, but Cleveland came back with a run in the fifth and sixth. It was still anyone's game.

Then came the play that people remembered. Franklin Gutierrez singled to short left and the speedy Kenny Lofton went from second to third. He might have been able to score, but third base coach Joel Skinner held him up. Casey Blake then hit into a double play, ending the rally.

Then Dustin Pedroia hit a two-run homer in the bottom of the seventh to make it 5-2, and Boston scored six runs in the bottom of the eighth. The Red Sox closed it out with a great catch by ex-Indian Coco Crisp in the ninth, and Cleveland had lost three in a row and the series.

October 21, 1984 — Steve Cox boots a 60-yard field goal to set a team record for the Browns, who still lose to Cincinnati by a score of 12-9. The game featured seven field goals and no touchdowns.

October 21, 1994 — The Cavaliers play their first game in the $152 million downtown facility named Gund Arena for team owner Gordon Gund. In 2005, under new team owner Dan Gilbert, the building's name is changed to Quicken Loans Arena. Then it is renamed Rocket Mortgage FieldHouse in 2019. Rocket Mortgage is a business unit of Gilbert's Quicken Loans company.

October 21, 2001 — The Browns defeat the Ravens, 24-14, for their first-ever win against the team that left Cleveland for Baltimore after the 1995 season.

22

October 22, 1984 — Browns dismiss Rutigliano

There was a sense of sadness among Browns fans when owner Art Modell decided to fire Sam Rutigliano on this day.

It had been a fun ride. Rutigliano was hired after Forrest Gregg was let go in 1977.

He made a commitment to quarterback Brian Sipe, and the 1978 draft that brought in linebacker Clay Matthews and tight end Ozzie Newsome laid the groundwork as the team forged its way to an 11-5 season of 1980. The team developed a knack for last-minute heroics – hence the nickname, "The Kardiac Kids" – but the results included plenty of happy endings for a team that was still waiting to achieve its first Super Bowl berth. Rutigliano's work off the field included helping start a substance abuse program for players that was informally called "The Inner Circle." It operated with the help of the Cleveland Clinic and it preserved players' anonymity.

But wins and losses on the field are how coaches are judged and the 1984 season began with a 1-7 start. Rutigliano finished with a 47-50 record in Cleveland.

TV work was a natural move for Sam at that point, and he stayed in that capacity until he took the head coaching job at Liberty University for 11 years. Rutigliano returned to Cleveland to analyze the Browns for some local television stations after that.

October 22, 1997 — The Indians and Marlins play the coldest game in World Series history. The 38-degree temperature doesn't bother Cleveland, which wins a 10-3 decision.

October 22, 2017 — Browns offensive left tackle Joe Thomas sees his consecutive snaps streak stopped at 10,363, when he suffers an injury to his left arm.

23

October 23, 1997 — Indians can't hold off Marlins

The fifth game of any best-of-seven playoff series in sports is usually considered pivotal, because the winner has two chances to wrap up the overall victory. Such was the description of Game 5 of this World Series between the Marlins and Indians.

The Indians sent Orel Hershiser to the mound on a 46-degree night, and he gave up a couple of runs in the second inning. Cleveland responded with four runs in their next two at-bats to take a 4-2 lead. Hershiser pitched well until the sixth, when Moises Alou hit a three-run homer for the Marlins as part of a four-run outburst.

Florida added single runs in the eighth and ninth innings, so it had an 8-4 lead entering the bottom of the ninth. That's a bleak picture, but Bip Roberts and Omar Vizquel reached base and David Justice singled them both home. Matt Williams hit into a force play, and Jim Thome singled Williams home. So it was 8-7 with two outs in the bottom of the ninth, with Sandy Alomar Jr. at the plate.

Could the Indians pull it out? For a split-second, it looked that way. Alomar hit the ball hard to deep right field. But the crowd of 44,888 exhaled when Gary Sheffield caught the ball short of the fence. The Marlins had escaped to win their third game of the series.

October 23, 2002 — Browns' owner Alfred Lerner dies; son Randy takes control of the team.

24

October 24, 1995 — Indians walk off a winner

Fans were thrilled when, after 41 years of waiting, Cleveland hosted its first World Series game since 1954. Imagine how they felt after the game.

Atlanta had won the first two games of the Series, so Cleveland needed a win. The Indians appeared in control of Game 3 with two innings to go. Charles Nagy had been effective, holding a 5-3 lead, and had thrown only 81 pitches. Manager Mike Hargrove saw no need to change pitchers, even though Nagy had given up runs in his previous two innings.

But Nagy only lasted two batters, giving up a double and a single that cut the lead to 5-4. Paul Assenmacher and Julian Tavarez couldn't slow the Atlanta attack either, and the Braves soon had a 6-5 lead. But Sandy Alomar doubled home Paul Sorrento in the bottom of the eighth to tie the game.

It stayed that way until the 11th. Carlos Baerga opened the inning for the Indians with a double, and Eddie Murray followed with the game-winning single. Cleveland had the win, 7-6.

October 24, 1953 — Art Hunter of Akron St. Vincent High School scores a touchdown as his Notre Dame team snaps Georgia Tech's 31-game unbeaten streak with a 27-14 victory.

October 24, 1993 — The Browns' Eric Metcalf returns two punts for touchdowns to tie an NFL record. The second came with 2:05 left and gave the Browns the lead for good. The returns, which went for 91 and 75 yards, allowed Cleveland to beat Pittsburgh, 28-23.

25

October 25, 2012 — A billion for the Browns

When the organization eventually known as the National Football League was formed more than 100 years ago, the cost of entry for a business was about $100. Jimmy Haslam paid a bit more than that to buy the Cleveland Browns from Randy Lerner. The price was $1.05 billion, and the transaction was completed on this day.

About 70% was paid immediately, and the rest came due in about four years. It was the second time that an NFL franchise had been sold for more than $1 billion; the Dolphins had fetched $1.1 billion in 2008.

Haslam had quite a business story to tell. He was one of the co-owners of the Pilot Flying J truck stop chain, one of the 10 biggest privately owned companies in the United States. At the time of the Browns' purchase, he had been a minority owner of the Steelers.

Randy Lerner took over in 2002 when his father Al died after winning the bidding in 1998 for the expansion team that began play in 1999. Randy Lerner also owned a team in the English Premier League, but sold the soccer club in 2016.

October 25, 1977 — Walt Frazier returns to Madison Square Garden in a Cleveland uniform, and leads the Cavs to a 117-112 overtime win over the Knicks.

October 25, 1997 — Pitcher Chad Ogea not only gets his second victory in the 1997 World Series as the Indians beat the Marlins, 4-1, in Game 6 to pull into a 3-3 tie, but he goes 2-for-2 at bat with two RBI and a run scored. Ogea was considered a possible series MVP winner until the Indians lost Game 7.

October 25, 2019 — Indians pitcher Carlos Carrasco wins the Roberto Clemente Award from Major League Baseball. It salutes players who have shown character, community involvement, philanthropy, and positive contributions, both on and off the field.

26

October 26, 1997 — No saving grace in Indians loss

How close can a team come without winning a championship? The Indians found out in the 1997 World Series.

They jumped out in front in Game 7 by 2-0 on a single by Tony Fernandez in the third. The lead held up as the innings went by. Bobby Bonilla got one of the runs back in the seventh with a homer off Jaret Wright. Still, the Indians clung to the lead, and got the game to the ninth inning. There the ball was handed to closer Jose Mesa.

Moises Alou and Charles Johnson put runners on the corners with one out. Craig Counsell's sacrifice fly drove home Alou with the tying run. Mesa avoided further damage, and it was on to extra innings.

Feelings of doom came true in the bottom of the 11th. Bonilla singled and Counsell reached on an error, followed by an intentional walk to Jim Eisenreich. Devon White grounded into a force play at home. The Indians were one out away from escaping the jam, but Edgar Renteria singled to drive home Counsell, and the Marlins were the first wild-card team to ever win a World Series.

October 26, 1980 — The Browns end a seven-game losing streak to the Steelers with a 27-26 win at Municipal Stadium.

October 26, 1995 — The Indians beat Greg Maddux and the Braves, 5-4, to stay alive in Game 5 of the World Series.

27

October 27, 2010 — No LeBron, no problem for Cavs

Was there life after LeBron James? The Cavaliers were about to find out.

James had left the Cavs as a free agent for Miami over the summer. The Cavaliers had to open the season against the Celtics, who had bounced them out of the playoffs in the second round the previous spring.

Quicken Loans Arena was quite noisy on opening night, and the fans had plenty of reason to be excited. It was a close game during the first three quarters, but the Cavs closed with a 27-14 edge in the fourth quarter for the 95-87 win. J.J. Hickson led Cleveland with 21 points.

"This was for the city," forward Antawn Jamison told the Associated Press. "It was for the fans to let them know the Cavs will survive and this is a place where you can still watch good basketball. And most of all, you can watch a team that wins."

October 27, 1974 — Greg Pruitt returns a punt 72 yards to set up the winning touchdown as the Browns edge the Broncos, 23-21.

October 27, 1974 — The first sporting event in the history of the Coliseum was supposed to be played on this night – a hockey game between the Crusaders and the Toronto Toros. However, problems with pipes leave the ice surface unplayable, and the game is postponed. Three days later, a second game has to be postponed for the same reason.

28

October 28, 1995 — Glavine shuts down Indians' offense

Most people figured that the 1995 World Series would come down to hitting versus pitching – the big bats of the Indians would face the fabled rotation of the Braves. In the end, pitching came out just ahead.

The Indians took the field for Game 6 in Atlanta facing a 3-to-2 series deficit. Future 300-game winner Tom Glavine took the mound for the Braves, opposed by Dennis Martinez. The teams traded zeroes on the scoreboards through five innings. Then in the bottom of the sixth, left-handed batter David Justice homered off left-handed Cleveland reliever Jim Poole.

It was up to Glavine to make it hold up. He threw one-hit ball for eight innings in perhaps the signature performance of his career. Then Mark Wohlers came on in relief. The Indians went down 1-2-3 in the ninth, and the Braves had a 1-0 win.

The Braves were in the midst of an amazing run. Throw out 1994, when the playoffs never happened because of labor problems, and Atlanta took part in the postseason for 14 straight times. However, this was the team's only World Series win.

October 28, 1970 — The Cavaliers play their first NBA game at home, and suffer a 110-99 loss to San Diego to drop to 0-8 on the season.

October 28, 2018 — Tyronn Lue is fired as coach of the Cavaliers after an 0-6 start to the 2018-19 season. In his three seasons, the Cavs won one championship and reached two other NBA Finals.

29

October 29, 1987 — Prince gets promotion and a title

"Prince" Charles Williams wasn't born in Mansfield, but he fought out of that city during his professional boxing career. The citizens of Mansfield should be proud of what one of their favorite sons accomplished.

Williams started his pro career with a loss and draw in 1978, which wasn't a good sign about his long-term prospects. He'd have to take the long way to success in the ring, which means plenty of bouts – most of them wins. Williams had won 14 in a row when he finally got his chance at fame, glory, and – of course – money.

The IBF light-heavyweight championship was on the line in Las Vegas when Williams took on champion Bobby Czyz. Williams was a big underdog, and that status seemed to be confirmed when Czyz knocked him down early in the bout. But Williams didn't give up, and damaged Czyz's eye to the point where his corner forced the champ to retire after the ninth round. The Prince was now the king of his division.

Williams never had that big life-changing bout during his time as the champion. But he successfully defended his title eight times through 1993, and finished his career with a 35-6-2 record.

October 29, 1989 — Ozzie Newsome fails to have a reception for the Browns in their game with the Houston Oilers, ending his streak of games with at least one catch at 150. The tight end hurt his ankle in the first half and decided not to play just for the purpose of keeping the streak alive.

October 29, 2003 — LeBron James makes his NBA debut in a 106-92 loss at Sacramento, scoring 25 points with six rebounds and nine assists in 42 minutes.

October 29, 2016 — The Indians move within a game of a championship by beating the Cubs, 7-2, to take a 3-1 lead in the World Series.

October 29, 2018 — The Browns fire head coach Hue Jackson and offensive coordinator Todd Haley after the team reaches the halfway point of the season with a 2-5-1 record. Jackson's career record was 3-36-1. Gregg Williams is named interim head coach.

30

October 30, 1980 — Cavaliers deal away their future

New Cavaliers Coach Bill Musselman came into his job wanting to win immediately. So when he looked at the team roster he inherited from former Coach Stan Albeck, he wanted to make changes to load up on size and play a physical style.

In preparation for the 1980-81 season, Musselman was part of a three-team trade that saw fan-favorite Campy Russell leave and forward Bill Robinzine come in. But only a month later, Robinzine had fallen out of favor with the coach. So he packaged together Robinzine and first-round draft picks in 1983 and 1986, sending those assets to Dallas for big men Richard Washington and Jerome Whitehead.

The Cavs' other moves included sending center Dave Robisch to the Denver Nuggets for backup center Kim Hughes and draft choices. Earlier in the summer, owner Ted Stepien had signed Robisch to a four-year, $1.3 million contract.

As for the result of the deal on this day, a NBA general manager put it this way to *Sports Illustrated*: "They'll be impressive walking through airports, but they won't play well."

Washington had been a star at UCLA in college, but averaged less than 10 points per game, and his career was over in 1982. Whitehead played in college at Marquette but was waived by the Cavs less than three weeks after he was acquired. Meanwhile, Dallas turned those draft picks into NBA All-Stars Derek Harper and Roy Tarpley.

October 30, 1995 — More than 50,000 turn out for a rally in Cleveland's Public Square to salute the Indians for their pennant-winning season – the team's first since 1954.

October 30, 1996 — The Cleveland Rockers are introduced as one of the founding franchises in the Women's National Basketball Association. Gordon Gund, the owner of the Cavaliers of the NBA, is the owner.

31

October 31, 1999 — Browns finally enter the win column

Four years is a long time to wait for a victory. Entering this game, the Browns hadn't posted a victory since 1995 – when the team moved to Baltimore. The rebooted version of the franchise came to life in 1999, but the Browns still hadn't won a game as October drew to a close.

Even so, this looked like a good opportunity for a change in fortune. The Saints were 1-5 entering their home game while the Browns were 0-6. It was a back-and-forth contest, and Cleveland had the lead for most of the fourth quarter.

That made the Saints' final possession tough to watch. Doug Brien kicked a 46-yard field goal for New Orleans to give it a 16-14 lead. The Browns only had 21 seconds to regain the lead.

After the kickoff and an incomplete pass, Cleveland's Tim Couch threw a 19-yard pass to Leslie Shepherd. The Browns still had 56 yards to go, and two seconds to do it. Couch threw a long pass into the end zone, and after a deflection, Kevin Johnson came up with the ball. Touchdown, Cleveland. It was the Browns' first of their two wins in the first year of their return.

October 31, 1972 — Gaylord Perry of the Indians wins the Cy Young Award as the best pitcher in the American League. He had a 24-16 record with a 1.92 ERA.

October 31, 2017 — The Browns work out a deal with the Bengals to acquire former Alabama quarterback A.J. McCarron for two draft choices. But the NFL nullifies the deal because the Browns did not submit the paperwork on the transaction by the 4 p.m. deadline.

1

November 1, 1959 — A shootout of superstars

Ted Williams or Joe DiMaggio? Bill Russell or Wilt Chamberlain? Well, if the argument was about pro football in the late 1950s and early 1960s, Jim Brown and Johnny Unitas certainly would have been in the conversation.

The two were in separate conferences, so they didn't play each other twice a year. But when their teams got together, the results could be special.

Take this day, when the Browns and Colts met in Baltimore's Memorial Stadium. There was a hint early in the second quarter when Brown went 70 yards on a run for a score. Unitas answered with a 3-yard touchdown pass to Lenny Moore.

That set the tone. In the end, the Browns won a 38-31 thriller. Brown finished with five touchdowns (an NFL record at the time) as he ran for 178 yards. Unitas was 23-for-41 for 397 yards and four touchdowns. The teams combined for 823 yards in total offense.

November 1, 1964 — Browns fullback Jim Brown surpasses 10,000 rushing yards for his NFL career, getting 149 as Cleveland beats the Steelers 30-17. The game marked the 47th time he had more than 100 yards in a game.

November 1, 1991 — Cleveland State celebrates the opening of its new 13,610-seat Convocation Center. The building's name was changed to the Wolstein Center in 2005.

November 1, 2009 — Ted Ginn Jr. returns two kickoffs for touchdowns (one for 101 yards and the other for 100) as the Miami Dolphins defeat the Chicago Bears, 30-25. Ginn played in high school for his father, Ted Ginn Sr., as head coach at Cleveland Glenville and then continued his career in college at Ohio State. He was a multiple state champion in track events in high school.

2

November 2, 2016 — Cubs edge Indians in Game 7

They are among the most special words in pro sports: "Game 7." And what a World Series matchup this was – the Chicago Cubs had not won a title since 1908, while the Cleveland Indians' last championship was in 1948. So no matter who won, the storyline was emotional.

It didn't take long to figure out that this would be a special night. The Cubs' Dexter Fowler opened the game with a home run. Chicago took leads of 5-1 and 6-3 as the game went along. It looked rather bleak for the Indians' faithful as they trailed by three in the bottom of the eighth inning.

But Cleveland gained a little hope when it put two runners on base. Then Rajai Davis came through with one of the most dramatic home runs in Indians' history, taking Aroldis Chapman deep to tie the game, 6-6. The tension grew when a 17-minute rain delay forced both teams to take a short break after the bottom of the ninth was completed.

The Cubs rebounded with two runs in the top of the 10th inning, but the Indians didn't roll over again. With two outs and no one on, Cleveland put together a walk, a base on defensive indifference and a single by Davis to get within one. But Kris Bryant threw out Michael Martinez on a nice play, and the Cubs' wait was over. Cleveland's drought continued.

November 2, 1970 — The Cavaliers, playing their 11th game of their expansion-year season, are clobbered by the 76ers, 141-87. Coach Bill Fitch of Cleveland fines his players $54 each for their play – $1 for each point in the defeat. The Cavs lost their first 15 games before finally getting a win.

November 2, 1974 — The third try is the charm as the Crusaders finally debut in the Coliseum with a 4-2 loss to the Edmonton Oilers. Ron Buchanan of the Oilers scored the first goal in the new arena's history. Ice problems had delayed the arena's opening.

3

November 3, 1946 — Pro basketball arrives in Cleveland

Once World War II had ended, pro sports entrepreneurs were anxious to create a professional basketball league that would be national in stature – the same as Major League Baseball and the National Football League. That included Al Sutphin, the owner of the Cleveland Arena. He liked the idea of having an attraction that could help fill vacant calendar dates in his building on a regular basis in the winter.

Therefore, the Cleveland Rebels were born. They were part of the Basketball Association of America, which in 1949-50 became the National Basketball Association. The BAA competed against another circuit called the National Basketball League, which probably had better players than its rival but played in smaller markets.

The BAA opened play on November 1, 1946, as the New York Knicks defeated the Toronto Huskies. Two nights later, the Huskies arrived in Cleveland to play the first game in the history of the Rebels. The crowd at the Arena was reported to be 7,594.

Cleveland earned a 71-60 win in its debut. Frankie Baumholtz got his season off to a great start with 25 points for the Rebels. The team only lasted one season, and Baumholtz – a second-team All-BAA selection – moved from basketball to baseball in the spring of 1947. He finished fifth in the baseball Rookie of the Year balloting at age 28 with the Reds, and stayed in that sport until 1957.

November 3, 1944 — Middleweight boxer George Kochan of Akron loses to Jake LaMotta for the second time in six weeks, with both bouts taking place at the Olympia in Detroit. LaMotta knocked Kochan down in the ninth round, and the bout was stopped soon thereafter. The two also fought on September 17, 1945, in Madison Square Garden in New York.

November 3, 2017 — LeBron James scores 57 points to tie Kyrie Irving's team record and sets a personal best as a member of the Cavaliers in a 130-122 win over the Wizards.

November 4, 1999 — Jacobs hands off to Dolan

The Indians announce the $323 million sale of the club by Richard Jacobs to fellow Clevelander Lawrence Dolan. The official change in control will take place two months later as Dolan announces that John Hart will continue as general manager.

Dolan, who is 68 at the time of the sale, is a lawyer with a degree from Notre Dame. He and his brother Charles Dolan (the founder of HBO), of New York, had attempted to acquire the expansion Cleveland Browns franchise that was awarded to Al Lerner in 1998 for $530 million.

Jacobs and his brother David were natives of Akron, where their father worked for Goodyear Tire & Rubber Co. One of Richard Jacobs' first jobs was at a Swenson's drive-in restaurant, a local chain famously patronized decades later by LeBron James. The brothers acquired the Indians in 1986 for a reported $45 million.

November 4, 1990 — The Browns learned all about the Buffalo Bills' powerful offense (they led the NFL in scoring) the hard way. In this game, Buffalo started with two short touchdown runs by Thurman Thomas of the Bills in the first half. Thomas added another score in the second half, and two other running backs added touchdowns. Cleveland native Darryl Talley iced the cake with a 60-yard interception for a score – his first such play in the NFL. It added up to a 42-0 shutout, the worst such loss in Cleveland's history and its most one-sided loss since 1969.

November 4, 2001 — The Browns blow a 21-7 lead with 32 seconds to play and fall to the Bears, 27-21, in overtime.

November 4, 2017 — Renee Powell, who grew up in Stark County's East Canton and was the second Black woman to play on the LPGA Tour, is inducted into the PGA of America Hall of Fame at a ceremony in Austin, Texas.

5

November 5, 1982 — Cavs become historically bad

The Cavaliers dropped a 99-91 decision to the Nets on this day. That wasn't a big surprise, since Cleveland had lost its previous four games in the young season already.

It was a typically depressing day for the Cavs, who had been having a lot of them since the 1980-81 season. Cleveland stayed close to New Jersey for a half, but a good third quarter gave the Nets enough of a margin to win. That was in spite of the fact that all five Cavs starters finished in double figures, led by 23 points from 7-foot center James Edwards.

It was Cleveland's 24th consecutive loss spread over two seasons. That total set an NBA record at the time. The first loss in the streak was back on March 19, 1982; the Cavs had defeated the equally dismal San Diego Clippers two days before that.

Cleveland's streak would end on November 10 with an overtime win over Golden State. Still, it would be an awful start for the Cavs, as they went 4-28 in their first 32 games.

November 5, 1950 — Defensive back Tommy James of the Browns intercepts three passes in a game against the Chicago Cardinals. James, from Massillon, played eight years for Cleveland and was the older brother of renowned college coach Don James.

November 5, 1961 — The Cleveland Pipers of the new American Basketball League play their first-ever game, losing to Pittsburgh, 87-82.

November 5, 1990 — The Browns fire Bud Carson as head coach with an 11-13-1 record, as he does not last two full seasons after succeeding Marty Schottenheimer. Jim Shofner is named the interim replacement.

6

November 6, 1995 — Browns say they're leaving Cleveland

Browns' owner Art Modell had been working for several years on a remodeled or new stadium. His temperature certainly rose a few degrees when the Indians moved out of Cleveland Stadium and played their first game in a new home, Jacobs Field, in 1994. Threats were made along the way about the Browns moving elsewhere, but most expected the situation to be worked out eventually.

But on this day, Modell stood in front of a site in Camden Yards in Baltimore, and announced he would be moving the Browns there in 1996. The Browns, out of Cleveland? Indeed. Cuyahoga County voters approved a referendum to pay for a remodeled facility a day later, but it was too late. The Browns were gone.

Cleveland Mayor Michael White was asked by Bob Costas of NBC-TV a few days later what he would say to Modell if he had the chance. "You've done a lot of good things in this town. But the very worst thing you've ever done in your life is what you did to Cleveland on November 6," White answered.

The announcement came 67 years to the day after Cleveland voters approved a bond issue that launched construction of Municipal Stadium.

November 6, 1878 — On its third day as a daily newspaper, the *Cleveland Press* contains the following report: "There was a meeting of the Cleveland baseball association last evening to decide the question of joining the league. The attendance was so small that the members thought it prudent to postpone the question." The reference was to baseball's National League that started in 1876 with teams in Cincinnati, Philadelphia, New York, Louisville, Boston, Hartford, St. Louis and Chicago. Cleveland would enter a team in 1879.

November 6, 1937 — The Barons make their hockey debut in Philadelphia, losing to the Ramblers, 5-1.

November 6, 1950 — The Indians report they will televise all home games in 1951 but only selected road games. Team president Ellis Ryan said he does not blame television for a home game attendance decline of just over 500,000 in 1950 compared with 1949.

November 6, 1980 — The NBA headquarters announces a ban on further player trades by the Cavaliers. Multiple rosters moves during the summer and fall saw Coach Bill Musselman swap Dave Robisch, Foots Walker, Campy Russell and first-round draft choices in 1983, '84 and '86. Team owner Ted Stepien says in response to the NBA edict: "If we get in the playoffs, just see if we do them (the NBA) any favors. I felt their actions were totally unfair."

November 7, 2010 — Browns rout powerful Patriots

The New England Patriots didn't win every game during the first two decades of the 21st century. It just seemed that way. They were the standard of excellence that the rest of the NFL tried to match.

One day in 2010, the Browns didn't just match the Patriots – they surpassed them by a wide margin. Cleveland came away with a shocking 34-14 win over New England. The victory came two weeks after the Browns had stunned the New Orleans Saints, so it was two straight wins over top-flight competition after a 1-5 start.

Peyton Hillis, who would be the selected player on the 2011 "Madden" video game cover, ran for 184 yards, a career best, and two touchdowns. Rookie quarterback Colt McCoy was efficient as his team bested Tom Brady's squad.

After the game, Browns coach Eric Mangini shook hands with Patriots coach Bill Belichick. They had worked together in New England, and this win meant Mangini was 3-5 against his former teacher and mentor.

November 7, 1954 — The Browns set a team record for points scored in beating Washington, 62-3. George Ratterman completes 10-of-11 pass attempts for 203 yards and three touchdowns while splitting quarterback duties with Otto Graham.

November 7, 1990 — Sandy Alomar Jr. of the Indians is a unanimous pick as the American League Rookie of the Year.

November 7, 1995 — Cuyahoga County voters approve by 72 to 28 percent a 10-year extension of a levy termed a "sin tax" on the sale of alcohol and tobacco products with the funds, estimated to total $150 million to $170 million, to be used for renovations of Cleveland Stadium, which opened on July 1, 1931. The first levy was passed in 1990 and was scheduled to expire in 1996. The day before the vote, Browns owner Art Modell announced Cleveland's NFL team would move to Baltimore in time for the 1996 season.

8

November 8, 1993 — Kosar suddenly cut by Browns

Most football teams simply change starting quarterbacks when they think they need better performance from that position. The Browns of 1993 weren't like most NFL teams.

The Browns made a shocking announcement the day after they lost to the Denver Broncos, 29-14. They released their starting quarterback, Bernie Kosar. Considering the amount of success that Kosar had enjoyed in Cleveland, and that he was a native of the area and enjoyed great popularity, it ranked as the biggest surprise in team history since Paul Brown was dismissed in 1963.

Owner Art Modell blamed Kosar's "declining physical condition" for the transaction. The phrase "diminishing skills" also came up and became famously repeated as the story was retold. Reportedly, Kosar and coach Bill Belichick hadn't been getting along and this was the final solution. With backup Vinny Testaverde hurt, Todd Philcox moved into the starting lineup for a while. Cleveland lost six of its last eight games and finished 7-9. In a five-year career, Philcox would appear in 15 NFL games and compile a 2-3 record as a starter.

Meanwhile, Kosar was immediately signed as a free agent by the Cowboys, and led Dallas to a victory less than a week after his release by the Browns. The Cowboys later won the Super Bowl, with Kosar earning a ring as a team member. He spent the final three seasons of his career as a backup in Miami.

November 8, 1994 — The Cavaliers open the newly built Gund Arena for basketball with a 100-98 loss to the Houston Rockets before a capacity crowd of 20,562.

9

November 9, 1969 — The Browns' touchdown streak ends

The Browns came into this game with the Vikings with a 5-1-1 record, while Minnesota was 6-1. Fans were expecting a great matchup, a potential preview of the NFL Championship game.

What those fans received was a mammoth blowout. The Browns were no match for the Vikings, dropping a stunning 51-3 game.

This one was pretty much over by halftime. Joe Kapp threw three touchdowns in the opening 30 minutes as Minnesota raced to a 27-3 lead. Cleveland native Clint Jones added some insurance with a short scoring run. The Browns had four turnovers and only earned 151 yards in total offense.

The game ended the Browns' streak of scoring a touchdown in 166 straight games. It began in 1957 in a Week 1 win over the Giants, and set an NFL record.

November 9, 1983 — The Cleveland Brewers claim the National Women's Football League championship with a 43-6 win over the Columbus Pacesetters.

10

November 10, 1937 — Opening Night for the Arena

The city of Cleveland didn't waste any time getting its brand new arena opened. A mere six months and two days after groundbreaking, the Cleveland Arena at 3717 Euclid

Avenue, not far from downtown, was open for business.

Most major cities around North America were constructing new arenas during the period from the late 1920s through the start of World War II. The Cleveland facility followed some of the design elements of Maple Leaf Gardens in Toronto.

The cost was a reported $1.5 million, and the man who did the financing was Al Sutphin, the owner of the Cleveland Barons of the American Hockey League. The building contained 700,000 bricks; a promotional flyer invited doubters to count them. The seating capacity for hockey was listed at 9,847, although it could hold 12,659 for boxing. Most of the seats were between the hockey goal lines, with a few located in the ends.

The first event in the building wasn't hockey or boxing. It was the Ice Follies of 1938, a traveling exhibition of figure skaters. Mayor Harold H. Burton paid a tribute to the "fighting heart of Al Sutphin" during the opening remarks.

In 1968, Cleveland sports entrepreneur Nick J. Mileti bought the building and the Barons. When Mileti was granted an NBA expansion franchise in 1970, the Arena was by then 33 years old and there were enough complaints about the plumbing that sometimes players from visiting teams declined to use the locker room showers. Mileti realized the Arena's heyday had come and gone. So Cleveland's NBA and pro hockey teams moved to the new $36 million facility he arranged to be built – the Coliseum in Richfield in northern Summit County, for the 1974-75 season. The downtown arena was demolished in 1977.

November 10, 1950 — The Indians fire manager Lou Boudreau, creating a storm of protest from fans remembering his role in the World Series title in 1948. Al Lopez is the replacement.

11

November 11, 1979 — Browns suffer damaging loss

The Browns were looking like playoff contenders in the middle of autumn. They had gone through the 1979 schedule under Coach Sam Rutigliano to this point with a 7-3 record, and appeared to have survived a three-game losing streak in midseason. They had won three in a row and were set to play an average Seahawks team at home.

However, Seattle forgot to follow the script. The Seahawks handed the Browns a damaging 29-24 loss.

This was a game of runs. Seattle scored the game's first 16 points, only to see Cleveland respond with 17. Mike Pruitt ran for two touchdowns, with one coming on a 65-yard gallop. The Browns looked to be in good shape entering the fourth quarter, but two Seahawks touchdowns proved to be insurmountable.

That was the moment when the team's postseason chances began to fade. Including the Seattle loss, Cleveland finished 2-4 to go 9-7 on the season. Denver had grabbed the last playoff spot even before losing on the season's final day.

November 11, 1986 — Cavaliers rookie guard Ron Harper breaks the 30-point mark in just his sixth game as a pro with 34 points against the Kings.

12

November 12, 1970 — Finally, the Cavaliers win

In recent years, expansion teams in pro sports have figured out how to be competitive quickly. The advent of free agency and financial rules mean there are no long building programs needed; it's possible to win from Day One.

That's not how it was in 1970 when the original Cavaliers were created. They came into the NBA with Buffalo and Portland as the league needed the dollars from expansion fees to fight off the threat of the rival American Basketball Association. The problem was the new teams received the lower echelon players from other teams' rosters. When Bill Fitch was named Cleveland's first coach after leaving the University of Minnesota, he said: "Just remember, the name's Fitch, not Houdini."

In 1970-71, Cleveland fell to the bottom of the league and stayed there. The Cavaliers lost their first 15 games, but finally earned a 105-103 win over the Trail Blazers on this day.

Walt Wesley led the Cavs with 21 points. The center from Kansas had the year of his life in his first year in Cleveland, averaging a career-high 17.7 points. McCoy McLemore had 19 points and John Warren added 18 for the Cavaliers.

November 12, 1957 — After dismissing Hank Greenberg, the Indians hire Frank "Trader" Lane as general manager. Lane had been GM of the St. Louis Cardinals starting in the 1956 season. Before that, he was the GM of the Chicago White Sox beginning in 1949. His tenure with Cleveland during the 1958, '59 and '60 seasons was marked by frequent player trades including sending away Roger Maris and Rocky Colavito.

November 12, 1970 — Dave Puddington announces he'll resign as Kent State football coach at the end of his third season with the Golden Flashes. Puddington said there was a "prevailing contagious negativism on campus and in the community" dating to the May 4, 1970, shooting deaths of four students by the National Guard during a campus protest. Puddington came to Kent State from Washington University, but went 9-21 with the Golden Flashes. The Canton native never was a head football coach again.

November 12, 1980 — South Euclid's Steve Stone, who pitched at Lyndhurst Brush High School and then at Kent State, receives the Cy Young Award in the American League after winning 25 games for the Baltimore Orioles in the 1980 season.

13

November 13, 1982 – Tragedy in the boxing ring

Ray "Boom Boom" Mancini of Youngstown only had been a World Boxing Association lightweight world champion for a handful of months when he accepted a nationally televised deal for his first title defense. The setting was before a crowd estimated at 6,500 at Caesars Palace in Las Vegas, and the opponent was a South Korean named Duk Koo Kim – a top contender who had never fought outside of Asia.

Mancini slowly took control of the fight, but Kim was determined and tough. Mancini hit him with 45 shots to the head in the 13th round alone, but Kim never went down. Then came Round 14. Mancini connected with a big right hook, and Kim finally hit the canvas. The challenger spun around to start to pull himself up, but then fell backward.

Kim went into a coma and was rushed to a hospital. He had 100 cubic centimeters of blood in his skull and underwent emergency brain surgery. It didn't help. Kim died four days later.

The repercussions were many. Kim's mother committed suicide. So did referee Richard Green. Mancini was never the same fighter. Championship bouts were soon reduced from a potential 15 rounds to 12, a change that still is in effect.

November 13, 1999 — The Cavaliers retire Mark Price's jersey No. 25.

November 13, 2007 — CC Sabathia of the Indians edges out Josh Beckett of the Red Sox to win the American League's Cy Young Award.

November 13, 2008 — Cliff Lee of the Indians picks up a second consecutive Cy Young Award for Cleveland's pitching staff.

14

November 14, 2019 — Garrett's stunning display of anger

The Browns play the Steelers on a Thursday night against Pittsburgh, and Cleveland comes up with a 21-7 win. That's cause for at least a smile from Cleveland-area fans, and yet no one was talking much about the game itself. It was completely overshadowed – some might say in typical Browns-Steelers fashion – by an incident on the field near the end of the contest.

The play started as Steelers quarterback Mason Rudolph went back to pass. Browns defensive lineman Myles Garrett applied pressure, and hit Rudolph after the pass was thrown. That started a wrestling match between the two. Eventually, Garrett pulled Rudolph's helmet off . . . and hit the Steeler in the head with it. Everyone was shocked – and memories came flooding back of "Mean" Joe Greene kicking Bob McKay, Joe "Turkey" Jones dumping Terry Bradshaw on his head, and James Harrison putting a vicious hit on Colt McCoy.

"I made a mistake," Garrett said to reporters after the game. "I lost my cool, and I regret it's gonna come back to hurt our team. The guys who jumped into the scrum, I appreciate my team having my back. But it should never have gotten that far. It's on me."

Garrett was suspended the rest of the season, and was reinstated the following February.

November 14, 1937 — It takes four games, but the Cleveland Barons earn their first-ever win in the American Hockey League, by 2-0 in Providence.

15

November 15, 1970 — Hats off to the Bengals' win

As the clock ticked down to zero, Cincinnati Bengals coach Paul Brown took off his hat and threw it into the air – sort of like Mary Tyler Moore at the beginning of her 1970s television series.

And why not? Brown had been waiting eight years for this moment. His Bengals had defeated the Cleveland Browns, 14-10, giving Brown a little revenge for his firing by team owner Art Modell in 1963. Brown returned to pro football in 1968 with an expansion team in the American Football League, but he didn't get to play his old team until the two leagues were fully merged in 1970.

The Browns had the better of the play in the early going. Leroy Kelly's touchdown run and Don Cockroft's short field goal gave Cleveland a 10-0 lead. Then Virgil Carter hit Jesse Phillips with a touchdown pass, and Paul Robinson ran it over the goal line to put the Bengals up, 14-10. That score held up through the end of the game.

"That's the greatest victory of my career," Brown said. And a rivalry was born.

November 15, 1979 — Cavaliers owner Nick Mileti and general manager Ron Hrovat say they are waiting for a reply from 43-year-old Wilt Chamberlain whether he will come out of a six-year NBA retirement to accept a two-year contract offer to make a comeback. He does not. During the negotiating process, the Cavs placed their contract offer in a gate at Chamberlain's home and later learned the document blew away and had to be retrieved on the lawn.

November 15, 2017 — Corey Kluber becomes the first Indians' pitcher to win two Cy Young Awards.

November 16, 1989 — Cavs add Ferry in major trade

It's been called the greatest trade in the history of the Clippers – which means things didn't balance out for the Cavaliers.

Los Angeles was sitting on an odd asset in the fall of 1989. It was in the form of Danny Ferry, the Clippers' first-round draft choice (second overall pick). The problem was that Los Angeles couldn't sign him to a contract; Ferry took off to play in Italy.

Meanwhile in Cleveland, the Cavaliers had a solid fourth-year guard in Ron Harper who had averaged about 20 points per game. But a problem arose. As Harper told *Akron Beacon Journal* pro basketball writer Terry Pluto, "They (the Cavaliers) didn't like some of my friends." There were suspicions about drugs but Harper denied the rumors. Owner Gordon Gund reportedly told general manager Wayne Embry to trade Harper. The Clippers were a willing partner, so Harper went west with a couple of first-round picks for Ferry's rights and guard Reggie Williams.

Ferry signed a 10-year contract worth up to $40 million upon returning, but his NBA game did not resemble the Larry Bird-like versatility he had shown at Duke his senior year when he averaged 22.6 points, 7.4 rebounds, and 4.7 assists. Danny shot 52.2 percent from the floor and 42.5 percent on three-pointers. Ferry averaged a little more than seven points per game in Cleveland. Harper spent almost five years as a Clipper, helping them become a playoff team. Then he went to Chicago, where he was part of the Chicago Bulls' dynasty. Harper was a part of five NBA championship teams.

November 16, 1929 — The Cleveland Indians, named after the baseball team, play the first pro hockey game in Cleveland's history. Their opponent is the London Tecumsehs in the International Hockey League.

17

November 17, 1929 — Friedman points to the NFL's future

Parts of America were already convinced that Benny Friedman was a great quarterback in the National Football League at this point. If fans in New York didn't realize that fact before this day, they received a good reminder by the end of it.

Friedman was a star athlete at Glenville High School in Cleveland, and went on to success at the University of Michigan. From there, he came home to play for Cleveland in 1927. That team moved to Detroit for the 1928 season. Friedman and the Wolverines earned a win and a tie against a good New York Giants team that year. Their owner, Tim Mara, was so impressed that he bought the Detroit franchise and then disbanded it, merging the two rosters.

Friedman and the reinforced Giants' roster started the season 8-0-1, and a 34-0 win over the Chicago Bears showed just how good Friedman was. He threw four touchown passes that afternoon, setting an NFL record. He also kicked three extra points. Friedman finished with 20 TD throws in the Giants' 13-1-1 season, a league record that lasted until 1942. He earned his third consecutive first-team All-Pro honor.

Friedman played five more years with the Giants and Dodgers, retiring after the 1934 season. He had opened up an innovation in pro football to the possibilities of the passing game. It took until 2005 for the Pro Football Hall of Fame to finally induct Friedman.

November 17, 1980 — Only 2½ weeks after trading for center Jerome Whitehead of the expansion Dallas Mavericks, Cavaliers coach Bill Musselman puts the former Marquette player on waivers.

November 17, 1992 — The Indians lose outfielder Darrell Whitmore and pitcher Jack Armstrong to Florida as well as pitcher Dennis Boucher to Colorado in baseball's expansion draft.

November 18, 1972 — Golden Flashes make history

Few expected the Kent State football team to do much in 1972. The team was coming off a 3-8 season, 0-5 in the Mid-American Conference. Don James had been hired as the team's new coach in 1971, leaving the defensive coordinator position at Colorado, and he obviously had a lot of work to do to make the Golden Flashes competitive. It was a homecoming of sorts for James, who was from nearby Massillon in Stark County.

James caught a break in an odd way when the team's middle linebacker gave up football before the season started. James decided to put his best defensive player in that position. The replacement player's name was Jack Lambert, and it was a great fit. Lambert, who came from Crestwood High School in the village of Mantua in Portage County, near Kent, now could roam all over the field in pursuit of ball carriers.

Kent State opened the season 1-3-1, but then the conference portion of the schedule kicked in. The Golden Flashes won four of five going into the last game of the season. One more win would mean the school's first Mid-American Conference title, and the Golden Flashes earned it going away, 27-9, over Toledo. Eddie Woodward went 95 yards with the second half kickoff to break the game open. The Flashes went on to their first-ever bowl game, the Tangerine Bowl.

The legacy of that team lasted for years. James left Kent after the 1974 season and had a great run as the coach at Washington. Lambert made the Pro Football Hall of Fame for his work with the Steelers. Another player on that team, Nick Saban, is considered by analysts to be the best college football coach of all time. He thanked James for giving him a chance in that profession. Meanwhile, a championship banner on the wall of Kent State's arena notes the school's MAC football titles, and 1972 was the only year on it after the 2022 season.

November 18, 1925 — Johnny Risko, who grew up in Cleveland, drops a decision to future heavyweight champion Gene Tunney in Cleveland. Tunney later calls Risko "the toughest man I ever fought."

November 18, 1954 — Outfielder Gene Woodling, an Akron native and graduate of East High School, is a key player in a record-setting 17-player trade between the New York Yankees and the Baltimore Orioles, who were new to that city after moving from St. Louis as the Browns. Woodling was a key platoon player for manager Casey Stengel as the Yankees won every American League pennant from 1949 to 1953.

November 18, 2007 — Phil Dawson's 51-yard tying field goal attempt against the Ravens is first called no good by officials, but then is called good after a long discussion. Then Dawson makes a 33-yard attempt in overtime to give Cleveland a 33-30 win.

19

November 19, 1976 — Garland signs rich deal with Indians

You have to say Wayne Garland was in the right place at the right time – financially. Garland had won a total of seven games in his first three seasons as a major leaguer in Baltimore, mostly pitching out of the bullpen. But in 1976, the Orioles put him in the starting rotation. He responded with a stunning 20-7 season with a 2.67 earned-run average. As for the timing, it was the second offseason for free agency in baseball, so Garland went on the market as being available to the highest bidder.

The Indians went all in on Garland, and signed him to a guaranteed 10-year deal worth $2.3 million. In the mid-'70s, Cleveland was known for mediocre teams and a big, empty ballpark, so the signing added to the shock of the deal. The owners of the team were a group led by Ted Bonda, and they were hoping to sell in the near future, so money was no object.

But there's no sure thing in the baseball pitching business. Garland pitched through a sore shoulder in 1977 and lost 19 games. Rotator cuff surgery followed. Garland hung around through 1981, when the Indians swallowed their losses and released him in January of 1982. He never pitched in the majors again.

November 19, 1961 — Jim Brown ties his personal best by rushing for 237 yards in a game against Philadelphia.

November 19, 1966 — One of the most famous games in college football history – the 10-10 tie between Notre Dame and Michigan State – has a Northeast Ohio connection. The Fighting Irish are coached by Ara Parseghian, a native of Akron. The Spartans' offense features halfback Clint Jones, a star athlete for Cathedral Latin High School in Cleveland.

November 19, 1996 — Albert Belle leaves the Indians and signs a five-year, $55-million deal with the White Sox as a free agent. The outfielder became the highest-paid player in baseball.

20

November 20, 1977 — Mays' efforts at QB can't save Gregg's job

The 1977 football season by the Browns offered a reminder of one of the basic truths of the sport in the modern era. When you lose your starting quarterback, you are in trouble.

Brian Sipe was in his second season as the Browns' starter in 1977. The 13th round draft pick (the selection process was 17 rounds in those days) out of San Diego State guided Cleveland to five wins in the first seven games and to playoff contention. But in Week 8, Sipe suffered a shoulder injury that sidelined him for the rest of the year.

Since Cleveland had traded its backup, Mike Phipps, to Chicago earlier in the season, the Browns had to turn to David Mays, who was also a practicing dentist, as the starting quarterback for a game with the New York Giants. It was his first start as a pro, and the Browns rallied around him. He was 13-for-24 for 138 yards and a touchdown, and the defense forced four turnovers – one of which was an interception returned for a touchdown by linebacker Gerald Irons – in a 21-7 win.

This game was Mays' only win as a starting NFL quarterback. The Browns lost their final four games and finished 6-8 and out of the playoffs. Forrest Gregg lost his head coaching job just before the end of the season.

November 20, 1937 — The Barons make their debut in an official American Hockey League game in Cleveland Arena, and tie Syracuse, 3-3.

November 21, 2018 — This time, LeBron is welcomed

LeBron James was the subject of scorn and hate the first time he returned to Cleveland as an ex-Cavalier. The second time went a great deal better.

James came back to face his old team with his new team, the Los Angeles Lakers. He was greeted by fans wearing his replica jersey, and received a long ovation when the starting lineups were introduced. But the best part came in the first quarter. During a timeout, the Cavaliers showed a video tribute to James, closing with the words "Thank you LeBron."

"They showed their appreciation," James said after the game. "And not only for myself, but for my friends and family that were at the game tonight. It was a great moment."

James played typically well – 32 points and 14 rebounds. Los Angeles picked up the 109-105 win, showing that LeBron still remembered how to win in Quicken Loans Arena.

November 21, 1949 — Bill Veeck sells the Indians to a syndicate headed by insurance company executive Ellis Ryan for an undisclosed figure estimated to be $2.2 million. Ryan, the incoming team president, says Hank Greenberg will continue to operate the club's minor-league system and Greenberg will be general manager.

November 22, 2009 — A shootout comes out of nowhere

A crowd of 43,170 bought tickets at Ford Field in Detroit for the game on this day between the Lions and the Browns.

Both teams had 1-8 records and were already out of the playoff hunt. Cleveland made an early statement by scoring 24 points in the first quarter alone. Brady Quinn threw three touchdowns within a span of 6:02. The Lions answered with three quick scores, but a Phil Dawson field goal put the Browns ahead, 27-24, at the half.

Cleveland took a 37-31 lead on Quinn's fourth touchdown pass of the day. But 5:44 remained in regulation, and that was plenty for Detroit's Matthew Stafford. He moved the Lions to the 1-yard line, and a Cleveland penalty meant there would be one final untimed play at the end of the game. Stafford hit Brandon Pettigrew with the scoring pass, his fifth such play of the day, and after the kick, Detroit was a 38-37 winner.

The teams combined for 902 yards in total offense. Stafford was 26-of-43 for 422 yards. "That was wild," the Lions QB said after the game.

November 22, 1945 — Rams' receiver Jim Benton makes 10 receptions for 303 yards as Cleveland wins 28-21 at Briggs Stadium in Detroit on Thanksgiving Day.

November 22, 1971 — Chris Chambliss of the Indians wins the American League's Rookie of the Year Award.

November 22, 2004 — Lou Holtz retires as South Carolina football coach, wrapping up a 33-year head coaching career that included stops with Notre Dame, Arkansas, and one partial season with the New York Jets. Holtz grew up in East Liverpool, Ohio, and earned his undergraduate degree in 1959 while playing college football at Kent State.

23

November 23, 1947 — Browns, Yankees tie one on

A crowd of 70,060 turned out in Yankee Stadium for what figured to be the game of the year in the All-America Football Conference. The Yankees were playing the powerful Cleveland Browns. New York was 9-2 and Cleveland was 10-1. The Browns were still a game ahead of the Yankees when the day was over, but they did it the hard way.

The Yankees thought they could take advantage of a weakness in the middle of the Browns' defensive line, so they ran the ball in that spot over and over again. It worked. Spec Sanders ran for three touchdowns, and Buddy Young added a fourth. It was 28-0 for New York before the end of the first half. Otto Graham threw a touchdown pass to Jim Boedeker to reduce that margin by seven at intermission.

The Browns moved closer in the third quarter, as Marion Motley scored two touchdowns. Jim Dewer added a 5-yard scoring run in the fourth quarter, and the Browns had come all the way back to tie the game at 28-28. But while the rally was one for the history books, it's not why the game is remembered.

In the final minute, the Yankees moved the ball into Cleveland territory. They ran the ball from the line of scrimmage at the 38-yard line, and then New York had a brain cramp. The Yankees forgot to call timeout, and time ran out before the Yanks could try a field goal, and the game ended in a tie.

November 23, 1905 — The first organized soccer game in Cleveland's history is played between immigrant teams representing England and Scotland.

November 23, 1907 — The Elysium opens at East 107th and Euclid Avenue in Cleveland. It was the city's first indoor ice skating arena, and was owned by Harry Humphrey.

November 23, 1968 — Brian Dowling, who played high school football for St. Ignatius, finishes his Yale college football career with one of the most famous ties in the sport's history. Harvard scores 16 points in the final 42 seconds to tie Yale, 29-29. Dowling, who spent three years on the rosters of two NFL teams, is the inspiration for the cartoon character named "B.D." in the political comic strip "Doonesbury," authored by fellow Yale student Garry Trudeau.

November 23, 1986 — The Browns finish their first sweep of the Steelers since 1969 with a 37-31 overtime win, as Bernie Kosar throws for 414 yards.

November 24, 1957 — Brown shows a sign of greatness

Jim Brown is considered one of the greatest college football players in history, if not the greatest. The Browns were lucky to take him with the sixth pick of the 1957 NFL draft. Once Brown arrived, it was Coach Paul Brown's assignment to translate his skills to the pro game.

Brown moved right into Cleveland's starting lineup, but it took him until the seventh game of the season to even break 100 yards in a game, and he fell short of that number in the next two games as well.

Then came Week 10 against Los Angeles. Call it Brown's coming-out party. He ran for 237 yards on 31 carries, and scored four touchdowns. Three scores came on short runs but one was a 69-yard gallop. Cleveland went on to win, 45-31.

Brown didn't break 100 yards in a game for the rest of the season. At the end of his rookie year, he had 942 yards, which led the league as he was named a first-team All-Pro. Other teams had learned quickly that they'd be trying to figure out how to stop him for the rest of his 9-year career.

November 24, 1970 — It's a career-ending day for Akron native Gene Mingo, considered the first Black kicker in pro football, as he is put on waivers by Coach Chuck Noll and the Pittsburgh Steelers. At 32, Mingo had played in the AFL and NFL since 1960 and never attended college after playing at Akron South High School and then serving in the Navy.

November 24, 1998 — The Indians bolster their infield with the free-agent signing of catcher Sandy Alomar's brother, Roberto, who will play second base. He receives a four-year contract estimated to be worth $32 million.

November 25, 1941 — Boudreau picked to be player / manager

The Indians had just kicked manager Roger Peckinpaugh upstairs to the job of general manager. That left an opening for a skipper. And regular shortstop Lou Boudreau thought he could handle the job, even though he was all of 24 years old.

To the surprise of most, even those who worked for the Indians, Boudreau got the job on this day. He was the youngest manager in baseball during the 20th century. Cleveland did give him some experienced coaches in Burt Shotton, Oscar Melillo and George Susce.

Only a couple of weeks after his appointment, World War II began for the U.S. That meant fans wouldn't know how good Boudreau really was as a player-manager until 1946.

He almost lost his job after the 1947 season, but Boudreau hung on and then had one of the great seasons in baseball history in 1948. He led the Indians to a world championship, and was named Most Valuable Player in the process.

Boudreau stayed in Cleveland for two more seasons and finished his career in Boston, where he later managed for a couple of years.

November 25, 1951 — Dub Jones scores six touchdowns (four rushing, two receiving) for the Browns in their game against the Chicago Bears. It's a league-record performance as he leads Cleveland to a 42-21 win. Jones reached the end zone the last five times he touched the ball.

November 25, 1966 — The Cincinnati Royals beat the New York Knicks, 115-109, at the Cleveland Arena. It's the first of 35 games played by the Royals in Cleveland through 1970, when the city was awarded a franchise.

November 25, 1996 — Demolition begins on the stadium first known as Municipal Stadium and later called Cleveland Stadium. The site-clearing would continue until March 1997.

November 26, 1956 — Browns hit jackpot in draft

When the National Football League met for the first four rounds of the annual draft, the teams probably knew there was some good talent out there. They might not have known just how good it was.

The Packers opened the proceedings by taking Paul Hornung, an all-around talent who won the Heisman Trophy from Notre Dame. The Rams followed with Jon Arnett, a halfback who could run and catch the ball. Third was San Francisco, and the 49ers took quarterback John Brodie of Stanford. Green Bay went again and with the fourth pick took end Ron Kramer of Michigan. That was followed by the Steelers' selection of quarterback Len Dawson of Purdue, a native of Alliance in Stark County. The Browns were hoping to take Dawson.

Hornung and Dawson later made the Hall of Fame, and the other three players were regulars on All-Pro or Pro Bowl lists. Who could be left for Cleveland, picking at No. 6? The answer was running back Jim Brown out of Syracuse. He probably should have won the Heisman Trophy in 1956, but many years later he was voted the greatest college football player in history.

Fullback Clarence Peaks went seventh to the Eagles, and he was merely "all right." But the next pick was Jim Parker, an offensive lineman who went to the Colts. Brown and Parker became Hall of Famers, so four of the first eight choices ended up in Canton. Five other lower draft picks joined them: Tommy McDonald, Sonny Jurgensen, Henry Jordan (fifth round to Cleveland), Gene Hickerson (seventh round to Cleveland), and Don Maynard. Three Hall of Famers in one draft was an amazing haul for the Browns.

November 26, 1967 — Carl Ward sets a team record with a 104-yard kickoff return for the Browns as Cleveland beats Washington, 42-37.

27

November 27, 1924 — The votes are in, and Cleveland wins it all

It had been an interesting year for the Cleveland Bulldogs and – no surprise – it ended in an unusual way.

The Cleveland Indians were the name of the NFL team in 1923, going 3-1-3. Owner Samuel Deutsch wasn't happy about that, so he bought the Canton franchise that had just won the '23 title, and merged it with his squad.

That worked out well. The team was renamed the Cleveland Bulldogs and it compiled a 7-1-1 season. The Bulldogs couldn't beat the Franklin Yellow Jackets, going 0-1-1 in two meetings. Otherwise, Cleveland was perfect. It finished on a high note on this day, blasting the Milwaukee Badgers, 53-10, in a game played in Canton.

Still, no one was certain at the end of the season who won the championship, as the NFL handled such situations in a very primitive manner. Ties didn't count in the standings, and the schedule was uneven among the teams. The Bulldogs, Chicago Bears (6-1-4), and Yellow Jackets (11-2-1) all had a case. But Cleveland had the best winning percentage, and it won the title on a vote of the teams.

November 27, 1946 — Municipal Stadium is filled with 70,955 fans for the annual charity football game. The high school battle ends with Cathedral Latin defeating Holy Name, 35-6.

November 27, 1952 — Could it be football legends George Blanda and George "Papa Bear" Halas on the field at the Rubber Bowl? With a reported 3,000 fans? In an NFL game? Believe it. But their Chicago Bears lost, 27-23, to the Dallas Texans in a Thanksgiving Day game moved to Akron because the Dallas franchise had come under the stewardship of the league. The win in Akron was the team's only one of the season. The team eventually moved to Baltimore and became the Colts.

November 27, 1953 — Al Rosen is a unanimous choice to win the American League's Most Valuable Player award. He hit .336 with 43 homers and 145 RBIs.

November 27, 1956 — Caldwell B. Esselstyn Jr., who received his medical doctor degree from Case Western Reserve University in Cleveland, claims a gold medal in rowing during the Olympic Games in Melbourne, Australia. Esselstyn is part of the men's coxed eight team for the United States, made up of rowers from Yale University. Esselstyn married Ann Crile, granddaughter of Dr. George Crile, who founded the Cleveland Clinic.

November 28, 1969 — Knicks make history in Cleveland

The New York Knickerbockers played one of the most famous games in their history in Cleveland, and they did it before the Cavaliers even existed. It's quite a story, even in a sport known for its spectacular finishes.

The Knicks came into the game in Cleveland Arena on a roll. It was a Cincinnati Royals' home game that was moved to Cleveland. New York had won 17 games in a row, tying the Boston Celtics' NBA record for consecutive victories. However, the streak appeared dead in the final minutes. Oscar Robertson had scored 33 points with 10 assists before fouling out with 1:39 left. Legendary star Bob Cousy, who was coaching the Royals, had activated himself at age 41 to the playing roster because of injuries. He hit two free throws to put Cincinnati up, 105-100, with 25 seconds left.

Then everything changed. Willis Reed sank two free throws to narrow the Royals' lead to three. Cousy called a timeout, and drew up an inbounds play – and then he threw the ball to New York's Dave DeBusschere, who scored to make it 105-104. Cincinnati used its last timeout, but Walt Frazier tipped Cousy's pass to Reed, who passed the ball back to Frazier. The Knicks' guard was fouled with two seconds to go. Frazier made both free throws to put New York ahead. Just to put icing on the cake, the Knicks made one last steal at the buzzer to come away with a 106-105 victory before a crowd of 10,438.

New York had scored six points in the last 16 seconds to win their 18th straight, breaking the record. The Knicks' brilliant run ended the next night at home against Detroit, but they went on to take the NBA title at the end of the 1969-70 season.

November 28, 1925 — Nels Stewart leaves his amateur hockey team in Cleveland to join the Montreal Maroons of the National Hockey League. He went on to lead the league in goals and points, capture the MVP trophy, and win the Stanley Cup in his rookie year.

November 28, 2001 — Warren Harding High School star running back Maurice Clarett is named Mr. Football for the state of Ohio. He would go on as a college freshman to lead Ohio State to the 2002 college football national championship.

29

November 29, 1971 — Gaylord becomes instant favorite

For most of the 1960s, Sam McDowell was one reason to see the Indians, because there was a good chance they might win while he was on the mound. McDowell was an All-Star six times during his seasons with Cleveland, and he led the American League five times in strikeouts. The nickname "Sudden Sam" was a good fit.

But during the Indians' years in the wilderness between pennants in 1954 and 1995, player trades involving a marquee name often provided the currency to keep fans' dreams alive. Think: Rocky Colavito (both going and coming), Luis Tiant, Graig Nettles, Chris Chambliss, Buddy Bell, Von Hayes, Dennis Eckersley . . . and so on.

So it was with McDowell, who went 13-17 in 1971 after a 20-win season the year before. The Giants offered veteran pitcher Gaylord Perry for McDowell. Perry was a few years older but they had similar records (133-109 for Perry, 122-109 for McDowell). The Indians had trouble reaching a contract agreement with McDowell, who, according to a report in the *Akron Beacon Journal*, had a salary in the $76,000 range. When the Giants threw in shortstop Frank Duffy, the Indians agreed.

Perry had three-plus sparkling seasons with Cleveland, winning 70 games and a Cy Young Award. Duffy was a regular at shortstop for six years, so the deal worked out fine for the Indians. Perry was then traded by Cleveland at the age of 36, but fooled many by pitching until he was 44 and ending up with 316 career wins and a ticket to Cooperstown.

McDowell won 10 games for the Giants in 1972 but never reached that total again. He drifted from the Giants to the Yankees and finished with the Pirates at age 32. He later acknowledged a substance problem, received help and became a counselor.

By the way, the character of Sam Malone on the television series "Cheers" is said to be based on McDowell.

November 29, 1926 — Tris Speaker resigns after serving as Indians manager since 1919, a tenure that included the World Series title in 1920. Speaker and Ty Cobb are later cleared in an investigation of charges of game-fixing.

November 29, 1984 — Peter Bavasi is hired as the new president of the Indians, as Gabe Paul moves into retirement, just a couple months away from turning 75. Bavasi had been an executive with the Toronto Blue Jays from 1977 to 1981.

30

November 30, 2015 — Browns find new way to lose

A game with the Baltimore Ravens – under the spotlight of *Monday Night Football* – was representative of the Browns' frustrations throughout the decade of the 2010s.

Baltimore had a 17-3 lead in the second quarter, but the Browns fought back to go ahead by a 20-17 lead on Karlos Dansby's 52-yard interception return. The Ravens answered with 10 points to go ahead, 27-20. However, Austin Davis threw a 42-yard pass to Travis Benjamin to tie the game with 1:47 to go. Overtime seemed likely.

Maybe . . . or maybe not. Here was the sequence of events: Matt Schaub of the Ravens threw an interception to Tramon Williams at midfield, but then Cleveland's Davis couldn't get anything going. Even so, the Browns still had a chance to win. Travis Coons lined up for a 51-yard field goal on the last play of regulation. Only two outcomes – a win or more football – seemed even possible.

Who would have believed there was an "Option C"? The kick was blocked by Brent Urban, and Will Hill ran 64 yards for the game-winning touchdown for Baltimore. Just like that, the Browns lost a game that in theory could not have been lost in such a rare occurrence, falling to 2-9 for the season. Fans instantly started to refer to the game as "The Block."

November 30, 1948 — Lou Boudreau of the Indians is picked as the American League's Most Valuable Player.

November 30, 1981 — Cavaliers owner Ted Stepien decides to make a coaching change after the team gets off to a 4-11 start under Don Delaney for the 1981-82 season. No candidate is named immediately as Stepien begins a search that includes Hubie Brown but leads to the hiring of Philadelphia 76ers assistant coach Chuck Daly.

1

December 1, 2005 — Akron wins the MAC title

The University of Akron moved into the Mid-American Conference in 1992 after becoming the first college program to jump from Division I-AA to Division I-A in football in 1987. It took some time for the Zips to claim a conference championship, and they had some challenges along the way.

Akron, coached by J.D. Brookhart, qualified for the MAC Championship game in 2005 by winning the East Division, and the reward was a date with West champion Northern Illinois. After a good start, Akron trailed, 24-10, after three quarters, and was still behind, 30-24, with 3:28 left.

But the Zips responded to the pressure, driving 81 yards in nine plays in a mere 91 seconds. The drive was capped by a 36-yard touchdown pass from Luke Getsy to Domenik Hixon with 10 seconds to go. Jason Swiger won the game with the extra point.

That meant Akron qualified for its first bowl game as a Division I NCAA member. It was the Motor City Bowl, which Akron lost, 38-31, to Memphis.

December 1, 1965 — The Indians acquire outfielder Jim Landis and pitcher Jim Rittwage from the Athletics for outfielder Joe Rudi and catcher Phil Roof. Rittwage was from the Cleveland suburb of Bedford and pitched in the Indians' system for nine seasons, appearing in the major leagues for eight games in 1970.

December 1, 2013 — Josh Gordon catches 10 passes for a team record 261 yards as his Browns lose to Jacksonville, 32-28.

2

December 2, 2010 — James comes back to play in Cleveland

As soon as LeBron James announced that he was leaving Cleveland to join the Miami Heat as a free agent, it was only a matter of time until he would return to Quicken Loans Arena for the first time in a visiting player's uniform.

This was the night, and the fans were ready to tell him what they thought of the move. "It was probably the loudest I've ever heard boos in my life," James said later to ESPN. Some fans even threw batteries on the court, which caused security to think about ending the game early.

The visitor got the last laugh, at least for this moment. James scored a season-high 38 points, including 24 in the third quarter, as the Heat beat the Cavs, 118-90.

Cleveland had to wait a while for a moment of revenge. It came on March 30, 2011, as the Cavaliers stunned the Heat, 102-90.

December 2, 1955 — Indians outfielder Al Smith finishes third in the American League Most Valuable Player voting behind winner Yogi Berra and Al Kaline. Smith, a former player in the Negro Leagues with the Cleveland Buckeyes, joined the major leagues with the Indians in 1953 at age 25.

December 2, 1963 — The Browns choose Warren native Paul Warfield of Ohio State as their first pick (11th overall) in the NFL Draft, and grab running back and return specialist Leroy Kelly of Morgan State in the eighth round. The No. 2 pick of the first round is offensive tackle Bob Brown of Nebraska by the Philadelphia Eagles. Brown is a Cleveland native who played at East Tech in high school. The 6-foot-4, 280-pounder would have a 10-year career with the Eagles, Raiders and Rams before becoming a Pro Football Hall of Fame inductee in 2004.

December 2, 1978 — Baldwin Wallace College, located west of Cleveland in Berea, claims an NCAA Division III national football championship by beating Wittenberg, 24-10, in the Amos Alonzo Stagg Bowl in Phenix City, Alabama. Coach Lee Tressel, father of future Ohio State coach Jim Tressel, guided the Yellow Jackets to an 11-0-1 season.

December 3, 1980 — Charboneau wins rookie award

Joe Charboneau had won two batting championships in the minor leagues before the 1980 season, but few expected him to make the Opening Day roster of the Indians that spring. Yet he beat the odds, moving into the starting lineup when Andre Thornton suffered an injury.

Charboneau hit a home run that day, and kept hitting for most of the rest of the regular season. He finished with a .289 average with 23 homers, picking up the nickname "Super Joe" from longtime sportswriter Terry Pluto along the way. The outfielder became a folk hero – as the song "Go Joe Charboneau" written about him hit the local charts. Charboneau was named American League Rookie of the Year on this day.

It appeared the Indians had found a diamond – acquiring Charboneau from the Philadelphia Phillies for minor league pitcher Cardell Camper.

Then Charboneau hurt his back during spring training in 1981, and was never really the same again. The Indians released him during the 1983 season. Joe stayed in the Cleveland area after retirement, and remains a fan favorite.

December 3, 1950 — The Browns beat Philadelphia, 13-7, without recording an official pass attempt on a rainy day. Cleveland did throw one pass, but it was wiped out by a penalty.

December 3, 1960 — Harvey Kuenn only stays with the Indians for less than a year after coming from Detroit the previous April in the Rocky Colavito deal. He is sent to San Francisco for pitcher Johnny Antonelli and outfielder Willie Kirkland.

December 3, 1967 — Frank Ryan hits Gary Collins for a 24-yard touchdown pass as the Browns beat the Giants, 24-14. It's the 49th and last time that the two team up on a scoring play that also sets a Cleveland team record.

December 4, 1961 — A meaningful draft-day deal

The Browns work out a trade shortly before the NFL Draft that turns out to be filled with meaning for both sides. It's quite a story.

The Redskins were the last team in the NFL that didn't have an African-American player on the roster. They were the subject of protests. Washington was building a new stadium that year, and since the federal government had oversight in the District of Columbia, the Redskins were told they couldn't use it unless they integrated the roster.

The best player in the draft was running back Ernie Davis of Syracuse. However, Washington owner George Preston Marshall wasn't sure he could sign him. The Buffalo Bills of the American Football League had drafted him as well. Just before the start of the draft, the Redskins agreed to send the top pick (Davis) to the Browns for established running back Bobby Mitchell and a first-round pick. In the draft, Washington formally took Davis and the Browns picked Leroy Jackson.

Soon, word of the trade leaked out. Davis signed with the Browns, and fans dreamed of a backfield featuring him and Jim Brown. Then Davis was diagnosed with leukemia and never played for Cleveland. Mitchell would play seven years for Washington and join Brown in the Hall of Fame.

December 4, 1957 — Frank Lane's first of many trades as the new Indians' general manager is a big one, as he acquires Minnie Minoso and Fred Hatfield from Chicago for Early Wynn and Al Smith.

December 4, 1979 — The Cavaliers retire uniform No. 7 to honor Bobby "Bingo" Smith, an original player on the 1970-71 expansion team.

December 4, 1981 — The Cavaliers hire Philadelphia 76ers assistant coach Chuck Daly as their new head coach for 93 days in the middle of the 1981-82 season, the second year of ownership under Ted Stepien. Daly's record in Cleveland would be 9-32.

December 4, 1984 — Forward Phil Hubbard hits 15 straight shots in a game with the Lakers to set a Cavs' team record. Hubbard is in the middle of his 10-year NBA career that began as a high school star at Canton McKinley in Stark County and continued at Michigan and with the gold-medal-winning 1976 U.S. Olympic team.

5

December 5, 1944 — Horvath takes the Heisman

Les Horvath is in a class by himself when it comes to college football. He's the only Heisman Trophy winner to take a "gap year" – as it's called today – during his collegiate career.

Horvath was born in South Bend, Indiana, but his family soon moved to Parma (in suburban Cleveland). There he was a three-sport standout, a star in football, basketball, and track. It earned him the attention of recruiters, and in the fall of 1939 Horvath arrived at Ohio State University. He was a sub in 1940 and 1941, but coach Paul Brown moved him into the starting lineup in the fall of 1942. That team went 9-1 and won the national championship.

You'd think that was the end of the story at Ohio State. Horvath enrolled at dental school and figured his playing days were over for the time being. But college football teams were shorthanded during World War II, and teams were allowed to give players an extra year of eligibility. Horvath agreed as long as his practice time was cut down to allow him enough time to do his schoolwork. The arrangement worked out fine for all concerned. Horvath piled up 1,200 all-purpose yards, and the Buckeyes went 9-0. The halfback became the first and only player to win the Heisman Trophy as the nation's best player while missing the preceding season; he received the award on this day.

Horvath joined the Navy after dental school and played for the Los Angeles Rams in 1947 and 1948. Then it was on to the Browns to wrap up his pro football career in 1949. Horvath and Billy Cannon are the only two Heisman winners to become dentists.

December 5, 1948 — The Browns finish a perfect regular season (14-0) with a 31-21 win in the All-America Football Conference over the Brooklyn Dodgers.

December 5, 1963 — Jim Brown finishes the NFL season with 1,863 yards, a career-best figure that stands as the league record for 10 seasons.

December 5, 1978 — The Indians send Alfredo Griffin and Phil Lansford to Toronto for pitcher Victor "Senor Smoke" Cruz. Griffin goes on to win the Rookie of the Year award for the Blue Jays in 1979.

6

December 6, 1989 — Carter trade boosts Indians

Indians' general manager Hank Peters could see his team's future after the 1990 season, and he didn't think Joe Carter would be a part of it. Carter had been one of the Indians' best players throughout the second half of the 1980s, but he was scheduled to be a free agent. Signing him would be very expensive.

So Peters went shopping. Many teams were anxious to acquire the outfielder, but Peters liked the chances for success with the offer from the Padres. Sandy Alomar Jr. was a great catching prospect, but he was stuck behind All-Star Benito Santiago. Infielder Carlos

Baerga (a rising minor-league prospect as a teenager in the Padres' system) and outfielder Chris James completed the three-for-one swap.

Alomar and Baerga led Cleveland out of the baseball wilderness and were part of some great teams during the 1990s. James spent two seasons in Cleveland, and was on eight different teams in a 10-year career.

December 6, 1947 — In the first and only Great Lakes Bowl featuring top colleges that would meet in Cleveland's Municipal Stadium, Kentucky (coached by the legendary Bear Bryant) defeats Villanova, 24-14.

December 6, 1959 — The Browns lose, 48-7, to the New York Giants at Yankee Stadium as fans storm the field, attacking the goal posts and causing Paul Brown to pull his team off the field with 1:53 remaining in the fourth quarter. The Giants blamed stadium management for not having enough security personnel to control the crowd of 68,436.

December 6, 1971 — A group led by George Steinbrenner reaches a handshake agreement from Vernon Stouffer's son Jim to buy the Indians for $8.6 million. However, the transaction falls through when Vernon backs out. Steinbrenner goes on to buy the New York Yankees in 1973.

December 6, 2020 — Cleveland State gives up 40 straight points in a 101-46 loss to Ohio University, as the teams set a record for the longest scoring run in basketball games involving Division I teams.

December 7, 2017 — Browns clean house

The calendar had turned to December, and the Browns still hadn't won a game yet. Everyone knew change was coming, and the team provided a double-barreled shot of it even before the season had ended.

The Browns started the day by firing general manager Sashi Brown. He had taken over the position less than two years earlier after a career that mostly dealt with legal work.

But Cleveland wasn't done yet. Later that day, longtime NFL executive John Dorsey was hired as the Browns' general manager. He had helped the Seahawks and Packers win two Super Bowls earlier in his career, and he had been the Chiefs' GM from 2013 to June 2017.

December 7, 1979 — The Indians deal outfielder Bobby Bonds to the Cardinals for pitcher John Denny and outfielder Jerry Mumphrey.

December 8, 1946 — A pile of points for the Browns

The Browns had enjoyed a spectacular start as a franchise in the All-America Football Conference by this time. They won their first six games, and were 11-2 entering the year's final regular season game against the Brooklyn Dodgers in Ebbets Field. It became the season's exclamation point.

The scoring started when Bud Schwenk hit Bill Lund for a 22-yard scoring pass to open the scoring. Marion Motley ran seven yards for a score a few minutes later, and the Browns had a 14-0 lead. Cleveland kept pouring on the points, leading by 28-7 at halftime and by 45-7 after three quarters.

But the Browns kept their foot on the gas after that. They put up three more touchdowns in a 66-14 win. Nine different Cleveland players had TDs, and the defense forced Brooklyn into six turnovers. The game set a franchise record that stood for decades.

December 8, 1930 — The Cleveland Rosenblums fold from the American Basketball League after winning three titles in five years. The team was named after its owner, Max Rosenblum, operator of a clothing store.

December 8, 1941 — One day after the Japanese attack on Pearl Harbor, Bob Feller of the Indians becomes one of the first pro baseball players to enlist in the United States armed forces.

December 8, 2021 — Indians' announcer Jack Graney wins the 2022 Ford C. Frick Award for excellence in baseball broadcasting.

9

December 9, 1923 — Another title for Canton

The Canton Bulldogs had enjoyed a terrific season in the National Football League in 1922. The team had won its final six games to finish 10-0-2. That was easily the best regular season of the 18 competing teams (there was no playoff system), and the Bulldogs were declared league champions.

What could they do for an encore in 1923? Be even better. Canton went 11-0-1, finishing as the only unbeaten team in the NFL again. The defense allowed only 19 points for the entire season. The Bulldogs' only blemish on the schedule was a 0-0 tie with the Buffalo All-Americans.

The Bulldogs finished the season on this date with a 10-0 win over the Columbus Tigers. Alas, that was the last highlight for the team. The Bulldogs had financial problems despite all the wins, and the team's assets were sold to Samuel Deutsch, owner of Cleveland's franchise.

New owners tried again to put a team in Canton for two years, but the city left the NFL for good after 1926. Still, the team's legacy remains. Six members of the Bulldogs have been inducted into the Pro Football Hall of Fame, which of course is located in Canton.

December 9, 1949 — Cleveland's spot in pro football is secured when the Browns, 49ers and Colts are accepted into the National Football League after a merger with the All-America Football Conference.

December 9, 1980 — The Indians trade Gary Alexander, Victor Cruz, Rafael Vasquez and Bob Owchinko to Pittsburgh for Bert Blyleven and Manny Sanguillen. Then, on August 1, 1985, in the middle of that year's pennant race (which does not involve the Indians), Blyleven is traded to Minnesota for Jay Bell, Curt Wardle, Jim Weaver and Rich Yett.

December 9, 1982 — The Indians trade arguably their best young player, outfielder Von Hayes, to the Phillies for Julio Franco, Manny Trillo, Jay Baller, George Vukovich and Jerry Willard. The deal earns Hayes the nickname "Five-For-One."

December 9, 2006 — Ohio State quarterback Troy Smith of Cleveland Glenville High is named college football's Heisman Trophy winner. The Buckeyes had a 12-1 season, losing, 41-14, to Florida in the BCS Championship game.

10

December 10, 1982 — Dokes wins boxing title quickly

Michael Dokes of South High School in Akron had the world heavyweight boxing title at one point in his career but there were some unusual circumstances.

Dokes had become one of the top contenders when he stepped into the ring with champion Mike Weaver at Caesars Palace in Las Vegas. Weaver was considered a slow starter, and Dokes went right to work. He delivered a solid left and then followed with a punch that knocked the champ down. Weaver got up quickly, and seemed to be defending himself well as Dokes tried to follow up.

Then came controversy. Referee Joey Curtis decided that Weaver had taken enough punishment and stopped the fight. Dokes was declared the winner at 63 seconds of the first round. It's been suggested that the referee remembered the then-recent death of Duk Koo Kim in a fight against Ray "Boom Boom" Mancini, and stopped it early. The night reached circus standards when the two fighters' handlers started a brawl before leaving the ring.

Weaver was still saying more than 35 years later that he was never hurt in the bout. Still, it went into the books as a win for Dokes.

December 10, 1922 — The Canton Bulldogs beat the Toledo Maroons, 19-0, to finish a 10-0-2 season – good enough to win the National Football League title.

December 10, 1936 — Baseball Commissioner Judge Kenesaw Landis rules that the Indians' contract with Bob Feller is valid and he could continue to play for Cleveland. The pitcher had signed with Fargo-Moorehead of the Northern League in 1935 at the age of 16, and the Des Moines team in the Western League had protested.

December 10, 1991 — The Indians complete one of the best deals in team history. They add Kenny Lofton, a future standout center fielder, and Dave Rohde in a trade with the Astros; Ed Taubensee and Willie Blair head for Houston.

11

December 11, 1949 — Farewell to the AAFC

Cleveland's Municipal Stadium must have had a bittersweet feeling in the air when it hosted the AAFC championship game between the Browns and the San Francisco 49ers. Those teams had been great rivals during the four years of the AAFC's existence, but the league was merging with the National Football League in 1950. This, then, was it.

The Browns had won the league's three previous titles, so it was only fitting to make it four straight. Cleveland was a 21-7 winner before a crowd of 22,550.

The key play came in the third quarter. The Browns were clinging to a 7-0 lead when Marion Motley ran 68 yards for a touchdown. Dub Jones added a 4-yard run for a score in the fourth quarter to wrap it up.

Cleveland's running game was the difference, with a total of 217 yards on 41 carries. Motley led the way with 75. San Francisco quarterback Frankie Albert was held to 9-of-24 passes for 108 yards.

December 11, 1976 — The University of Akron football team loses 24-13 to Montana State in the NCAA Division II title game called the Pioneer Bowl in Wichita Falls, Texas. To reach the game, Akron defeated the University of Nevada-Las Vegas (quarterbacked by future Dallas Cowboy Glenn Carano) 27-6 and Northern Michigan 29-26 (quarterbacked by future NFL head coach Steve Mariucci) in previous rounds, both at the Rubber Bowl.

December 11, 1986 — The American League formally approves the sale of the Indians to a group headed by Cleveland real estate developer Dick Jacobs, an Akron native.

December 11, 2000 — Outfielder Manny Ramirez leaves the Indians to sign an eight-year, $160 million deal with the Red Sox as a free agent.

December 11, 2001 — The Indians trade Roberto Alomar and Mike Bacsik to the Mets for Alex Escobar, Matt Lawton and three other players.

12

December 12, 1920 — Akron tops the football world

The American Professional Football Association, which eventually became the National Football League, was born in September of 1920. The teams in the new league went right to work, starting the season in early October.

The Akron Pros had been playing football since 1904, and even won a couple of titles in their league. They had done some rebuilding for the 1920 season, and were obviously ready for the start. They beat the Wheeling Stogies, 43-0, in the opener. Akron marched through the rest of the season unbeaten, and was entering its last game with an 8-0-2 record. Avoid losing that last game, and the title probably would be theirs. Decatur coach George Halas, who would become more famous later with the Chicago Bears, had signed future Hall of Famer Paddy Driscoll to play in that one game for them, even though the backfield standout usually suited up for the Chicago Cardinals.

Sure enough, the Akron defense pitched its sixth straight shutout on this day. The Pros only gave up seven points in the entire season, and this whitewashing gave them a 0-0 tie with the Staleys. The 8-0-3 record was considered better than Decatur's 10-1-2 (ties were ignored), and the Pros were eventually declared league champions by a vote of the team managers.

December 12, 1937 — In his final game, Cliff Battles of Akron earns a championship title in the Washington Redskins' 28-21 NFL win over the Chicago Bears at Wrigley Field. Battles rushes 17 times for 53 yards and catches three passes for 80 yards. Quarterback Sammy Baugh finishes with 335 yards passing and three TDs. Battles had previously played at Akron Kenmore High School. He was inducted into the Pro Football Hall of Fame in 1968.

December 12, 1964 — Frank Ryan throws five touchdown passes in leading the Browns to a 52-20 win over the Giants. Cleveland led, 45-7, after three quarters.

13

December 13, 2018 — Indians reacquire Santana

There are many moving parts when three teams get together to trade players. But the headline for Cleveland on this day was that Carlos Santana was coming back to town. Santana had been an Indian for eight seasons from 2010 to 2017, and he was in double figures in home runs in the last seven of them when he was a regular. Santana's peak power season was in 2016 with 34 homers.

But he left Cleveland at the end of the 2017 season and signed as a free agent with the Phillies. Santana still hit for power in Philadelphia, but his average hit a career low of .229. In early December of 2018, the Phillies traded him to Seattle. He wasn't there long.

The Indians received Santana from the Mariners and outfielder Jake Bauers from the Rays. Cleveland sent Yandy Diaz and Cole Sulser to Tampa Bay, while slugger Edwin Encarnacion was dealt by the Indians to Seattle.

December 13, 1977 — Forrest Gregg resigns as the Browns' head coach when he finds out he will be fired at the end of the season. Dick Modzelewski takes over as interim coach for the team's final game of the season.

December 13, 1989 — At age 60, Glenn "Bo" Schembechler, a native of Barberton in Summit County, announces his retirement as Michigan football coach after 21 seasons. Schembechler had served as an assistant on Woody Hayes' staff at Ohio State, and the Buckeyes' games with Hayes matched against his former staff member became known as "The Ten Year War." His overall record was 234-64-8 in 27 seasons.

December 13, 2003 — Mount Union College, located in the Stark County city of Alliance, wins its 55th straight football game – a 66-0 triumph over Bridgewater. The Raiders break their own NCAA record for consecutive wins, set in 1999.

14

December 14, 1958 — Summerall's kick defeats Browns

Yankee Stadium hosted a lot of football drama in December of 1958. The Giants' championship game against the Colts at the end of the month is one of the NFL's most famous games. But this contest earlier in the month was another classic.

The situation for the Browns was simple. They were 9-2 entering the last game of the regular season, while the Giants were 8-3. If Cleveland won or tied, it would win the division and advance to the title game. The two teams were greeted by snow when they took the field, and a defensive battle was the result.

Jim Brown gave Cleveland an early lead on a 65-yard run, but New York later tied the game, 10-10, on an option pass from Frank Gifford to Bob Schnelker. As time ran down into the final minutes, the Giants' apparent last hope to avoid a tie was a long field goal through the snow and wind. Pat Summerall had missed a field goal kick with less than five minutes left from 31 yards away. Now the clock was down under two minutes, and because of the snow on the ground, no one could be sure how far the kick would be.

Somehow, Summerall, who would go on to a lengthy broadcasting career, made it. The Browns ended up on the wrong end of the 13-10 decision and the play became one of the most famous kicks in football history.

December 14, 1947 — The Browns defend their AAFC championship with a 14-3 win over the New York Yankees.

December 14, 1948 — The Indians complete a good trade with the Senators, adding pitcher Early Wynn and first baseman Mickey Vernon. The price tag was Eddie Robinson, Joe Haynes and Eddie Klieman. Haynes was the son-in-law of Senators owner Clark Griffith, who didn't like Indians' owner Bill Veeck, and didn't want his relative playing for the Indians.

December 14, 1991 — Desmond Howard of Michigan wins the Heisman Trophy as the nation's top college football player. He had been a star high school athlete for Villa Angela-St. Joseph in Cleveland, scoring 18 touchdowns and intercepting 10 passes as a senior. He would go on to be named MVP of the 1997 Super Bowl for the Green Bay Packers.

December 14, 2020 — The Indians announce that they will drop the franchise's nickname, which had been used since 1915.

December 15, 2019 — Kluber dealt to the Rangers

One of the sad realities of modern day baseball is that only large market teams can keep their stars in one place for most of their careers. The story of Indians pitcher Corey Kluber is one example.

In a perfect world, Kluber would have been an Indian forever. The right-handed pitcher came to the organization as a minor leaguer in a trade with the Padres. It took him a couple of years to fulfill his potential, but he moved into the starting rotation in 2013 and went 11-5. Kluber's career took off after that, as he won the Cy Young Award in 2014 and 2017.

But Kluber had misfortunes beginning in 2019. He was hit by a line drive in Miami on May 1 and suffered a broken bone in his arm. Kluber tried to come back in the minors in August, but suffered a muscle injury and had to be shut down for the season.

The Indians decided to move Kluber after the season, and the Rangers gave up outfielder Delino DeShields and prospect Emmanuel Clase for him. The trade made sense for baseball and financial reasons, but reminded Cleveland fans of their inability to keep stars like Albert Belle, Jim Thome, CC Sabathia, Manny Ramirez – and, more recently, Francisco Lindor – in the past.

December 15, 1957 — Jim Brown runs for 78 yards on 15 carries in the Browns' 34-28 win over the Giants. Brown's total for the season is 942 yards in 12 games, good for his first NFL rushing title.

December 15, 1963 — Jim Brown rushes 28 times for 125 yards in the Browns' 27-20 victory over the Washington Redskins in the final regular-season game, giving him an NFL single-season record of 1,863 yards. He would capture the league's MVP award later in his career.

December 15, 1982 — New Cavaliers General Manager Harry Weltman trades guard Ron Brewer to Golden State for World B. Free.

December 15, 2008 — Cedric Jackson's three-quarter court shot at the buzzer gives Cleveland State a shocking 72-69 win over No. 11 Syracuse in the Carrier Dome. It is the first time that the Vikings have ever beaten a Top 25 team on the road.

16

December 16, 2001 — A not-so-instant replay for Browns

Welcome to "Bottlegate," one of the most amazing losses in Browns' history – which is saying something.

Cleveland trailed Jacksonville, 15-10, with 68 seconds left, but had the ball. On a fourth-and-2 play, Tim Couch hit Quincy Morgan for three yards and a first down on the Jaguars' 12. The Browns quickly moved to the line of scrimmage, and Couch spiked the ball.

But wait! Referee Terry McAuley ruled that the Browns' completion was under review. Apparently he was buzzed from the press box that a review was forthcoming, and had to check to see if the buzz took place before Couch's spike.

Then the ruling was announced: the fourth down pass was incomplete, and the Jaguars were awarded the ball. Cleveland fans littered the field with debris, including brown plastic beer bottles. That led the officials to declare the game forfeited to Jacksonville with 48 seconds left. Then NFL Commissioner Paul Tagliabue called the referees and told them to finish the game, and the teams did so while dodging objects on the playing surface.

December 16, 1945 — The Cleveland Rams beat Washington, 15-14, for the NFL championship on a minus-8 degree day in Cleveland. It was the last home game ever played by the Rams in Ohio, as they moved to Los Angeles for the 1946 season.

December 16, 1956 — The Browns lose to the Chicago Cardinals, 24-7, and finish with a 5-7 record for the season. It's the first time the franchise had a losing record.

December 16, 1974 — The Browns fire head coach Nick Skorich. He had a 30-24-2 record in the regular season, and lost both of his playoff games.

December 16, 1984 — Doug Dieken starts for the Browns for the 194th and last time in a 27-20 win over Houston. Dieken also played in 203 straight games for Cleveland. He immediately began a 34-season career as a team broadcaster in 1985.

17

December 17, 1995 — Last call for the Browns

The Browns' played their last home game in Cleveland Stadium on this date. It means nothing in the NFL standings, but touches the emotion of fans everywhere.

It was announced five weeks earlier on November 6 that they would be moving to Baltimore after the 1995 season, ending a 50-year run. Fittingly, the December 17 opponents were the Cincinnati Bengals, founded by former Browns coach and executive Paul Brown.

Cleveland lived up to its side of the bargain, playing inspired football in a 26-10 win to break a six-game losing streak. Vinny Testaverde was 22-for-32 for 241 yards and two scores for the Browns, who never trailed.

When the game was over, the Browns players headed for the famous Dawg Pound section of the stadium and accepted the cheers of the 55,875 in the building. "I will take away with me the sight of tears streaming down a young lady's face," running back Earnest Byner told the *Plain Dealer*.

December 17, 1950 — The Browns capture the NFL East Division title by beating the Giants, 8-3, in a playoff game at Municipal Stadium. Defensive lineman Bill Willis saves the game for Cleveland by catching the Giants' Gene "Choo-Choo" Roberts from behind on a fourth-quarter run.

December 17, 1952 — Archie Moore wins a unanimous 15-round decision over Cleveland's Joey Maxim to capture the world light-heavyweight boxing championship in a bout staged in St. Louis.

December 17, 1991 — The Cavs record the most one-sided win in NBA history by beating Miami, 148-80, at the Coliseum. Cleveland outscored Miami, 75-27, in the second half. The record lasts 30 years until Oklahoma City loses by 73 points to Memphis in 2021.

18

December 18, 1952 — Lions surprise the Browns

The Browns were playing in the NFL championship game in 1952. So what else was new? It was their third such appearance in three years in the league. This time, their opponents were the Detroit Lions, and it was an unusual game.

The Lions only had 10 first downs despite rushing for 199 yards and committing no turnovers. Yet Detroit had enough offense to lead the entire game on the way to a 17-7 win. Once they took a 14-0 lead on a 67-yard touchdown run by Doak Walker, the Lions' offense turned conservative as the coaching staff figured the lead was in good hands with a sturdy Detroit defense.

Browns quarterback Otto Graham was 20-for-35 for 191 yards. Chick Jagade had 15 carries for 104 yards and a touchdown. But two turnovers hurt, and the Browns were without wide receivers Mac Speedie and Dub Jones because of injuries.

After the game, kicker Lou Groza revealed that he was playing with torn cartilage in his ribs. He would not use that as an excuse for his three missed field goals, saying that poor footing on the somewhat frozen field was a problem for what he called a bad day.

December 18, 1977 — The Cavaliers retire uniform No. 42, worn by Akron's Nate Thurmond, during his two seasons with the team in 1975-76 and '76-77.

December 18, 1985 — Gerry Faust, fresh off serving for five years as head football coach at Notre Dame, takes the same job at the University at Akron as the college prepares to move up to the NCAA Division I level.

December 18, 1988 — Don Strock, who came out of retirement to join the Browns earlier in the season, leads Cleveland to 21 straight points down the stretch and a 28-23 win over the Oilers to gain a playoff berth. At 38, he becomes the fourth-oldest quarterback to start an NFL playoff game.

December 18, 2013 — London Fletcher announces his retirement from the NFL after a career spanning 16 seasons with St. Louis, Buffalo and Washington that included four Pro Bowl selections and a Super Bowl championship. Fletcher played in high school at Cleveland Villa Angela-St. Joseph and in college at Division III John Carroll University in the Cleveland suburb of University Heights.

19

December 19, 1948 — Browns finish a perfect season

The All-America Football Conference was unbalanced in talent in this particular season. The Browns finished 14-0, while the San Francisco 49ers – another team from the West Conference – was 12-2. No other team in the league was above the .500 mark.

But some opposition was needed for the AAFC championship game, and the Buffalo Bills were that team. The Bills and Baltimore Colts both finished 7-7 to tie for the East title, and Buffalo took the playoff game.

The potential for a mismatch certainly was present, and the Browns turned it into reality. Cleveland overwhelmed the Bills, 49-7, before 22,981 in Municipal Stadium. The Browns broke open the game with two touchdowns early in the third period to take a 28-0 lead, and it was a matter of running out the clock from there. Lou Saban, who would go on to coach the Bills twice, ended the scoring with a 39-yard interception return.

The win gave the Browns football perfection – a 13-0 record. No team would do it better until the 1972 Miami Dolphins went 17-0 in winning an NFL crown.

December 19, 1975 — The first double overtime game in Cavaliers history has a happy ending, as Cleveland's 128-124 win over Phoenix sets a team record for consecutive victories with six.

December 19, 1999 — Browns offensive tackle Orlando Brown is hit accidentally in the eye by a penalty flag thrown by a referee. He would miss three seasons with vision problems.

20

December 20, 1997 — Another title for Tressel's Penguins

Winning became a habit at Youngstown State while Jim Tressel was coaching football there. Four national championships built a reputation that led to Tressel later being hired at Ohio State.

The fourth came when the Penguins knocked off McNeese State, 10-9. Youngstown State had won titles in 1991, 1993 and 1994. It was a terrific football game with a dramatic ending. With about seven minutes left to play, Demond Tidwell threw a 9-yard touchdown pass to Renauld Ray to tie the game, 9-9. Mark Griffith kicked the extra point to give the Penguins the lead. McNeese failed to move the ball in its last two possessions, and Youngstown State ran out the clock to celebrate the win in a game played in Chattanooga, Tennessee.

Tressel stayed at YSU through 2000, and then landed at Ohio State, where he won a national championship along with six Big Ten titles. The coach left that position in 2011, and he eventually became the president of Youngstown State.

December 20, 1970 — Blanton Collier coaches his final game with the Browns, a 27-13 win over Denver. Collier finishes with a 76-34-2 record in eight years, including the 1964 NFL title.

December 20, 1997 — Bill Borchert, the quarterback for Mount Union College's football team, is named the first two-time winner of the Melberger Award as the top player in the NCAA Division III category. Borchert, who played at Parma Holy Name in high school, led Mount Union (located in Alliance) to national titles in both 1996 and '97.

December 20, 2009 — Josh Cribbs returns two kickoffs for touchdowns, and Jerome Harrison runs 28 yards for the winning touchdown in the Browns' 41-34 win over Kansas City.

December 20, 2019 — Kent State wins its first football bowl game, a 51-41 decision over Utah State in the Frisco Bowl in Frisco, Texas.

December 21, 1980 — More thrills for the 'Kardiac Kids'

The Browns had been winning games in a dramatic way throughout 1980. It's not a surprise, then, that the team known as the "Kardiac Kids" would go down to the wire in their last game of the regular season.

The Browns beat the Bengals, 27-24, to improve to 11-5 and win the AFC Central title for the first time since 1971 and reach the postseason for the first time since 1972. The teams exchanged scores throughout the game, and were tied with about six minutes left.

That's when the Browns moved down the field, arriving at the Cincinnati 5 with two minutes to go. Three plays went nowhere before Don Cockroft kicked a field goal from the 22 to give Cleveland the lead. But it wasn't over yet. Cincinnati had 1:18 left and advanced the ball quickly to the Browns' 11, but Ron Bolton tackled Steve Kreider on the game's final play to run out the clock.

Brian Sipe became the third quarterback in NFL history to total 4,000 passing yards in a season, thanks to a 308-yard day. The game sent the Browns into the playoffs with a first-round matchup at home against Oakland.

December 21, 1958 — The Browns fall short in their second of two straight chances to beat the Giants and advance to the NFL Championship game. This time in a special playoff game, New York wins by a 10-0 count, as Cleveland finishes with seven first downs and 24 rushing yards.

December 21, 1968 — The Browns stop the Cowboys from appearing in the NFL championship game for the third consecutive time with a 31-20 upset win.

December 21, 2009 — Browns owner Randy Lerner shakes up the team's front office by hiring Mike Holmgren as the team's new president. The contract reportedly is for five years and $40 million. Previously, in a head coaching role, Holmgren had led the Green Bay Packers to a title in Super Bowl XXXI.

22

December 22, 2015 — Zips finally go bowling

Football fans at the University of Akron will never forget the Zips' first bowl victory. That's especially true for the game's Most Valuable Player.

Akron earned a trip to Boise, Idaho, to play Utah State in the Famous Idaho Potato Bowl. There were a couple of lead changes in the contest, but a field goal by Robert Stein with 8:15 left gave the Zips a 23-14 lead. That proved important when the Aggies scored a late touchdown to come within two points, giving Akron the 23-21 win.

Stein earned Most Valuable Player honors for the game, as his three field goals proved crucial. It was quite a finish to a career that began when Stein didn't kick well and lost his scholarship. However, he didn't go anywhere and fought back to regain the kicker's job.

By the way, the 46-yard field goal that was the difference in the game gave Stein 268 career points and made him the leading scorer in school history.

December 22, 1946 — The Browns beat the New York Yankees, 14-9, in the first-ever AAFC championship game.

December 23, 1951 — Rams win thriller over Browns

It was not a surprise that the Browns were playing for another championship since they had been around for five previous title games, and won them all. Considering that Cleveland went 11-1 in the regular season, another championship seemed like a good probability.

The Los Angeles Rams, however, had other ideas. They had an 8-4 record, but were playing on their home field and hosted the Browns as the nation watched the first coast-to-coast television broadcast of an NFL game in history. The Dumont Network did the honors.

America watched a close contest. The lead flipped a few times, and the score was tied in the fourth quarter. Then Norm Van Brocklin of the Rams hit Tom Fears with what was called a perfect pass, and Fears galloped 73 yards for a touchdown. The Browns couldn't score on their final two possessions, and the Rams were 24-17 winners.

There must have been fans back in Cleveland who had mixed emotions after the game. The Rams, remember, had moved from Cleveland to Los Angeles after winning the 1945 title.

December 23, 1989 — Kevin Mack goes four yards for a touchdown with 39 seconds left to lift the Browns to a 24-20 win over the Oilers and an AFC Central title.

December 24, 1950 — Browns, Rams stage a classic

The Browns had proved they belonged in the National Football League after moving over from the All-America Football Conference in 1950. But the new challenge was to prove they could be the best in the NFL. The Browns, who still had 11 players from the initial AAFC team from 1946, were about to find out.

The Los Angeles Rams provided the opposition on an above-freezing day at Municipal Stadium, and they set the tone early. Bob Waterfield hit Glenn Davis with an 82-yard touchdown pass for the first score of the game. It was back and forth from there. Dante

Lavelli scored on two touchdown passes from Otto Graham. Still, the Rams had a 28-20 lead after three quarters.

Graham hit Otto Bumgardner with a 14-yard scoring pass to cut the lead to one point. Cleveland got the ball back on its own 31 when Graham went to work with 1:49 left. The Browns moved straight down the field, and Lou Groza kicked a 16-yard field goal to give Cleveland the lead.

The Browns' Warren Lahr ended the hopes of Los Angeles with his second interception of the game, and Cleveland was a 30-28 winner. Browns coach Paul Brown said later in his career that this was the greatest game he had ever seen.

December 24, 1967 — The Browns are bounced out of the NFL playoffs, emphatically losing to the Dallas Cowboys, 52-14, for the right to play Green Bay for the title. It is Lou Groza's last game after 21 seasons for Cleveland. Groza, from Martins Ferry, Ohio, joined the Browns in 1946 as a lineman and kicker. He was a member of four NFL title teams and a nine-time Pro Bowl selection.

December 24, 1972 — The Browns give the Dolphins – fresh off a perfect regular season (14-0) – a bit of a scare by leading, 14-13, in the fourth quarter of their playoff matchup. But Miami answers and wins, 20-14.

December 24, 1988 — The Oilers have just enough to beat the Browns, 24-23, in a wild-card game in Cleveland. Houston's Tony Zendejas kicks a 49-yard field goal with a little less than two minutes left to give the Oilers enough to win.

December 24, 2016 — San Diego kicker Josh Lambo's last-second missed field goal attempt gives the Browns a 20-17 win over the Chargers. It's Cleveland's first win after 14 losses that season and 17 consecutive defeats overall.

December 25, 2016 — Cavaliers win a rematch

Christmas Day in the sports world has belonged to the NBA the past several years, and the schedule-makers always try to offer good matchups. And there were few better matchups in the 2010s than when the Cavaliers and Warriors got together.

This regular season game had a little added juice to it, because the teams had played for the NBA championship earlier in the year. The Cavs had won the title, but Golden State had added superstar Kevin Durant since then.

It was a close game for most of the first three quarters, but the Warriors pulled out to a 14-point lead early in the fourth. But Cleveland would not let Golden State get out of reach. Down by a point, Kyrie Irving hit a short jumper over the Warriors' Klay Thompson to give the Cavs the lead with 3.4 seconds left.

Golden State had one last chance to win, but Durant couldn't get off a shot at the buzzer. The Cavs had held on to bragging rights with a 109-108 win. LeBron James had 31 points and 13 rebounds for Cleveland.

December 25, 1970 — The Cavaliers play their first game on Christmas in their first season, dropping a 117-100 decision to the Cincinnati Royals. Cleveland falls to 3-37.

26

December 26, 1955 — Going out with a win

You can argue about who has been pro football's greatest player. However, there's not much argument about the greatest winner in the sport's history. It has to be Otto Graham.

Graham had come out of retirement to play one last year. His Browns sailed through the 1955 season with a 9-2-1 record, finishing the regular season by scoring at least 30 points in their last four games. That set up a championship game with the Rams in Los Angeles.

It wasn't much of a game. Cleveland pulled away in the third quarter and won by a score of 38-14. Graham was 14-for-25 for 209 yards and two touchdowns, and he also ran for two scores. The defense did the rest, forcing seven Los Angeles turnovers.

The Browns quarterback played 10 seasons. Graham's teams reached the playoffs 10 times, and won seven championships. In six years in the NFL, the Browns went 57-13-1 with Graham behind center. He was a three-time league MVP.

December 26, 1954 — Lou Groza sets a title game record with eight extra points as the Browns clobber Detroit, 56-10, for the NFL championship before 43,827 in Municipal Stadium.

December 26, 1978 — The Cleveland Force makes its debut in the Major Indoor Soccer League, losing to the Houston Summit by a score of 10-3.

December 26, 2003 — The Rockers of the WNBA fold when new ownership cannot be found for the team. Gordon and George Gund, owners of the Cavs, announced earlier in the year that they would no longer operate the franchise. The Rockers were an original member of the league when it was formed and played six seasons.

December 27, 1964 — Browns erupt to beat Colts

Consider this game a worthy accomplishment for a Browns team that had beaten the best pro football had to offer for almost 20 years, starting with their birth in the All-America Football Conference in 1946. No team in the NFL had a better all-time record than the Browns at the time this game was played.

The Browns had a good team in 1964, going 10-3-1 to win the East Division under coach Blanton Collier, who had succeeded franchise creator Paul Brown in 1963. Jim Brown was on the roster, of course, and he was still one of the league's great players eight years into his career. Frank Ryan had become a solid quarterback, and he had excellent receivers in Gary Collins and rookie Paul Warfield. The defense was solid and experienced. Still, they would have to beat the Baltimore Colts to win the NFL championship. The West champs were 12-2 and featured Johnny Unitas in his prime.

The Colts were favored (by seven points, according to betting line reports), so it was something of a surprise that the contest was scoreless at halftime. Then the Browns erupted and played one of the great halves in their history. Ryan hit Collins with three touchdown passes, and Lou Groza kicked two field goals.

Meanwhile, the Colts could do little on offense. Unitas only threw for 95 yards, and Lenny Moore ran for a mere 40 yards. It had been nine years since 1955, but Cleveland celebrated its latest championship for a major sports team. No one could have known the next one would not arrive for almost 52 years.

December 27, 1953 — Bobby Layne hits Jim Doran with a 33-yard touchdown pass with about two minutes left, and the Lions edge the Browns, 17-16, in the NFL Championship game.

December 27, 1983 — Brian Sipe, the NFL's Most Valuable Player in 1980, jumps from the Browns to the New Jersey Generals of the United States Football League. The Generals, owned by New York real estate investor Donald Trump, sign Sipe to a three-year, $1.9 million deal, fully guaranteed, according to an *Akron Beacon Journal* report.

December 27, 1988 — Marty Schottenheimer resigns as the Browns' head coach, after he and owner Art Modell disagreed on whether Schottenheimer should continue in his other role as offensive coordinator. Schottenheimer's decision comes after a turmoil-filled season in which, because of injuries, the Browns needed to use four quarterbacks to make the playoffs.

28

December 28, 1969 — A shocking win by the Browns

The Dallas Cowboys figured to be in ill humor when they played the Browns in the first round of the playoffs after the 1969 season. The Cowboys had one of their best teams ever the previous year, but they were shocked by the Browns in the first round of the playoffs. Dallas was still good in 1969, though, turning in an 11-2-1 record. But the Browns were still good, too. Bill Nelsen, Leroy Kelly and Paul Warfield were all headed to the Pro Bowl, and the defense was solid with players such as Jack Gregory, Jim Houston and Walter Johnson.

Still, no one was prepared for what happened. Bo Scott opened the scoring with a 2-yard run, and Nelsen hit Milt Morin for another score. Don Cockroft added a field goal before halftime to make it a stunning 17-0 lead. When Scott started the second half with another touchdown run, it was simply a matter of running out the clock. Walt Sumner's 88-yard interception return completed Cleveland's scoring in a 38-14 win.

In a sense, this win was the last gasp of the long run of great Cleveland teams. The Browns didn't win another playoff game until 1987, and their next road postseason win came a little more than 50 years later.

December 28, 1952 — The Detroit Lions hand the Browns a 17-7 loss in the NFL title game, which was played in Cleveland.

December 28, 1974 — The Browns hire former Packers' lineman Forrest Gregg as head coach.

December 28, 2008 — Andy McCollum, an offensive lineman from Summit County's Revere High School and Toledo, ends his 14th and final NFL season as a member of the Detroit Lions' 0-16 team. McCollum won a Super Bowl ring in 2000 with the St. Louis Rams.

29

December 29, 2002 — Browns earn a playoff spot

It almost felt like old times for the Browns. The reborn franchise was in the midst of a fight for a playoff berth, and a crowd of more than 73,000 turned out on a cold day in Cleveland Browns Stadium to see if their favorite team could beat the Falcons. It was a necessary first step to reach the postseason, which required some help from other teams. Atlanta also needed a win to keep its playoff hopes alive.

It was a suitably tense contest. Kelly Holcomb hit Kevin Johnson with a 15-yard scoring pass to give Cleveland the lead, and William Green ran 64 yards for an insurance score. Still, the Browns' lead was only eight points, and the Falcons had four minutes to send the game into overtime.

Four times, the Falcons tried to score from inside the Cleveland 5, and four times the Browns' defense held – three of them coming on the 1-yard line. Cleveland escaped with a 24-16 win. The Patriots already had won their game, so the Browns needed the Jets to win their game to reach the playoffs.

Play-by-play announcer Jim Donovan of the Browns was listening to the Jets-Packers game on the radio in the parking lot when another car pulled up next to him. It was Cleveland coach Butch Davis, asking for help on how to find out what was going on in New York. They listened as the Jets blasted the Packers, 42-17. The Browns were in the playoffs.

December 29, 1957 — The Lions take a 31-7 halftime lead and roll to a 59-14 win over the Browns in the NFL championship game in Detroit

December 29, 1968 — The Colts come to Cleveland and blank the Browns, 34-0, to earn a date in Super Bowl III against quarterback Joe Namath and the New York Jets.

December 29, 1972 — Tampa defeated Kent State, 21-18, in the Tangerine Bowl college football game in Orlando before a crowd of 20,062. Tampa was coached by Earle Bruce, who had previously been at Massillon High School.

December 29, 2019 — This day continues to be bad luck for Browns' head coaches, as Freddie Kitchens is dismissed by the team. Romeo Crennel (2008) and Rob Chudzinski (2013) also were fired on December 29.

30

December 30, 2018 — Browns fall short against Baltimore

It had been a long, frustrating and difficult decade for the Browns. They hadn't had a winning season since 2007, and they were on their seventh coach in that drought as they finished the 2018 season. A record above .500 would be a good sign of progress, and Cleveland could improve to 8-7-1 for the year with a win over the Ravens.

Baltimore, however, had a bigger goal than a moral victory in mind for this game. A win would give them a division championship. The Ravens got off to a good start before their home fans, and led 20-7 at the half. Lamar Jackson ran for two touchdowns. But the Browns weren't through yet. Baker Mayfield hit Antonio Callaway with a 1-yard pass to cut the Ravens' lead to 26-24.

The Browns got the ball back and moved to the Baltimore 39 with 1:20 left. A year earlier, Baltimore had been eliminated from the postseason on a late scoring pass by the Bengals. There was no replay this time. Mayfield's fourth-down pass was intercepted by C.J. Mosley, and Baltimore could exhale and head for the playoffs.

December 30, 1978 — Mohammed Attiah of Ghana pops in the game-winning goal as the Cleveland Force indoor soccer team beats the Pittsburgh Spirit, 7-6, before 10,199 in its first-ever home game.

December 30, 2001 — The Browns rally from a 38-24 deficit in the final 10 minutes to defeat the Titans, 41-38. Phil Dawson's 44-yard field goal with 55 seconds left is the difference.

31

December 31, 2017 — A perfectly winless season

It's not easy to have a winless season in the National Football League. The league has a number of devices designed to level the competition, such as scheduling and the college draft. Still, a few teams have done it since the end of World War II. The first-year Dallas Cowboys stumbled to a 0-11-1 record in 1960. The expansion Tampa Bay Buccaneers were 0-14 in 1976. The Detroit Lions became the first 0-16 team in 2008.

Certainly the Browns did not want to add their names to the list in 2017, but it was staring them in the face whenever they looked in the standings before the season's last game against Pittsburgh. The Steelers even sat out some of their stars to give them a rest for the playoffs.

It didn't help the Browns. The Steelers jumped out to a 14-0 lead early in the second period, and had a 21-7 margin midway through the second quarter. DeShone Kizer threw two touchdown passes for Cleveland to tie the game. But JuJu Smith-Schuster returned a kickoff 96 yards for a score to give Pittsburgh the lead for good.

The Browns did have one last chance to win the game in the fourth quarter, but Kizer's pass bounced off the hands of one-time first-round draft pick Corey Coleman and fell incomplete. It had been 372 days since Cleveland walked off the field as a winner, and now the Browns would have to wait at least eight more months to do so.

December 31, 2012 — It wouldn't be a happy New Year for Browns coach Pat Shurmur and general manager Tom Heckert, as both are fired – two months after new owner Jimmy Haslam takes over the franchise. Shurmur went 9-23 in his two seasons in Cleveland after being brought in by team president Mike Holmgren.

Book Sources

Bellamy II, John Stark. *Cleveland's Greatest Disasters.* Gray & Company, 2009.

Boyer, Mary Schmitt. *The Good, the Bad, and the Ugly.* Triumph, 2008.

Coughlin, Dan. *Crazy, With The Papers To Prove It.* Gray & Company, 2010.

Coughlin, Dan. *Pass The Nuts.* Gray & Company, 2011.

Coughlin, Dan. *Let's Have Another.* Gray & Company, 2015.

Coughlin, Dan. *Just One More Story …* Gray & Company, 2018.

Crippen, Kenneth R., and Reaser, Matt. *The All-American Football Conference.* McFarland, 2018.

Dolgan, Bob. *Heroes, Scamps and Good Guys,* 1971-2003, The Plain Dealer. Gray & Company.

Dyer, Bob. *Cleveland Sports Legends.* Gray & Company, 2003.

Eckhouse, Morris. *Legends of the Tribe.* SporTraditions, 2000.

Eckhouse, Morris, and Crouse, Greg. *Where Cleveland Played.* History Press, 2010.

Epplin, Luke. *Our Team.* Flatiron Books. 2021.

Finnan, Bob. *100 Things Cavaliers Fans Should Know and Do Before They Die.* Triumph, 2016.

Fitch, Jerry. *Cleveland's Greatest Fighters of All Time.* Arcadia, 2002.

Gallagher, Robert C. *Ernie Davis: The Elmira Express.* Bartleby, 1999.

Gay, Timothy M. *Tris Speaker.* Lyons, 2005.

Gordon, Roger. *Tales from the Cleveland Cavaliers.* Sports Publishing LLC, 2004.

Gordon, Roger. *Cleveland Browns A-Z.* Sports Publishing, 2015.

Gordon, Roger. *The Miracle of Richfield.* Black Squirrel Books, 2016.

Gordon, Roger. *So You Think You're A Cleveland Browns Fan?* Sports Publishing, 2017.

Heaton, Chuck. *Browns Scrapbook.* Gray & Company, 2007.

Hodermarsky, Mark (editor). *The Cleveland Sports Legacy, 1900-1945.* Cleveland Landmarks Press, 1992.

Hudak, Mike. *The Cleveland Sports Wiz Trivia Quiz.* Saddle River, N.J.: Red-Letter Press, 2000.

Knight, Jonathan. *Classic Browns.* Kent State University Press, 2008.

Knight, Jonathan. *Classic Cavs.* Kent State University Press, 2009.

Knight, Jonathan. *Classic Tribe.* Kent State University Press, 2009

Lebovitz, Hal. *The Best of Hal Lebovitz.* Gray & Company, 2004.

Livingston, Bill. *George Steinbrenner's Pipe Dream.* Black Squirrel Books, 2015.

Livingston, Bill, and Brinda, Greg. *The Great Book of Cleveland Sports Lists.* Running Press, 2008.

Lloyd, Jason. *The Blueprint.* Dutton, 2017.

Longert, Scott H. The Best They Could Be. Potomac, 2013.

O'Connor, Ian. *Belichick The Making Of The Greatest Football Coach Of All Time.*
Houghton Mifflin Harcourt, 2018.

Owens, Thomas S. *Basketball Arenas.* Milbrook, 2002.

Pappas, George Christian. *A Tribe Reborn.* Sports Publishing, 2019.

Pellowski, Michael J. *The Little Giant Book of Baseball Facts.* Sterling, 2007.

Piascik, Scott. *The Best Show in Football.* Taylor, 2010.

Pluto, Terry. *Dealing.* Gray & Company, 2008.

Pluto, Terry, and Tait, Joe. *Joe Tait, It's Been A Real Ball.* Gray & Company, 2011.

Pluto, Terry. *The Comeback: LeBron, The Cavs & Cleveland.* Gray & Company, 2016.

Pluto, Terry. *The Browns Blues.* Gray & Company, 2018.

Pluto, Terry. *Vintage Cavs.* Gray & Company, 2019.

Schaap, Dick. *Steinbrenner!* Avon Books, 1982.

Schneider, Russell. *Tribe Memories, The First Century.* Moonlight Publishing, 2000.

Schneider, Russell. *Tales from the Tribe Dugout.* Sports Publishing LLC, 2002.

Schneider, Russell. *The Cleveland Indians Encyclopedia.* Sports Publishing LLC, 2004.

Schneider, Russell. *What Ever Happened to Super Joe?* Gray and Company, 2006.

Sulecki, James C. *The Cleveland Rams.* McFarland, 2016.

Wancho, Joseph. *So You Think You're a Cleveland Indians Fan?* Sports Publishing, 2018.

Wiggins, Robert Peyton. *The Federal League of Baseball Clubs.* McFarland & Co, 2011.

Index

March 29, 1971 – Cavs grab Carr with first overall pick
March 30, 1978 – Indians trade Eckersley to Red Sox
March 31, 1976 – Cavaliers sew up a playoff spot

April 1, 1998 – Meno ranks with skating's best
April 2, 1993 – For once, the Price is wrong
April 3, 1966 – Indians miss out on Seaver
April 4, 1994 – Indians open Jacobs Field in style
April 5, 2001 – Hart decides to leave Indians
April 6, 1975 – Cavs are close, but no cigar
April 7, 1946 – Keiser wins Masters championship
April 8, 1975 – Robinson helps his own cause
April 9, 1962 – Pipers win ABL championship
April 10, 1976 – Cavaliers earn a banner with win
April 11, 1948 – Barons start a winning streak
April 12, 1916 – Speaker debuts for Indians
April 13, 2011 – Joe Tait's last game
April 14, 1925 – Indians, Browns open with slugfest
April 15, 1976 – Bingo! Cavs win first playoff game!
April 16, 1940 – Feller opens with a no-hitter
April 17, 1960 – Indians trade Rocky Colavito
April 18, 1960 – Score dealt to White Sox
April 19, 1969 – Harrelson comes to Cleveland
April 20, 1945 – The Cleveland Browns' birthday
April 21, 1991 – Browns take Turner second overall
April 22, 1976 – More thrills for the Cavaliers
April 23, 1902 – Welcome, Cleveland Bronchos
April 24, 1982 – Browns acquire Cousineau
April 25, 1890 – Infants put one in the win column
April 26, 2018 – Browns take Mayfield first in draft
April 27, 1994 – Crunch claims a championship
April 28, 2006 – James takes another step forward
April 29, 1976 – The Miracle of Richfield is born
April 30, 1996 – Cleveland State hires Massimino

May 1, 1879 – Cleveland debuts in the National League
May 2, 1930 – Sewell's streak snapped at 1,103
May 3, 1994 – Jordan-less Bulls still beat Cavs
May 4, 1871 – Cleveland baseball leads the way
May 5, 2005 – James' shot is decisive for Cavs
May 6, 2016 – Frye's shooting stops Hawks
May 7, 1989 – "The Shot" beats Cavaliers at buzzer
May 8, 2014 – Browns gamble, take Manziel
May 9, 1983 – Stepien Era ends for Cavs
May 10, 1969 – Browns agree to switch conferences
May 11, 1970 – Cavs assemble team in expansion draft
May 12, 1973 – Johnson exits basketball on top
May 13, 2010 – James' time with Cavs starts to run out
May 14, 1968 – Browns add insurance at quarterback
May 15, 1981 – Barker is perfect in win over Jays
May 16, 1962 – Lucas pulls shocker by joining Pipers
May 17, 1925 – Speaker celebrates No. 3,000
May 18, 2008 – Pierce tops James in duel
May 19, 2016 – Lue sets record for coaching wins
May 20, 1983 – Dokes keeps title with draw
May 21, 1979 – Fitch leaves Cavaliers' job
May 22, 2003 – Cavs win an important lottery
May 23, 1972 – Indians reach a peak, if only briefly
May 24, 1993 – Wilkens walks away from Cavs
May 25, 1935 – Owens has an hour to remember
May 26, 2015 – James returns to finals with Cavs
May 27, 1972 – Penske gets his first Indy 500 win
May 28, 1966 – Indians continue surprising start
May 29, 1974 – Indians have big brawl in Texas
May 30, 1937 – Shute doubles his fun at PGA
May 31, 2007 – James scores final 25 points in win

June 1, 1984 – Mancini loses his boxing title
June 2, 2007 – Gibson plays the starring role in win
June 3, 2018 – Curry guns down the Cavaliers
June 4, 1944 – The NFL gets some competition
June 5, 2016 – Women's soccer draws a crowd
June 6, 1983 – Gorman comes stormin' into town
June 7, 1936 – No bullpens needed in marathon
June 8, 2018 – King James exits with loss to Warriors
June 9, 2003 – Rupp has goal of a lifetime for Devils
June 10, 1959 – The Rock hits four big knocks
June 11, 1995 – Kilbane joins boxing's best in Hall
June 12, 1880 – Sheffield's Richmond has perfect day
June 13, 1984 – Indians help Cubs reach postseason
June 14, 1978 – Barons pack for Minnesota
June 15, 1958 – Indians trade a future two-time MVP
June 16, 1986 – Sixers do the Cavs a big favor
June 17, 2002 – Mexico can't break through "Human Wall"
June 18, 1950 – Indians score two early touchdowns
June 19, 2016 – Cleveland has a world champion at last
June 20, 1998 – Lemon's No. 21 goes out of circulation
June 21, 1946 – Indians return to life through new owner
June 22, 2016 – N.E. Ohio celebrates a championship
June 23, 2011 – Cavs take Kyrie Irving first overall
June 24, 2007 – Tracy closes the show with a third win
June 25, 1952 – Maxim earns TKO of exhausted Robinson
June 26, 2003 – Pick of James starts new era for Cavs
June 27, 2002 – Colon brings a haul of talent from Expos
June 28, 1922 – Graney completes his first act
June 29, 1934 – A baseball founding father dies
June 30, 1948 – Lemon turns out the lights on Detroit

July 1, 2018 – Thanks for everything, LeBron
July 2, 1951 – The NHL rejects Cleveland's bid

Oct. 8, 1895 – Spiders win a title, sort of
Oct. 9, 1910 – A batting race to the finish and beyond
Oct. 10, 1920 – An eventful day at the ballpark
Oct. 11, 1948 – Indians rule the baseball world
Oct. 12, 1920 – Coveleski gives Indians first title
Oct. 13, 2007 – Indians explode in Boston
Oct. 14, 1970 – Cavs begin with a loss
Oct. 15, 1899 – Spiders limp to the finish line
Oct. 16, 1957 – Indians make a change at the top
Oct. 17, 1995 – A pennant for the Indians
Oct. 18, 1989 – Replacement Browns earn a win
Oct. 19, 2016 – Indians advance to Series
Oct. 20, 1968 – Browns hand Colts a rare loss
Oct. 21, 2007 – Indians let opportunity get away
Oct. 22, 1984 – Browns dismiss Rutigliano
Oct. 23, 1997 – Indians can't hold off Marlins
Oct. 24, 1995 – Indians walk off a winner
Oct. 25, 2012 – A billion for the Browns
Oct. 26, 1997 – No saving grace in Indians' loss
Oct. 27, 2010 – No LeBron, no problem for Cavs
Oct. 28, 1995 – Glavine shuts down Indians' offense
Oct. 29, 1987 – Prince gets promotion and a title
Oct. 30, 1980 – Cavaliers deal away their future
Oct. 31, 1999 – Browns finally enter the win column

Nov. 1, 1959 – A shootout of superstars
Nov. 2, 2016 – Cubs edge Indians in Game 7
Nov. 3, 1946 – Pro basketball arrives in Cleveland
Nov. 4, 1999 – Jacobs hands off to Dolan
Nov. 5, 1982 – Cavs become historically bad
Nov. 6, 1995 – Browns say they're leaving Cleveland
Nov. 7, 2010 – Browns rout powerful Patriots
Nov. 8, 1993 – Kosar suddenly cut by Browns
Nov. 9, 1969 – Browns' touchdown streak ends
Nov. 10, 1937 – Opening Night for the Arena
Nov. 11, 1979 – Browns suffer damaging loss
Nov. 12, 1970 – Finally, the Cavaliers win
Nov. 13, 1982 – Tragedy in the boxing ring
Nov. 14, 2019 – Garrett's stunning display of anger
Nov. 15, 1970 – Hats off to the Bengals win
Nov. 16, 1989 – Cavs add Ferry in major trade
Nov. 17, 1929 – Friedman points to NFL's future
Nov. 18, 1972 – Golden Flashes make history
Nov. 19, 1976 – Garland signs rich deal with Indians
Nov. 20, 1977 – Mays does enough at quarterback
Nov. 21, 2018 – This time, LeBron is welcomed
Nov. 22, 2009 – A shootout comes out of nowhere
Nov. 23, 1947 – Browns, Yankees tie one on
Nov. 24, 1957 – Brown shows a sign of greatness
Nov. 25, 1941 – Boudreau picked to be player/manager
Nov. 26, 1956 – Browns hit jackpot in draft
Nov. 27, 1924 – The votes are in, and Cleveland wins it all
Nov. 28, 1969 – Knicks make history in Cleveland
Nov. 29, 1971 – Gaylord becomes instant favorite
Nov. 30, 2015 – Browns find new way to lose

Dec. 1, 2005 – Akron wins the MAC title
Dec. 2, 2010 – James comes back to play in Cleveland
Dec. 3, 1980 – Charboneau wins rookie award
Dec. 4, 1961 – A meaningful draft-day deal
Dec. 5, 1944 – Horvath takes the Heisman
Dec. 6, 1989 – Carter trade boosts Indians
Dec. 7, 2017 – Browns clean house
Dec. 8, 1946 - A pile of points for the Browns
Dec. 9, 1923 – Another title for Canton
Dec. 10, 1982 – Dokes wins boxing title quickly
Dec. 11, 1949 – Farewell to the AAFC
Dec. 12, 1920 – Akron tops the football world
Dec. 13, 2018 – Indians reacquire Santana
Dec. 14, 1958 – Summerall's kick defeats Browns
Dec. 15, 2019 – Kluber dealt to Rangers
Dec. 16, 2001 – A not-so-instant replay for Browns
Dec. 17, 1995 – Last call for the Browns
Dec. 18, 1951 – Lions surprise the Browns
Dec. 19, 1948 – Browns finish perfect season
Dec. 20, 1997 – Another title for Tressel's Penguins
Dec. 21, 1980 – More thrills for the 'Kardiac Kids'
Dec. 22, 2015 – Zips finally go bowling
Dec. 23, 1951 – Rams win a thriller over Browns
Dec. 24, 1950 – Browns, Rams stage a classic
Dec. 25, 2016 – Cavaliers win a rematch
Dec. 26, 1955 – Going out with a win
Dec. 27, 1964 – Browns erupt to beat Colts
Dec. 28, 1969 – A shocking win by the Browns
Dec. 29, 2002 – Browns earn a playoff spot
Dec. 30, 2018 – Browns fall short against Baltimore
Dec. 31, 2017 – A perfectly winless season

About the Authors

Pantages is the former managing editor at *The Gazette* in Medina, Ohio, and served as sports editor at the *Akron Beacon Journal* from 1998 to 2006 with special coverage of: the Cleveland Browns as an expansion team; the high school career and early Cavaliers seasons of LeBron James; profiles of athletes of the century from Akron and Summit County, and the 50th anniversary of professional golf tournaments at Firestone Country Club. He was also part of the *Akron Beacon Journal*'s newsroom staff that won a Pulitzer Prize in 1987 for its coverage of an attempted corporate takeover of Goodyear Tire & Rubber Co.

Bailey has been part of the Western New York sports media for more than 40 years, including a long stint as a reporter and editor of *The Buffalo News*. He also worked as a reporter and talk-show host for WEBR Radio, and as Director of Information for the Buffalo Sabres. Now retired, Budd still covers events on a free-lance basis in the Buffalo area. This is his 14th book.